Ultimate CNAPP for Next-Gen Multi Cloud Security

Master CNAPP to Secure Your Cloud-Native Applications with Unified Visibility, Compliance, and Multi-Cloud Protection

Ravi Kumar Malhotra

www.orangeava.com

First Published: October 2025

Published By: Orange Education Pvt Ltd, AVA®

Address: 9, Daryaganj, Delhi, 110002, India

275 New North Road Islington Suite 1314 London,
N1 7AA, United Kingdom

ISBN (PBK): 978-93-49888-08-1
ISBN (E-BOOK): 978-93-49888-84-5

Scan the QR code to explore our entire catalogue

www.orangeava.com

Dedicated To

My Beloved Parents,

Shri Krishan Lal Malhotra and Raj Rani Malhotra,

My Wife, Monika, My Daughter, Ruhin, My Son, Manthan Malhotra

And

My Younger Brother, Nitin.

About the Author

Ravi Kumar Malhotra is a cybersecurity strategist and cloud security consultant with over two decades of experience and expertise in architecting and implementing secure cloud-native environments. His journey into cybersecurity is a story of transformation – beginning with a **bachelor's degree in commerce**, **Ravi made a deliberate shift into the world of technology.** Through relentless self-learning and hands-on experience, he evolved into a respected expert across **network security**, **cybersecurity**, and **cloud security** domains.

Currently, working as **Senior Manager - Consulting | Cloud Security**, Ravi leads enterprise security transformations across **multi-cloud infrastructures**, combining strategy with implementation.

His expertise spans across all major Firewalls, Web Application Firewalls (WAFs), WAN Accelerator, Data Loss Preventions (DLPs), and also the entire CNAPP landscape – from **Cloud Security Posture Management (CSPM)**, **Cloud Workload Protection Platforms (CWPP)**, and **Kubernetes Security Posture Management (KSPM)** to **Data Security Posture Management (DSPM)** and **DevSecOps**.

Ravi has successfully designed and deployed secure architectures across **Microsoft Defender for Cloud**, **Azure**, **GCP**, **OCI**, **Zscaler ZIA/ZPA**, and **Barracuda Firewall solutions**. His passion lies in breaking down complex cloud security concepts into actionable steps that enable teams to scale securely and confidently.

In the book, *Ultimate* CNAPP *for Next-Gen Multi Cloud Security*, Ravi distils years of field experience into an accessible, practical resource – packed with real-world scenarios, guided labs, and proven frameworks to help readers implement modern cloud security controls. A recognized community voice, Ravi engages with a growing network of **18,000+ professionals on LinkedIn**, where he regularly shares insights, visual explainers, and thought leadership on emerging security trends. His content empowers professionals across industries to build strong foundations in cloud security, one concept at a time.

Ravi's professional credentials include **Checkpoint CCSA, CCSE, CCSE+**, **CCIE Security**, **JNCIA**, **AWS**, **Azure**, and **GCP** cloud certifications. His Zero Trust and access management knowledge are validated by **Zscaler ZIA and ZPA** credentials, along with certification in **Barracuda technologies**. He is currently pursuing a **master's degree in Cybersecurity**, demonstrating his belief in lifelong learning.

About the Technical Reviewer

Ravi Bindra has over 30 years experience in IT and Cyber Security including roles as Global Head of Risk Management and Security at a global pharmaceutical enterprise in Switzerland (Roche) and as Global Head of Security Architecture at another (Novartis). He has led the transformation of security infrastructure in these companies in the domains of Network Security, IAM, Application Security, SIEMs, IT Service Continuity and Data Centre Security, where he designed the security controls that would allow a regulated industry to securely use cloud services. His core princiala are "get the basics right" and "process is more important than technology".

He currently serves is as the CISO for SoftwareOne, which transformed fully to a cloud-only model between 2020 to 2023. During this transformation, he collaborated with Ravi Malhotra, who led network security architecture, to implement security controls that enabled the rapid adoption of transformational technologies. His current focus is on ensuring the safe use of AI.

Acknowledgments

The journey of writing this book, ***Ultimate CNAPP for Next-Gen Multi Cloud Security*** has been both intellectually rewarding, and personally enriching. I am profoundly grateful to the many individuals who supported, inspired, and empowered me throughout this process.

I thank **my parents**, whose unwavering belief in me has been my silent strength. Their values, encouragement, and quiet resilience continue to shape every chapter of my life, including this salient one!

I thank **my wife, daughter and son**, whose curiosity, questions, and innocent perspectives reminded me why simplification and clarity matter, even in the most complex of subjects. This book carries their silent imprint.

A special acknowledgment goes to **Mr. Ravi Bindra**, whose discerning and technical eye as well as encouragement brought both precision and perspective to this work. His input ensured that the book remains not only comprehensive, but also credible and relevant.

I am also truly thankful to **Mr. Lalit Kalra**, my mentor and thought partner, for his constant support and valuable guidance. His insights and encouragement helped me think more clearly, and improve the quality of this book.

I extend my sincere appreciation to the cybersecurity community, whose collective spirit of knowledge-sharing fuelled the foundation of this book. My deep gratitude also goes to the practitioners and engineers building the future of CNAPP. Their work inspired every lab, concept, and the practical insight captured here.

I thank the publishing team at **Orange Education Pvt Ltd**, whose professionalism, patience, and meticulous attention to detail transformed this manuscript into a finished work, I am truly proud of. Lastly, to the unsung contributors – the community forum responders, open-source contributors, cloud evangelists, and the countless voices in the background – a big thank you! Their passion for securing the cloud-native world made this book possible.

Preface

As organizations accelerate their adoption of cloud-native technologies, the need to secure dynamic, distributed, and hybrid environments has never been more critical. This book, ***Ultimate CNAPP for Next-Gen Multi Cloud Security*** was born out of this urgent need – to demystify the evolving concept of Cloud-Native Application Protection Platforms (CNAPP), and to serve as a practical guide for both security practitioners and modern DevSecOps professionals.

The book provides a comprehensive understanding of CNAPP – not just as a buzzword, but as an integrated security strategy combining multiple cloud security pillars such as CSPM, CWPP, CIEM, KSPM, and DevSecOps with CNAPP, CSNS, DSPM, and Centralized Compliance Management. Through real-world examples, hands-on labs, and industry insights, the book bridges the gap between theory and application.

With the rise of containerized workloads, multi-cloud adoption, and continuous integration pipelines, security cannot remain an afterthought. CNAPP offers a unified approach to secure every layer of the cloud-native stack – from code to runtime. This book explores these layers in depth, empowering readers to assess, implement, and operationalize CNAPP effectively.

Hence, whether you are a security architect, cloud engineer, SOC analyst, compliance lead, or a curious learner looking to upskill, this guide walks you through essential concepts, modern tools, and hands-on configurations to build robust cloud security postures. The content has been carefully organized into chapters that progressively cover foundational knowledge, technical implementation, and real-world use cases – ensuring both breadth and depth of understanding.

This book is divided into 11 focused chapters that together form a unified CNAPP journey:

Chapter 1. Understanding Cloud Computing, Cloud-Native Applications Security and Challenges: In this chapter, readers will gain a comprehensive understanding of the fundamental concepts related to cloud computing offerings across various platforms. We will explore the different types of cloud computing environments, including private, public, and hybrid models. Additionally, we will delve into the various service models such as Infrastructure as a Service (IaaS), Platform as a Service (PaaS), and Software as a Service (SaaS).

Chapter 2. Understanding Cloud Native Application Protection Platform (CNAPP): In this chapter, readers will understand the meaning of cloud native assets, their risks and vulnerabilities, as well as the need to secure cloud native assets. As there are many different types of cloud-native assets, organizations have footprints with multi-cloud and hybrid environments. To protect applications spread across public, private and hybrid clouds, security teams typically must use multiple security tools. These multiple security tools have different DNAs and development methods, so that they do not collaborate with each other.

Chapter 3. A Practical Guide to Onboarding CNAPP: Understanding Microsoft Defender for Cloud is a comprehensive Cloud-Native Application Protection Platform (CNAPP) designed to secure your cloud environments. It provides robust security features that protect against a wide range of threats, ensuring that your applications and data remain safe. Hence, by integrating seamlessly with Azure, AWS, GCP, Azure DevOps, Docker, and GitHub, it offers a unified security solution across multiple platforms.

Chapter 4. Understanding Cloud Security Posture Management (CSPM): In today's digital age, cloud computing has become the backbone of many organizations. With this shift, ensuring the security of cloud environments is more important than ever. This is where Cloud Security Posture Management (CSPM) comes into play. CSPM is a set of tools and practices designed to continuously monitor and improve the security of cloud infrastructures.

Chapter 5. Understanding Cloud Workload Protection Platform (CWPP): In this chapter, we will explore CWPP concepts, technologies, and industry best practices, followed by hands-on labs using Microsoft Defender for Cloud to implement both agent-based and agentless security for servers and serverless workloads.

Chapter 6. Understanding Cloud Infrastructure Entitlement Management (CIEM): As cloud technology continues to transform how organizations operate, securing cloud environments has become more crucial than ever. This chapter takes you on a journey into Cloud Infrastructure Entitlement Management (CIEM), a key component of modern cloud security.

Chapter 7. Understanding Kubernetes Security Posture Management (KSPM): Kubernetes is everywhere–from start-ups to enterprises–powering modern apps in the cloud. But with all that flexibility and scale comes a big challenge, that is Security. That is where Kubernetes Security Posture Management (KSPM) comes in. In fact, KSPM helps you find and fix misconfigurations, identify risks before attackers do, and monitor your cluster setup against security best practices.

Chapter 8. Understanding DevSecOps with CNAPP: This chapter introduces the principles and practices of DevSecOps in the context of cloud-native development, breaking down how security is automated, enforced, and monitored at every phase of the software lifecycle. This is where DevSecOps comes in – a modern cultural and technical shift that integrates security practices directly into DevOps workflows.

Chapter 9. Understanding Cloud Service Network Security (CSNS): Within a CNAPP framework, Cloud Service Network Security (CSNS) functions as a foundational layer focused on securing network-level communications. It ensures protected traffic flows, enforces controlled access paths, and safeguards infrastructure across multi-cloud and hybrid environments.

Chapter 10. Centralized Compliance Management Using CNAPP: As cloud environments grow in scale and complexity, maintaining regulatory compliance across services, workloads, and subscriptions becomes a critical challenge for modern enterprises. This section provides hands-on experience in managing compliance centrally, using Microsoft Defender for Cloud.

Chapter 11. Understanding Data Security Posture Management (DSPM): Data is the heart of every modern business, and keeping it safe in the cloud is more important than ever. Companies store vast amounts of sensitive data such as customer records, financial details, and intellectual property across multiple cloud platforms. But without the right security measures, this data can be exposed, misused, or even stolen.

To sum up, this book serves as a trusted companion in your cloud security journey, and empowers you to secure what matters most – confidently, effectively, and continuously.

Get a Free eBook

We hope you are enjoying your recently purchased book! Your feedback is incredibly valuable to us, and to all other readers looking for great books.

If you found this book helpful or enjoyable, we would truly appreciate it, if you could take a moment to leave a short review with a 5 star rating on Amazon. It helps us grow, and lets other readers discover our books.

As a thank you, we would love to send you a free digital copy of this book, and a **30%** discount code on your next cart value on our official websites:

www.orangeava.com

www.orangeava.in (For Indian Subcontinent)

☑ **Here's how:**

Leave a review for the book on Amazon.

Take a screenshot of your review, and send an email to **info@orangeava.com** (it can be just the confirmation screen).

Once, we receive your screenshot, we will send you the digital file, within 24 hours.

Thank you so much for your support – it means a lot to us!

Colored Images

Please follow the links or scan the QR codes to download the ***Images*** of the book:

You can find code bundles of our books on our official Github Repository. Go to the following link to and QR code to explore the further:

https://github.com/orgs/ava-orange-education/repositories

Please follow the link to download the Colored Images of the book:
https://rebrand.ly/9571da

In case there's an update to the code, it will be updated on the existing GitHub repository.

Errata

We take immense pride in our work at **Orange Education Pvt Ltd,** and follow best practices to ensure the accuracy of our content to provide an indulging reading experience to our subscribers. Our readers are our mirrors, and we use their inputs to reflect and improve upon human errors, if any, that may have occurred during the publishing processes involved. To let us maintain the quality and help us reach out to any readers who might be having difficulties due to any unforeseen errors, please write to us at :

errata@orangeava.com

Your support, suggestions, and feedback are highly appreciated.

DID YOU KNOW

Did you know that Orange Education Pvt Ltd offers eBook versions of every book published, with PDF and ePub files available? You can upgrade to the eBook version at **www.orangeava.com** and as a print book customer, you are entitled to a discount on the eBook copy. Get in touch with us at: **info@orangeava.com** for more details.

At **www.orangeava.com**, you can also read a collection of free technical articles, sign up for a range of free newsletters, and receive exclusive discounts and offers on Print Books and eBooks.

PIRACY

If you come across any illegal copies of our works in any form on the internet, we would be grateful if you would provide us with the location address or website name. Please contact us at **info@orangeava.com** with a link to the material.

ARE YOU INTERESTED IN AUTHORING WITH US?

If there is a topic that you have expertise in, and you are interested in either writing or contributing to a book, please write to us at **business@orangeava.com**. We are on a journey to help developers and tech professionals to gain insights on the present technological advancements and innovations happening across the globe and build a community that believes Knowledge is best acquired by sharing and learning with others. Please reach out to us to learn what our audience demands and how you can be part of this educational reform. We also welcome ideas from tech experts and help them build learning and development content for their domains.

REVIEWS

Please leave a review. Once you have read and used this book, why not leave a review on the site that you purchased it from? Potential readers can then see and use your unbiased opinion to make purchase decisions. We at Orange Education would love to know what you think about our products, and our authors can learn from your feedback. Thank you!

For more information about Orange Education, please visit **www.orangeava.com**.

Table of Contents

Chapter 1
Understanding Cloud Computing, Cloud-Native Applications Security and Challenges

Introduction

Cloud Computing has fundamentally disrupted the whole IT Economy, bringing significant changes and opportunities on a massive scale!

Before we delve into the arsenal of tools designed to fortify cloud security, let us take a moment to revisit the **fundamentals of cloud computing**.

This chapter will cover all the basic concepts which are necessary to learn about cloud computing. Remember that cloud computing is indeed a methodology, rather than a single tool.

It is a suite which contains different types and models of cloud computing platforms, various types of cloud service providers, different types of cloud computing deployment models, most common cloud computing characteristics, and many different types and categories of cloud computing services.

As you embark on this journey through my book, I hope you find the insights and stories both enlightening and enjoyable. Each chapter is crafted to provide valuable knowledge, and a fresh perspective on CNAPP, making it a resource you will want to revisit time and again.

Structure

In this chapter, the following topics will be covered:

- Introduction to Cloud Computing
- Cloud Computing Deployment Models
- Cloud Computing Service Models
- Cloud Computing Platforms Service Providers
- Cloud Computing Characteristics
- Enhanced Native Security Solutions in Cloud Computing
- Categories of Services in Cloud Computing Platforms
- Market Trends for Cloud Computing

Introduction to Cloud Computing

Welcome to Cloud Computing, **a definitely new era of Computing**. Believe me, one of the only strong buzzes in the IT industry these days is something known as "*Cloud Computing*".

Cloud computing is a new methodology to manage day-to-day operations and much more. It revolutionizes how we handle data, applications and IT infrastructure **by leveraging the power of the Internet** which is now easily available in every corner of the universe.

Along with the cloud computing demand rising day by day, the market has indeed evolved to address the complexity of cloud computing security and operations.

Look at this business report from "*Gartner*" **emphasizing on the IT landscape, shifting from traditional IT to Cloud Computing**.

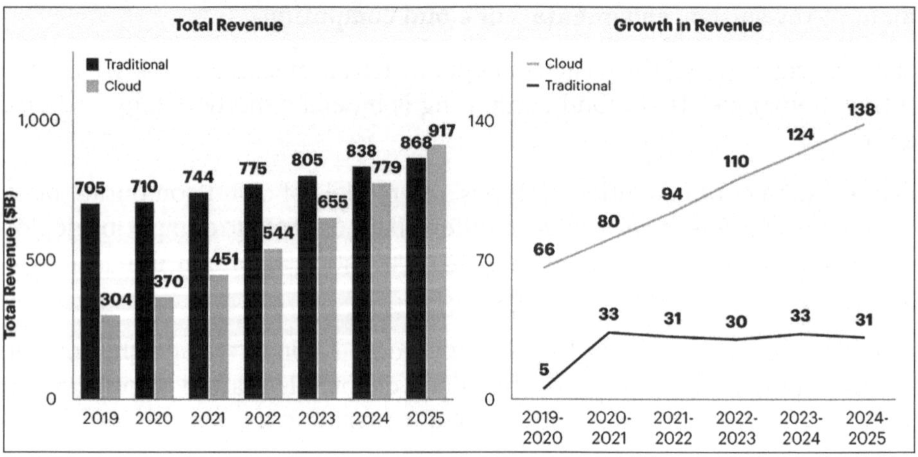

Figure 1.1: *Client–Server Model*

Prior to engaging with cloud computing concepts like cloud computing deployment models (public vs private cloud) and cloud computing service models (IaaS, PaaS, and SaaS), it is imperative to possess a comprehensive understanding of the prevalent concepts that define the contemporary cloud computing landscape.

These are some of the concepts that are commonly used in today's cloud computing world. We will talk about:

- On-Premises Infrastructure
- Shared-Responsibility Model
- CapeX vs OpeX

Traditional On-Premises Infrastructure

You all are aware about this traditional concept known as On-Premises. This has been the only service model available till the beginning and adoption of cloud computing. On-Premises refers to all compute, storage, database, networking resources, and other infrastructure located physically within an organization's physical boundaries, their own facilities, and buildings, rather than hosted remotely.

Organizations need to purchase all the necessary and desired equipment through the procurement processes which is operationally complex, and time-sensitive too. There is a chance that the equipment will arrive on schedule, but there is also a possibility, it might be delayed, which may cause you loss. Organizations must also invest in physical spaces, buildings with special needs for the purpose of data centers, and specialized rooms with HVAC capabilities. Then you also need a pool of resources, which means lots of people, for you to design the whole network, and to run this network design securely and smoothly over the time. Believe me, this all is challenging, and difficult.

Scalability, Agility and High Availability have always been difficult factors in setting up on-premises infrastructure. It is very difficult to scale up, in case there is a sudden spike, and current provisioned infrastructure runs out of capacity. And the other side of the coin is also dangerous, which means you also may pay extra for overprovisioning the infrastructure which is never used/utilized at the expected level.

There are many other challenges in setting up the on-premises infrastructure which is resolved by adapting some of the cloud computing service models such as IaaS, PaaS, and SaaS.

Understanding Shared-Responsibility Model

Before you begin your journey as a cloud administrator, you must understand the key concepts such as "*cloud service providers*" and "*cloud consumers*". Equally important is a thorough understanding of your responsibilities as a cloud consumer, and what all you get as a service from the cloud service provider. Remember, as an organization utilizing cloud services accessible via the Internet, you are identified as a cloud consumer.

This foundational knowledge is indispensable for distinguishing between different service models such as Infrastructure as a Service (IaaS), Platform as a Service (PaaS), and Software as a Service (SaaS).

There exists a distinct delineation between your role as a cloud consumer, and that of the cloud service provider, a boundary that is meticulously outlined within the framework of the "*shared responsibility model*."

The shared responsibility model stands as a pivotal tenet, elucidating the demarcation of duties between the cloud consumer and the cloud service provider.

CapEx versus OpEx

Think, why would you as an organization opt for cloud computing?

The pay-as-you-go model, which is actually an OpEx model, is indeed one of the significant factors in the whole disruption strategy caused by cloud computing. It is really important for you to enable yourself with these two highly used terms in cloud computing. This understanding will help directly manage your finance spent on IT Infrastructure procurement.

Most of you believe that cloud computing works on the OpeX model, but remember that cloud computing operates at both CapEx and OpeX models such as the "*Public Cloud Computing Platform*" operates at OpEx model, while the "*Private Cloud Computing Platform*" operates at the CapEx model.

You will not be able to understand these terms better wearing a hat of a cloud engineer or analyst, you need to have some finance related knowledge, and you will have to wear a hat of the "*Cloud Finance Officer*" or "*Chief Technology Officer*" to understand these terms better.

CapEx

CapeX means Capital Expenditure. It simply means an upfront payment.

Capex was the only one of the heavily used payment methods for procuring IT assets such as industrial buildings, data-centers, racks, servers, software licenses, network and security equipment, as well as other IT assets before Cloud Computing disrupted the whole IT economy.

With the Capex model, all the money is spent in one go to buy and procure different types of IT assets. These are heavy and large investments which provide benefits over a long period.

The private cloud deployment model leverages CapEx business expense model.

OpeX

OpeX means operational expenditure. These are all day to day running expenses required to effectively run a business.

Public cloud deployment model leverages OpeX business expense model.

Scalability and Flexibility in Cloud Economics

One of the most compelling advantages of cloud computing–especially under the OpEx model–is its **inherent scalability**. Organizations can easily upscale or downscale their IT resources based on real-time demand, **without being locked into long-term hardware investments**.

This is particularly beneficial for startups and growing businesses which often face unpredictable workloads and limited capital. **Instead of investing heavily in infrastructure they might not need immediately**, they can start small and expand month by month, aligning costs directly with usage.

This flexibility not only optimizes financial planning, but also accelerates innovation and responsiveness.

Cloud Computing Deployment Models

Cloud Computing is a diverse set of tools and technologies. It is a suite of tools and technologies. It is not just limited to one specific set of models, rather it offers various deployment models that can be stitched as per an organization's individual and unique needs. It encompasses a varied spectrum of tools and technologies.

The first thing to begin in understanding cloud computing is the "*Cloud Computing Deployment Models*". We ensure that we will share industry-wide accepted and engaging use cases, and self-explanatory theories to make the concept easy to digest.

Public Cloud

A Public Cloud platform is public which means that all the different types of services offered such as Compute, Storage, Databases, Machine Learning and Analytics services are public in nature, and provided over the INTERNET by the cloud service provider. Remember that, being public, all these services are exposed over to the INTERNET. It is available to everyone, provided they have the correct authentication medium and valid credentials.

It is important to understand that while **public cloud platforms are available to everyone (typically with a credit card and valid credentials), this does not mean that the resources you deploy are automatically exposed to the Internet.**

The term "*public*" refers to the accessibility of the cloud infrastructure itself–not the visibility of your applications or data.

As a cloud consumer, you are responsible for configuring access controls, network security, and ensuring that only the necessary components are made publicly accessible.

This is a key part of the Shared Responsibility Model, where the cloud provider secures the infrastructure, and you are responsible for securing your environment within it.

These are the most popular Public Cloud Service Providers worldwide:

1. Amazon Web Services (AWS)
2. Microsoft Azure
3. Google Cloud Platform
4. Alibaba Cloud
5. Oracle Cloud
6. IBM Cloud

These are some of the core and inherent benefits of adapting the public cloud deployment model:

- **Cost Efficiency:** I would say this is one of the most ultimate benefits of adapting to the public cloud computing platform. This has disrupted the whole IT industry.

  It offers a Pay-as-you-go pricing model in which you only pay for the **resources you have used** and **provisioned**, avoiding the high upfront cost of setting up traditional infrastructure. While the public cloud offers a pay-as-you-go model, it is important to note that **you typically pay for the resources you provision, not just what you use.**

  For example, if you provision a high-performance server with 256GB RAM and 128 CPUs, you are billed for that configuration–even if it is underutilized. However, cloud platforms offer features like auto-scaling which allow you to start with a smaller setup, and scale up only when needed. This way, you pay more only when your resource usage increases, making it a cost-effective strategy for dynamic workloads.

- **Scalability:** Scalability means an ability to efficiently and dynamically adjust computing and other relevant resources such as disks, NIC cards, and IP addresses to meet the changing demands. Remember that autoscaling capability can both increase and decrease as per the demands. Autoscaling feature is available to cloud consumers as a managed service, which means you do not need to worry about the underlying infrastructure.

Scaling capabilities relies on (i) continuous health and performance monitoring, and (ii) pre-defined threshold parameters to add or remove additional resources, based on usage metrics of the CPU, memory, hard-disk, and network traffic.

- **Threshold Parameters:** Threshold parameters are conditions which can trigger the scaling actions.
- **Vertical Scaling (Scaling Up/Down):** It means upgrading and degrading resources such as vCore, RAM, and Hard Disks into an existing running virtual machine to handle the actual demand. If the demand increases, then the virtual machine is scaled up, and when the demand decreases then the virtual machine is scaled down. Scale up means that now you need to pay extra for the compute resources, and scale down means that you pay less. This whole process is automated and triggered with the help of some pre-configured threshold settings.
- **Horizontal Scaling (Scaling Out/In):** This means adding/removing more similar configuration virtual machines into an existing pool. For example, increasing more servers to meet the sudden spike to the web application due to festival evening, and then removing extra servers to meet the actual traffic. Here again, you pay more, when more similar virtual machines are working in the pool, and you pay less, when few virtual machines are running in the pool. This whole process is automated and triggered with the help of some pre-configured threshold settings.

Use case: The demand for Pizza increases during Christmas worldwide, therefore, the backend infrastructure should be capable of detecting these rise in demands, and accordingly scale up or scale out, and then automatically scale down and scale in, when the demand has decreased.

- **Agility:** There is a famous saying that "*Being agile is a powerful capability that enables individuals and teams to adapt swiftly to changes, innovate continuously, and deliver high quality results efficiently. It fosters resilience, encourages proactive problem-solving, and enhances the overall productivity.*"

  Agility in cloud computing is the ability to adapt to changes by efficiently deploying, managing and scaling applications and resources.

- **Ease of Management and Maintenance:** Adopting the public cloud fundamentally transforms the ease of management and maintenance for organizations. By leveraging cloud service provider's robust infrastructure and advanced management tools, businesses can significantly reduce the complexity of their day-to-day IT operations. The public cloud offers automated updates, seamless scaling, and comprehensive monitoring, while collectively minimizing the need for manual interventions, and reducing the risk of human errors. It is a pretty streamlined approach, which not only enhances operational efficiency, but also allows IT teams to focus on strategic initiatives, rather than routine maintenance tasks. Furthermore, the public cloud's inherent flexibility and accessibility enable rapid deployment of applications and services, ensuring that businesses can swiftly adapt to the changing market demands, and maintain a competitive edge.

- **Improved Security:** Adapting the public cloud significantly enhances an organization's security posture. Cloud service providers invest heavily in advanced security technologies and practices, offering robust protection that often surpasses what many businesses can achieve on their own. These providers implement multi-layered security measures, including encryption, identity and access management, and continuous monitoring to safeguard data and applications. Additionally, the public cloud's inherent scalability allows for rapid deployment of security updates and patches, ensuring that systems remain protected against emerging threats. By leveraging the experience and resources of cloud providers, organizations can achieve a higher level of security, reduce the risk of breaches, and maintain compliance with industry standards and regulations, all while focusing on their core business objectives.
- **Faster Time to Market:** Adopting the public cloud accelerates an organization's time to market by streamlining the development and deployment processes. The cloud's on-demand resources and scalable infrastructure enable teams to quickly provision and configure environments, eliminating the delays associated with traditional hardware procurement and setup. Additionally, cloud-native tools and services such as Continuous Integration and Continuous Development (CI/CD) pipelines, facilitate rapid development cycles and automated testing, ensuring that new features and updates can be rolled out swiftly and reliably. This agility allows businesses to respond faster to market demands, innovate continuously, and maintain a competitive edge. By leveraging the public cloud, organizations can significantly reduce the time it takes to bring new products and services to market, driving growth and customer satisfaction.
- **Global Reach:** Adopting the public cloud empowers organizations with unparalleled global reach, enabling them to deploy applications and services closer to their users, regardless of their geographic location. Cloud service providers operate extensive networks of data centers around the world, allowing businesses to leverage these distributed resources to ensure low-latency access and high availability. This global infrastructure supports seamless

scalability and redundancy, ensuring that applications remain performant and resilient, even during peak demand periods. By utilizing the public cloud, organizations can easily expand into new markets, deliver consistent user experiences across regions, and meet local compliance requirements. This capability to operate on a global scale not only enhances customer satisfaction, but also drives business growth and competitive advantage.

In summary, adopting the public cloud offers a multitude of core benefits that drive operational excellence and business growth. From the ease of management and maintenance to improved security, faster time to markct, and global reach, the public cloud empowers organizations to innovate and scale with unprecedented agility. By leveraging the advanced capabilities of and extensive infrastructure of cloud service providers, businesses can focus on their strategic objectives, enhance customer experiences, and maintain a competitive edge in an ever-evolving digital landscape.

Embracing the public cloud is not just a technological shift, but a strategic enabler that transforms how organizations operate and deliver values.

Private Cloud

It is different from the public cloud in many ways. It is as simple as the word, "*Private*" in English. Yes, it is your own cloud environment, you build this infrastructure, you make this heavy investment to host your servers, databases, applications, and other digital IT assets, as well as finally, you manage it. CapeX business expense is leveraged for setting up the private cloud.

These are the most popular Public Cloud service providers worldwide:

1. Amazon Web Services (AWS)
2. Microsoft Azure
3. Google Cloud Platform
4. VMware
5. IBM Cloud
6. OpenStack

Interesting to see that AWS falls under both public and private cloud deployment models. Yes, that is correct. AWS primarily operates as a public cloud provider, offering a wide range of services accessible over the Internet. However, AWS also provides private cloud solutions through services like "AWS *Outposts*" which bring AWS infrastructure and services to on-premises environments allowing for a hybrid cloud setup. It is an actual and practical use case of Hybrid Cloud Computing platform.

The same is true for Microsoft Azure which offers both public and private cloud solutions. Azure offers private cloud services through "*Azure Stack*", which allow you to run Azure services in your own data center. It is an actual and practical use case of Hybrid Cloud Computing platform.

These are the major pillars of a private cloud computing platform:

- **Enhanced Security:** Private cloud offers the most robust security control for your own organization, including dedicated servers and racks with dedicated network and security gears, dedicated redundant Internet provider links, and dedicated dual water and power supplies.
- **Customization:** Private cloud offers the highest customization capabilities. This enables organizations to stitch the infrastructure and services as per the actual business needs.
- **Greater Control:** You being the sole owner of the private cloud infrastructure, you have full control on all physical as well as logical IT assets, including the building, physical security controls (CCTV, fencing) data center, racks, and logical security controls.
- **Cost Predictability:** The private cloud deployment model offers much better cost optimization and predictability compared to the public cloud deployment model. You can well plan your investment as per the future trend, and the needs of your business.

  Private cloud platforms offer a level of cost predictability by allowing organizations to plan their IT investments upfront and amortize them over several years–typically three to five. This model helps to fix your minimum costs, and aligns well with long-term budgeting. However, it is important to note that this predictability comes with trade-offs. If your business needs change, or you require an upgrade, you may face significant downtime, or lose part of your earlier investment. Unlike public cloud, scaling in private cloud environments is not as seamless, and often involves additional infrastructure planning and capital expenditure.
- **Reliability:** Reliability is the cornerstone of private cloud computing, ensuring that services and applications are consistently available, and perform optimally. In a private cloud environment, reliability encompasses several critical aspects: High Availability, Disaster Recovery, Fault Tolerance, Scalability and Elasticity.

Hybrid Cloud

The hybrid cloud model represents a strategic blend of public and private cloud environments, offering organizations the flexibility to optimize their IT infrastructure. By integrating on-premises resources with cloud services, businesses can leverage the best of both worlds – scalability and cost-efficiency of the public cloud, combined with the control and security of private infrastructure. This approach allows for seamless data and application mobility, enabling organizations to dynamically allocate resources, based on workload demands and regulatory requirements. The hybrid cloud not only enhances operational agility, but also supports innovation by providing a versatile platform for deploying and managing diverse applications. As enterprises navigate the complexities of digital transformation, the hybrid cloud emerges as a powerful solution to achieve a balanced, resilient, and future-ready IT ecosystem.

Community Cloud

A community cloud is a collaborative cloud infrastructure designed to meet the specific needs of a group of organizations with shared concerns such as security, compliance or performance requirements. This model allows multiple organizations to share resources and infrastructure, benefiting from economies of scale, while maintaining a higher level of control and customization compared to public clouds. Community clouds are particularly advantageous for sectors with stringent regulatory requirements such as healthcare, finance and government where data privacy and compliance are paramount. The community cloud fosters collaboration and innovation among its members, enabling them to leverage collective expertise, and address common challenges more effectively. This model not only enhances operational efficiency, but also supports the development of industry-specific solutions tailored to the unique needs of the community.

If you ask us, which one is better, Public Cloud, Private Cloud or Hybrid Cloud. Seriously, we do not have a one-word answer for you. Because each of these deployment models serve different purposes, and can be adapted to fulfill very specific needs. Look at these simple examples here:

We would prefer a public cloud, if we need immediate infrastructure setup, on-demand access to services, pay-as-you-go pricing model, instead of upfront, and unlimited scaling capabilities. On the other hand, we would prefer a private cloud, if we want full control over the underlying hardware infrastructure.

Cloud Computing Service Models

Now, it is the time for the second gear!

This section of the chapter is exceptionally important and informative. It is crucial to read and understand it with great care.

A cloud computing service model is a framework that offers various mechanisms to access a wide range of resources, including compute, storage, database, analytics, and machine learning services over the Internet. Each service model is distinct, with its own set of advantages and disadvantages. The following are the most popular and widely discussed cloud computing service models adopted in the industry:

- Infrastructure-as-a-service (IaaS)
- Platform-as-a-service (PaaS)
- Software-as-a-service (SaaS)

Bonus Topic: These are some of the less common cloud computing service models that organizations are gradually adopting. It is a bonus topic. Exploring these will deepen your understanding, and make you feel even more confident navigating the vast universe of cloud computing.

- Function as a Service (FaaS)
- Container as a Service (CaaS)
- Database as a Service (DBaaS)
- Storage as a Service (STaaS)
- Network as a Service (NaaS)
- Security as a Service (SECaaS)
- Monitoring as a Service (MaaS)
- Anything as a Service (XaaS)

Infrastructure as a Service (IaaS)

IaaS is the most popular, and one of the three main categories of cloud computing services, alongside SaaS and PaaS. IaaS provides virtualized computing resources over the Internet, allowing businesses to rent servers, storage and networking, on-demand. This model offers flexibility and scalability, enabling organizations to quickly adjust their infrastructure to meet the changing needs. With IaaS, organizations can avoid the costs and complexities of managing physical hardware, focusing instead on their core operations. It empowers businesses to innovate and grow without the constraints of traditional IT infrastructure. In the previous section, we delved into the intricacies of the "*Shared Responsibility Model*," exploring its fundamental principles and applications. Now, let us shift our focus, and examine this model through the lens of IaaS:

Responsibilities	Cloud Service Provider	Customer
Physical Infrastructure	Manages physical servers, storage, and networking	Not Responsible
Virtualization	Provides and maintains virtualization layer	Not Responsible
Operating System	Provides optional OS images	Manages and maintains the OS

Middleware	Not Responsible	Installs and manage middleware
Applications	Not Responsible	Develops, deploys, and manages applications
Data	Not Responsible	Manages data, including security and privacy
Security	Secure physical infrastructure	Secure OS, applications, and data
Compliance	Ensures infrastructure compliance with regulations	Ensures application and data compliance with regulations
Networking	Manages core networking infrastructure	Configures and manages virtual networks
Monitoring and Logging	Provides basic monitoring tools	Monitors and logs application performance

***Table 1.1**: Shared Responsibility Model for IaaS Service Model*

This table clearly delineates the division of responsibilities, ensuring both the cloud service provider and the customer understand their roles in managing a secure and efficient IaaS environment.

Platform as a Service (PaaS)

Platform as a Service (PaaS) provides a cloud-based environment where developers can build, deploy and manage applications, without worrying about the underlying infrastructure. It offers those tools and services that streamline the development process, enabling faster innovation, and reducing operational complexity. This model empowers developers to focus on coding and creativity, while the platform handles the heavy lifting of infrastructure management.

Responsibilities	**Cloud Service Provider**	**Customer**
Infrastructure Management	Manages physical servers, storage, and networking	Not Responsible
Platform Maintenance	Updates and maintains the platform software	Not Responsible
Application Development	Provides development tools and environment	Develops and maintains application
Data Management	Ensures data storage and backup solutions	Manages data, including security and privacy
Security	Secures the platform and infrastructure	Secures applications and data

Compliance	Ensures platform compliance with regulations	Ensures application compliance with regulations
Scalability	Provides scalable infrastructure	Manages application scalability
Monitoring and Logging	Monitors platform performance	Monitors application performance

Table 1.2: *Shared Responsibility Model for PaaS Service Model*

This table highlights the division of responsibilities, ensuring that both parties understand their roles in maintaining a secure and efficient PaaS environment.

Software as a Service (SaaS)

Software as a Service (SaaS) delivers software applications over the Internet, allowing users to access them via a web browser, without the need for the local installation or maintenance. This model offers convenience and scalability, as updates and security patches are managed by the service provider, ensuring that users always have access to the latest features. SaaS solutions are typically subscription-based, providing cost-effective access to powerful software tools that can be used from anywhere with an Internet connection. This approach simplifies IT management, and enables businesses to focus on their core activities, while leveraging advanced software capabilities.

Responsibilities	**Cloud Service Provider**	**Customer**
Application Management	Develops, maintains and updates the application	Uses the application and manages user settings
Data Management	Ensures data storage and backup solutions	Manages data input, access and privacy
Security	Secures the application and underlying infrastructure	Manages user access and data security within the application
Compliance	Ensures application compliance with regulations	Ensures data compliance with regulations
Infrastructure Management	Manages servers, storage and networking	Not responsible
Operating System	Manages and updates the OS	Not responsible
Middleware	Manages and update middleware	Not responsible
Networking	Manages core networking infrastructure	Not responsible

Monitoring and Logging	Monitors application performance and infrastructure	Monitors user activity and data usage

Table 1.3: *Shared Responsibility Model for SaaS Service Model*

This table highlights the division of responsibilities, ensuring that both the cloud service provider and the customer understand their roles in maintaining a secure and efficient SaaS environment.

Function as a Service (FaaS)

FaaS allows developers to execute the code in response to events, without managing server workloads or the infrastructure. **This serverless model simplifies deployment and scaling, enabling rapid development, and cost efficiency by charging only for the compute time used.**

Container as a Service (CaaS)

CaaS provides a platform for managing and deploying containerized applications. It offers orchestration, scaling, and security features, **allowing developers to focus on building applications, while the platform handles the underlying infrastructure.**

Database as a Service (DBaaS)

DBaaS delivers database management capabilities over the cloud. It simplifies database setup, maintenance, and scaling, providing automated backups, updates and high availability, **allowing businesses to focus on data utilization, rather than infrastructure management.**

Storage as a Service (STaaS)

STaaS offers scalable and flexible cloud storage solutions. It enables organizations to store, manage and access data remotely, providing cost-effective storage options, with built in redundancy and security features to ensure data integrity and availability.

Network as a Service (NaaS)

NaaS provides virtualized network infrastructure over the cloud. It allows businesses to configure and manage network resources dynamically, offering flexibility, scalability and enhanced security, without the need for physical hardware.

Security as a Service (SECaaS)

SECaaS delivers security solutions through the cloud. It includes services like threat detection, identity management, and data protection, enabling organizations to enhance their security posture with scalable, up-to-date defenses managed by experts.

Monitoring as a Service (MaaS)

MaaS provides cloud-based monitoring tools for IT infrastructure and applications. It offers real-time insights, alerts and analytics, helping organizations to ensure optimal performance, detect issues early, and maintain system reliability.

Anything as a Service (XaaS)

XaaS encompasses a broad range of services delivered over the cloud. It includes various "*as a service*" models, providing comprehensive solutions that enable businesses to access and manage IT resources flexibly and cost-effectively, driving innovation and efficiency.

Serverless Architecture

Serverless architecture is transforming the landscape of application development by eliminating the need for developers to manage the underlying infrastructure. In this model, cloud providers automatically allocate resources as needed, allowing developers to focus solely on wiring code. This approach is particularly advantageous for event-driven applications such as real-time data processing, where functions are triggered by specific events and scale automatically to handle the varying loads. By adapting serverless architecture, organizations can achieve greater agility, reduce operational costs, and accelerate innovation, making it an ideal choice for modern cloud-native applications.

Use case → For example, in a real-time analytics system, serverless functions can process incoming data streams, perform computations, and store results, without any manual intervention. Another compelling use case is in the realm of IoT, where serverless architecture can efficiently handle data from numerous devices, processing and responding to events in real-time.

Cloud Computing Platforms Service Providers

Cloud computing platforms are not just tools, they are ecosystems that empower developers and businesses to build, deploy and secure applications in ways that were unimaginable, just a few years ago.

In the vast and ever evolving universe of technology, cloud computing platforms stand out as the stars that guide businesses towards innovation and efficiency. The list of these platforms is not just long; it is growing at an unprecedented pace, expanding day by day, month by month.

The following is a list of cloud computing platforms:

- Amazon Web Services (AWS)
- Microsoft Azure
- Google Cloud Platform (GCP)
- Oracle Cloud
- Alibaba Cloud
- IBM Cloud
- VMware Cloud

As we delve into the intricacies of Cloud-Native Application Protection Platform (CNAPP), it becomes essential to understand the key players in the space. Among the myriad of options, three giants have emerged as the most influential and widely adopted: Amazon Web Services (AWS), Microsoft Azure, and Google Cloud Platform (GCP). Cloud computing platforms are not just tools, they are ecosystems that empower developers and businesses to build, deploy and secure applications in ways that were unimaginable, just a few years ago.

AWS with its pioneering spirit, offers a comprehensive suite of services that cater to every conceivable need. Azure, seamlessly integrating with Microsoft's extensive product line, provides unparalleled hybrid cloud capabilities. GCP with its innovative approach, excels in data analytics and machine learning. Each platform has carved out its niche, offering unique strengths that cater to different aspects of cloud-native security.

In this section, we will explore these platforms in detail, uncovering the features that make them indispensable.

Amazon AWS

AWS, the trailblazer in cloud computing, boasts a comprehensive suite of services that span across all aspects of IT infrastructure. Its maturity and extensive global network make it a reliable choice for businesses of all sizes. AWS excels in providing scalable compute power, storage solutions, advanced devops, and machine learning capabilities. A standout feature is AWS Lambda which enables serverless computing by allowing developers to run code, without managing servers infra. AWS security offerings such as AWS shield for DDOS protection and AWS WAF for web application security, provides robust defenses against cyber threats.

Microsoft Azure

Azure, Microsoft's cloud platform is renowned for its seamless integration with other Microsoft products and services. This makes it an ideal choice for enterprises already invested in the Microsoft ecosystem. Azure offers a rich array of services, including Azure DevOps for CI/CD pipelines and Azure Active Directory for identity management. One of Azure's key strengths is its hybrid cloud capabilities which allows businesses to integrate on-premises infrastructure with cloud resources seamlessly. This hybrid approach is particularly beneficial for CNAPP, as it offers greater control and flexibility over data and applications. Azure security features, such as Azure Security Center, provide comprehensive monitoring and threat protection.

Google GCP

GCP, while newer to the cloud market, has quickly gained a reputation for its innovation and expertise in data analytics and machine learning. Google Cloud's strengths lie in its powerful data processing tools such as BigQuery for data warehousing and TensorFlow for machine learning. GCP's most famous Kubernetes Engine simplifies the management of containerized applications which is a critical component of CNAPP. Google's commitment to open-source technologies and its robust security infrastructure, including the BeyondCorp security model, make GCP a strong contender for modern cloud-native applications. GCP's emphasis on zero-trust security principles ensures that applications and data are protected against evolving threats.

Cloud Computing Characteristics

Cloud computing revolutionizes the way we think about IT infrastructure by offering unparalleled flexibility, scalability, and efficiency. At its essence, cloud computing provides on-demand access to a vast array of configurable resources such as computing power, storage and applications which can be quickly adjusted to meet the varying demands. This elasticity ensures that businesses can scale their operations seamlessly, optimizing both performance and cost. Furthermore, cloud platforms are designed with high availability and reliability in mind, incorporating data redundancy and robust disaster recovery solutions to safeguard against potential disruptions. Security is a fundamental aspect, with advanced features such as encryption, identity and access management, and compliance as well as industry standards, ensuring that data and applications remain protected. There are many more cloud computing characteristics explained in this section.

These characteristics make cloud computing an ideal foundation for Cloud-Native Application Protection Platform (CNAPP), empowering organizations to innovate securely and efficiently in an ever-evolving digital landscape.

- **On-Demand Self-Service:** On-demand self-service is a fundamental characteristic of cloud computing that empowers users to provision and manage computing resources independently, without requiring human intervention from the service provider. This capability allows users to quickly and efficiently access resources such as virtual machines, storage, and applications through a user-friendly interface, typically a web portal or API. By providing immediate resource allocation, on-demand self-service enhances operational agility, and reduces the time and effort needed to deploy and scale services.
- **Broad Network Access:** Cloud services are accessible over the network through standard mechanisms, promoting use by heterogeneous thin or thick client platforms (for example, mobile phones, tablets, laptops, and workstations). This ensures that services are available from anywhere with an Internet connection, enhancing accessibility and convenience.
- **Resource Pooling:** Cloud providers use a multi-tenant model to serve multiple customers with dynamically assigned resources according to the demand. This pooling of resources leads to economies of scale, as physical and virtual resources are allocated and reallocated efficiently, ensuring optimal utilization.
- **Rapid Elasticity:** Cloud services can be elastically provisioned and released to scale rapidly outward and inward commensurate with demand. For users, this means that they can quickly scale up resources to handle peak loads, and scale down when demand decreases, ensuring that they only pay for what they use.
- **Measured Services:** Cloud systems automatically control and optimize resource use by leveraging a metering capability at some level of abstraction appropriate to the type of service (for example, storage, processing, and bandwidth). This transparency in resource usage helps in monitoring, controlling, and reporting, providing accountability and billing, based on actual consumption.
- **Cost Efficiency:** Cloud computing reduces the need for significant Capital Expenditure (CapEx) on hardware and software. Instead, it shifts costs to Operational Expenditure (OpEx), where users pay for services on a subscription or pay-per-use basis. This model can lead to significant cost savings, especially for small and medium-sized enterprises.
- **Security:** Cloud providers implement stringent security measures, including encryption, access controls, and regular security audits, to protect the data and applications. While security is a shared responsibility between the provider and the user, cloud services often offer advanced security features that might be cost-prohibitive for individual organizations to implement on their own.
- **Reliability:** Cloud providers offer robust disaster recovery and backup solutions, ensuring high availability and reliability of services. Data is often

replicated across multiple geographic locations, reducing the risk of data loss and downtime.

- **Flexibility:** Cloud computing offers flexibility in terms of resource allocation and usage. Users can choose from a variety of service models (IaaS, PaaS, and SaaS) as well as deployment models (public, private, and hybrid) to best meet their specific needs. This flexibility allows organizations to tailor their cloud strategy to their unique requirements.
- **CapEx versus OpEx:** Capital Expenditure (CapEx) involves upfront costs for physical infrastructure, while Operational Expenditure (OpEx) involves the ongoing costs for services and maintenance. Cloud computing shifts the financial burden from CapEx to OpEx, allowing businesses to avoid large upfront investments, and instead pay for services as they use them.
- **Economies of Scale:** Cloud providers achieve economies of scale by serving a large number of customers with shared infrastructure. This leads to cost savings that are passed on to customers, making cloud services more affordable than traditional on-premises solutions.
- **Compliance and Governance:** Cloud providers often comply with industry standards and regulations, offering services that meet various compliance requirements (example, GDPR, HIPAA). They provide tools and features that help organizations maintain governance over their data and applications, ensuring compliance with legal and regulatory obligations.

Enhanced Native Security Solutions in Cloud Computing

As we have come to understand, cloud computing is far more than a mere tool; it is an intricate ecosystem, a harmonious suite of diverse technologies working in concert. Before delving into the extensive array of security solutions available within cloud computing, it is essential to grasp the concept of "*Native Security*." Native Security refers to the comprehensive security measures provided inherently by public or private cloud platforms. These platforms offer a plethora of services, including Compute, Database, Storage, DevOps, Networking, Containerization, Analytics, Data Warehousing, and Machine Learning. Alongside these services, they also deliver robust security solutions. There is no need to depend on third-party providers to secure your cloud assets; instead, you can leverage the security solutions offered directly by your cloud service provider. Hence, these are aptly termed Native Security solutions. These native security solutions are integral to building a secure cloud environment, ensuring that data and applications are protected against evolving threats. Here are some enhanced native security solutions commonly found in cloud computing:

- Automated and Advanced Threat Detection and Response

- Identity and Access Management
- Encryption
- Compliance and Governance
- Security Information and Event Management
- Web Application Firewall
- Distributed Denial of Service (DDoS) Protection
- Endpoint Protection
- Network Security
- Container Security
- Kubernetes Security
- Zero Trust Security

In this section, we will delve deeper into some of these solutions, not all.

Automated and Advanced Threat Detection and Response

This being a native security solution leverages machine learning techniques to continuously monitor and analyze cloud environments, swiftly identifying and neutralizing potential threats, before they can cause harm. By automating the detection process, it reduces the time to respond to incidents, minimizing potential damage, and ensuring continuous protection.

Identity and Access Management

An IAM system enforces stringent authentication and authorization protocols, ensuring that only verified and legitimate users can access sensitive cloud resources, thereby safeguarding against unauthorized access. These systems also provide detailed audit logs and access controls, enabling organizations to manage user permissions effectively, and maintain compliance with security policies.

Encryption

Encryption secures data by converting it into a coded format, both at rest and in transit, ensuring that even if intercepted, the information remains unreadable, without the proper decryption keys in possession. This process protects sensitive information from unauthorized access and breaches, maintaining data integrity and confidentiality across the cloud infrastructure.

Compliance and Governance

These tools help organizations adhere to industry standards and regulatory requirements by providing continuous monitoring, reporting and automated compliance checks, within the cloud environment. They simplify the process of maintaining compliance, reducing the risk of penalties and ensuring that the security practices align with the legal and industry standards.

Security Information and Event Management

The SIEM solution is no secret; it is well-known and widely recognized by all of us. SIEM solutions aggregate and analyze security data in the shape of logs and events from various sources like servers, routers, switches, firewalls, endpoints, applications and database servers, enabling real-time threat detection, incident response and comprehensive security management. By correlating data from different systems, SIEM provides a holistic view of the security landscape, helping organizations to identify and respond to threats more effectively.

Web Application Firewall

These WAF protect web applications by filtering and monitoring HTTP traffic, blocking malicious requests, and safeguarding against common web exploits like SQL injection and cross site scripting. They act as a shield between the web application and the Internet, ensuring that only legitimate traffic reaches the application, thereby enhancing its security.

Distributed Denial of Service (DDoS) Protection

This solution defends against DDoS attacks by absorbing and mitigating malicious traffic, ensuring that legitimate users can access cloud services without interruption. It uses many advanced static and dynamic algorithms to detect and filter out attack traffic, maintaining the availability and performance of cloud applications even under attack.

Endpoint Protection

Endpoint protection secures devices such as laptops, desktop and mobile devices against threats, ensuring that all endpoints connected to the cloud are protected from malware and other attacks. It includes features such as antivirus, anti-malware, and firewall protection, providing a comprehensive defense for all endpoint devices.

Network Security

Network security encompasses measures such as Virtual Private Networks (VPNs), firewalls and Intrusion Detection/Prevention Systems (IDS/IPS) to protect the data as it travels across the cloud network. These tools ensure secure communication channels, prevent unauthorized access, and detect suspicious activities, maintaining the integrity and confidentiality of data in transit.

Container Security

Container security involves scanning for vulnerabilities, enforcing runtime protection, and ensuring compliance, thereby securing containerized applications throughout their lifecycle. It includes monitoring container behavior, managing container images, and implementing security policies to protect against threats specific to container environments.

Kubernetes Security

This solution secures kubernetes cluster by implementing policies and controls to manage access, monitor activity, and protect workloads from threats within the container orchestration environment. It includes Role-Based Access Control (RBAC), network policies, and security configurations to ensure that Kubernetes deployments are secure and resilient.

Zero Trust Security

Zero trust security operates on the principle that no entity is trusted by default, requiring continuous verification for access to resources, thereby minimizing the risk of unauthorized access and breaches. It involves strict identity verification, micro-segmentation, and real-time monitoring to ensure that only authenticated and authorized users can access the sensitive data and applications.

Categories of Services in the Cloud Computing Platforms

Cloud computing offers a vast array of services that can be broadly categorized into several key areas. Understanding each or some of these categories is essential for leveraging the full potential of the cloud environments ecosystem, especially when implementing Cloud-Native Application Protection Platform (CNAPP). Each category encompasses a range of services designed to address the specific needs and challenges.

Compute Services

Compute services are the backbone of cloud platforms, providing the processing power required to run applications and workloads. These compute services include Virtual Machines (VMs), containers, and serverless computing. Each of these services have their own pros and cons, and their own specific use cases. Virtual machines offer scalable and customizable environments, while containers provide lightweight, portable solutions for deploying applications. Serverless computing such as AWS Lambda or Azure Functions, allow developers to run a code without managing the server and underlying hardware or virtual infrastructure, enabling rapid scaling and cost efficiency.

As we continue our journey into understanding CNAPP, it is necessary to take a practical approach and familiarize ourselves with some of the commonly used compute services across the three major cloud computing platforms. The following is a table listing ten widely utilized compute services for each of these cloud giants:

AWS Compute Services	Azure Compute Services	GCP Compute Services
1. Amazon Elastic Compute Cloud (EC2) 2. Amazon EC2 Autoscaling 3. AWS Lambda 4. Amazon Elastic Container Service (ECS) 5. Amazon Elastic Kubernetes Services (EKS) 6. AWS Fargate 7. Amazon Lightsail 8. Amazon Elastic Beanstalk 9. Amazon Elastic Container Registry (ECR) 10. AWS App Runner	1. Azure Virtual Machines 2. Azure Virtual Machine Scale Sets 3. Azure Functions 4. Azure Kubernetes Services (AKS) 5. Azure Container Instances (ACI) 6. Azure App Service 7. Azure Logic Apps 8. Azure Container Registry (ACR) 9. Azure Spring Apps 10. Azure Dedicated Host	1. Google Compute Engine 2. Google Kubernetes Engine (GKE) 3. Google App Engine 4. Google Cloud Functions 5. Google Cloud Run 6. Google Cloud Batch 7. Google Anthos 8. Google Cloud Build 9. Google Cloud Scheduler 10. Google Cloud Run

Table 1.4: *Widely Used Compute Services in AWS, Azure and GCP Cloud Platforms*

In conclusion, the compute services provided by AWS, Azure, and GCP each offer distinct advantages that cater to a variety of computational needs. **AWS EC2** is renowned for its extensive range of instance types, ensuring flexibility and scalability for diverse workloads. **Azure's Virtual Machines** seamlessly integrate with Microsoft's ecosystem, making them an ideal choice for enterprises already utilizing Microsoft technologies. On the other hand, **GCP's Compute Engine** excels with its customizable virtual machines and robust container orchestration, particularly through its **Kubernetes Engine**.

By leveraging these advanced compute services, organizations can optimize their performance, enhance scalability, and foster innovation within their cloud infrastructure. Staying informed about these offerings is necessary for harnessing the full potential of cloud computing in an ever-evolving digital landscape.

Storage Services

Storage services in the cloud offer scalable and durable solutions for storing and managing data. These services include object storage, block storage, and file storage. Object storage like S3 or Google Cloud Storage is ideal for storing unstructured data such as media files and backups, as well as images. Block storage such as Azure Disk Storage, provides high-performance storage for applications requiring low-latency access. And, the last File Storage services such as Amazon EFS or Azure Files, offer shared file systems accessible from multiple instances.

It is equally important to understand different types of data like structured data, unstructured data and semi-structured data.

Structured Data

Structured data is highly organized and easily searchable, typically stored in relational databases or spreadsheets with predefined schemas such as SQL databases. This type of data is characterized by its strict format which allows for efficient querying and analysis. Structured data is often used in business applications where data integrity and consistency are crucial. Examples include customer information, transaction records, and inventory management systems. The predefined schema ensures that the data is entered in a consistent manner, making it easier to manage and analyze large datasets. Additionally, structured data can be easily integrated with various data analysis tools and business intelligence platforms, enabling organizations to derive valuable insights, and make data-driven decisions.

Unstructured Data

Unstructured data is the most flexible, but also the most challenging to manage, as it does not follow any predefined format or structure. This category includes a vast array of data types such as text documents, images, videos and social media posts. In the context of CNAPP, the ability to effectively handle and secure these diverse data types is paramount, as each type presents unique challenges and opportunities for data protection and threat detection. For instance, text documents may contain sensitive information that needs encryption, while images and videos require robust storage solutions, and advanced analysis tools to detect anomalies. Social media posts, on the other hand, can provide valuable insights into user behavior, but also pose significant security risks, if not properly monitored.

By leveraging advanced technologies such as machine learning and artificial intelligence, organizations can better manage unstructured data, ensuring that it is both secure and accessible for analysis.

Semi-Structured Data

Semi-structured data, on the other hand, lacks a rigid schema, but still contains tags or markers to separate data elements, making it more flexible, yet still somewhat organized. Examples include JSON and XML files which are commonly used in web applications and APIs.

Let us familiarize ourselves with some of the commonly used storage services across the three major cloud computing platforms. The following is a table listing ten widely utilized compute services for each of these cloud giants:

AWS Storage Services	Azure Storage Services	GCP Storage Services
1. Amazon Simple Storage Service (S3) 2. Amazon Elastic Block Store (EBS) 3. Amazon Elastic File Systems (EFS) 4. Amazon FSx 5. AWS Backup 6. AWS Storage Gateway 7. AWS Snow Family 8. AWS DataSync 9. Amazon S3 Glacier 10. AWS Transfer Family	1. Azure Blob Storage 2. Azure Disk Storage 3. Azure Files 4. Azure Queue Storage 5. Azure Table Storage 6. Azure Data Lake Storage 7. Azure NetApp Files 8. Azure Backup 9. Azure Archive Storage 10. Azure Storage Explorer	1. Google Cloud Storage 2. Google Persistent Disk 3. Google Cloud Filestore 4. Google Cloud Bigtable 5. Google Cloud Spanner 6. Google Cloud SQL 7. BigQuery 8. Google Cloud Firestore 9. Google Cloud Memorystore 10. Google Transfer Appliance

Table 1.5: *Most Used Storage Services in AWS, Azure and GCP Cloud Platforms*

In conclusion, the diverse storage solutions offered by AWS, Azure, and GCP provide robust, scalable, and secure options tailored to meet the needs of any organization. Whether it is the extensive ecosystem of **AWS S3**, the seamless integration of Azure **Blob Storage** with Microsoft's suite of services, or the innovative features of **Google Cloud Storage**, each platform brings unique strengths to the table.

By leveraging these cloud storage services, businesses can enhance their data management strategies, ensure high availability, and drive innovation. As cloud technology continues to evolve, staying informed about these offerings will be crucial for maximizing efficiency, and maintaining a competitive edge in the digital landscape.

Database Services

Database services in the cloud provide managed solutions for storing and querying structured data. These services include relational databases, NoSQL databases, and data warehousing. NoSQL databases like Amazon DynamoDB or Google Cloud Firestore, are designed for flexible, schema-less data storage. Relational databases such as Amazon RDS or Azure SQL Database, offer traditional SQL-based with high availability and scalability. Data warehousing services, such as Amazon Redshift or Google BigQuery, enable large-scale data analysis and reporting.

Let us explore some of the frequently used database services offered by the leading cloud computing platform. The following table highlights ten popular database services by each of these cloud giants:

AWS Database Services	Azure Database Services	GCP Database Services
1. Amazon Relational Database Service (RDS) 2. Amazon DynamoDB 3. Amazon Aurora 4. Amazon Redshift 5. Amazon ElastiCache 6. Amazon Neptune 7. Amazon DocumentDB 8. Amazon Timestream 9. AWS Glue 10. AWS Quantum Ledger Database (QLDB)	1. Azure SQL Database 2. Azure SQL Managed Instance 3. Azure SQL Server on Azure Virtual Machine 4. Azure Database for PostgreSQL 5. Azure Database for MySQL 6. Azure Database for MariaDB 7. Azure CosmosDB 8. Azure Cache for Redis 9. Azure Synapse Analytics 10. Azure Data Explorer	1. Google Cloud SQL 2. Google Cloud Spanner 3. Google Cloud Firestore 4. Google Cloud BigTable 5. Google BigQuery 6. Google Cloud MemoryStore 7. Google Cloud Datastore 8. Google Cloud SQL for postgreSQL 9. Google Cloud SQL for MysQL 10. Google Cloud SQL for SQL Server

Table 1.6: *Most Used Database Services in AWS, Azure and GCP Cloud Platforms*

In conclusion, the database services offered by AWS, Azure, and GCP each provide powerful and versatile solutions tailored to meet the diverse business needs. **AWS's Amazon RDS** stands out with its extensive support for various database engines, and seamless scalability. **Azure's SQL Database** offers deep integration with Microsoft's ecosystem, making it an excellent choice for enterprises already leveraging Microsoft technologies. Meanwhile, **GCP's Cloud SQL** excels with its robust performance and strong emphasis on data analytics as well as machine learning capabilities.

By utilizing these advanced database services, organizations can ensure high availability, robust security, and efficient data management. Staying informed about these offerings is crucial for optimizing database performance, and driving innovation in today's data-driven world.

Networking Services

Networking services in the cloud platforms facilitate secure and efficient communication between resources. These services include Virtual Private Clouds (VPCs), load balancers, and Content Delivery Networks (CDNs). VPCs like AWS VPC or Azure Virtual Network, provide isolated network environments for deploying resources. Load balancers distribute the incoming traffic across multiple instances to ensure high availability and reliability. CDNs such as Amazon CloudFront or Azure CDN, accelerate content delivery by caching data at edge locations closer to users.

Let us now explore some of the frequently used networking services offered by the leading cloud computing platform. The following table highlights ten popular networking services by each of these cloud giants:

AWS Networking Services	Azure Networking Services	GCP Networking Services
1. Amazon Virtual Private Cloud (VPC)	1. Azure Virtual Network (VNet)	1. Google Virtual Private Cloud (VPC)
2. Amazon CloudFront	2. Azure Load Balancer	2. Google Cloud Load Balancing
3. AWS DirectConnect	3. Azure Application Gateway	3. Google Cloud Interconnect
4. AWS TransitGateway	4. Azure VPN Gateway	4. Google Cloud VPN
5. Elastic LoadBalancing (ELB)	5. Azure ExpressRoute	5. Google Cloud Content Delivery Network (CDN)
6. AWS Global Accelerator	6. Azure Traffic Manager	6. Google Cloud DNS
7. AWS PrivateLink	7. Azure Front Door	7. Google Cloud NAT
8. Amazon Route53	8. Azure DNS	8. Google Cloud Armor
9. AWS VPN	9. Azure Bastion	9. Google Cloud Network Intelligence Center
10. AWS App Mesh	10. Azure Firewall	10. Google Cloud Router

Table 1.7: *Most Used Networking Services in AWS, Azure and GCP Cloud Platforms*

AWS's Virtual Private Cloud (VPC) excels with its extensive features for creating isolated networks and secure connections. **Azure's Virtual Network (VNet)** offers seamless integration with Microsoft's ecosystem and hybrid cloud capabilities, making it a strong choice for enterprises. **GCP's Virtual Private Cloud (VPC)** stands out with its global reach and innovative networking features such as Cloud Interconnect and Cloud DNS.

By leveraging these advanced networking services, organizations can ensure high performance, secure connectivity, and efficient management of their cloud environments.

Security Services

Security services in cloud services ensure the protection of data and applications. These services include Identity and Access Management (IAM), encryption and threat detection. IAM services like AWS IAM or Azure Active Directory manage user permissions, and access controls. Encryption services protect the data at rest and in transit, ensuring confidentiality and integrity. Threat detection services such as AWS GuardDuty or Azure Security Center, continuously monitor for suspicious activities and vulnerabilities.

Let us delve into some of the commonly utilized security services provided by top cloud computing platforms. The following table showcases ten widely-used security services from each of these major cloud providers.

AWS Security Services	Azure Security Services	GCP Security Services
1. AWS Identity and Access Management 2. Amazon GuardDuty 3. AWS Key Management Service (KMS) 4. AWS Shield 5. AWS Web Application Firewall (WAF) 6. Amazon Macie 7. AWS CloudTrail 8. AWS Config 9. AWS Security Hub 10. AWS Inspector	1. Microsoft Defender for Cloud 2. Microsoft Sentinel 3. Azure Key Vault 4. Azure Active Directory (AD) 5. Azure Security Center 6. Azure DDoS Protection 7. Azure Firewall 8. Azure Policy 9. Azure Information Protection 10. Azure Bastion	1. Google Cloud Identity and Access Management (IAM) 2. Google Cloud Key Management Service (KMS) 3. Google Cloud Armor 4. Google Cloud Security Command Center (SCC) 5. Google Cloud Audit Logs 6. Google Cloud Data Loss Prevention (DLP) 7. Google Cloud Identity-Aware Proxy (IAP) 8. Google Cloud Security Scanner 9. Google Cloud VPC Service Control 10. Google Cloud Operations Suite (formerly stackdriver)

Table 1.8: *Most Used Security Services in AWS, Azure and GCP Cloud Platforms*

In the realm of cloud security, AWS, Azure, and GCP each offer comprehensive solutions designed to protect data and applications. AWS provides robust security features such as **Identity and Access Management (IAM)**, **network firewalls**, and **encryption** in transit and at rest. Azure enhances security with its **Azure Security Center** which offers advanced threat protection and continuous security assessments. GCP stands out with its **Security Command Center**, providing centralized visibility and control over security policies and threats.

By leveraging these advanced security services, organizations can ensure their cloud environments are well-protected against evolving cyber threats, maintaining data integrity and compliance.

DevOps Services

In the rapidly evolving landscape of cloud computing, DevOps has emerged as a critical practice for accelerating software delivery and enhancing operational efficiency. All three major and leading cloud providers offer a comprehensive suite of DevOps services designed to streamline the development lifecycle, automate workflows, and ensure robust application performance. AWS leads with its extensive range of tools like CodePipeline and CloudFormation, enabling seamless integration and deployment. Azure Stands out its integrated DevOps solutions such as Azure pipelines and Azure Repos, fostering collaboration and continuous delivery. GCP, with its innovative offerings like Cloud Build and Google Kubernetes Engine, empowers developers to build, test, and deploy applications with agility and precision. Together, these platforms provide the foundational infrastructure that drives modern Devops practices, making them indispensable for organizations aiming to achieve continuous innovation and operational excellence.

Let us embark on a journey through some of the most esteemed DevOps services offered by the foremost cloud computing platforms. The following table illuminates ten prominent database services provided by each of these cloud titans:

AWS DevOps Services	Azure DevOps Services	GCP DevOps Services
1. AWS CodePipeline	1. Azure Boards	1. Google Cloud Build
2. AWS CodeBuild	2. Azure Pipelines	2. Google Cloud Source Repositories
3. AWS CodeDeploy	3. Azure Repos	3. Google Cloud Deploy
4. AWS CodeCommit	4. Azure Artifacts	4. Google Cloud Operations Suite
5. AWS CodeStar	5. Azure Test Plans	5. Google Cloud Artifact Registry
6. AWS CloudFormation	6. Azure DevTest Labs	6. Google Cloud Scheduler
7. AWS Elastic Beanstalk	7. Azure Monitor	7. Google Cloud Tasks
8. Amazon CloudWatch	8. Azure Automation	8. Google Cloud Pub/Sub
9. AWS OpsWorks	9. Azure Resource Manager	9. Google Cloud Functions
10. AWS X-Ray	10. Azure Blueprints	10. Google Kubernetes Engine (GKE)

Table 1.9: *Most Used DevOps Services in AWS, Azure and GCP Cloud Platforms*

In conclusion, the DevOps services provided by AWS, Azure, and GCP each offer comprehensive tools to streamline and enhance the software development lifecycle. **AWS DevOps** stands out with its robust suite of tools such as **AWS CodePipeline**, **CodeBuild**, and **CodeDeploy** which facilitate **Continuous Integration** and **Continuous Delivery (CI/CD)**. Azure DevOps offers a rich set of features, including **Azure Pipelines**, **Azure Repos**, and **Azure Boards**, providing seamless integration with Microsoft's ecosystem, and supporting agile project management. GCP's DevOps services such as **Cloud Build and Cloud Deploy**, excel in automating the build, test, and deployment processes, particularly for containerized applications.

By leveraging these advanced DevOps services, organizations can accelerate their development cycles, improve collaboration, and ensure high-quality software delivery. Staying informed about these offerings is essential for optimizing DevOps practices, and driving innovation in the fast-paced world of cloud computing.

Artificial Intelligence and Machine Learning (AIML) Services

Artificial Intelligence and Machine Learning services enable the extraction of insights, and the development of intelligent applications. These services include data processing, machine learning models, and Artificial Intelligence (AI) tools. Data processing services like AWS Glue or Google Dataflow, transform and prepare data for analysis. Machine learning services such as Amazon SageMaker or Azure Machine Learning, provide tools for building, training and deploying models. AI services such as Google Cloud AI or Azure Cognitive Services, offer pre-built models for tasks such as image recognition and natural language processing.

Let us explore some of the frequently used artificial intelligence and machine learning services offered by the leading cloud computing platform. The following table highlights ten popular AIML services by each of these cloud giants:

AWS AIML Services	Azure AIML Services	GCP AIML Services
1. Amazon Sage Maker	1. Azure Machine Learning	1. Vertex AI
2. AWS Deep Learning AMIs	2. Azure AI Services	2. AutoML
3. AWS Deep Learning Containers	3. Azure Databricks	3. BigQuery ML
4. Amazon Comprehend	4. Azure Cognitive Services	4. AI Platform Notebooks
5. Amazon Recognition	5. Azure AI Bot Service	5. Cloud Natural Language API
6. Amazon Polly	6. Azure AI Metrics Advisor	6. Cloud Vision API
7. Amazon Lex	7. Azure AI Content Safety	7. Cloud Speech-to-Text
8. Amazon Transcribe	8. Azure AI Video Indexer	8. Cloud Text-to-Speech
9. Amazon Translate	9. Azure AI Custom Vision	9. Cloud Translation API
10. Amazon Textract	10. Azure AI Document Intelligence	10. AI Hub

Table 1.10: *Most Used AIML Services in AWS, Azure and GCP Cloud Platforms*

AWS's SageMaker provides a comprehensive suite for building, training, and deploying machine learning models at scale. **Azure's Machine Learning** service integrates seamlessly with Microsoft's ecosystem, offering robust tools for automated ML and model management. GCP stands out with its **AI Platform**, leveraging TensorFlow and custom TPUs for high-performance machine learning tasks.

Thus, by utilizing these advanced AI and ML services, organizations can unlock new insights, enhance decision-making, and stay competitive in the rapidly evolving tech landscape.

Market Trends for Cloud Computing

The market trends in cloud computing reflect a dynamic shift towards more integrated, efficient, and secure solutions. From the rise of hybrid and multi-cloud strategies to the advent of edge computing and AI integration, these trends are not just shaping the future of IT infrastructure, but are also driving significant advancements across various industries. This section delves into the most influential trends in cloud computing, offering insights into how they are transforming the digital ecosystem, and setting the stage for the next wave of technology breakthroughs.

Hybrid and Multi-Cloud Strategies

Organizations are increasingly adopting hybrid and multi-cloud strategies to leverage the best features of different cloud providers. This approach enhances flexibility, reduces dependency on a single vendor, and optimizes costs.

Edge Computing

Edge computing is gaining traction as it brings computation and data storage closer to the location where it is needed, or to be consumed. This provides benefits to businesses which have latency sensitive applications. This reduces latency and bandwidth use, making it ideal for applications like IoT, autonomous vehicles, and real-time analytics.

Zero Trust Architecture

In this era of cloud computing, Zero Trust Architecture (ZTA) has emerged as a pivotal trend, fundamentally transforming how organizations approach security. Unlike traditional models that assume that everything inside the network is trustworthy, ZTA operates on the principle that no entity, whether inside or outside the network, should be trusted by default. This paradigm shift involves a rigorous verification process for every access request, ensuring that only authenticated and authorized users and devices can interact with sensitive data and systems. By employing techniques such as continuous monitoring, micro-segmentation, and adaptive access controls, ZTA provides a robust defense against sophisticated cyber threats. As organizations increasingly migrate to cloud environments, the adoption of Zero Trust Architecture is essential for safeguarding digital assets, and maintaining trust in a zero-trust world.

Serverless Computing

Serverless computing is becoming more popular due to its in-built cost-efficiency and scalability. It allows developers to focus on writing code, without worrying about infrastructure management, leading to faster deployment and innovation.

Micro Services

Microservices refer to an architectural style where applications are composed of small, independent services that communicate over well-defined APIs. Each microservice is designed to perform a specific business function, and can be developed, deployed and scaled independently. By leveraging microservices, organizations can build more agile, scalable, and resilient cloud-native applications, driving efficiency and innovation in their cloud environment.

Microservices architecture is transforming the cloud computing landscape by enabling the development of applications as a collection of loosely coupled, independently deployable services. This architecture promotes continuous delivery and deployment, as updates to individual services can be made without disrupting the entire application.

Let us explore some of the frequently used microservices offered by the leading cloud computing platform:

Microservices in AWS	Microservices in Azure	Microservices in GCP
1. Amazon ECS (Elastic Container Service) 2. Amazon EKS (Elastic Kubernetes Service) 3. AWS Lambda 4. Amazon API Gateway 5. AWS Fargate 6. Amazon SQS (Simple Queue Service) 7. Amazon SNS (Simple Notification Service) 8. Amazon DynamoDB 9. Amazon RDS (Relational Database Service) 10. AWS Step Functions	1. AKS (Azure Kubernetes Service) 2. Azure Functions 3. Azure Service Fabric 4. Azure API Management 5. Azure Logic Apps 6. Azure Event Grid 7. Azure Event Hubs 8. Azure Cosmos DB 9. Azure SQL Database 10. Azure Container Instance (ACI)	1. Google Kubernetes Engine (GKE) 2. Cloud Functions 3. Cloud Run 4. Google Cloud Endpoints 5. Pub/Sub 6. Cloud Tasks 7. Firestore 8. Cloud SQL 9. BigQuery 10. Dataflow

Table 1.11: *Most Used Microservices in AWS, Azure and GCP Cloud Platforms*

All these services help in building, deploying and managing microservices architecture efficiently on their respective cloud platforms.

Sustainability and Green Cloud

Sustainability is a growing concern, and cloud providers are investing in green technologies and practices. This includes using renewable energy sources, optimizing data center efficiency, and developing carbon-neutral cloud services. These initiatives not only minimize the carbon footprint of cloud operations, but also inspire broader industry adoption of eco-friendly practices. By prioritizing sustainability, cloud providers are helping to drive a global shift towards eco-friendlier and responsible computing solutions. With this, cloud providers are paving the way for a greener future, demonstrating that technological advancements and environmental responsibility can go hand in hand.

Quantum Computing

Quantum Computing is on the horizon with cloud providers investing in research and development. While still in its early stage, quantum computing promises to solve complex problems that are currently beyond the capabilities of classical computers/ traditional computing. This revolutionary technology leverages the principle of quantum mechanism, such as superposition and entanglement, to process information and data in fundamentally new ways. As a result, it has the potential to transform industries, ranging from cryptography and materials science to pharmaceuticals and artificial intelligence. Major tech companies and startups are racing to build practical quantum computers, aiming to unlock unprecedented computational power. The future of quantum computing holds the promise of breakthroughs that could redefine our understanding of computation and problem-solving. As research continues to advance, the day when quantum computers become a mainstream tool for solving the world's most complex problems is drawing close.

The following is a list of the most popular and most used quantum computing services which are leading the way in making quantum computing more accessible and practical for researchers, developers, and businesses:

- IBM Quantum Experience
- Google Quantum AI
- Amazon Bracket
- Microsoft Azure Quantum
- Rigetti Computing
- D-Wave Leap
- IonQ

Data Sovereignty and Localization

Data sovereignty refers to the concept that digital data is subject to the laws and governance structures within the nation where it is collected. This means that countries can assert control over data within their borders, influencing how it is stored, processed and transferred. This is **crucial for ensuring compliance with local regulations and protecting national security interests.**

Data localization, on the other hand, involves policies that require data to be stored and processed within a specific geographic location. These measures can often be implemented to enhance data security, protect privacy, and ensure that data remains under the jurisdiction of local laws. However, data localization can also pose challenges, such as increased costs for businesses, and potential barriers to global data flow.

The interplay between data sovereignty and localization is becoming increasingly significant as more countries adopt stringent data protection laws. With increasing regulations around data privacy and sovereignty, cloud providers are offering localized data centers to comply with regional laws. This trend ensures that data remains within specific geographic boundaries.

Conclusion

Having completed this chapter, we now have a solid grasp of basic cloud computing concepts. We understand the origins of cloud computing and the challenges associated with traditional on-premises IT infrastructure. We have explored the shared responsibility model, and the financial distinctions between CapEx and OpEx.

We have also identified the major cloud service providers–AWS, Azure, and GCP–and delved into the different cloud service models: IaaS, PaaS, and SaaS. Additionally, we have distinguished between public and private cloud service providers. Our exploration covered various service categories offered by cloud providers, including compute, storage, database, networking, security, Artificial Intelligence, Machine Learning, and Microservices.

In the next chapter, we will delve into Cloud Native Application Protection Platform (CNAPP). This chapter delves into the intricacies of CNAPP, exploring how it integrates various security tools and practices to provide holistic protection. As organizations increasingly adopt cloud-native technologies, the need for robust security measures has never been more critical. Enter the Cloud Native Application Protection Platform (CNAPP), a comprehensive solution designed to safeguard cloud-native applications throughout their lifecycle. From securing code during development to monitoring applications in production, CNAPP offers a unified approach to cloud security, ensuring that businesses can innovate with confidence, while maintaining a strong security posture. Join us as we uncover the essential components and benefits of CNAPP, and learn how it can transform your approach to cloud security.

Points to Remember

- Public vs Private vs Hybrid cloud computing service models.
- Shared responsibility model.
- Differences between IaaS, PaaS, and SaaS.

- Cloud Service Provider and customer responsibilities in IaaS, PaaS, and SaaS models.
- Serverless architecture, microservices, and edge computing.

Multiple-Choice Questions

1. What is the primary reason for the emergence of public cloud computing?
    a. To reduce the cost of hardware
    b. To address the limitations of traditional on-premises IT infrastructure
    c. To increase the complexity of IT systems
    d. To eliminate the need for software updates
2. Which of the following is NOT a major cloud service provider?
    a. AWS
    b. Azure
    c. GCP
    d. Mozilla Firefox
3. What does the shared responsibility model in cloud computing refer to?
    a. The division of security responsibilities between the cloud provider and the customer.
    b. The sharing of financial costs between multiple customers.
    c. The distribution of computing resources across different regions.
    d. The collaboration between different cloud service providers.
4. Which cloud service model provides the highest level of control over the underlying infrastructure?
    a. SaaS
    b. PaaS
    c. IaaS
    d. FaaS

5. Which of the following is a benefit of cloud-native applications?
    a. Increased latency
    b. Reduced scalability
    c. Enhanced flexibility and efficiency
    d. Higher maintenance costs

Answers

1. b
2. d
3. a
4. c
5. c

Questions

1. What is cloud computing?
2. Why did cloud computing emerge?
3. What are the main challenges of traditional on-premises IT infrastructure?
4. What is the shared responsibility model in cloud computing?
5. How do CapEx and OpEx differ in the context of cloud computing?
6. Name the three major cloud service providers.
7. What are the three main cloud service models?
8. How do public and private cloud service providers differ?
9. What types of services do cloud providers offer in the Compute category?
10. How do Artificial Intelligence and Machine Learning integrate with cloud services?

Key Terms

- **Cloud Computing Deployment Models:** It includes terms such as Public Cloud, Private Cloud, Hybrid and Community Cloud.
- **Cloud Computing Service Models:** It includes terms such as IaaS, PaaS, SaaS, FaaS, CaaS, DBaaS, STaaS, NaaS, SECaaS, MaaS, and XaaS.
- **Cloud Service Providers:** It includes Amazon AWS, Microsoft Azure and Google GCP.

CHAPTER 2
Understanding Cloud Native Application Protection Platform (CNAPP)

Introduction

As organizations increasingly adopt cloud-native technologies to drive innovation and efficiency, the need for robust security measures has never been more critical. This chapter delves into the concept of Cloud Native Application Protection Platform (CNAPP), exploring their essential role in safeguarding modern cloud environments. We will examine the architecture and components of CNAPP, understand why it is indispensable for an organization, and provide insights into selecting and scaling these platforms. By the end of this chapter, readers will have a comprehensive understanding of CNAPP, and its significance in the ever-evolving landscape of cloud security.

Structure

In this chapter, the following topics will be covered:

- Understanding Cloud Native Application Protection Platform (CNAPP)
- Understanding CNAPP Architecture Flow
- The Importance of CNAPP for an Organization
- Overview of Leading CNAPPs
- Selection Strategies before You Procure CNAPP
- Understanding Cloud Security Posture Management (CSPM)

- Understanding Cloud Workload Protection Platform (CWPP)
- Understanding Cloud Infrastructure Entitlement Management (CIEM)
- Understanding Cloud Service Network Security (CSNS)
- Understanding Kubernetes Security Posture Management (KSPM)
- Understanding Data Security Posture Management (DSPM)
- Understanding Infrastructure-as-Code (IaC) Scanning
- Understanding Centralized Compliance Dashboard
- Real-World Case Studies for CNAPP
- The Future of CNAPP

Understanding CNAPP Platform

In this cloud computing ecosystem, security still remains a paramount concern. Remember that traditional security controls and measures fall short in addressing the complexities of cloud-native environments. This is exactly where Cloud Native Application Protection Platform (CNAPP) comes into play. The CNAPP emerges as a sophisticated guardian, designed to safeguard the intricate architectures of modern applications. CNAPPs are designed to provide comprehensive security solutions tailored specifically for cloud-native applications. CNAPP addresses this need by integrating various security measures and tools into a cohesive platform, ensuring robust protection across the entire application lifecycle.

The Evolution of Cloud Security

To appreciate the significance of CNAPP, one must first understand the evolution of cloud security. Traditional security models, designed for static, on-premises environments, are ill-suited for the dynamic and distributed nature of cloud-native applications. The shift towards microservices, containers and serverless architectures has necessitated a new approach to security – one that is as agile and scalable, as the environment it protects.

Microservices architecture, with its modular approach, allows developers to build and deploy applications as a collection of loosely coupled services. While this enhances flexibility and scalability, it also introduces new security challenges. Each microservice, potentially running its own containers, must be individually secured, monitored, and managed. And this complexity is further compounded by the ephemeral nature of containers which can be spun up and down in response to demand.

Defining CNAPP

A Cloud Native Application Protection Platform (CNAPP) is an integrated security solution that combines multiple security functions to protect cloud-native applications. This CNAPP platform is designed to address the unique challenges posed by modern cloud architectures such as microservices, containers and serverless functions. CNAPP offers a holistic approach to security, ensuring that applications are protected throughout their entire lifecycle, from development to deployment and beyond.

Core Components of CNAPP

CNAPP solution is designed to address these challenges through a multi-faceted approach, integrating several key components to provide comprehensive protection:

- **Cloud Security Posture Management:** Cloud Security Posture Management (CSPM) continuously monitors cloud environments to ensure compliance with security policies and standards. It identifies and mitigates potential vulnerabilities and misconfigurations in real-time, providing automated remediation to enhance the overall security posture of cloud infrastructure. CSPM offers comprehensive visibility into cloud assets, enabling proactive threat management. By integrating CSPM, organizations can significantly reduce the risk of data breaches, and ensure regulatory compliance, thereby safeguarding their cloud operations effectively.
- **Workload Security:** To begin with, let us clarify our understanding of the term, "*workload*." This concept encompasses a variety of computing environments including containers, virtual machines, and serverless architecture. At the heart of CNAPP is workload security, which is fundamentally responsible for the protection of the applications running in containers, virtual machines, and serverless architecture. This includes sub-components such as runtime protection, vulnerability management, compliance monitoring, and much more. By continuously scanning for vulnerabilities, and ensuring compliance with industry standards, CNAPP helps maintain the integrity and security of workloads.
- **Identity and Access Management (IAM):** Effective IAM is crucial for securing cloud-native applications. CNAPP leverages advanced IAM capabilities to manage user identities and control access to resources. This includes implementing least privilege access, multi-factor authentication, and role-based access controls. By ensuring that only authorized users can access sensitive data and systems, CNAPP mitigates the risk of unauthorized access and potential breaches.
- **Network Security:** CNAPP employs sophisticated network security measures to protect the communication between workloads (virtual machines, containers, and microservices). This includes network segmentation, which

isolates different parts of the application to prevent lateral movement of threats, and the use of encryption to protect data in transit. Additionally, CNAPP integrates intrusion detection and prevention systems to identify and respond to malicious activities in real-time.

- **Data Security:** Protecting data is a fundamental aspect of CNAPP. This involves securing data at rest and in transit through encryption, data masking and tokenization. By ensuring that sensitive information is protected, CNAPP helps organizations comply with data protection regulations, and safeguard against data breaches.
- **Threat Detection and Response:** Protecting data in a CNAPP integrates advanced threat detection and response capabilities, leveraging machine learning and artificial intelligence to identify and respond to threats. By analyzing patterns and behaviors, CNAPP can detect anomalies easily, and orchestrate automated responses to neutralize threats before they can cause harm. This proactive approach to security helps organizations stay ahead of emerging threats.

Key Features of CNAPP

The Cloud Native Application Protection Platform (CNAPP) offers a comprehensive suite of features **designed to enhance cloud security**. These features provide robust protection, streamline compliance, and ensure the integrity of cloud-native applications. Let us now explore the key capabilities that make CNAPP an essential component of modern cloud security strategies.

- **Artifact Scanning: CNAPP performs automated scanning of everything** like compute, storage, database, user-accounts, roles and permissions, virtual machines, containers, serverless functions, APIs, and Keys in your cloud accounts to **identify vulnerabilities**. This comprehensive approach ensures that potential security gaps are detected and addressed, combining robust protection with streamlined compliance management.
- **Security Guardrail:** These are **predefined security policies and protocols** that **ensure applications adhere to the best practices** and compliance requirements. **Security guardrails help prevent misconfigurations and enforce consistent security standards.**
- **Configuration and Compliance Management:** CNAPP provides tools to manage and enforce secure configurations across cloud environments. They also help organizations maintain compliance with industry standards and regulations by continuously monitoring and reporting on compliance status.
- **Risk Detection and Prioritization:** By leveraging **advanced analytics and machine learning, CNAPPs can identify and prioritize security risks.** This allows organizations to focus on addressing the most critical threats, first.

- **Compliance Management:** CNAPP streamlines compliance **by providing automated tools to ensure adherence to regulatory standards** such as GDPR, HIPAA, and PCI DSS. It continuously monitors cloud environments, identifies compliance gaps, and generates detailed reports, enabling organizations to maintain robust security postures, and meet the regulatory requirements effortlessly.
- **User Behavior Analysis: CNAPPs use AI and machine learning to analyze user behavior, and detect anomalies that may indicate security threats.** This helps in identifying potential insider threats and compromised accounts.
- **Unified Security:** CNAPPs integrate multiple security functions into a single platform, providing comprehensive visibility and control over cloud environments. This unified approach simplifies security management, and reduces the complexity associated with using multiple disparate tools.
- **Proactive Threat Management:** By identifying and mitigating security risks early in the development lifecycle, CNAPPs enable organizations to adopt a proactive approach to threat management. This reduces the likelihood of security incidents, and minimizes their impact.

Processes for Implementing CNAPP in Your Organizations

Implementing **CNAPP starts with assessing your security posture to identify gaps.**

Develop a strategy, select the right solution, and establish monitoring processes. Begin with critical applications, train your team, and enforce policies. Continuously review and refine your approach to stay ahead of threats.

The following are the high-level processes for implementing a Cloud Native Application Protection Platform (CNAPP) in your organization:

1. **Assessment:** A CNAPP begins by evaluating your current security posture, and identifying gaps that CNAPP can address. This involves understanding your cloud architecture, the type of applications you are running, and the specific security challenges you face.

2. **Planning:** Develop a strategy for integrating CNAPP into your existing security framework. This includes selecting the right CNAPP solution, defining security policies, and establishing processes for continuous monitoring and improvement.

3. **Adoption:** Gradually implemented CNAPP, starting with critical applications and expanding as needed. Ensure that your team is trained on how to use the platform effectively, and that security policies are consistently enforced.

4. **Monitoring and Improvement:** Continuously monitor the effectiveness of CNAPP, and make adjustments to improve security outcomes. This involves regularly reviewing security metrics, conducting audits, and staying updated on the latest security threats and best practices.

CNAPP versus Traditional Security Approaches

Traditional security approaches often involve using siloed tools that may not be effective for dynamic, distributed and scalable cloud-native environments. These tools are typically designed for static, on-premises infrastructure, and lack the flexibility needed to secure modern cloud applications. In contrast, CNAPPs offer an integrated, real-time security approach tailored to the unique challenges of cloud-native applications. This makes CNAPPs more effective in providing comprehensive protection for cloud environments.

Understanding CNAPP Architecture Flow

In the sophisticated landscape of cloud-native security, the architecture flow of the Cloud-Native Application Protection Platform (CNAPP) is a critical aspect that ensures seamless protection across various stages of application deployment and operation. This section delves into the intricate flow of CNAPP, elucidating how its components interact to provide a comprehensive security framework.

To fully comprehend the CNAPP architecture flow, it is crucial to first understand the lifecycle of cloud-native applications. This lifecycle generally encompasses the following stages:

1. **Development:** The initial phase where application code is written and tested.
2. **Build:** The process of compiling the code, and creating deployable artifacts.
3. **Deployment:** The stage where the application is released to the production environment.
4. **Runtime:** The period during which the application is actively running and serving users.
5. **Monitoring and Maintenance:** Ongoing activities to ensure that the application remains secure, performs well, and is updated as needed.

Understanding the lifecycle of cloud-native applications is fundamental to grasping the CNAPP architecture flow. Each stage of this lifecycle plays a crucial role in ensuring the security, performance, and reliability of the application. Let us explore these stages in detail to see how they contribute to the overall architecture and functionality of CNAPPs.

- **Development Phase:** This is the phase where applications are designed and coded. CNAPP promotes secure coding practices by integrating security tools into the development environment. This includes Static Application Security Testing (SAST) tools that analyze code for vulnerabilities as it is written. Cloud-Native Application Protection Platform (CNAPP) provides resources and training for developers to understand and implement security best practices, ensuring that security is embedded from the ground up.
- **Build Phase:** During the **build process**, CNAPP performs automated security scans using tools like Software Composition Analysis (SCA) to identify vulnerabilities in third-party libraries and dependencies. CNAPP ensures that building configurations adhere to security policies, preventing misconfigurations that could lead to vulnerabilities.
- **Deployment Phase:** During the **deployment phase**, CNAPP integrates with IaC tools to ensure that the infrastructure is deployed securely. This includes scanning IaC templates for security issues before deployment. CNAPP also secures CI/CD pipeline by incorporating security checks at each stage, ensuring that only secure code is deployed to production.
- **Runtime Phase:** During the runtime phase, CNAPP provides continuous runtime protection by monitoring applications for suspicious activities and anomalies. This includes detecting and mitigating threats in real-time. CNAPP secures the communication between microservices through network segmentation, encryption, and Intrusion Detection System (IDS).
- **Monitoring and Maintenance Phase:** During the monitoring and maintenance phase, CNAPP continuously monitors the application and its environment for security threats. This includes log analysis, threat intelligence integration, and anomaly detection. In the event of a security incident, CNAPP orchestrates a coordinated response, including isolating affected components, applying patches, and conducting forensic analysis. CNAPP equally ensures that the application remains compliant with regulatory requirements by conducting regular audits, and generating compliance reports.
- **Continuous Improvement and Adaptation:** During the continuous improvement and adaptation phase, CNAPP leverages feedback from threat detection and response activities to refine its algorithms and policies. This adaptive approach ensures that the platform evolves in response to emerging threats and changing environments. Continuous improvement enhances the effectiveness of CNAPP, providing robust protection for cloud-native applications.

By understanding the architecture flow of CNAPP, organizations can appreciate the comprehensive and dynamic nature of cloud-native security. Each component plays a vital role in ensuring that the application remains secure, compliant, and resilient in the face of evolving threats.

The Importance of CNAPP for an Organization

In today's fast paced digital landscape, security is not just a priority–it is a necessity.

In this dynamic and fast-paced world of cloud computing, organizations are increasingly turning to cloud-native technologies to drive innovation, scalability, and operational efficiency. And with this ongoing migration to the cloud, the complexity of managing and securing cloud-native applications grows exponentially. And, this shift brings with it a host of new security challenges that traditional security measures are ill-equipped to handle. This is where a Cloud-Native Application Protection Platform (CNAPP) becomes indispensable. The Cloud-Native Application Protection Platform (CNAPP) emerges as a comprehensive solution designed to address these challenges, providing robust security for cloud-native environments. In this digital age, where agility and innovation are the cornerstones of success, securing cloud-native applications is akin to safeguarding a treasure trove.

Imagine your organization as a bustling city. Each application is a building, each user is a resident, and each data packet is a vehicle navigating streets in the city. Without proper security measures, this city is vulnerable to threats, from petty thefts to major heists. CNAPP acts as the city's comprehensive security system, ensuring every building is fortified, every resident is safe, and every vehicle is monitored.

This section explores all the critical reasons why any organization needs CNAPP to safeguard their digital assets, and ensure operational resilience. These are some of the reasons why you would opt for CNAPP as an organization:

- **A Holistic Security Approach:** One of the primary reasons organizations need CNAPP is its holistic approach to security. CNAPP suite is capable of integrating multiple security controls and functions into a single platform, providing end-to-end protection for cloud-native applications.
    - **Workload Protection:** CNAPP secure workload running in containers, virtual machines and serverless environments. It provides runtime protection, vulnerability management, and compliance monitoring, ensuring that workloads remain secure and compliant with regulatory standards.
    - **Identity and Access Management:** CNAPP offers robust IAM capabilities, managing user identities, and controlling access to resources. This includes implementing least privilege access, multi-factor authentication, and role-based access controls, mitigating the risk of unauthorized access and potential breaches.
    - **Network Security:** CNAPP employs advanced network security measures to protect the communication between microservices. This includes

network segmentation, intrusion detection and prevention, and encryption to safeguard data in transit.

- **Data Security:** CNAPP protecting data is a fundamental aspect of CNAPP. This involves encryption, data masking, and tokenization to ensure that sensitive information remains secure and inaccessible to unauthorized parties.
- **Threat Intelligence and Responses:** CNAPP integrates threat intelligence and response capabilities to detect and respond to emerging threats in real-time. By leveraging machine learning and artificial intelligence, CNAPP can identify anomalous behavior and orchestrate automated responses to neutralize threats, before they can cause harm.

- **Enhanced Visibility and Control:** In Cloud-native environments, visibility and control are paramount. Organizations need to have a clear understanding of their security posture, and the ability to respond swiftly to incidents. CNAPP provides enhanced visibility into the security status of cloud-native applications through comprehensive monitoring and reporting tools. This includes real-time dashboards, detailed logs, and automated alerts that keep security teams informed and empowered to take action.

  Moreover, CNAPP offers granular control over security policies and configurations. Organizations can define and enforce security policies across their entire cloud environment, ensuring consistency and compliance. This level of control is essential for maintaining a robust security posture in the face of evolving threats.

- **Scalability and Flexibility:** As organizations grow and their cloud environments expand, scalability and flexibility become critical. CNAPP is designed to scale with the needs of the organization, providing consistent security coverage, regardless of the size or complexity of the environment.

  Whether an organization is running a few microservices or thousands of containers, CNAPP can adapt to provide the necessary protection.

  Additionally, CNAPP's flexibility allows it to integrate with a wide range of cloud platforms and services. This ensures that organizations can leverage their existing investments in cloud infrastructure, while enhancing their security capabilities. CNAPP supports multi-cloud and hybrid environments, providing a unified security framework that spans across different cloud providers and on-premises systems.

- **Proactive Security Posture: In today's threat landscape, a reactive approach to security is no longer sufficient. Organizations need to adopt a proactive security posture that anticipates and mitigates threats, before they can cause damage.** CNAPP enables this proactive approach through advanced threat detection and response capabilities. By leveraging machine learning and AI, CNAPP can identify patterns and anomalies that indicate potential threats, allowing security teams to respond swiftly and effectively.

Furthermore, CNAPP's continuous monitoring and automated response mechanisms ensure that threats are detected and neutralized in real-time. **This reduces the window of opportunities for attackers, and minimizes the impact of security incidents.**

- **Compliance and Regulatory Requirements:** Compliance with regulatory requirements is a critical concern for organizations across industries. CNAPP helps organizations meet these requirements by providing comprehensive compliance monitoring and reporting tools. This includes automated compliance checks, detailed audit trails, and customizable reports that demonstrate adherence to industry standards and regulations.

  By ensuring that cloud-native applications remain compliant with regulatory requirements, CNAPP helps organizations avoid costly fines and reputational damage. It also provides peace of mind, knowing that their security practices are aligned with the best practices and legal obligations.

- **Future-Proofing Security:** Compliance. As cloud-native technologies continue to evolve, so too will the threat landscape. CNAPP is designed to be future-proof, incorporating the latest advancements in security technology to stay ahead of emerging threats. This includes the integration of quantum cryptography for enhanced data security, the use of blockchain for immutable audit trails, and the incorporation of more sophisticated AI-drive analytics for threat detection and response.

By adopting CNAPP, organizations can ensure that their security measures are not only effective today, but also capable of adapting to the challenges of tomorrow. This future-proofing is essential for maintaining a robust security posture in an ever-changing digital landscape.

Overview of Leading CNAPPs

In the rapidly evolving landscape of cloud computing, ensuring the security of cloud-native applications has become a paramount concern for organizations worldwide. Cloud-Native Application Protection Platforms (CNAPPs) have emerged as essential tools, providing comprehensive security solutions tailored to the unique challenges of cloud environments. This section delves into the most widely adopted CNAPPs, highlighting their deployment models, licensing types, and subscription details.

As organizations increasingly migrate their workloads to the cloud, the need for robust security measures becomes ever more critical. CNAPPs are designed to address the complexities of cloud-native environments, **offering a unified approach to security that spans across development, deployment, and runtime phases.** These platforms integrate seamlessly with various cloud service providers, enabling continuous monitoring and protection of cloud resources. **By leveraging advanced technologies such as machine learning, artificial intelligence, and behavioral analytics, CNAPPs can detect and respond to threats in real-time, minimizing the risk of data breaches and other security incidents**.

Understanding the nuances of these CNAPPs is crucial for organizations aiming to bolster their cloud security posture. By leveraging the capabilities of these platforms, businesses can proactively identify and mitigate potential threats, ensuring the integrity and confidentiality of their cloud-native applications. This comprehensive overview serves as a valuable resource for decision-makers seeking to navigate the complex landscape of cloud security solutions, and select the most suitable CNAPP for their specific requirements.

Moreover, CNAPPs provide valuable insights into the security posture of cloud environments, helping organizations maintain compliance with industry standards and regulations. Features such as automated vulnerability scanning, configuration management, and policy enforcement ensure that security best practices are consistently applied across all cloud assets. This proactive approach not only enhances the overall security of cloud-native applications, but also reduces the operational burden on security teams, allowing them to focus on more strategic initiatives.

The table below presents **a detailed comparison** of **ten leading CNAPP providers**, each renowned for their robust security features and industry expertise. These platforms offer a range of deployment options, including Software as a Service (SaaS), desktop applications, agent-based, agentless, and hybrid models, catering to diverse organizational needs. Additionally, the licensing types and subscription models vary, **with some providers offering perpetual licenses alongside subscription-based services.**

SentinelOne, Prisma Cloud by Palo Alto Networks, Microsoft Defender for Cloud, Wiz, Lacework, Sysdig Secure, Trend Vision One - Cloud Security, Orca Security, Aqua Security, and Check Point CloudGuard are among the top CNAPP providers trusted by industry experts. Each of these platforms brings unique strengths to the table, from advanced threat detection and automated compliance to seamless integration with existing cloud infrastructure. The following table enumerates the licensing and subscription details for top ten CNAPPs providers with their business web link:

CNAPP Provider	Licensing Type	Deployment Model	Subscription Details	Perpetual License	Main Web Link
SentinelOne	Proprietary	SaaS	Subscription-based	No	SentinelOne

Prisma Cloud by Palo Alto Networks	Proprietary	SaaS, Desktop	Subscription-based	Yes	Prisma Cloud
Microsoft Defender for Cloud	Proprietary	SaaS	Subscription-based	No	Microsoft Defender for Cloud
Wiz	Proprietary	SaaS	Subscription-based	No	Wiz
Lacework	Proprietary	SaaS, Agent-based	Subscription-based	No	Lacework
Sysdig Secure	Proprietary	SaaS, Agent-based	Subscription-based	No	Sysdig Secure
Trend Vision One - Cloud Security	Proprietary	SaaS, Hybrid	Subscription-based	No	Trend Vision One
Orca Security	Proprietary	SaaS, Agentless	Subscription-based	No	Orca Security
Aqua Security	Proprietary	SaaS, Agent-based	Subscription-based	No	Aqua Security
Check Point CloudGuard	Proprietary	SaaS, Hybrid	Subscription-based	No	Check Point CloudGuard

Table 2.1: *Top Ten CNAPPs with Deployment and Subscription Details*

Please refer to the following links for detailed information about specific CNAPP providers. Use these resources to familiarize yourself with the ecosystem of these providers.

- https://www.sentinelone.com/lp/cloudprotection/
- https://www.paloaltonetworks.com/prisma/cloud
- https://learn.microsoft.com/en-us/azure/defender-for-cloud/defender-for-cloud-introduction
- https://www.wiz.io/platform
- https://www.lacework.com/cnapp
- https://sysdig.com/cloud-native-application-protection/
- https://www.trendmicro.com/en_us/business/products/one-platform.html
- https://orca.security/platform/cnapp-cloud-security-platform/
- https://www.aquasec.com/
- https://www.checkpoint.com/cloudguard/cnapp/

When exploring Cloud Native Application Protection Platform (CNAPP) providers, it is essential to understand their varied pricing models. Each provider has distinct features and pricing structures tailored to different needs and budgets.

The following table highlights the top 10 CNAPP providers, offering a comprehensive comparison to help you make an informed decision. Here is a table with the estimated costs for each of the CNAPP providers.

Please note that the actual costs can vary based on specific requirements, usage, and subscription plans. It is always the best to contact the providers directly for the most accurate pricing.

CNAPP Provider	Estimated Cost	Main Web Link
SentinelOne	Custom pricing based on deployment size and features	SentinelOne
Prisma Cloud by Palo Alto Networks	Starts at $1,000 per month for small deployments	Prisma Cloud
Microsoft Defender for Cloud	Starts at $15 per resource per month	Microsoft Defender for Cloud
Wiz	Custom pricing based on cloud usage and environment	Wiz
Lacework	Custom pricing based on the number of vCPUs	Lacework
Sysdig Secure	Custom pricing based on the number of hosts	Sysdig Secure
Trend Vision One - Cloud Security	Custom pricing based on deployment and features	Trend Vision One
Orca Security	Custom pricing based on the number of workloads	Orca Security
Aqua Security	Custom pricing based on the number of workloads and repositories	Aqua Security
Check Point CloudGuard	Custom pricing based on deployment and features	CheckPoint CloudGuard

Table 2.2: *Top Ten CNAPPs with Pricing Models*

These prices are indicative, and can vary significantly based on the specific needs and scale of deployment. For precise pricing, it is recommended to request a quote from the respective providers. These platforms are widely used across multiple cloud environments such as AWS, Azure, GCP OCI, IBM and Alibaba Cloud, providing comprehensive security solutions for cloud-native applications.

In summary, the adoption of CNAPPs is a strategic investment for organizations looking to secure their cloud-native applications effectively. By choosing the right CNAPP, businesses can achieve a higher level of security, operational efficiency, and compliance, ultimately driving greater confidence in their cloud transformation journey.

Selection Strategies before You Procure CNAPP

In the quest to secure cloud-native environments, selecting the right Cloud-Native Application Protection Platform (CNAPP) is a critical decision that can significantly impact an organization's security posture. With a myriad of options available, it is necessary to adopt a strategic approach to ensure that the chosen CNAPP aligns with the organization's specific needs and objectives. This chapter outlines the key selection strategies that organizations should consider before procuring a CNAPP. This strategic approach should consider the following major highlights as minimum:

- Understanding Organizational Requirements
- Evaluating CNAPP Features and Capabilities
- Integration and Operability
- Vendor Reputation and Support
- Cost Considerations
- Endorsement from Industry Leaders

Understanding Organizational Requirements

The first step in selecting a CNAPP is to thoroughly understand the organization's unique requirements, **unique means which are very specific to the organization.**

Every organization has different unique requirements.

Gathering these organization's specific requirements is accomplished by performing a comprehensive assessment of the current cloud environments, security challenges, and future goals.

Understanding organizational requirements is crucial when procuring a Cloud Native Application Protection Platform (CNAPP). This involves a thorough assessment of the organization's current security posture, identifying specific needs such as compliance mandates, threat detection capabilities, and data protection requirements. It is necessary to ensure that the CNAPP solution can seamlessly integrate with the existing cloud infrastructure and security tools, providing scalability to accommodate future growth. Evaluating the vendor's reputation, support services, and the total cost of ownership, including maintenance and training, is also vital. Thus, by comprehensively understanding these requirements, organizations can select a CNAPP solution that effectively enhances their security posture, and aligns with their operational goals.

Evaluating CNAPP Features and Capabilities

When evaluating CNAPP features and capabilities, it is essential to conduct a thorough assessment to ensure that the platform meets your organization's security needs, and supports its long-term growth.

- Start by examining the comprehensive protection offered by the CNAPP. This includes features such as runtime protection which safeguards applications during execution, and vulnerability management which identifies and mitigates potential security risks.
- Compliance monitoring is also crucial, as it ensures your applications adhere to industry standards and regulations.
- Scalability is another key factor to consider; the CNAPP should be capable of growing with your organization, handling increased workloads, and maintaining performance without degradation.
- Additionally, the ease of use of the platform can significantly impact operational efficiency.
- A user-friendly interface with intuitive dashboards can streamline security management, making it easier for your team to monitor and respond to incidents.
- Look for features that simplify complex security tasks, and provide clear and actionable insights.
- Furthermore, consider the platform's integration capabilities. It should seamlessly integrate with your existing cloud infrastructure and tools, offering robust API support and automation features to enhance security operations.
- Interoperability across different cloud environments is also important if your organization employs a multi-cloud strategy.

By thoroughly evaluating these features and capabilities, you can select a CNAPP that not only provides robust security, but also aligns with your organization's growth and operational needs. This comprehensive approach will help you make an informed decision, ensuring that the CNAPP you choose delivers maximum value and protection for your cloud-native applications.

Integration and Interoperability

When considering the integration and interoperability of a CNAPP, it is vital to ensure that the platform can seamlessly blend with your existing cloud infrastructure and tools.

Effective **integration** means that the CNAPP should support robust **API capabilities**, allowing for smooth communication and data exchange between different systems. **This is crucial for automating security processes, and enhancing operational efficiency.** Additionally, the CNAPP should be able to integrate with third-party security tools and services, providing a unified view of your security posture, and enabling comprehensive threat detection and response.

Furthermore, the platform should support **continuous integration and continuous deployment (CI/CD)** pipelines, ensuring that security is embedded throughout the software development lifecycle. This integration helps in identifying and mitigating vulnerabilities early in the development process, reducing the risk of security breaches.

Interoperability, on the other hand, ensures that the **CNAPP can function across various cloud environments,** which is particularly important for organizations employing a **multi-cloud strategy**. This capability allows for consistent security policies and monitoring across different platforms, reducing the complexity and potential security gaps that can arise from managing multiple environments.

By focusing on these aspects of **integration and interoperability**, organizations can ensure that their CNAPP not only enhances security, but also aligns with their operational workflows and strategic goals, providing a scalable and efficient solution for protecting cloud-native applications.

Vendor Reputation and Support

When evaluating the reputation and support of a CNAPP vendor, it is crucial to delve into several key aspects to ensure that you choose a reliable partner for your cloud security needs.

- Start by researching the vendor's track record in the industry.
- Look for customer reviews, case studies, and testimonials that highlight their performance and reliability. A vendor with a strong history of successful deployments and satisfied customers is often a good indicator of their capability to deliver on promises.
- Additionally, consider the vendor's commitment to innovation and staying ahead of emerging threats.
- Vendors that actively participate in the security community, contribute to open-source projects, and regularly update their platforms with new features and improvements demonstrate a proactive approach to security.
- Customer support is another critical factor. Evaluate the quality and availability of their support services, including response times, expertise, and the range of support options available. A vendor that offers 24/7 support, dedicated account managers, and comprehensive training resources can significantly enhance your experience as well as ensure that you get the most out of your CNAPP investment.

- Furthermore, consider the vendor's ecosystem and partnerships. Vendors with strong alliances with other technology providers can offer more integrated and comprehensive solutions, enhancing the overall effectiveness of your security strategy.
- Lastly, assess the vendor's financial stability and long-term viability.

By thoroughly evaluating these aspects, you can select a CNAPP vendor that not only meets your current needs, but also supports your organization's growth and adapts to the ever-changing security landscape. This comprehensive approach will help you build a resilient and effective cloud security posture, backed by a trusted and capable vendor.

Cost Considerations

When evaluating the cost considerations of a Cloud-Native Application Protection Platform (CNAPP), **it is essential to look beyond the initial purchase price and consider the total cost of ownership (TCO).**

- This includes not only the **licensing fees** but also the costs associated with **implementation, integration, and ongoing maintenance.** Start by assessing the **licensing model** offered by the vendor. **Some CNAPPs may have subscription-based pricing, while others might offer perpetual licenses.** It is important to choose a model that aligns with your budget and usage patterns.
- Additionally, consider the costs of integrating the CNAPP with your existing infrastructure. This might involve expenses related to custom development, consulting services, or additional hardware and software.
- Operational costs are another critical factor. These include the resources required to manage and maintain the CNAPP, such as personnel, training, and support services.
- Furthermore, consider the potential savings that a CNAPP can offer. By consolidating multiple security tools into a single platform, you can reduce the complexity and costs associated with managing disparate systems. This consolidation can lead to lower licensing fees, reduced maintenance costs, and improved operational efficiency.
- It is also important to factor in the long-term financial benefits of enhanced security. A robust CNAPP can help prevent costly security breaches, reduce downtime, and ensure compliance with industry regulations, which can save your organization significant amounts of money in the long run.
- Lastly, look for vendors that offer flexible pricing options, such as pay-as-you-go models or tiered pricing based on usage. This flexibility can help you manage costs more effectively and scale your investment as your organization grows.

By thoroughly evaluating these cost considerations, you can make an informed decision that balances upfront expenses with long-term value, ensuring that your investment in a CNAPP delivers maximum return on investment.

Bonus Topic: Endorsement from Industry Leaders

Industry leaders play a crucial role in evaluating and endorsing CNAPP providers. These organizations, including Gartner, Forrester, Frost, Sullivan, and others, provide comprehensive analyses, reviews, and ratings that help businesses make informed decisions.

- **Gartner**, known for its Magic **Quadrant reports**, is highly regarded for its in-depth market research and analysis.
- **Forrester** offers valuable insights through its Wave reports.
- **Frost and Sullivan** provides strategic market analysis and growth consulting.
- **KuppingerCole**, **PeerSpot**, **MITRE Engenuity**, **G2**, **IDC**, **GigaOm**, and **Omdia** also contribute significantly by offering expert evaluations and user reviews.

These industry leaders ensure that CNAPP providers meet high standards of security, compliance, and performance, guiding organizations in selecting the best solutions for their cloud-native environments. These industry leaders provide valuable insights and evaluations that help in assessing the strengths and capabilities of each CNAPP provider. Use this table to understand the backing each provider has received and make an informed decision based on these endorsements.

The following table highlights the top 10 CNAPP providers and the industry leaders that endorse them. These endorsements come from reputable organizations such as Gartner, Frost & Sullivan, and MITRE Engenuity, among others.

Here is the corrected table with the industry leaders backing each CNAPP provider:

CNAPP Provider	**Industry Leaders Backing**
SentinelOne	PeerSpot, Gartner, MITRE Engenuity12
Prisma Cloud by Palo Alto Networks	Frost & Sullivan34
Microsoft Defender for Cloud	Frost & Sullivan56
Wiz	G2, Frost & Sullivan78
Lacework	KuppingerCole, Frost & Sullivan910
Sysdig Secure	Gartner, KuppingerCole1112
Trend Vision One - Cloud Security	Gartner1314
Orca Security	Gartner1516

Aqua Security	Gartner1718
Check Point CloudGuard	Frost & Sullivan, GigaOm1920

Table 2.3: *Top 10 CNAPP Providers with Their Industry Endorsements*

In conclusion, leveraging insights from top industry leaders ensures that you select the most reliable and effective CNAPP provider for your needs.

Understanding CSPM

Cloud Security Posture Management (CSPM) emerges as a critical solution, designed to address the unique security challenges posed by the cloud infrastructures. This chapter delves into the essence of CSPM, exploring its significance, core functionalities, and the transformative impact, it has on cloud security.

Introduction to CSPM

Cloud Security Posture Management refers to a set of automated tools and processes that continuously monitor cloud environments to detect and remediate security risks. Unlike traditional security measures, CSPM is specifically tailored for the dynamic and scalable nature of cloud infrastructures. It provides organizations with real-time visibility into their cloud security posture, ensuring that configurations adhere to the best practices and compliance standards.

As organizations are continuously increasingly migrating their traditional and on-premises workloads (application and database servers) to the cloud.

As more companies move to the cloud, the risk of security breaches increases. Traditional security tools are not always effective in the cloud because they were designed for on-premises environments. CSPM is specifically built for the cloud, making it essential for modern businesses. It helps prevent data breaches, protects sensitive information, and ensures compliance with regulations. Here are 10 things you can do with the help of CSPM:

- Continuous Monitoring
- Automated Remediation
- Compliance Management
- Risk Assessment
- Policy Enforcement
- Configuration Management
- Threat Detection
- Visibility and Reporting

- Integration with Cloud Providers
- Incident Response
- In practice, web servers are a combination of different servers, where each will handle a specific task.
- The client will initiate communication and choose what operation will be performed on a resource.
- The client can use multiple servers, and the servers can serve multiple clients.
- REST and HTTP are not the same. REST is an architectural style, while HTTP is a resource exchange protocol often used in applications designed by REST guidelines.
- The JSON format is easy to understand; when we see text in JSON format, it is clear which object the text represents.

Cloud Security Posture Management stands as the most extensively utilized module within the CNAPP.

This prominence is vividly illustrated by the following date chart, which underscores its critical role in maintaining robust security posture across diverse cloud cnvironments.

The widespread adoption of CSPM highlights its effectiveness in identifying and mitigating potential vulnerabilities, ensuring compliance, and enhancing overall cloud security.

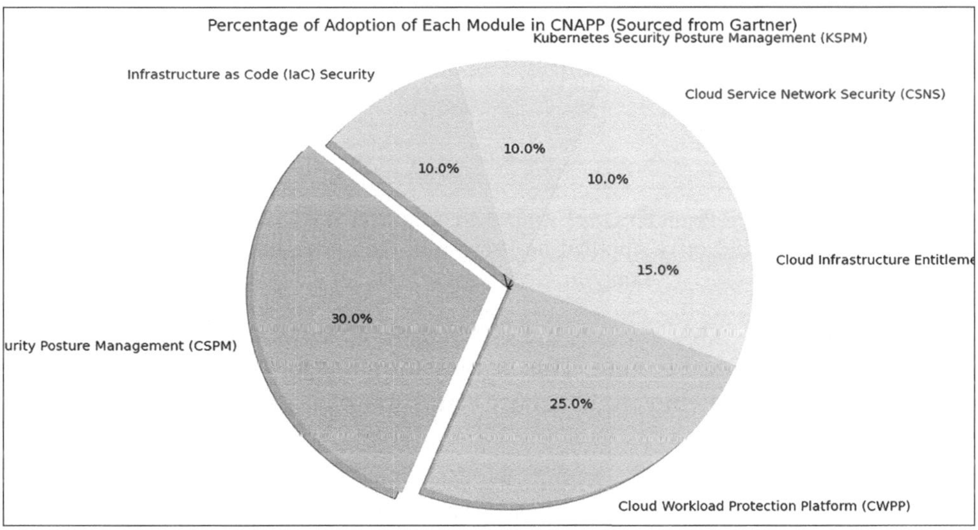

Figure 2.1: *Percentage of Adoption of Each Module in CNAPP Suite Model*

Top 10 CNAPP Providers with Their Adoption Rate

To illustrate the growing importance and adoption of Cloud Native Application Protection Platforms (CNAPP), the following graph highlights the top 10 CNAPP providers, and their respective increases in adoption over the past five years. Based on insights from Gartner, this data underscores the rapid growth and significant market presence of leading CNAPP solutions such as Palo Alto Networks, CrowdStrike, and Wiz. These trends reflect the increasing reliance on robust cloud security measures to protect modern cloud-native applications and environments.

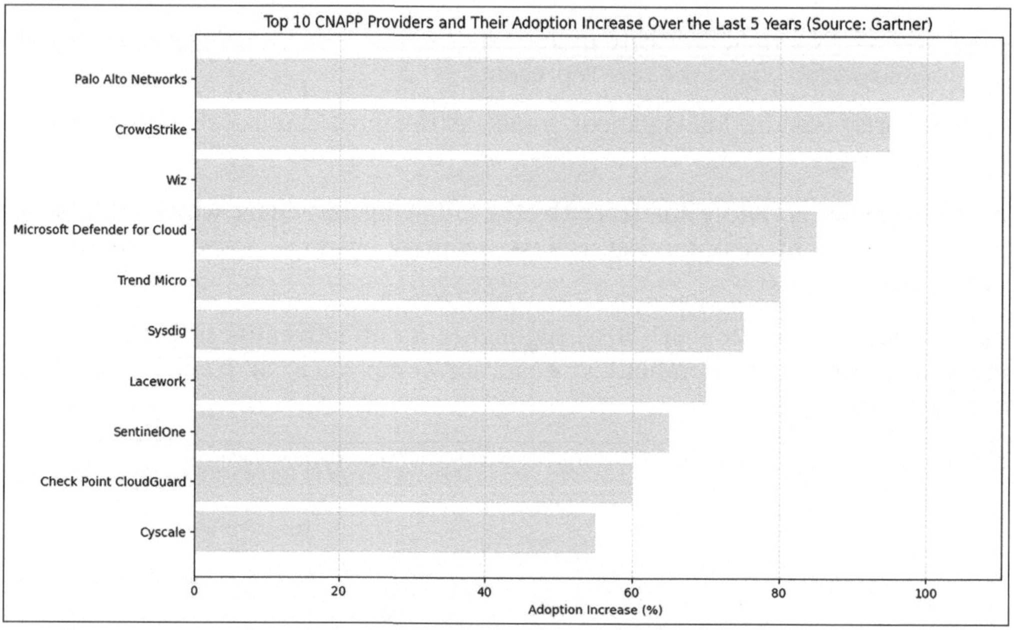

Figure 2.2: *Top 10 CNAPP Providers and Their Adoption over the Last 5 Years. (source: Gartner Market Guide for Cloud-Native Application Protection Platforms, Link: https://www.gartner.com/en/documents/5605291*

As illustrated in the pie chart above, the CSPM module alone accounts for 30% of the utilization within the CNAPP suite. This significant adoption underscores the critical role CSPM plays in enhancing cloud security and compliance.

This section served as an introductory overview of the "*Cloud Security Posture Management* (CSPM)" module. In the upcoming dedicated chapter, "*Understanding Cloud Security Protection Management* (CSPM)," we will delve deeper into various concepts, explore advanced topics, and engage in hands-on labs as well as exercises to enhance our understanding of CSPM.

Understanding CWPP

In the era of digital transformation, organizations are increasingly leveraging cloud technologies to enhance agility, scalability, and innovation. However, this shift to the cloud introduces new security challenges that traditional security measures are not equipped to handle.

Cloud Workload Protection Platforms (CWPP) have emerged as a critical solution to address these challenges, providing comprehensive security for cloud workloads.

Introduction to CWPP and WAAS

As organizations migrate their applications and data to the cloud, they encounter a diverse range of workloads, including virtual machines, containers, and serverless functions. Each of these workloads presents unique security challenges that require specialized protection. Traditional security tools, designed for static, on-premises environments, are often inadequate for the dynamic and distributed nature of cloud workloads. The Cloud Workload Protection Platform (CWPP) addresses this gap by providing a unified platform that offers comprehensive protection for all types of cloud workloads. By integrating security into the cloud environment, CWPP ensures that workloads are protected throughout their lifecycle, from development to deployment and runtime. This holistic approach to security is essential for maintaining a robust security posture in the cloud.

Cloud-native applications are increasingly distributed across Virtual Machines (VMs), hosts, containers, Kubernetes, and serverless architectures, each with unique security requirements. Ensuring consistent workload protection across these diverse environments is a significant challenge. The Web Application and API Security (WAAS) module is designed to provide robust protection against a wide range of cyber threats. By leveraging advanced machine learning algorithms, WAAS can detect and mitigate vulnerabilities in real-time, safeguarding your digital assets from potential breaches. This module seamlessly integrates with your existing infrastructure, enhancing both security and performance, and allowing your business to operate with confidence in an interconnected world.

As businesses increasingly rely on web applications and APIs to drive innovation and customer engagement, the need for robust security measures has never been greater. The WAAS module stands at the forefront of this defense, offering unparalleled protection through its sophisticated threat detection and mitigation capabilities. Utilizing the state-of-the-art machine learning techniques, WAAS continuously monitors and adapts to emerging threats, ensuring your applications and APIs remain secure and resilient. By integrating effortlessly with your existing systems, WAAS not only fortifies your security posture, but also enhances the overall performance and reliability of your digital infrastructure. Additionally, CNAPP's Cloud offers both agent-based and agentless protection within a single interface, providing teams with flexible deployment options that fit each unique environment.

Core Components of CWPP

CWPP encompasses several core components that work together to provide end-to-end protection for cloud workloads. These components include:

- **Workload Visibility and Discovery:** One of the foundational aspects of CWPP is the ability to provide visibility into all cloud workloads. This involves discovering and inventorying workloads across different cloud environments, including public, private, and hybrid clouds. By maintaining an up-to-date inventory of workloads, CWPP ensures that security teams have a comprehensive view of the cloud environment, and can identify potential security risks.
- **Vulnerability Management:** CWPP solutions continuously scan cloud workloads for vulnerabilities, including misconfigurations, outdated software, and known security flaws. By identifying and prioritizing vulnerabilities, CWPP enables organizations to take proactive measures to mitigate risks. Automated vulnerability management ensures that workloads remain secure and compliant with the industry standards.
- **Runtime Protection:** Protecting workloads during runtime is a critical function of CWPP. This involves monitoring workloads for suspicious activities and behaviors that may indicate a security threat. Runtime protection includes capabilities such as intrusion detection and prevention, behavioral analysis, and anomaly detection. By continuously monitoring workloads, CWPP can detect and respond to threats in real-time, minimizing the impact of security incidents.
- **Compliance and Governance:** CWPP helps organizations maintain compliance with regulatory requirements and industry standards. This includes automated compliance checks, policy enforcement, and audit reporting. By ensuring that workloads adhere to security policies and compliance frameworks, CWPP reduces the risk of non-compliance and associated penalties.
- **Threat Intelligence and Response:** Integrating threat intelligence into CWPP enhances the ability to detect and respond to emerging threats. This involves leveraging threat intelligence feeds to stay informed about the latest threats and vulnerabilities. CWPP solutions use this information to enhance threat detection capabilities, and orchestrate automated responses to neutralize threats, before they can cause harm.
- **Micro-Segmentation:** Micro-segmentation is a security technique used to isolate workloads, and limit the lateral movement of threats within the cloud

environment. CWPP solutions implement micro-segmentation by creating granular security policies that control communication between workloads. This reduces the attack surface, and prevents the spread of threats across the cloud environment.

Benefits of CWPP

Implementing CWPP offers numerous benefits to organizations, enhancing their ability to secure cloud workloads, and achieve operational resilience. Key benefits include:

- **Comprehensive Protection:** CWPP provides end-to-end protection for all types of cloud workloads, including virtual machines, containers, and serverless functions. By integrating security into the cloud environment, CWPP ensures that workloads are protected throughout their lifecycle.
- **Enhanced Visibility:** CWPP solutions offer comprehensive visibility into cloud workloads, enabling security teams to identify and address potential security risks. Enhanced visibility ensures that organizations have a clear understanding of their security posture, and can take proactive measures to mitigate risks.
- **Automated Security:** Automation is a key feature of CWPP, reducing the manual effort required to manage cloud security. Automated vulnerability management, compliance checks, and threat response enhance operational efficiency, and allow security teams to focus on strategic initiatives.
- **Improved Compliance:** CWPP helps organizations maintain compliance with regulatory requirements and industry standards. Automated compliance checks and audit reporting simplify the process of demonstrating adherence to security policies and frameworks.
- **Reduced Risk:** By continuously monitoring workloads and implementing proactive security measures, CWPP reduces the risk of data breaches and other security incidents. This proactive approach to security ensures that vulnerabilities are addressed before they can be exploited by malicious actors.
- **Scalability:** CWPP solutions are designed to scale with the needs of the organization, providing consistent security coverage, regardless of the size or complexity of the cloud environment. This scalability ensures that organizations can secure their workloads as they grow and evolve.

Agent-Based and Agentless Workload Protection in CWPP

In the realm of Cloud Workload Protection Platforms (CWPP), **both agent-based and agentless solutions offer distinct advantages and limitations. Agent-based**

protection involves deploying software agents directly onto workloads, providing continuous visibility, real-time threat detection, and robust runtime protection.

This approach ensures comprehensive security coverage, but can be resource-intensive, and may require significant maintenance and updates.

On the other hand, **agentless protection leverages cloud provider APIs and non-invasive methods to monitor workloads**, offering seamless visibility and easier deployment **without the need for installing agents on each device.**

While agentless solutions are simpler to implement and maintain, they may not provide the same depth of real-time protection, and detailed monitoring as agent-based solutions. An ideal CWPP strategy often combines both approaches, utilizing agent-based solutions for critical workloads requiring stringent security and agentless solutions for broader visibility and ease of management.

In conclusion, CWPP are essential for organizations seeking to secure their cloud environments, and maintain a robust security posture. By providing comprehensive protection for all types of cloud workloads, CWPP addresses the unique security challenges posed by cloud infrastructures.

Implementing CWPP offers numerous benefits, including enhanced visibility, automated security, improved compliance, reduced risk, and scalability. As cloud adoption continues to grow, the importance of CWPP in ensuring cloud security will only become more critical.

As illustrated in the pie chart above in the previous section, "*Introduction to CSPM*", you can see that the **CWPP module alone accounts for 25% of the utilization within the CNAPP suite**. This significant adoption underscores the critical role CWPP plays in enhancing cloud security and compliance.

This section served as an introductory overview of the "*Cloud Workload Protection Platform* (CWPP)" module. In the upcoming dedicated chapter, "Understanding Cloud Workload Protection Platform (CWPP)," we will delve deeper into various concepts, explore advanced topics, and engage in hands-on labs and exercises to enhance our understanding of CWPP.

Understanding Cloud Infrastructure Entitlement Management (CIEM)

As organizations increasingly adopt cloud technologies, managing access and entitlements within cloud environments has become a critical aspect for maintaining security and compliance. **Cloud Infrastructure Entitlement Management (CIEM) is an emerging discipline that addresses the complexities of managing identities, and access rights in cloud infrastructures.** This chapter delves into the intricacies of CIEM, exploring its significance, core components, and the benefits it offers to organizations striving to secure their cloud environments.

Introduction to CIEM

We all know that in cloud environments, the traditional perimeter-based security model is no longer sufficient. The dynamic and distributed nature of cloud infrastructures **requires a new approach to managing identities and access rights. Misconfigurations, excessive permissions, and lack of visibility into access entitlements can lead to significant security risks, including unauthorized access and data breaches.**

CIEM addresses these challenges by **providing a comprehensive framework for managing and governing access entitlements across cloud infrastructures.**

By ensuring that identities have the appropriate level of access, and that access rights are continuously monitored and adjusted, CIEM helps organizations to maintain a robust security posture as well as reduce the risk of security incidents.

Core Components of CIEM

CIEM encompasses several core components that work together to provide a holistic approach to managing cloud access entitlements. These components include:

- **Identity Discovery and Inventory:** One of the foundational aspects of CIEM is the ability to discover and inventory all identities within the cloud environment. This includes human users, service accounts, and machine identities. By maintaining an up-to-date inventory of identities, CIEM ensures that security teams have a comprehensive view of who has access to what resources.
- **Access Rights Management:** CIEM solutions provide tools for managing access rights and entitlements across cloud environments. This includes defining and enforcing policies that govern who can access specific resources, and what actions they can perform. Access rights management ensures that identities have the minimum necessary permissions to perform their tasks, following the principle of least privilege.
- **Continuous Monitoring and Analytics:** Continuous monitoring is a critical function of CIEM, providing real-time visibility into access activities and entitlements. CIEM solutions use advanced analytics to detect anomalies and potential security risks such as excessive permissions or unusual access patterns. By continuously monitoring access rights, CIEM helps organizations identify and mitigate risks, before they can be exploited.
- **Automated Remediation:** When security risks or policy violations are detected, CIEM solutions can automatically remediate the issues. This includes revoking

excessive permissions, adjusting access rights, and enforcing compliance policies. Automated remediation reduces the time and effort required to address security risks, and ensures that access entitlements remain aligned with security policies.

- **Compliance and Reporting:** CIEM helps organizations maintain compliance with regulatory requirements and industry standards. This includes generating detailed reports and audit trails that demonstrate adherence to access management policies and compliance frameworks. By providing comprehensive compliance management, CIEM simplifies the process of passing security audits, and meeting regulatory obligations.

Benefits of CIEM

Implementing CIEM offers numerous benefits to organizations, enhancing their ability to manage access entitlements, and achieve operational resilience. Key benefits include:

- **Improved Security Posture:** CIEM provides continuous monitoring and automated remediation, ensuring that access entitlements are managed effectively and securely. By proactively identifying and addressing security risks, CIEM helps organizations maintain a strong security posture, and reduce the likelihood of unauthorized access and data breaches.
- **Enhanced Visibility:** CIEM solutions offer comprehensive visibility into access entitlements and activities, enabling security teams to identify and address potential security risks. Enhanced visibility ensures that organizations have a clear understanding of their access management landscape, and can take proactive measures to mitigate risks.
- **Operational Efficiency:** Automation is a key feature of CIEM, reducing the manual effort required to manage access entitlements. Automated discovery, monitoring, and remediation enhance operational efficiency, and allow security teams to focus on strategic initiatives.
- **Improved Compliance:** CIEM helps organizations maintain compliance with regulatory requirements and industry standards.
- **Reduced Risk:** By continuously monitoring access entitlements and implementing proactive security measures, CIEM reduces the risk of unauthorized access and data breaches.
- **Scalability:** CIEM solutions are designed to scale with the needs of the organization, providing consistent access management coverage, regardless of the size or complexity of the cloud environment. This scalability ensures that organizations can manage access entitlements as they grow and evolve.

In conclusion, Cloud Infrastructure Entitlement Management (CIEM) is an essential solution for organizations seeking to manage access entitlements, and maintain a robust security posture in cloud environments. By providing comprehensive visibility, automated remediation, compliance management, and enhanced security, CIEM addresses the unique challenges of managing identities and access rights in the cloud. Implementing CIEM offers numerous benefits, including improved security posture, enhanced visibility, operational efficiency, improved compliance, reduced risk, and scalability. As cloud adoption continues to grow, the importance of CIEM in ensuring cloud security will only become more critical.

As illustrated in the pie chart above in the previous section, "Introduction to CSPM", you can see that the **CIEM module alone accounts for 15% of the utilization within the CNAPP suite**. This significant adoption underscores the crucial role CIEM plays in enhancing cloud security and compliance.

This section served as an introductory overview of the "*Cloud Infrastructure Entitlement Management* (CIEM)" module. In the upcoming dedicated chapter, "*Understanding Cloud Infrastructure Entitlement Management* (CIEM)," we will delve deeper into various concepts, explore advanced topics, and engage in hands-on labs and exercises to enhance our understanding of CIEM.

Understanding Cloud Service Network Security (CSNS)

In the realm of cloud-native applications, network security is a critical component **that ensures the integrity, confidentiality, and availability of data as it traverses various cloud environments.** The **"*Cloud Service Network Security*" module within the Cloud-Native Application Protection Platform (CNAPP) is designed to address the unique challenges posed by cloud networking,** providing robust security measures to safeguard cloud infrastructure and applications.

Introduction to CSNS

In today's rapidly evolving digital landscape, the security and compliance of cloud-native applications have become paramount. As organizations increasingly migrate their workloads to the cloud, they face a myriad of complex security challenges and regulatory requirements. The dynamic nature of cloud environments, characterized by their scalability, flexibility, and distributed architecture, introduces new vulnerabilities and attack vectors that traditional security measures may not adequately address. Consequently, there is a pressing need for robust and comprehensive security solutions that can adapt to the unique demands of cloud infrastructure. **The "Cloud Service Network Security" module within the Cloud-Native Application Protection Platform (CNAPP) is specifically designed to meet these challenges head-on.**

This module provides a suite of advanced security tools and practices tailored to protect cloud networks, ensuring the integrity, confidentiality, and availability of data as it traverses various cloud environments. By integrating these capabilities into a unified platform, CNAPP offers organizations a holistic approach to securing their cloud-native applications, enabling them to maintain a strong security posture while adhering to critical regulatory standards.

Cloud network security encompasses a range of practices and technologies aimed at protecting data, applications, and resources within a cloud environment.

Unlike traditional on-premises networks, cloud networks are dynamic, scalable, and often span multiple regions and providers. **This complexity necessitates a comprehensive approach to security that can adapt to the fluid nature of cloud infrastructure.**

Key Components of CSNS

Understanding the essential elements of cloud network security is crucial for safeguarding data and maintaining robust defenses against evolving threats. Let us explore some of the key components for cloud service network security:

- **Network Segmentation:** One of the foundational principles of cloud network security is **segmentation. By dividing the network into smaller, isolated segments, organizations can limit the spread of potential threats and contain breaches.**
- **Firewalls and Security Groups: Firewalls and security groups** are essential tools for controlling inbound and outbound traffic to and from cloud resources. These tools enable organizations to **define rules that permit or deny traffic based on various criteria** such as IP addresses, ports, and protocols. Advanced firewalls can also provide deep packet inspection and threat intelligence integration.
- **Encryption: Encrypting data in transit and at rest is a critical measure** to protect sensitive information from unauthorized access. Cloud service providers offer various encryption options, including **Transport Layer Security (TLS) for data in transit and server-side encryption for data at rest**. Organizations should implement strong encryption practices to ensure data confidentiality.
- **Intrusion Detection and Prevention Systems (IDPS):** IDPS solutions **monitor network traffic for signs of malicious activity** and can automatically take action to prevent or mitigate threats. These systems use a **combination of signature-based and anomaly-based detection methods** to identify potential attacks and respond in real-time.
- **Virtual Private Networks (VPNs):** VPNs provide secure, encrypted

connections between remote users and cloud resources. **By establishing a VPN, organizations can ensure that data transmitted over public networks remains protected from eavesdropping and interception.**

- **Zero Trust Architecture: The Zero Trust model operates on the principle of "*never trust, always verify.*"** In a cloud context, this means that every access request is authenticated, authorized, and encrypted, regardless of the source. **Implementing Zero Trust requires robust identity and access management (IAM) practices, multi-factor authentication (MFA), and continuous monitoring.**

Best Practices for CSNS

Implementing the best practices in cloud network security ensures a resilient and secure environment, protecting sensitive information and maintaining compliance with regulatory standards. Let's explore some of the best practices for cloud service network security:

- **Implement Least Privilege Access:** Grant users and applications the **minimum level of access necessary to perform their functions.** This **reduces the risk of unauthorized access,** and limits the potential impact of compromised credentials.
- **Regularly Update and Patch Systems:** Keeping systems and applications up to date with the latest security patches is crucial for protecting against known vulnerabilities. Automated patch management solutions can help streamline this process.
- **Monitor and Log Network Activity: Continuous monitoring and logging of network activity** provide visibility into potential security incidents. Organizations should implement centralized logging solutions, and use security information and event management (SIEM) tools to analyze and respond to threats.
- **Conduct Regular Security Assessments:** Periodic security assessments, including vulnerability scans and penetration testing, help identify and address weaknesses in the network. These assessments should be part of a broader security strategy that includes regular audits and compliance checks.
- **Educate and Train Staff:** Human error is a significant factor in many security breaches. Providing ongoing security training and awareness programs for staff can help mitigate this risk, and foster a culture of security within the organization.

The Role of CNAPP in Cloud Network Security

The Cloud-Native Application Protection Platform (CNAPP) integrates these network security components into a unified solution, offering organizations a comprehensive approach to securing their cloud environments. CNAPP provides centralized management and visibility, enabling security teams to monitor and control network traffic, enforce security policies, and respond to threats in real-time.

By leveraging CNAPP, organizations can achieve a higher level of security and compliance, ensuring that their cloud-native applications are protected against evolving threats. The platform's advanced features such as automated compliance checks, threat intelligence integration, and real-time monitoring, empower businesses to maintain a robust security posture, while focusing on innovation and growth.

In conclusion, cloud service network security is a vital aspect of protecting cloud-native applications. The "*Cloud Service Network Security*" module within CNAPP offers a comprehensive suite of tools and practices designed to address the unique challenges of cloud networking. By implementing these measures, organizations can safeguard their data, maintain compliance with regulatory standards, and create a secure and resilient cloud environment.

As illustrated in the pie chart above in the previous section, "*Introduction to CSPM*", you can see that the **CSNS module alone accounts for 10% of the utilization within the CNAPP suite**. This significant adoption underscores the critical role CSNS plays in enhancing cloud security and compliance.

This section served as an introductory overview of the "*Cloud Service Network Security* (CSNS)" module. In the upcoming dedicated chapter, "*Understanding Cloud Service Network Security* (CSNS)," we will delve deeper into various concepts, explore advanced topics, and engage in hands-on labs as well as exercises to enhance our understanding of CSNS.

Understanding KSPM

Before delving into Kubernetes Security Posture Management (KSPM), it is crucial to have a foundational understanding of containers and Kubernetes. Containers are lightweight, portable units that package an application and its dependencies, enabling consistent execution across different environments. Kubernetes, on the other hand, is an open-source platform designed to automate the deployment, scaling, and management of containerized applications. Understanding these core concepts will provide the necessary context for comprehending the intricacies of KSPM which focuses on securing and maintaining the integrity of Kubernetes environments.

Understanding Kubernetes

Kubernetes is an open-source, container orchestration platform for managing containerized application workloads and services. Kubernetes is in charge of container deployment and also manages the software-defined networking layer that allows containers to talk to one another. The platform is portable and facilitates declarative configuration and automation.

The official kubernetes website states, "*The name Kubernetes comes from Greek, meaning helmsman or pilot.*" Google open-sourced the kubernetes project in 2014. Kubernetes combines over 15 years of Google's experience running production workloads at scale with best-of-breed ideas and practices from the community.

Kubernetes plays a critical role in managing the scale and complexity of containerized applications by grouping and managing the various containers that run your applications. Containers are constantly being spun up and replaced. So, Kubernetes will immediately swap a container to ensure there is no down time.

The Fundamentals of KSPM

Kubernetes Security Posture Management (KSPM) is the process of putting into place a system for ensuring the defenses of Kubernetes – also referred to as K8s. Securing the management of containerized workloads across environments include practices like leveraging role-based access control (RBAC), limiting API access, ensuring Kubernetes itself is up to date, and performing proactive scanning and monitoring.

As organizations increasingly adopt Kubernetes for orchestrating their containerized applications, ensuring the security of these environments has become a critical concern. KSPM is an emerging discipline that focuses on securing Kubernetes clusters by continuously monitoring and managing their security posture. This chapter delves into the intricacies of KSPM, exploring its significance, core components, and the benefits it offers to organizations striving to secure their Kubernetes environments.

Kubernetes has become the de facto standard for container orchestration, enabling organizations to deploy, scale, and manage containerized applications efficiently. However, the complexity and dynamic nature of Kubernetes environments introduce unique security challenges. Misconfigurations, inadequate access controls, and lack of visibility can lead to vulnerabilities that are easily exploitable by malicious actors.

KSPM addresses these challenges by providing a comprehensive framework for managing and improving the security posture of Kubernetes clusters. By continuously monitoring configurations, access controls, and runtime activities, KSPM helps organizations identify and mitigate security risks, ensuring that their Kubernetes environments remain secure and compliant.

Core Components of KSPM

KSPM encompasses several core components that work together to provide a holistic approach to securing Kubernetes environments. These components include:

- **Configuration Management:** One of the foundational aspects of KSPM is the ability to manage and enforce secure configurations for Kubernetes clusters. This involves continuously scanning cluster configurations to identify misconfigurations and deviations from security best practices. Configuration management ensures that clusters are configured securely from the outset, and remain compliant with security policies over time.
- **Access Control and Identity Management:** Effective access control is critical for securing Kubernetes environments. KSPM solutions provide tools for managing access controls and identities within Kubernetes clusters. This includes implementing role-based access control (RBAC), managing service accounts, and enforcing the principle of least privilege. By ensuring that only authorized users and services have access to sensitive resources, KSPM reduces the risk of unauthorized access and potential breaches.
- **Runtime Security:** Protecting Kubernetes workloads during runtime is a key function of KSPM. This involves monitoring the behavior of containers and pods to detect and respond to suspicious activities. Runtime security includes capabilities such as anomaly detection, intrusion detection and prevention, and behavioral analysis. By continuously monitoring runtime activities, KSPM can detect and mitigate threats in real-time, minimizing the impact of security incidents.
- **Network Security:** Kubernetes environments rely on complex networking configurations to facilitate communication between containers, pods, and external services. KSPM solutions provide tools for securing these network communications, including network segmentation, encryption, and network policy enforcement. By securing network traffic, KSPM helps prevent lateral movement of threats within the cluster and protects data in transit.
- **Compliance and Governance:** KSPM helps organizations maintain compliance with regulatory requirements and industry standards. This includes automated compliance checks, policy enforcement, and audit reporting. By ensuring that Kubernetes clusters adhere to security policies and compliance frameworks, KSPM reduces the risk of non-compliance and associated penalties.
- **Threat Intelligence and Response:** Integrating threat intelligence into KSPM enhances the ability to detect and respond to emerging threats. This involves leveraging threat intelligence feeds to stay informed about the latest threats and vulnerabilities. KSPM solutions use this information to enhance threat

detection capabilities and orchestrate automated responses to neutralize threats before they can cause harm.

Benefits of KSPM

Implementing KSPM offers numerous benefits to organizations, enhancing their ability to secure Kubernetes environments, and achieve operational resilience. The key benefits include:

- **Improved Security Posture:** KSPM provides continuous monitoring and automated remediation, ensuring that Kubernetes clusters remain secure and compliant. By proactively identifying and addressing security risks, KSPM helps organizations maintain a strong security posture and reduce the likelihood of security incidents.
- **Enhanced Visibility:** KSPM solutions offer comprehensive visibility into Kubernetes environments, enabling security teams to identify and address potential security risks. Enhanced visibility ensures that organizations have a clear understanding of their security posture and can take proactive measures to mitigate risks.
- **Operational Efficiency:** Automation is a key feature of KSPM, reducing the manual effort required to manage Kubernetes security. Automated configuration management, compliance checks, and threat response enhance operational efficiency and allow security teams to focus on strategic initiatives.
- **Improved Compliance:** KSPM helps organizations maintain compliance with regulatory requirements and industry standards. Automated compliance checks and detailed reports simplify the process of demonstrating adherence to security policies and frameworks.
- **Reduced Risk:** By continuously monitoring Kubernetes environments and implementing proactive security measures, KSPM reduces the risk of data breaches and other security incidents. This proactive approach to security ensures that vulnerabilities are addressed before they can be exploited by malicious actors.
- **Scalability:** KSPM solutions are designed to scale with the needs of the organization, providing consistent security coverage regardless of the size or complexity of the Kubernetes environment. This scalability ensures that organizations can secure their Kubernetes clusters as they grow and evolve.

Kubernetes Security Posture Management (KSPM) is an essential solution for organizations seeking to secure their Kubernetes environments and maintain a robust security posture. By providing comprehensive visibility, automated remediation, compliance management, and enhanced security, KSPM addresses the unique challenges of managing Kubernetes security. Implementing KSPM offers numerous benefits, including improved security posture, enhanced visibility, operational efficiency, improved compliance, reduced risk, and scalability. As Kubernetes adoption continues to grow, the importance of KSPM in ensuring Kubernetes security will only become more critical.

As illustrated in the pie chart above in the previous section "*Introduction to* CSPM" you can see that the **KSPM module alone accounts for 10% of the utilization within the CNAPP suite.** This significant adoption underscores the critical role KSPM plays in enhancing cloud security and compliance.

This section served as an introductory overview of the "*Kubernetes Security Posture Management* (KSPM)" module. In the upcoming dedicated chapter, "*Understanding Kubernetes Security Posture Management* (KSPM)," we will delve deeper into various concepts, explore advanced topics, and engage in hands-on labs and exercises to enhance our understanding of KSPM.

Understanding DSPM

Data Security Posture Management (DSPM) is a holistic strategy aimed at **protecting an organization's sensitive data** from unauthorized access, exposure, modification, or destruction.

Introduction to DSPM

DSPM integrates various security measures such as data classification, encryption, access controls, data loss prevention (DLP), and continuous monitoring.

By adopting these measures, organizations can build and sustain a robust data security posture, ensuring compliance with privacy and security regulations, preventing data breaches, and safeguarding their brand reputation. DSPM addresses the security challenges posed by the widespread distribution of sensitive data across diverse environments.

It offers a structured approach to securing cloud data by ensuring that sensitive and regulated information maintains the appropriate security posture, regardless of its location or movement. As a data-centric approach to securing an organization's assets, both in the cloud and on-premises, DSPM emphasizes the protection of data itself, rather than just the systems housing it.

This makes DSPM a vital component of any data security strategy, particularly in cloud-first and cloud-native environments where traditional security measures may fall short.

Highlighted in Gartner's 2022 Hype Cycle for Data Security, DSPM technology automates the detection and protection of data, addressing the primary challenge of visibility in secure data management.

Through DSPM, organizations can gain crucial insights into:

- The **locations** of the sensitive data.
- **Who** has **access** to it?
- **How** the data is being **utilized?**
- The security posture of the data stores or applications.

Functioning of DSPM

DSPM uses data flow analysis techniques to understand how data moves within an organization to identify potential risks and vulnerabilities. These are the key steps involved in the overall DSPM process:

- **Data Discovery:** Data Security Posture Management (DSPM) initiates its process by meticulously identifying and cataloging data sources across the organization, including databases, file systems, cloud storage, and third-party applications. This comprehensive inventory enables organizations to gain a clear understanding of the locations and contexts of their sensitive data.
- **Data Classification:** Upon identifying data sources, DSPM meticulously classifies the data based on its sensitivity and significance. This classification process determines whether the information is personally identifiable information (PII), financial data, intellectual property, or other sensitive categories. By doing so, DSPM ensures that data protection efforts are prioritized effectively and aligned with regulatory compliance mandates.
- **Data Flow Mapping:** DSPM meticulously charts the flow of sensitive data across the organization's infrastructure, encompassing servers, databases, and applications. This mapping process enables organizations to visualize data access, processing, and transmission pathways, thereby uncovering potential vulnerabilities and weak points.
- **Risk Assessment:** Through comprehensive analysis of data flow, DSPM pinpoints potential risks and vulnerabilities, including unauthorized access, data leakage, and insufficient encryption. This detailed insight allows organizations to prioritize their security initiatives, and address the most critical threats effectively.
- **Security Control Implementation:** Based on the risk assessment, organizations can deploy suitable security controls to safeguard their data. These controls may include encryption, access management, and data loss prevention (DLP) strategies to ensure the protection of sensitive information as it traverses the organization.
- **Monitoring and Auditing:** DSPM continuously monitors data flow to identify anomalies, potential threats, and policy violations. Regular audits are

conducted to verify the effectiveness of security controls, and ensure that the organization remains compliant with data protection regulations.

- **Incident Response and Remediation:** In the event of a security incident, DSPM delivers salient information to swiftly identify the compromised data, evaluate the breach's extent, and execute remediation measures to mitigate the impact.

By leveraging data flow analysis, DSPM empowers organizations to gain a holistic understanding of how the sensitive data traverses and interacts within their infrastructure. This insight enables businesses to identify and mitigate potential risks, ensuring the protection of valuable data assets, and maintaining regulatory compliance.

DSPM Capabilities

According to Gartner's projections, by 2026, over 20% of organizations will have implemented Data Security Posture Management (DSPM). This surge is driven by the critical need to uncover previously unidentified data repositories and their geographic locations, thereby mitigating security and privacy risks.

- **Comprehensive Data Discovery:** By scanning both cloud environments and on-premises data stores, DSPM tools are necessary for uncovering shadow data and helping organizations understand their attack surface. Shadow data includes information created, stored, and processed outside official IT systems, often without IT department awareness. DSPM's data discovery capabilities allow organizations to identify these shadow data sources across unauthorized cloud services, personal devices, and third-party applications. Achieving visibility into all organizational data, including shadow data, is crucial for understanding the data landscape and implementing appropriate security controls like encryption, access management, and Data Loss Prevention (DLP).
- **Data Classification Advantage:** DSPM's active data classification allows organizations to prioritize security resources on critical information assets, ensuring that the sensitive data is adequately protected. This process also aids in regulatory compliance by identifying specific security controls required for different data types, enabling tailored protective measures.
- **Access Governance:** Access governance is a crucial aspect of DSPM, managing data access based on the principle of least privilege. DSPM ensures individuals access only the data necessary for their roles by providing visibility into access controls and identifying excessive or inappropriate access.
- **Vulnerability and Misconfiguration Detection and Remediation:** A key strength of DSPM is its robust risk detection capability. By continuously scanning data sources like databases, file systems, and cloud storage, DSPM tools uncover hidden vulnerabilities and misconfigurations that could expose

sensitive data. DSPM also detects abnormal user behavior, access patterns, and data movement, signaling potential insider threats or external attacks. With real-time alerts and actionable insights, DSPM enables swift responses to emerging risks, preventing data breaches before they occur.

- **Compliance Support:** Noncompliance with regulations like GDPR, HIPAA, and CCPA can result in hefty fines. DSPM provides visibility into data assets and security controls, helping organizations meet standards like PCI DSS and other data protection regulations. It also monitors for noncompliance, alerting security teams to address issues promptly.
- **Static Risk Analysis:** DSPM tools employ static risk analysis to identify potential data risks by examining data at rest. This process identifies sensitive information, assesses its risk level, and ensures adequate protection. By pinpointing data risks, organizations can prioritize security efforts and mitigate these risks effectively.
- **Policy Controls:** DSPM offers robust policy control capabilities, enabling organizations to define security policies for data protection and access. It applies controls such as encryption, tokenization, and access restrictions, enforcing them across data stores to ensure consistent data protection, and minimize unauthorized access risks.

Understanding Infrastructure-as-Code (IaC) Scanning

In the past, setting up and managing IT systems was a labor-intensive, manual task. Teams would designate an engineer to provision a server for a new application, database, or file storage. This process often included lengthy discussions about naming the new server, and many lower-level configuration tasks such as IP address, roles, and permissions.

Today, those days are behind us. With the advent of distributed architectures, ephemeral cloud resources, and global scalability, modern development teams rely on code and automation to configure their systems. **This approach, known as Infrastructure as Code (IaC), accelerates infrastructure setup and minimizes errors.** For organizations managing complex systems, IaC is a significant advantage.

Before we explore IaC scanning, it is vital to first grasp the fundamentals of Infrastructure as Code (IaC).

The Fundamentals of IaC

In a very simple definition, IaC is a modern approach to managing and provisioning computing infrastructure through machine-readable scripts, rather than through manual processes.

Imagine you could set up your entire computer network, including servers, databases, and networking equipment, just by writing a few lines of code. That is essentially what IaC allows you to do.

By defining your infrastructure in code, you can automate the setup, configuration, and management of your IT resources, making it faster, more reliable, and less prone to human errors.

Think of IaC as creating a blueprint for your infrastructure. Just like an architect designs a building with detailed plans, you write scripts that describe how your infrastructure should look and behave. These scripts can be version-controlled, shared, and reused, ensuring consistency across different environments (like development, testing, and production).

In this modern era of cloud computing and DevOps, IaC has revolutionized the way organizations manage and deploy their IT infrastructure. By treating the infrastructure configuration as code, IaC enables automation, consistency, and scalability.

This approach not only saves time but also enhances collaboration among teams, as everyone can see and modify the infrastructure code. In essence, IaC transforms infrastructure management into a software engineering practice, bringing the benefits of automation, scalability, and repeatability to the world of IT operations.

However, this shift also introduces new security challenges that require specialized solutions.

Popular IaC Languages Used by Industry Experts

Infrastructure as Code (IaC) has revolutionized the way organizations manage and provision their IT infrastructure. **By treating infrastructure configurations as code, IaC enables automation, consistency, and scalability, significantly reducing the time and effort required for manual setup and management.**

AWS CloudFormation and Azure Resource Manager are two of the most renowned IaC techniques widely adopted by cloud experts across the industry. However, the landscape of IaC tools and technologies is vast, offering numerous options for automating and managing cloud IT infrastructure.

Industry experts rely on a variety of IaC languages and tools to streamline their workflows and ensure reliable, repeatable infrastructure deployments. Following is a list of some of the most commonly used IaC languages and tools in the industry. Following is a list of IaC tools and technologies commonly used by industry professionals:

- **Terraform:** Developed by **HashiCorp**, Terraform is a widely-used open-source tool that allows you to define and provision infrastructure across multiple cloud providers using a simple, declarative language.
- **AWS CloudFormation (JSON/YAML):** This is Amazon Web Services' **(AWS)** native IaC tool, which enables you to model and set up your AWS resources using JSON or YAML templates. It integrates seamlessly with other AWS services.
- **Azure Resource Manager (ARM):** Microsoft's **(Azure)** IaC solution for managing Azure resources. ARM templates are written in JSON and allow you to deploy, manage, and monitor resources as a group.
- **Google Cloud Deployment Manager (JSON/YAML): Google's** IaC tool that uses YAML, Python, or Jinja2 templates to define and deploy Google Cloud resources.
- **Pulumi (Multiple Languages):** A modern IaC tool that supports multiple programming languages like JavaScript, TypeScript, Python, Go, and C#. Pulumi allows you to use familiar languages to define and manage cloud infrastructure.
- **Ansible (YAML):** An **open-source automation tool** that can be used for configuration management, application deployment, and IaC. Ansible uses YAML to define automation jobs, making it easy to read and write.
- **Chef (Ruby):** A powerful configuration management tool that uses Ruby-based DSL for writing configuration "recipes." Chef is used to automate infrastructure provisioning and management.
- **Puppet (DSL):** Similar to Chef, Puppet is a configuration management tool that uses its own declarative language to manage infrastructure. It is known for its robust reporting and compliance features.
- **SaltStack:** An open-source configuration management and orchestration tool that uses Python to define infrastructure states. SaltStack is known for its speed and scalability.
- **Vagrant:** A tool for building and managing virtualized development environments. Vagrant provides easy-to-configure, reproducible, and portable work environments.
- **Kubernetes Operators:** These are custom controllers that extend the Kubernetes API to manage complex applications and their dependencies using custom resources.
- **Crossplane:** An open-source project that extends Kubernetes to manage infrastructure across multiple cloud providers using Kubernetes-native APIs.

- **AWS CDK (Cloud Development Kit):** Allows you to define cloud infrastructure using familiar programming languages like TypeScript, JavaScript, Python, Java, and C#.
- **Spacelift:** A management platform that supports multi-IaC workflows, integrating with tools like Terraform, Pulumi, and Kubernetes to provide a unified management experience.

In summary, the adoption of IaC languages and tools has become essential for modern IT operations. By leveraging these powerful IaC solutions, organizations can achieve greater efficiency, consistency, and scalability in their infrastructure management. Embracing these tools not only streamlines operations but also paves the way for innovation and agility in the ever-evolving landscape of cloud computing.

The Fundamentals of IaC Scanning

However, simply declaring and codifying the desired state of infrastructure does not ensure it is free from errors or security vulnerabilities.

This is where IaC scanning becomes necessary. IaC scanning examines the code for security risks and rule violations before deployment.

IaC scanning is a crucial practice in modern cloud computing that ensures the security and correctness of your infrastructure configurations. **Infrastructure as Code (IaC) is a method of managing and provisioning computing infrastructure through machine-readable configuration files, rather than physical hardware configuration or interactive configuration tools.**

These are the benefits of using IaC Scanning:

- **Early Detection of Issues:** By scanning IaC code early in the development process, teams can catch and fix problems, before they affect live environments.
- **Enhanced Security:** IaC Scanning helps maintain a secure infrastructure by identifying vulnerabilities, and ensuring compliance with security standards.
- **Consistency and Reliability:** Automated scanning ensures that infrastructure configurations are consistent and reliable across different environments.

Understanding Shift-Left Security

IaC Scanning represents the principle of "*shift-left security*" which involves embedding security checks early in the software development lifecycle. This strategy allows for the early detection and mitigation of risks.

Integrating IaC Scanning into your development process ensures that your cloud infrastructure remains secure, compliant, and devoid of critical errors. This forward-thinking approach not only conserves time and resources, but also significantly boosts the reliability of your cloud deployments.

Understanding Policy as Code (PaC) Concept

Policy as Code (PaC) is a fundamental aspect of IaC scanning. Similar to how we define infrastructure configurations through IaC, PaC involves codifying security policies for that infrastructure. By expressing these security policies in a machine-readable format, teams can utilize IaC scanning tools to ensure compliance with security rules across all infrastructure deployments. This approach guarantees that every piece of deployed infrastructure adheres to the organization's security standards.

As illustrated in the pie chart above in the previous section "*Introduction to* CSPM" you can see that the **IaC Scanning module alone accounts for 10% of the utilization within the CNAPP suite**. This significant adoption underscores the critical role IaC Scanning plays in enhancing cloud security and compliance.

This section served as an introductory overview of the "*Infrastructure as Code* (IaC) *Scanning*" module. In the upcoming dedicated chapter, "*Understanding Infrastructure as Code (IaC) Scanning*," we will delve deeper into various concepts, explore advanced topics, and engage in hands-on labs and exercises to enhance our understanding of IaC Scanning.

Understanding Centralized Compliance Dashboard

Imagine navigating a vast ocean without a compass. That's what managing cloud compliance can feel like without a Centralized Compliance Dashboard. This powerful tool acts as your navigational beacons, guiding you through the complexities of cloud compliance with precision and ease.

A Centralized Compliance Dashboard is more than just a monitoring tool; it is the heartbeat of your cloud security strategy. It pulses with real-time data, ensuring that every beat aligns with your compliance standards. This dynamic interface brings together disparate data streams into a cohesive, actionable format.

In today's digital age, organizations are increasingly migrating their operations to the cloud, seeking the agility and scalability it offers. **However, this shift brings with it a complex web of compliance requirements that must be meticulously managed.** Enter the Centralized Compliance Dashboard—a revolutionary tool designed to simplify and streamline compliance management in cloud environments.

As its core, the Centralized Compliance Dashboard serves as the nerve center for all compliance-related activities.

Benefits of Centralized Compliance Dashboard

In the fast-paced world of cloud-native applications, keeping up with numerous regulatory standards can be a challenging task for a cloud administrator. **A centralized compliance dashboard module within a Cloud-Native Application Protection Platform (CNAPP) emerges as a game-changer, offering unparalleled visibility and control over compliance status across the entire cloud environment. This innovative tool consolidates compliance data from various sources into a single, intuitive interface, enabling organizations to monitor, manage, and report on compliance with ease.**

By providing real-time insights and automated alerts, a centralized compliance dashboard not only simplifies the compliance process but also enhances the organization's ability to swiftly address potential issues, thereby reducing the risk of non-compliance. This unique capability empowers businesses to stay ahead of regulatory requirements, ensuring that their cloud-native applications remain secure and compliant in an ever-evolving digital landscape.

Through this book, we will explore the transformative impact of centralized compliance dashboards on cloud security strategies, highlighting their critical role in fostering a robust and resilient cloud infrastructure.

These are some of the notable primary features of Centralized Compliance Dashboard:

- **Enhanced Visibility:** Provides clear insights into compliance status, making it easier for security teams to maintain and demonstrate compliance. A centralized compliance dashboard provides a comprehensive view of compliance status across all cloud-native applications. This holistic perspective allows organizations to quickly identify and address compliance gaps, ensuring that no aspect of their cloud environment is overlooked.
- **Streamlined Reporting:** With all compliance data aggregated in one place, generating reports becomes a seamless process. This not only saves time but also ensures accuracy, making it easier for organizations to demonstrate compliance to auditors and regulatory bodies.
- **Proactive Issue Resolution:** Real-time alerts and notifications enable organizations to detect and resolve compliance issues before they escalate. This proactive approach minimizes the risk of non-compliance and helps maintain a robust security posture.
- **Improved Efficiency**: Streamlines the compliance management process, saving time and resources. By automating compliance monitoring and reporting, a centralized dashboard reduces the manual effort required to manage compliance. This frees up valuable resources, allowing teams to focus on more strategic initiatives.
- **Cost Saving:** Centralized compliance management can lead to significant cost

savings by reducing the need for multiple compliance tools, and minimizing the risk of costly fines and penalties. This streamlined approach ensures that compliance efforts are both effective and economical.

- **Simplified Audits:** A centralized dashboard simplifies the audit process by providing easy access to all necessary compliance documentation and evidence. This makes it easier for organizations to prepare for and pass audits, reducing the stress and complexity associated with compliance assessments.
- **Continuous Improvement:** By providing ongoing insights into compliance performance, a centralized dashboard supports continuous improvement efforts. Organizations can use this data to refine their compliance strategies, and enhance their overall security posture over time.
- **Enhanced Collaboration:** A centralized compliance dashboard fosters collaboration among different teams by providing a shared platform for compliance management. This ensures that everyone is on the same page, and working towards common compliance goals, improving overall organizational alignment.
- **Real-Time Monitoring:** The dashboard continuously tracks compliance metrics, ensuring that any deviations from established standards are promptly identified and addressed.
- **Unified View:** It integrates data from different cloud services and security tools, presenting a holistic view of compliance across the entire cloud infrastructure.
- **Automated Reporting:** Automated compliance reports can be generated, helping organizations to meet the regulatory requirements and internal policies efficiently.
- **Risk Management:** By identifying potential compliance risks early, the dashboard enables proactive risk management, reducing the likelihood of security breaches and non-compliance penalties.
- **Customizable Alerts:** Users can set up customizable alerts for specific compliance issues, ensuring that critical events are not missed.
- **Proactive Security:** Helps in identifying and mitigating risks, before they escalate into significant issues.

In summary, a Centralized Compliance Dashboard is an indispensable tool for organizations leveraging CNAPP to maintain robust security and compliance in their cloud environments.

Key Compliances Managed by a Centralized Compliance Dashboard

In today's digital landscape, securing and ensuring compliance for cloud-native applications is essential. The Cloud-Native Application Protection Platform (CNAPP) integrates advanced security tools and compliance capabilities into a single platform, offering comprehensive protection throughout the application lifecycle. **CNAPP ensures adherence to standards like GDPR, HIPAA, and PCI DSS, helping businesses to protect the sensitive data, and streamline compliance efforts.** This book explores CNAPP's key features, benefits, and its vital role in modern cloud security strategies. Join us to discover how CNAPP is revolutionizing cloud-native application protection. Here are some key IT standards and compliance frameworks that can be monitored through a centralized Compliance Dashboard:

- **ISO/IEC 27001:** Specifies requirements for establishing, implementing, maintaining, and continually improving an information security management system (ISMS).
- **NIST Cybersecurity Framework (CSF):** Provides a policy framework of computer guidance for how private sector organizations in the U.S can assess and improve their ability to prevent, detect, and respond to cyber-attacks.
- **Control Objectives for Information and Related Technologies (COBIT):** A framework created by ISACA for IT management and IT governance, providing a set of best practices for managing IT processes.
- **General Data Protection Regulation (GDPR):** Ensure data protection and privacy for individuals within the European Union, impacting how organizations handle personal data.
- **Health Insurance Portability and Accountability Act (HIPAA):** Protects sensitive patient health information in the healthcare industry, ensuring data privacy and security provisions.
- **Payment Card Industry Data Security Standard (PCI DSS):** Ensures secure handling of credit card information, crucial for organizations that process card payments.
- **Cybersecurity Maturity Model Certification (CMMC):** A framework to assess the cybersecurity maturity of contractors working with the U.S. Department of Defense.
- **Federal Risk and Authorization Management Program (FedRAMP):** Provides a standardized approach to security assessment, authorization and continuous monitoring for cloud products and services used by U.S. federal agencies.
- **Sarbanes-Oxley Act (SOX):** Mandates strict reforms to improve financial disclosure and prevent accounting fraud, impacting IT systems that handle the financial data.

These standards help organizations ensure they are compliant with various regulatory requirements, thereby reducing risks and enhancing their security posture. The

Centralized Compliance Dashboard provides a unified view to track adherence to these standards, making compliance management more efficient and effective.

This section served as an introductory overview of the "*Centralized Compliance Dashboard*" module. In the upcoming dedicated chapter, "*Centralized Compliance Management*," we will delve deeper into various concepts, explore advanced topics, and engage in hands-on labs and exercises to enhance our understanding of Centralized Compliance Management.

Real-World Case Studies for CNAPP

To illustrate the transformative power of a Cloud-Native Application Protection Platform (CNAPP), **let's delve into some real-world case studies.** These examples showcase how organizations have leveraged CNAPP to enhance their cloud security posture, streamline compliance, and mitigate risks effectively.

Case Study 1: Global Retailer

A global retailer **faced significant challenges in managing security and compliance across its multi-cloud environment**. With a diverse range of applications and services, maintaining visibility and control was a daunting task.

By implementing a CNAPP, the retailer achieved comprehensive visibility into their cloud assets and vulnerabilities. The platform's automated risk prioritization and remediation capabilities enabled the security team to focus on critical issues, reducing the time to resolve vulnerabilities by 60%. This proactive approach not only improved their security posture but also ensured continuous compliance with industry standards like PCI DSS and GDPR.

Additionally, **the CNAPP's integration with the retailer's existing security tools and workflows** streamlined incident response processes. The centralized dashboard provided a unified view of security events, allowing the team to quickly correlate and investigate incidents. **This integration led to a 30% reduction in incident response times**, and enhanced collaboration across the security and IT operations teams, ultimately fortifying the retailer's overall security framework.

Case Study 2: Financial Institution

A leading financial institution **required a robust solution to manage compliance with multiple regulatory frameworks**, including SOX and ISO/IEC 27001. The institution's cloud environment was complex, with numerous applications and services spread across different providers.

Implementing a CNAPP allowed the institution to integrate data from various

sources into a single, unified platform. This integration provided a holistic view of their compliance landscape, enabling real-time monitoring and automated compliance checks. The institution experienced a 40% improvement in audit readiness and a significant reduction in manual compliance tasks, freeing up resources to focus on strategic initiatives.

In addition, the CNAPP's detailed audit trails and comprehensive reporting capabilities simplified the audit process. Auditors could easily access and review compliance records, reducing the time and effort required for audits. The platform's continuous compliance monitoring ensured that the institution remained audit-ready at all times, minimizing the risk of non-compliance penalties. This enhanced audit readiness not only improved regulatory relationships, but also provided a competitive edge in the financial market by demonstrating a strong commitment to security and compliance.

These expanded case studies highlight the significant benefits and real-world impact of implementing a CNAPP. By providing comprehensive visibility, automated risk management, and streamlined compliance processes, CNAPPs empower organizations to maintain robust security and compliance in their cloud environments.

The Future of CNAPP

As we look towards the future of cloud security, the evolution of Cloud Native Application Protection Platforms (CNAPP) stands out as a pivotal development. The rapid adoption of cloud-native technologies has transformed the way organizations build, deploy, and manage applications.

With this transformation comes a new set of security challenges that traditional security measures struggle to address. CNAPPs are designed to meet these challenges head-on, providing a comprehensive and integrated approach to securing cloud-native environments.

One of the most exciting prospects for the future of CNAPP is the integration of emerging technologies such as quantum cryptography and advanced AI-driven analytics. Quantum cryptography promises to revolutionize data encryption, making it virtually unbreakable and ensuring the highest level of data protection. Meanwhile, AI-driven analytics will enhance CNAPP's ability to detect and respond to threats in real-time. **By analyzing vast amounts of data and identifying patterns that indicate potential security breaches, AI can help organizations stay one step ahead of cybercriminals.**

The future of CNAPP will also see a greater emphasis on **proactive threat detection and response. Traditional security measures often rely on reactive approaches, addressing threats only after they have been identified.** In contrast, CNAPPs will leverage real-time threat intelligence and behavioral analytics to anticipate and neutralize potential attacks before they can cause harm. This proactive approach will not only enhance security but also minimize downtime and operational disruptions, ensuring business continuity.

Moreover, CNAPPs will become increasingly integrated with DevSecOps practices, embedding security into every stage of the application development lifecycle. This seamless integration will foster a culture of security awareness among development teams, enabling them to build and deploy secure applications from the ground up. **By incorporating security into the development process, organizations can reduce the risk of vulnerabilities and ensure that their applications are resilient against emerging threats.**

Another key aspect of the future of CNAPP is its role in compliance management. As data protection regulations continue to evolve, organizations must ensure that they remain compliant with standards such as GDPR, HIPAA, and PCI DSS. CNAPPs will provide automated tools to monitor compliance, identify gaps, and generate detailed reports. This will enable organizations to maintain robust security postures and avoid the significant fines and penalties associated with noncompliance.

Furthermore, the future of CNAPP will likely involve greater collaboration and information sharing among organizations. **By sharing threat intelligence and best practices, organizations can collectively enhance their security postures and better defend against common threats.** This collaborative approach will be particularly important as cyber threats become more sophisticated and widespread.

In conclusion, the future of CNAPP is bright and full of potential. As cloud-native technologies continue to evolve, CNAPPs will play an increasingly vital role in securing cloud environments. By integrating advanced technologies, adopting proactive security measures, and fostering a culture of security awareness, CNAPPs will help organizations navigate the complexities of cloud security and fully realize the benefits of cloud-native applications. The continued development and adoption of CNAPPs will be crucial in ensuring that organizations can protect their data, maintain compliance, and stay ahead of the ever-changing threat landscape.

Conclusion

In conclusion, the introduction to Cloud Native Application Protection Platform (CNAPP) has provided a foundational understanding of its critical role in modern cloud security. As organizations increasingly adopt cloud-native architectures, the need for robust security measures becomes paramount.

CNAPP addresses this need by integrating various security components, including Cloud Security Posture Management (CSPM), Cloud Workload Protection Platform (CWPP), Web Application and API Security (WAAS), Cloud Infrastructure Entitlement

Management (CIEM), Cloud Service Network Security (CSNS), Data Security Posture Management (DSPM), Kubernetes Security Posture Management (KSPM), and Infrastructure as Code (IaC) Scanning.

Each module plays a vital role in ensuring comprehensive protection across the entire cloud environment. By leveraging CNAPP, organizations can achieve enhanced visibility, proactive threat detection, and automated remediation, ultimately leading to a more secure and compliant cloud infrastructure. As we move forward, understanding and implementing CNAPP will be vital for safeguarding cloud-native applications, and maintaining a strong security posture in the ever-evolving digital landscape.

In this next chapter, we will delve into the practical aspects of onboarding a CNAPP. We will guide you through the essential steps, from initial setup to full integration, ensuring that your cloud environments are secure and compliant. You will also learn how to configure CNAPP to meet your organization's specific needs, streamline security operations, and leverage advanced features to protect against emerging threats. By the end of this chapter, you will have a comprehensive understanding of how to effectively deploy and manage CNAPP, empowering your team to safeguard your cloud-native applications with confidence.

Points to Remember

- Core components of CNAPP include Cloud Security Posture Management, Workload Security, Identity and Access Management, Network Security, Data Security, and Threat Detection and Response.
- Modules in CNAPP include CSPM, CWPP, WAAS, CIEM, CSNS, DSPM, KSPM, IaC Scanning and Centralized Compliance Dashboard.
- High-level processes for implementing CNAPP include Assessment, Planning, Adoption, and Monitoring and Improvement.
- CNAPP architecture workflow includes Development, Build, Deployment, Runtime, and Monitoring and Maintenance.
- Top 10 leading CNAPP providers include SentinelOne, Prisma Cloud by Palo Alto Networks, Microsoft Defender for Cloud, Wiz, Sysdig, Lacework, Trend Vision One Cloud Security, Orca Security, Aqua Security, and Checkpoint CloudGuard.
- Cloud Security Posture Management refers to a set of automated tools and processes that continuously monitor cloud environments to detect and remediate security risks.
- Cloud Workload Protection Platforms (CWPP) have emerged as a critical solution to address these challenges, providing comprehensive security for cloud workloads.

- The Web Application and API Security (WAAS) module is designed to provide robust protection against a wide range of cyber threats.
- Cloud Infrastructure Entitlement Management (CIEM) is an emerging discipline that addresses the complexities of managing identities, and access rights in cloud infrastructures.
- The "*Cloud Service Network Security*" module within the Cloud-Native Application Protection Platform (CNAPP) is designed to address the unique challenges posed by cloud networking, providing robust security measures to safeguard cloud infrastructure and applications.
- Kubernetes Security Posture Management (KSPM) is the process of putting into place a system for ensuring the defenses of Kubernetes – also referred to as K8s.
- Data Security Posture Management (DSPM) is a holistic strategy aimed at protecting an organization's sensitive data from unauthorized access, exposure, modification, or destruction.
- Infrastructure as Code (IaC) Scanning is a crucial practice in modern cloud computing that ensures the security and correctness of your infrastructure configurations. IaC scanning examines the code for security risks, and rules violations before deployment.
- A Centralized Compliance Dashboard is more than just a monitoring tool; it is the heartbeat of your cloud security strategy. It pulses with the real-time data, ensuring that every beat aligns with your compliance standards.

Multiple-Choice Questions

1. What does CNAPP stand for?
   a. Cloud Native Application Protection Platform
   b. Cloud Network Application Protection Platform
   c. Cloud Native Applied Protection Platform
   d. Cloud Network Applied Protection Platform
2. Which of the following is a core component of CNAPP?
   a. Workload Security
   b. Data Encryption
   c. User Authentication
   d. Network Monitoring

3. What is the primary function of Cloud Security Posture Management (CSPM) in CNAPP?
   a. Monitoring network traffic
   b. Ensuring compliance with security policies
   c. Managing user identities
   d. Encrypting data at rest
4. Which module in CNAPP is responsible for scanning Infrastructure as Code (IaC) templates?
   a. CWPP
   b. WAAS
   c. KSPM
   d. IaC Scanning
5. What is a key benefit of integrating CSPM into CNAPP?
   a. Enhanced visibility into cloud assets
   b. Improved user experience
   c. Faster data processing
   d. Reduced hardware cost

Answers

1. a
2. a
3. b
4. d
5. a

Questions

1. What does CNAPP stand for?
2. Which CNAPP module is responsible for managing cloud security configurations?
3. What is the primary function of Cloud Workload Protection Platform (CWPP)?

4. Which module in CNAPP focuses on securing web applications and APIs?
5. What does CIEM stand for in the context of CNAPP?
6. How does Cloud Service Network Security (CSNS) contribute to CNAPP?
7. Which CNAPP component ensures data security and privacy in cloud environments?
8. What is the role of Kubernetes Security Posture Management (KSPM) in CNAPP?
9. Which CNAPP module is responsible for scanning Infrastructure as Code (IaC) templates?
10. How does CNAPP help in threat detection and response?

Key Terms

- **CNAPP**: Cloud Native Application Protection Platform
- **CSPM**: Cloud Security Posture Management
- **CWPP**: Cloud Workload Protection Platforms
- **WAAS**: Web Application and API Security
- **CSNS:** Cloud Service Network Security
- **CIEM**: Cloud Infrastructure Entitlement Management
- **KSPM**: Kubernetes Security Posture Management
- **DSPM**: Data Security Posture Management
- **IaC**: Infrastructure-as-Code
- **IaC Scanning:** Infrastructure-as-Code Scanning

CHAPTER 3
A Practical Guide to Onboarding CNAPP

Introduction

This chapter serves as a practical guide to onboarding CNAPP, with a specific focus on **Microsoft Defender for Cloud**. As a leading CNAPP solution, Microsoft Defender for Cloud offers extensive capabilities to secure your cloud-native applications across multiple environments. Whether you are a seasoned IT professional or a newcomer to cloud security, this guide aims to equip you with the knowledge and tools necessary to protect your cloud-native applications effectively.

We will delve into the intricacies of integrating Microsoft Defender for Cloud with various cloud environments, including Azure, AWS, and Google Cloud Platform (GCP). Additionally, we will explore how to secure your CI/CD pipelines with Azure DevOps, and protect your containerized applications as well as code repositories within Docker and GitHub. By providing detailed instructions and best practices, this chapter will help you navigate the complexities of cloud security, and ensure that your infrastructure is resilient against evolving cyber threats.

By the end of this chapter, you will have a thorough understanding of how to effectively onboard and utilize Microsoft Defender for Cloud to secure your cloud-native applications across various environments. Let us embark on this journey to fortify your cloud infrastructure, and ensure its resilience against evolving cyber threats.

In this chapter, we will successfully onboard three (3) Azure subscriptions, one (1) AWS account, and one (1) GCP account to Microsoft Defender for Cloud. The onboarding process is demonstrated with clear, step-by-step instructions, and actual screenshots. Here is how the environment page will look after Azure, AWS, and GCP cloud platforms are onboarded to Microsoft Defender for Cloud.

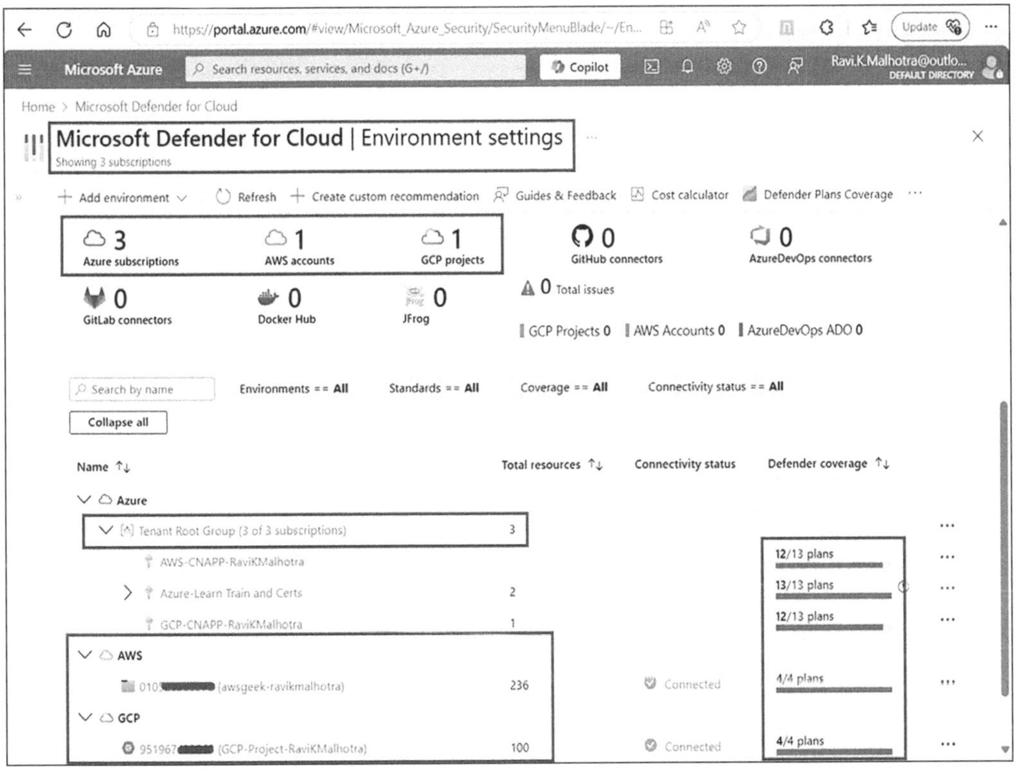

Figure 3.1: *Page Showing Azure, AWS and GCP Onboarded Successfully to Defender for Cloud*

To make this chapter more insightful, we have included **Six (6) hands-on labs**, providing **live demonstrations,** using **`Microsoft Defender for Cloud`**. The following is the list of **all hands-on demonstrations covered in this chapter**:

- **Lab # 1:** Automatic Onboarding of Foundational CSPM to the Azure Cloud Platform
- **Lab # 2:** Manual Onboarding of Defender CSPM to the Azure Cloud Platform
- **Lab # 3:** Manual Onboarding of Server CSPM Plans to the Azure Cloud Platform
- **Lab # 4:** Onboarding Multiple Subscriptions using Azure Policy
- **Lab # 5:** Defender for Cloud to the AWS Cloud Platform
- **Lab # 6:** Onboarding Defender for Cloud to the GCP Cloud Platform

These labs are designed to **bridge the gap between theory and real-world application**, enabling you to **strengthen cloud security posture** across **multi-cloud environments**.

Structure

Get ready for a fun adventure with Cloud Computing and Security in my book! I cannot wait for you to enjoy every page. So, here is what you can expect: A well-structured journey through key cloud security concepts, hands-on labs, and real-world insights. Each section builds upon the previous one, ensuring a smooth learning curve. From foundational principles to advanced security strategies, this chapter is designed to enhance your understanding and practical skills in onboarding the most popular public cloud platforms to Microsoft Defender for Cloud CNAPP. Let us dive in! The following topics will be covered in this chapter:

- CNAPP: Microsoft Defender for Cloud
- Understanding Subscriptions and Licensing for Defender for Cloud
- CNAPP Onboarding Labs

CNAPP: Microsoft Defender for Cloud

Microsoft Defender for Cloud is a comprehensive Cloud-Native Application Protection Platform (CNAPP) designed to secure your cloud environments. It provides robust security features that protect against a wide range of threats, ensuring that your applications and data remain safe. By integrating seamlessly with Azure, AWS, GCP, Azure DevOps, Docker, and GitHub, it offers a unified security solution across multiple platforms.

This section will guide you through the essential steps to onboard and utilize Microsoft Defender for Cloud effectively.

Understanding Microsoft Defender for Cloud

Microsoft Defender for Cloud is a comprehensive CNAPP designed to safeguard cloud-based applications against a wide array of cyber threats and vulnerabilities. This platform integrates several key security solutions:

- **DevSecOps Integration:** It offers a unified security management approach at the code level, seamlessly operating across multi-cloud and multiple-pipeline environments.
- **Cloud Security Posture Management (CSPM):** This component identifies and recommends preventive actions to mitigate potential breaches.
- **Cloud Workload Protection Platform (CWPP):** It provides specialized protection for various workloads, including servers, containers, storage, and databases.

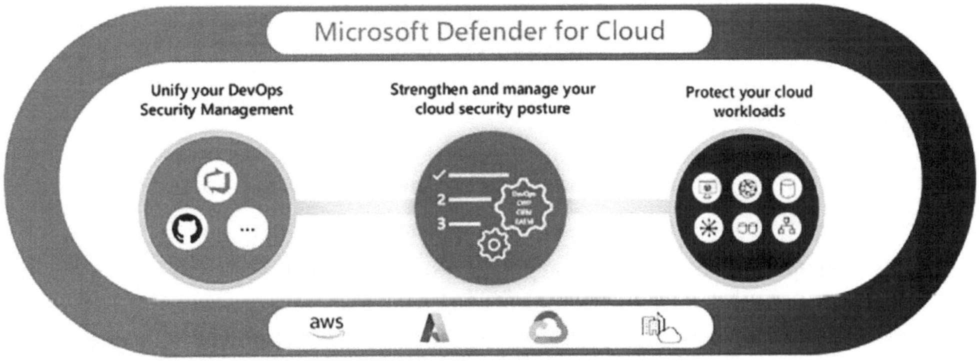

Figure 3.2: *Microsoft Defender for Cloud CNAPP Solution (source: https://learn.microsoft.com/en-us/azure/defender-for-cloud/defender-for-cloud-introduction)*

When you activate Defender for Cloud, you also gain automatic access to **Microsoft Defender XDR**. This extended detection and response (XDR) solution enhances your security posture by providing comprehensive threat detection and response capabilities across your entire environment.

Understanding Subscriptions and Licensing for Defender for Cloud

Microsoft Defender for Cloud offers a comprehensive approach to cloud security through its flexible subscription and licensing models. These models are designed to cater to the diverse security needs of modern enterprises, ensuring robust protection, while aligning with operational and financial strategies.

Subscription Models

Microsoft Defender for Cloud presents a range of subscription models designed to cater to various security requirements. These models offer extensive protection, ensuring that cloud environments remain secure and resilient. Grasping these options is essential for maximizing the value of cloud security investments.

- **Free Tier:** This tier provides basic security features at no cost, making it ideal for organizations starting their cloud security journey. It includes continuous security assessments, actionable recommendations, and a Secure Score to help gauge and enhance your security posture.
- **Pay-As-You-Go:** This model charges based on actual usage, offering flexibility for varying workloads. It is suitable for organizations that need to scale their security measures in tandem with their growth.
- **Commitment Tiers:** These tiers offer discounts for pre-purchased usage,

providing cost savings for consistent, high-volume usage. This model is beneficial for organizations with predictable security needs.

Licensing Models

Understanding these are the available licensing models supported for Microsoft Defender for Cloud:

- **Per-Resource Licensing:** Charges are based on the specific resources being protected such as Virtual Machines (VMs), containers, and databases. Each resource type has its own pricing model, allowing for tailored security solutions.
- **Bundled Licensing:** This model offers a package of security features for multiple resources, often at a discounted rate compared to purchasing each feature separately. It is ideal for organizations looking for comprehensive security coverage.
- **Standalone Licensing:** Allows you to purchase individual security features or protections as needed, without bundling them with other services. This model provides flexibility to address specific security requirements.
- **Enterprise Agreements:** These agreements provide customized licensing options for large organizations, often including volume discounts and additional benefits. They are tailored to the specific needs and usage patterns of the enterprise.

Subscription Details

Exploring the subscription details of Microsoft Defender for Cloud unveils a robust array of features tailored to diverse security needs. Each subscription level is meticulously crafted to deliver specific protections and capabilities, empowering organizations to select the ideal solution for their cloud security framework. Mastering these details is pivotal for fully harnessing the power of Defender for Cloud.

- **Pay-As-You-Go:** This subscription model offers flexible billing based on actual usage, making it suitable for organizations with varying workloads. It ensures that you only pay for what you use, providing cost-effective security solutions.
- **Pre-Purchase Plans:** These plans offer cost savings for consistent, high-volume usage by providing discounts for committing to a certain level of usage over a specified period. This model is beneficial for organizations with predictable security needs.
- **Free Trial:** Microsoft Defender for Cloud offers a 30-day free trial for new users. During this period, you can explore the features and capabilities of the platform, without incurring any charges. After the trial period, charges will apply based on the plans enabled in your environment.

Licensing Details

Understanding the licensing details of Microsoft Defender for Cloud is crucial for effective cloud security management. Each licensing option is designed to offer specific features and benefits, ensuring organizations can select the most suitable plan for their security needs. Mastering these details enables organizations to optimize their investment, and enhance their cloud security posture.

- **Defender for Servers:**
  - **Plan 1**: Focuses on endpoint detection and response (EDR) capabilities provided by the Defender for Endpoint integration. It offers robust protection against a wide range of threats.
  - **Plan 2**: Includes all features of Plan 1 plus additional advanced threat protection capabilities, compliance assessments, and premium vulnerability management.
- **Defender for Containers:** Protects containerized environments, including Kubernetes clusters, with advanced threat detection and security recommendations.
- **Defender for SQL:** Provides advanced threat protection for SQL databases, including vulnerability assessments and threat detection.
- **Defender for Storage:** Offers threat detection and security recommendations for storage accounts.
- **Defender for App Service:** Protects web applications hosted on Azure App Service with advanced threat detection and security recommendations.
- **Defender for Key Vault:** Provides advanced threat protection for Azure Key Vault, including anomaly detection and security recommendations.
- **Defender for Resource Manager:** Protects Azure Resource Manager with advanced threat detection and security recommendations.

Free Tier Offerings

The Free Tier of Microsoft Defender for Cloud offers foundational Cloud Security Posture Management (CSPM) features at no additional cost. This tier provides continuous security assessments, actionable recommendations, and a Secure Score to help you gauge and enhance your security posture. It supports resources across Azure, AWS, and Google Cloud, giving you a comprehensive view of your cloud security landscape. Ideal for organizations beginning their cloud security journey, the Free Tier delivers valuable insights and tools to strengthen your defenses, without any financial commitment.

Paid Plans

- **Defender for Servers Plan 1:** This plan is designed as an entry-level solution, focusing on essential Endpoint Detection and Response (EDR) capabilities. It integrates seamlessly with Microsoft Defender for Endpoint to provide robust protection against a wide range of threats.
- **Defender for Servers Plan 2:** This plan builds on the capabilities of Plan 1, offering a comprehensive suite of advanced security features designed to provide enhanced protection and compliance. It includes agentless scanning, compliance assessments, premium vulnerability management, and much more.

Decoding Pricing Plans

- **Free Tier: Foundational CSPM** features at no cost, including continuous assessments, security recommendations, and secure score visibility.
- **Defender CSPM:** Advanced capabilities for enhanced security and governance, priced at $15 per billable resource per month.

Defender for Servers:

- **Defender for Servers Plan 1:** Priced at $5 per server per month, focusing on essential EDR capabilities.
- **Defender for Servers Plan 2:** Priced at $15 per server per month, including advanced security features such as agentless scanning and Just-in-Time (JIT) VM access.
- **Pre-Purchase Plan:** Offers discounts for committing to a specific amount of Defender for Cloud Commit Units (DCUs) for one year, providing significant cost savings.

Here is a detailed table for comprehensive understanding:

Plan/Features	**Description**	**Azure**	**GCP**
◍ ☑ Free Tier (CSPM)	Foundational Cloud Security Posture Management (CSPM) features to monitor and secure your environment.	Free	☑ Basic security recommendations ☑ Secure Score visibility
◍ ☑ Defender CSPM	Advanced CSPM capabilities for enhanced security and governance.	$15 per billable resource/ month	☑ Attack path analysis ☑ Sensitive data discovery ☑ Cloud security graph

◍ ☑ Defender for Servers	Endpoint protection and advanced threat detection for virtual machines.	Plan 1: $5/ server/month Plan 2: $15/ server/month	Plan 1: ☑ Integration with Microsoft Defender for Endpoint Plan 2: ☑ Agentless scanning, JIT access
◍ ☑ Pre-Purchase Plan	Discounted pricing by committing to a specific amount of Defender for Cloud Commit Units (DCUs).	Discounts vary by commitment level	☑Predictable budgeting ☑Volume-based discounts
◍ ☑ Defender for Containers	Protect containerized applications across Kubernetes and container registries.	$0.006 per vCore/hour	☑ Vulnerability scanning ☑ Kubernetes cluster threat detection
◍ ☑ Defender for Databases	Advanced protection for relational and non-relational databases.	$0.02 per resource/ hour	☑ SQL vulnerability assessments ☑ Threat detection for databases

***Table 3.1**: Pricing Table for Each Plan in Microsoft Defender for Cloud*

Notes:

- **CSPM Features**: The foundational CSPM features are available for free, but advanced capabilities under Defender CSPM are charged.
- **Flexibility**: Microsoft Defender for Cloud offers a pay-as-you-go model to scale with your needs, and a pre-purchase plan for cost optimization.
- **Trial**: A 30-day free trial is available for all Defender plans, enabling organizations to evaluate features.

Cost Estimation and Savings

Microsoft provides a Cost Estimation Dashboard that helps organizations estimate their Defender for Cloud costs based on their specific resource usage. This tool allows users to select the subscriptions and Defender plans they wish to estimate costs for, providing a consolidated view of the estimated expenses. By leveraging the cost estimation tools and pre-purchase plans, businesses can effectively manage their security investments, while ensuring comprehensive protection across their cloud environments.

CNAPP Onboarding Labs

Embarking on the journey to secure your cloud infrastructure with Microsoft

Defender for Cloud is both an exciting and crucial step in fortifying your digital environment. As organizations increasingly migrate their workloads to the cloud, the need for robust security measures becomes paramount. Get ready to dive into the practical side of cloud security with our comprehensive "*Onboarding* CNAPP *Labs*" section. This part of the chapter is designed to provide you with hands-on experience through a series of meticulously crafted labs. Each lab focuses on a specific aspect of onboarding Cloud Native Application Protection Platforms (CNAPPs) to various cloud environments, ensuring that you gain practical skills and real-world insights.

In Lab #1, you will start with the Automatic Onboarding of Foundational CSPM to the Azure Cloud Platform, where you will learn how to streamline the onboarding process, using automated tools. Moving on to Lab #2, you will tackle the Manual Onboarding of Defender CSPM to the Azure Cloud Platform, giving you a deeper understanding of the manual steps involved in securing your cloud environment. Lab #3 will guide you through the Manual Onboarding of Server CSPM Plans to the Azure Cloud Platform, focusing on server-specific security measures.

Next, Lab #4 covers Onboarding Multiple Subscriptions using Azure Policy, teaching you how to manage and secure multiple cloud subscriptions efficiently. In Lab #5, you will expand your skills to the Defender for Cloud to the AWS Cloud Platform, exploring the nuances of integrating security tools with AWS. Finally, Lab #6 will take you through the Onboarding Defender for Cloud to the GCP Cloud Platform, ensuring that you are well-versed in securing Google Cloud environments.

Each lab is designed to build on the previous one, providing a cohesive and comprehensive learning experience. By the end of this section, you will have a solid foundation in onboarding CNAPP across different cloud platforms, equipped with the knowledge and skills to implement robust security measures in your cloud environments. Let us dive in and start this exciting journey together!

Lab # 1: Automatic Onboarding of Foundational CSPM to the Azure Cloud Platform

Embarking on the journey to secure your cloud infrastructure with Microsoft Defender for Cloud is both an exciting and crucial step in fortifying your digital environment. As organizations increasingly migrate their workloads to the cloud, the need for robust security measures becomes paramount.

Microsoft Defender for Cloud offers a comprehensive suite of tools designed to protect your Azure and hybrid resources from evolving threats. When it comes to securing your Azure environment, Microsoft Defender for Cloud offers a robust solution.

However, it's important to understand that not all subscriptions are automatically onboarded with full capabilities. These are some of the key points to remember before onboarding:

When you first access Microsoft Defender for Cloud in the Azure portal, **the basic features (Foundational Cloud Security Posture Management or CSPM) are automatically enabled for your subscription. This includes basic security assessments and recommendations.**

For this, you must have (1) an active Microsoft Azure subscription, and (2) you must be assigned the Owner, Contributor or Reader's role for the subscription, or for the resource group.

Follow these steps to observe the automatic onboarding process, where no action is required on your part. You will notice that the Foundational CSPM is automatically enabled for your Azure subscriptions:

1. Login into the **`Azure`** portal, and check if you have any active subscriptions, and you can see that we have three (3) active azure subscriptions in the cloud account.

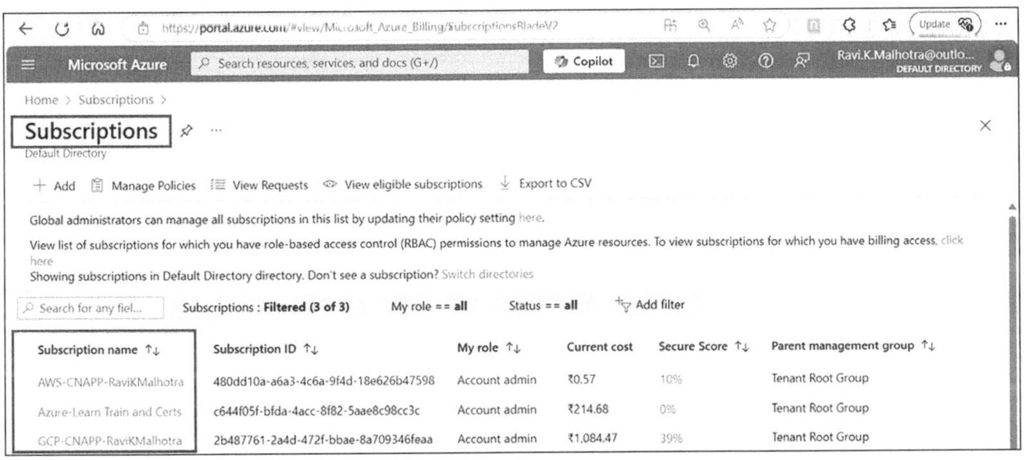

Figure 3.3: *Active Subscriptions in the Azure Account*

2. Next, check if you have got appropriate roles (**`Owner`**, **`Contributor`**, or **`Reader`**) assigned. For this:

    a. Click on any of the subscriptions, then click on **`Access Control (IAM)`** tab.

    b. Go to the **`Check Access`** tab, and refer to the following screenshot:

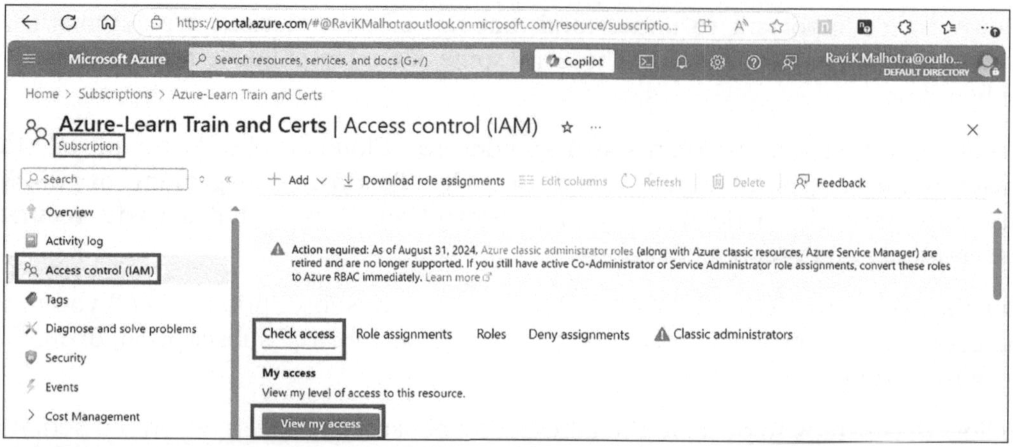

Figure 3.4: *Access Control (IAM) for the Azure Subscription*

c. Click on **`View my access tab`**, and there you will see the role assignment.

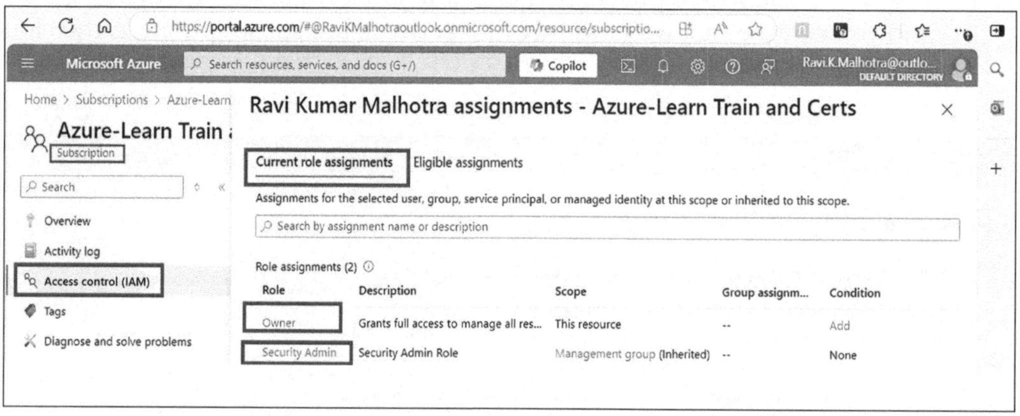

Figure 3.5: *Current Role Assignments for the Azure Subscription*

3. You can see that the role, '**`Owner`**' is assigned to the root user.
4. Search for and select **`Microsoft Defender for Cloud`**. By default, the **`Overview`** tab is displayed.
5. Go to **`Management`** → **`Environment Settings`** tab, and click on any subscriptions.
6. There, you will see that '**`Foundational CSPM`**' is automatically enabled, which cannot be disabled.
7. Foundation CSPM is enabled on all active subscriptions in the Azure account.
8. This concludes the lab.

Lab # 2: Manual Onboarding of Defender CSPM to the Azure Cloud Platform

To leverage the full spectrum of Microsoft Defender for Cloud's capabilities, including advanced security features like **Defender for Servers** or **Defender for Storage**, you must **manually enable these plans for each subscription**. That means if you have more than 1 subscription, then you need to go into each subscription, and enable the desired Defender plan. These steps ensure that your resources are protected with the most comprehensive security measures available. Let us follow these steps to see the manual onboarding process for the desired subscription:

1. Login into the Azure portal, and sign in with your Azure account credentials.
2. Once logged in, verify if you have any active subscriptions.
3. Navigate to Environment Settings.
    a. On the left-hand side, expand the **`Management`** tab.
    b. Click on **`Environment`** settings.
    c. This page allows you to integrate environments from leading cloud service providers such as AWS, GCP, GitHub, Azure DevOps, GitLab, Docker Hub, and JFrog. Scroll to the bottom right of the page.
    d. Expand Azure, then expand **`Tenant Root Group`**, which is a management group.
    e. Here, you will see all your active subscriptions detected by Microsoft Defender for Cloud. It will also display the currently active plans.

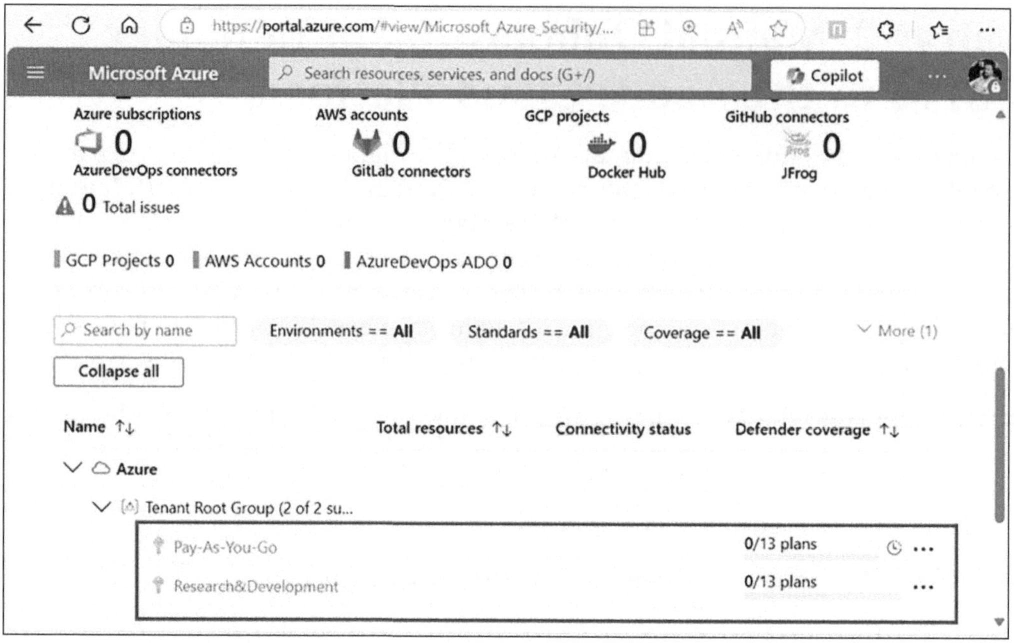

Figure 3.6: *No Defender Plans Activated on Both Azure Subscriptions*

4. You can observe that there are currently **two** active subscriptions, and no Defender plans have been enabled yet. **`The plan coverage is displayed as 0 out of 12`**.

5. Next, click on the **`Defender Plan Coverage`** option located in the top right corner of the screen. This feature offers **three** distinct types of coverage to address various business and leadership needs: **`Relative`** Coverage, **`Absolute`** Coverage, and **`Detailed`** Coverage.

   - **Relative Coverage** provides a comparative view of your security posture against industry benchmarks and peers.
   - **Absolute Coverage** gives a straightforward assessment of your current security status, highlighting areas that are fully protected versus those that need attention.
   - **Detailed Coverage** offers an in-depth analysis of your security measures, breaking down the specifics of each Defender plan and its impact on your overall security posture. At this moment, you will not see any details because the Defender CSPM plan has not yet been enabled on any of your subscriptions. Once enabled, these coverage types will provide valuable insights to help you justify security investments and strategies to your business and leadership teams.

6. Return to the **`Environment settings`** main page and select any subscription. Here, you'll find a comprehensive list of all Defender plans, along with their

current status. **You have the flexibility to enable any individual plan as needed, or you can streamline the process by clicking on** '`Enable All Plans`' to activate all available plans simultaneously.

7. We selected an active subscription from our account named **"`Research & Development`"**. In the following screenshot, you can observe the following:
    - The **Foundational CSPM** status is set to **`On`** by default, with **Monitoring Coverage** marked as **Full**, and it falls under the **`Free`** pricing tier.
    - The **Defender CSPM** status, however, is set to **`Off`** by default, with the **`Resource Quantity`** displayed as **Zero (0)** and a pricing structure of **$5 per billable resource per month**. Refer to the following screenshot:

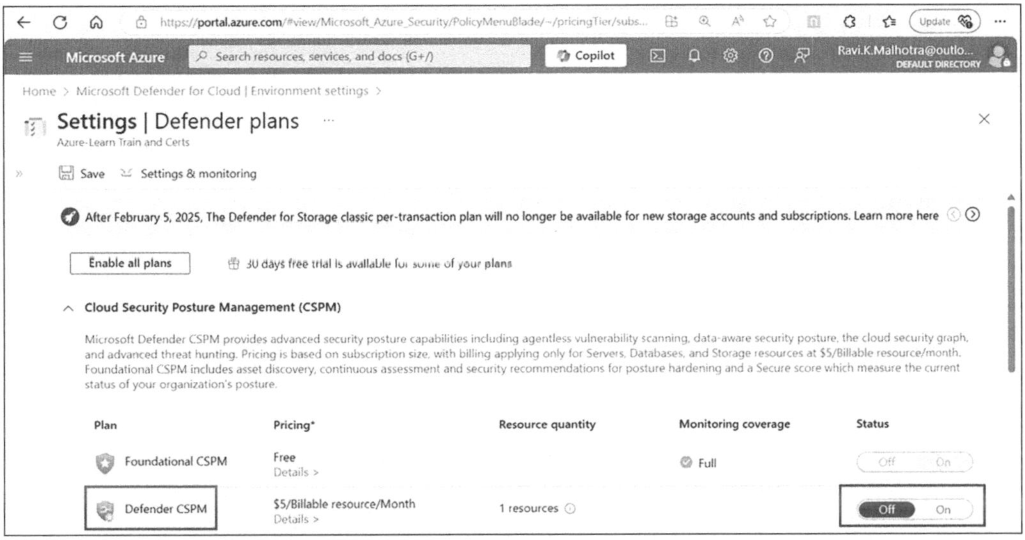

Figure 3.7: *Status of Foundational CSPM and Defender CSPM*

8. Now, we will enable the **`Defender CSPM`** feature manually.
9. Enabling this feature **'`Defender CSPM`'** unlocks a comprehensive suite of advanced security capabilities, including:
    a. Agentless VM vulnerability scanning
    b. Agentless VM secrets scanning
    c. Attack path analysis
    d. Risk prioritization
    e. Risk hunting with Security Explorer
    f. Code-to-cloud mapping for containers
    g. Code-to-code mapping for IaC
    h. PR annotations

   i. Internet exposure analysis
   j. **External attack surface management (EASM)**
   k. **Permissions Management (CIEM)**
   l. Regulatory compliance assessments
   m. ServiceNow Integration
   n. Critical assets protection
   o. Governance to drive remediation at-scale
   p. AI Security Posture Management
   q. Data-aware security posture, Sensitive data scanning
   r. K8S API access
   s. Agentless code-to-cloud containers vulnerability assessment
   t. API Security Posture Management

10. Go to **`Environment Settings`** >> Select the desired subscription >> **`toggle`** the switch to on against **Defender CSPM**.

11. Click on the **`'Save'`** button on top. Wait for some time.

12. Upon returning to the Environment settings page, you will observe that 1 out of 12 plans is now activated. Please refer to the following screenshot for further details:

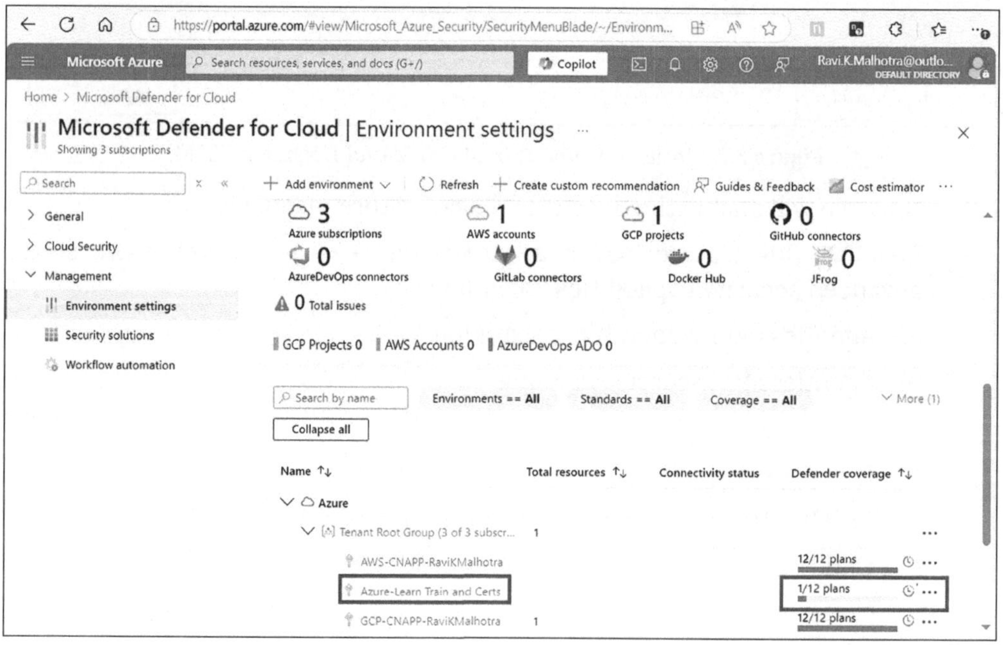

Figure 3.8: *Defender Coverage Status after Enabling Defender CSPM Plan*

13. This concludes the lab.

Lab # 3: Manual Onboarding of Server CSPM Plans to the Azure Cloud Platform

At the bottom of the same screen, you will find a comprehensive list of **Defender for Cloud plans**, designed to offer security across development and runtime in both single- and multi-cloud environments. Each plan is **Off** by default but can be activated easily by toggling the **On** option. Pricing details for each plan are also displayed, allowing you to assess their costs.

Before enabling any of these plans, ensure that you fully understand the potential commercial impact on your organization. Refer to the following screenshot for quick visibility to comprehensive Defender protection plans:

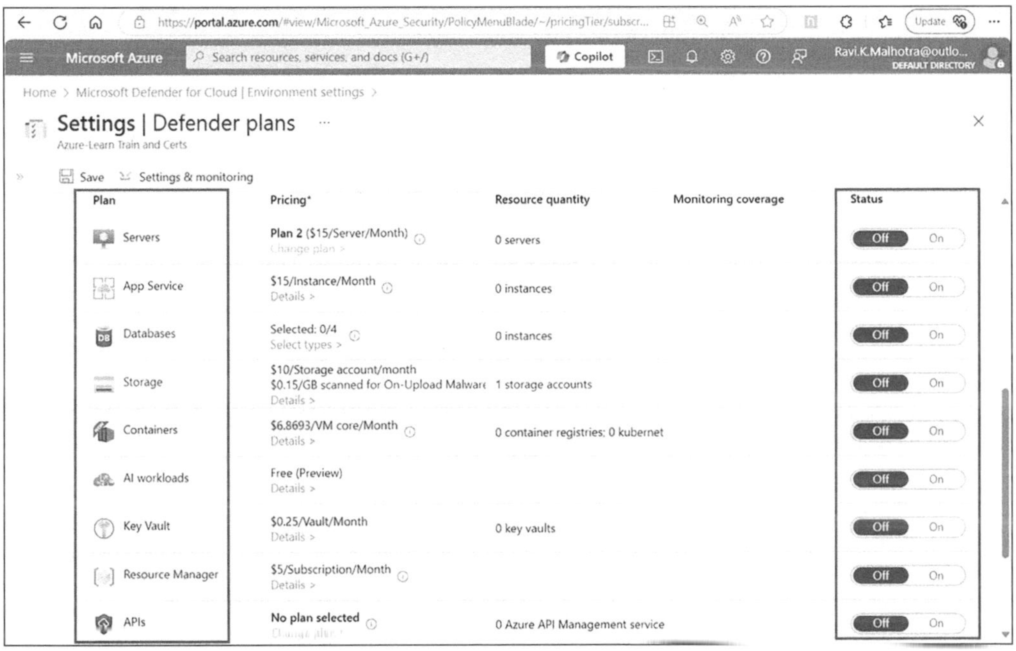

Figure 3.9: *Default Status of Multiple Azure Defender Plans*

You can streamline the process by clicking on '**Enable All Plans**' to activate all available plans simultaneously.

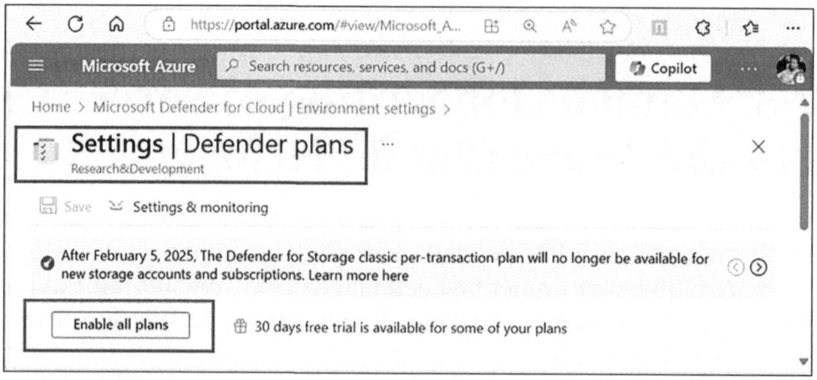

Figure 3.10: *Enable All Plans Buttons for the Current Azure Subscription*

Let us enable the following Defender protection plans only on 'Research and Development' subscription.

- Defender Plan 2 for Servers
- Defender for Containers
- Defender for Storage

Perform these steps to enable these Defender plans on the '**`Research and Development`**' subscription.

1. Toggle the switch to **`On for Defender for Servers`**, **`Defender for Storage`**, and **`Defender for Containers`**, then click on the **`Save`** button. See the following screenshot for reference:

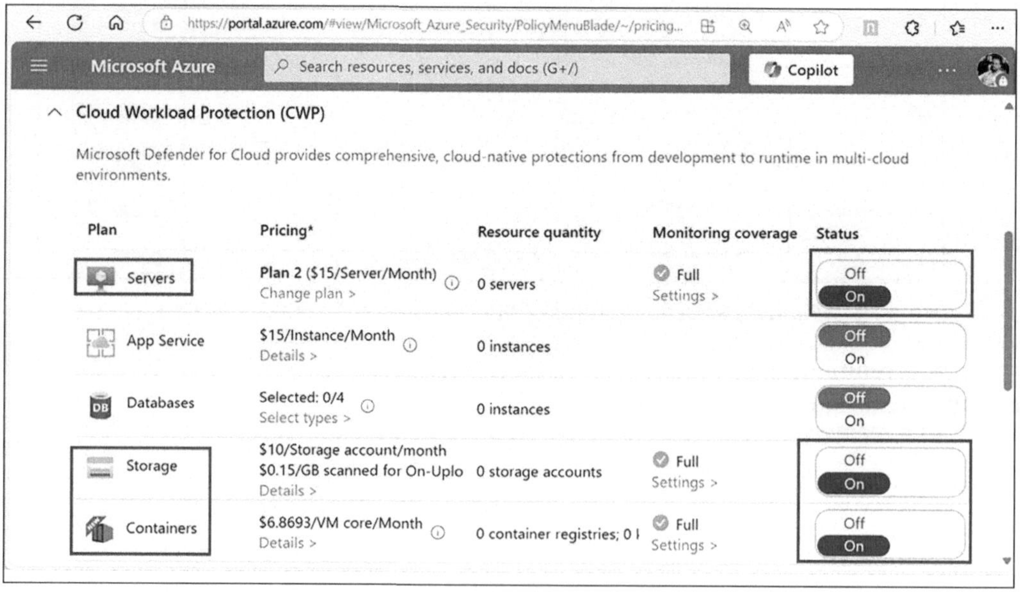

Figure 3.11: *Enabling Some of the Individual Defender CSPM Plans*

2. Upon revisiting the Environment settings page, **you will notice that 4 out of 12 plans are now activated**. This indicates that plans can be activated or deactivated based on the specific use cases and needs of the organization. Please refer to the following screenshot for further details:

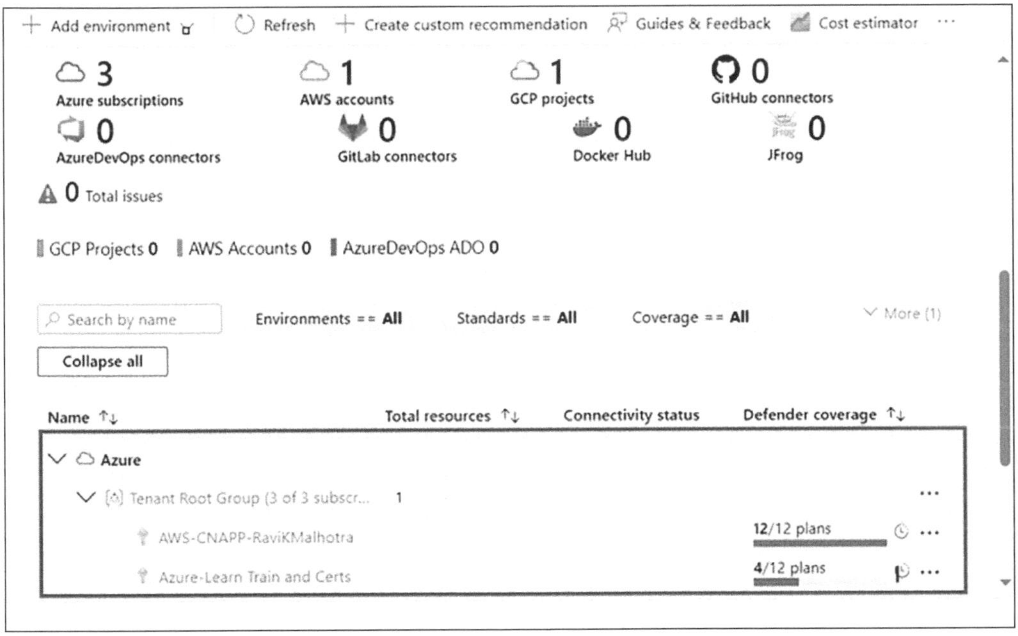

***Figure 3.12:** Defender Coverage Status after Enabling Defender CSPM and Individual Server Plans*

3. However, if you examine the **'AZ-900' subscription or any other subscription in your account, you will notice that 0 out of 12 plans are activated. This indicates that with the manual approach, each plan must be selected individually for each subscription.**

4. For organizations managing hundreds of subscriptions, this task can become exceedingly cumbersome. This challenge can be effectively addressed by managing multiple subscriptions, **using Azure Policy**, which we will explore in the next topic.

5. This concludes the lab.

Lab # 4: Onboarding Multiple Subscriptions Using Azure Policy

For organizations managing multiple Azure subscriptions, the process can be streamlined **using Azure Policy**. Managing multiple subscriptions can be a daunting task, especially when it comes to ensuring consistent security policies across all of them. **Azure Policy provides a powerful solution to streamline this process for Microsoft Defender for Cloud.**

By **applying a policy at the management group level**, you can ensure that all subscriptions within that group are onboarded to Microsoft Defender for Cloud. This approach simplifies the onboarding process, and ensures consistent security across your entire Azure environment. Here is how you can efficiently manage multiple subscriptions:

1. Login into the Azure portal:
    a. Open your web browser, and navigate to the **`Azure`** portal.
    b. Sign in with your Azure account credentials.
2. Open Azure Policy:
    a. Navigate to the Azure Policy service in the Azure portal.

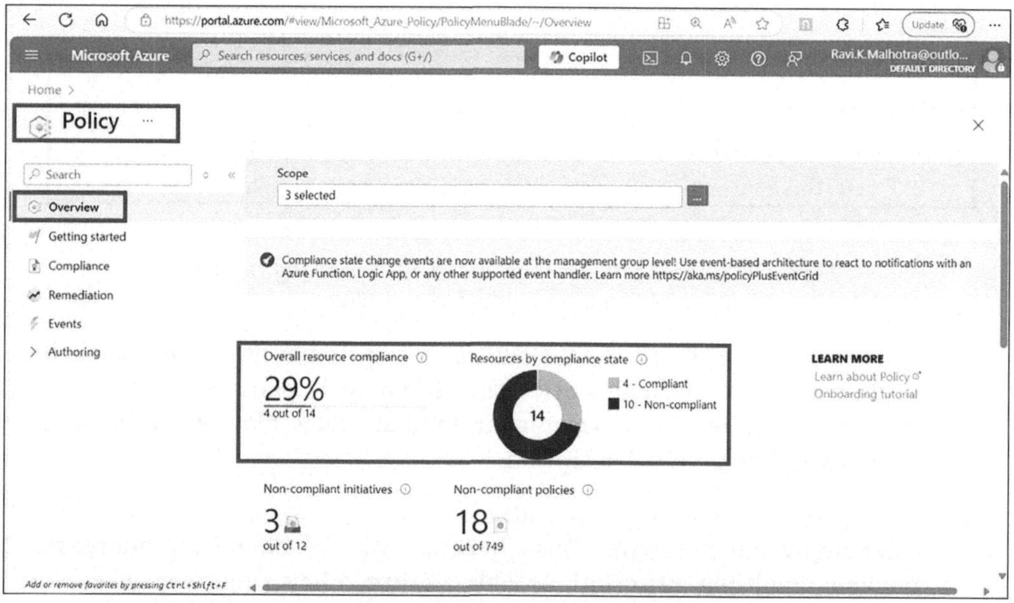

Figure 3.13: *Microsoft Defender for Servers Overview Page*

3. Search for Policy Definition:
    a. In the Azure Policy blade, go to '**`Definitions`**' tab on the left side of the screen.
    b. Search for the built-in definition "**`Enable Microsoft Defender for cloud on your subscription`**".

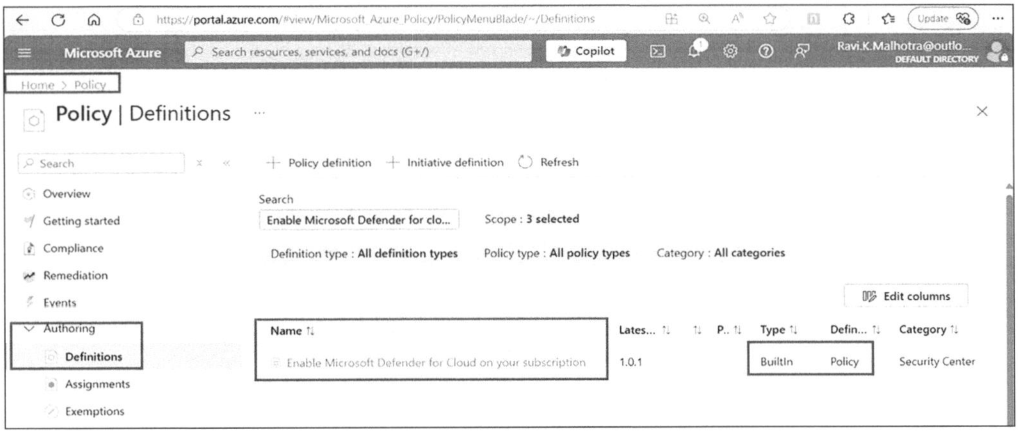

Figure 3.14: *Azure Policy Definition for Enabling Defender for Cloud on Subscriptions*

4. Assign the Policy: Follow these steps to assign the policy:
    a. Select the policy definition, and click on **`Assign Policy`** button.
    b. Set the scope to the desired Management Group (MG) level to apply the policy across all subscriptions within the group.
    c. Select all other settings as it is.
    d. Click on **`Review + Create`**.
    e. Click on **`Create`**.
5. Validate the Policy assignment:
    a. Click on **`Assignments`** tab.
    b. Here, you can see the assigned policy.

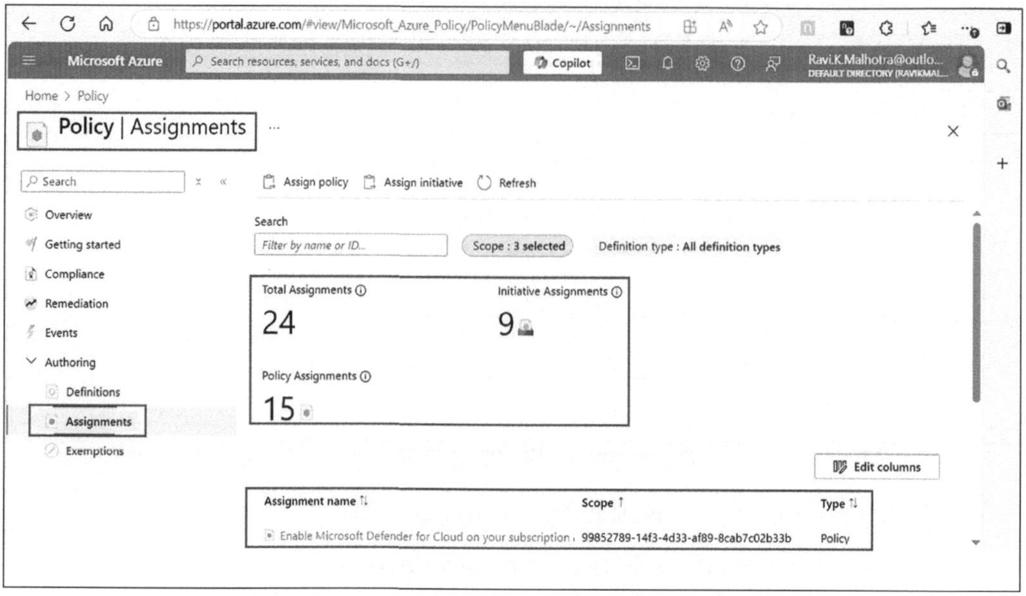

Figure 3.15: *Status after Enabling Defender for Cloud Policy*

6. Configure Remediation:

   In the Remediation tab, select Create a remediation task. This ensures that all the existing subscriptions that do not have Microsoft Defender for Cloud enabled will be onboarded automatically.

7. Validation:

   a. Search for '**`Microsoft Defender for Cloud`**' service, and select the service.

   b. Go to **`Environment settings`** tab.

   c. Ensure that Microsoft Defender for Cloud is now enabled across all subscriptions in your account. Remember, without using Azure Policy, you would need to manually enable Microsoft Defender for each subscription individually.

   In conclusion, leveraging Azure Policy for managing Microsoft Defender for Cloud across multiple subscriptions ensures a streamlined, consistent, and automated security posture. This approach not only saves time but also enhances compliance and reduces the risk of manual errors, making it an essential strategy for any organization.

8. This concludes the lab.

In summary, while Microsoft Defender for Cloud provides automatic onboarding for basic security features, additional steps are required to fully enable its advanced capabilities. By understanding and implementing these steps, you can ensure that your Azure environment is comprehensively protected.

Lab # 5: Onboarding Defender for Cloud to the AWS Cloud Platform

To keep your AWS account safe, you can connect it to Microsoft Defender for Cloud. Here is a step-by-step guide to seamlessly onboard your AWS account:

1. **Prerequisites:** Before diving in, ensure that you have the essentials:
    - An active Microsoft Azure subscription.
    - Microsoft Defender for Cloud set up on your Azure account.
    - Access to the AWS account, you wish to secure.
    - Contributor level permissions for the relevant Azure subscription.
2. **Connecting Your AWS Account:** You should be able to connect to the AWS Account to perform these steps:
    - **Open Defender for Cloud:** Start by navigating to Microsoft Defender for Cloud in the Azure portal.
    - **Add AWS Environment:** Head to `'Environment Settings'` and select `'Add Environment'`. Choose '`Amazon Web Services (AWS)`'. We will explore this section with screenshots in the following section.
    - **Authenticate:** Utilize federated authentication between Microsoft Defender for Cloud and AWS. This involves deploying a CloudFormation template that establishes an identity provider and IAM roles.
3. **Deploying the CloudFormation Template:** This step entails initially generating the CloudFormation Template within the Azure environment, followed by its concurrent deployment in the AWS environment. The high-level points are outlined below:
    - **Generate Template:** In the Azure portal, generate the necessary CloudFormation template.
    - **Deploy Template:** Deploy this template in your AWS account to create the required IAM roles and policies.
    - **Validate Setup:** Confirm that the roles and policies are correctly configured, and that your AWS account is now connected to the Defender for Cloud.

4. **Selecting Defender Plans:** Choose the desired plans as per the organization needs.
    - **Choose Plans:** During the setup, select the Defender for Cloud plans that best suit your AWS resources.
    - **Configure Settings:** Tailor the settings to align with your specific security needs.
5. **Integration and Automation**
    - **CI/CD Integration:** Integrate Defender for Cloud with your CI/CD pipelines to ensure continuous security checks.
    - **Terraform Automation:** For those managing multiple AWS accounts or seeking streamlined processes, use Terraform templates to automate the onboarding.
6. **Monitoring and Maintenance**
    - **Continuous Monitoring:** Regularly monitor your AWS resources through Defender for Cloud to maintain a strong security posture.
    - **Update Policies:** Keep your security policies and configurations up to date to counter new threats.

Please perform these steps to onboard your AWS account to the Microsoft Defender for Cloud:

1. Login into the Azure portal.
    a. Open your web browser and navigate to the Azure portal.
    b. Sign in with your Azure account credentials.
2. Login into the AWS portal, and sign in with your AWS root account credentials.
3. Get the AWS account ID.

    Click on your account name in the top navigation bar, and find the account ID next to "**`Account ID`**" under "**`Account Settings`**". Account ID is a **12-digit long character**. We will use this Account ID in later steps. See the following screenshot:

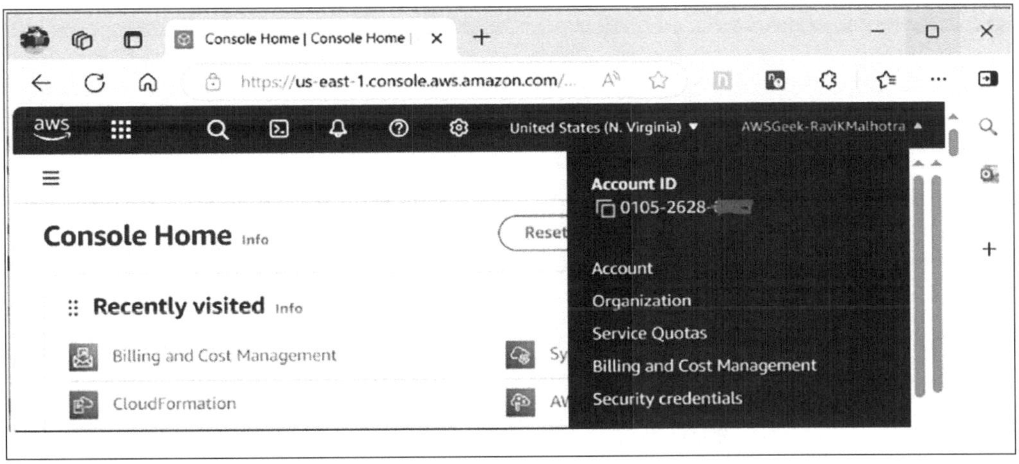

Figure 3.16: *AWS Account ID Details in Portal*

4. Check for active subscriptions in the **`Azure`** portal.

   Once logged in, verify if you have any active subscriptions. If possible, create a new subscription in your Azure account before onboarding your AWS account to Microsoft Defender for Cloud. This dedicated subscription will help you manage and track all billing related to this integration more effectively. I have created an exclusive subscription before onboarding the AWS account, please refer to the following screenshot:

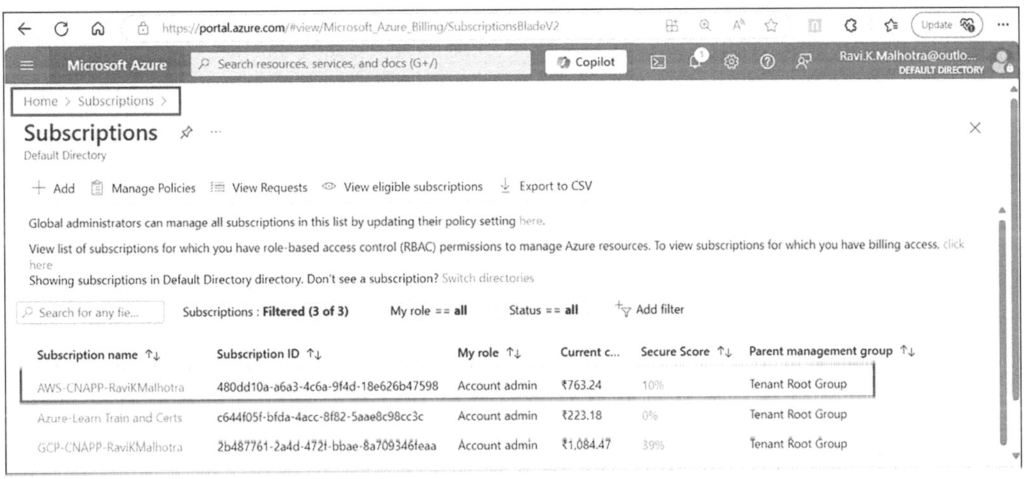

Figure 3.17: *Dedicated Subscription before Onboarding an AWS Account*

5. Navigate to **`Setup`** Tab in the **`Microsoft Defender for Cloud`** in Azure.

   This page allows you to integrate environments from leading cloud service providers such as AWS, GCP, GitHub, Azure DevOps, GitLab, Docker Hub, and JFrog. Refer to the following screenshot:

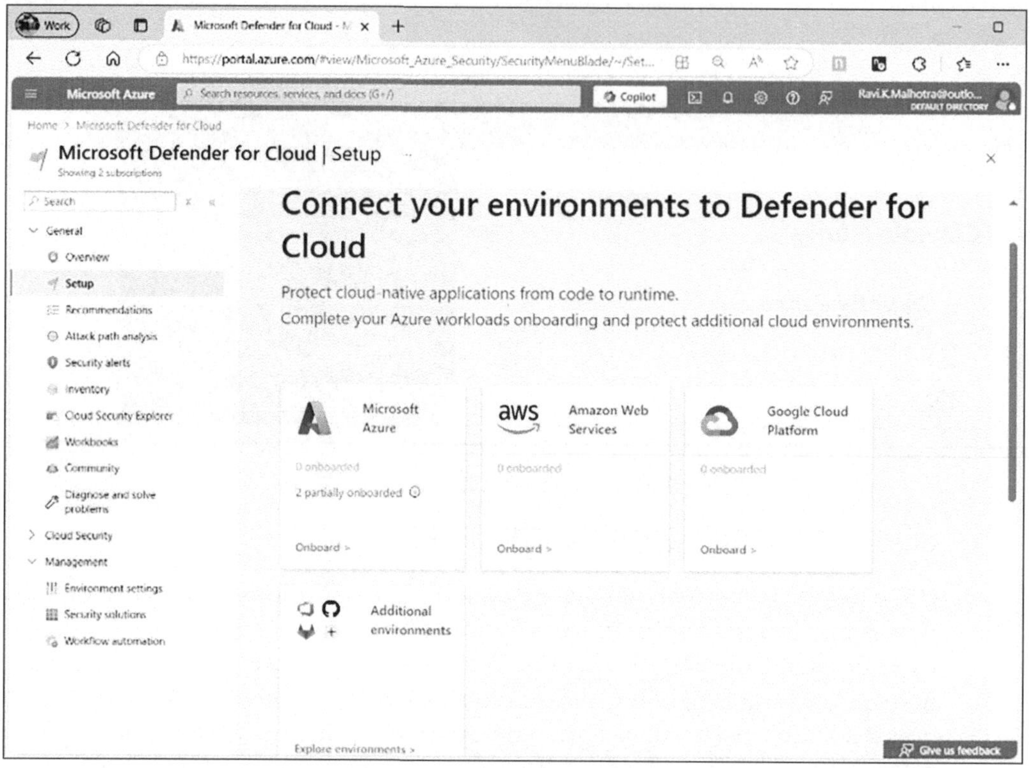

***Figure 3.18:** None of the Accounts have been Onboarded to Defender for Cloud yet*

6. Onboard the AWS account.

   Click on Onboard in the '**`Amazon Web Services`**' tile. Fill the Account Details as follows:

   - **Connector Name: `CNAPP-for-AWSAccount`.**
   - **Onboard:** Select the **`Single`** Account.
   - **AWS Region:** Leave it as it is, no changes or select the desired region.
   - **Subscription:** Select the subscription that you have created. In my case, I have selected '**`AWS-CNAPP-RaviKMalhotra`**'.
   - **Resource Group:** Click on '**`Create New`**', and create a new Resource Group.
   - Location: Select the desired location.
   - **Scan Interval:** Leave it as it is.
   - **AWS Account ID:** Provide the AWS account ID that you copied in the above steps.
   - Click on **`Next: Select Plans`** >. Refer to the following screenshot:

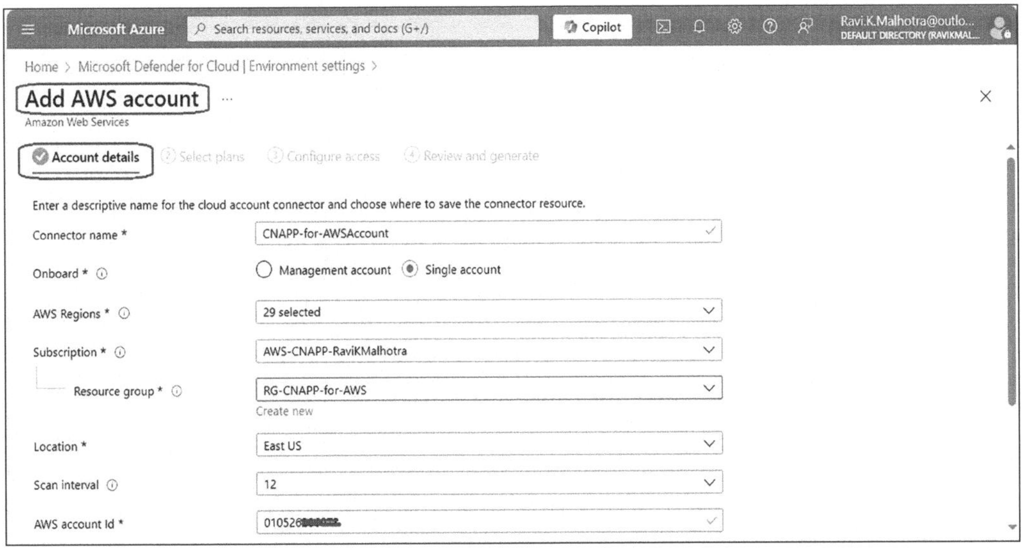

Figure 3.19: *Onboarding AWS Account to the Defender for Cloud*

7. Select the **`Plan`** >> **`Enable`** all the options under CSPM modules as follows:

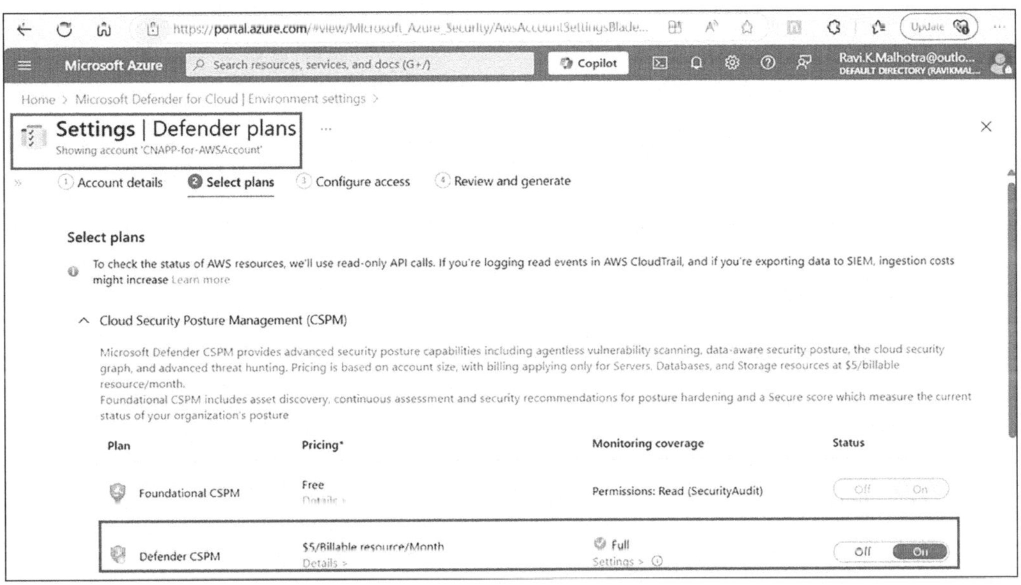

Figure 3.20: *Selecting Defender for Cloud Plan for an AWS Account*

8. Select the **`Plan`** >> **`Enable`** all the options under CWPP modules as follows:

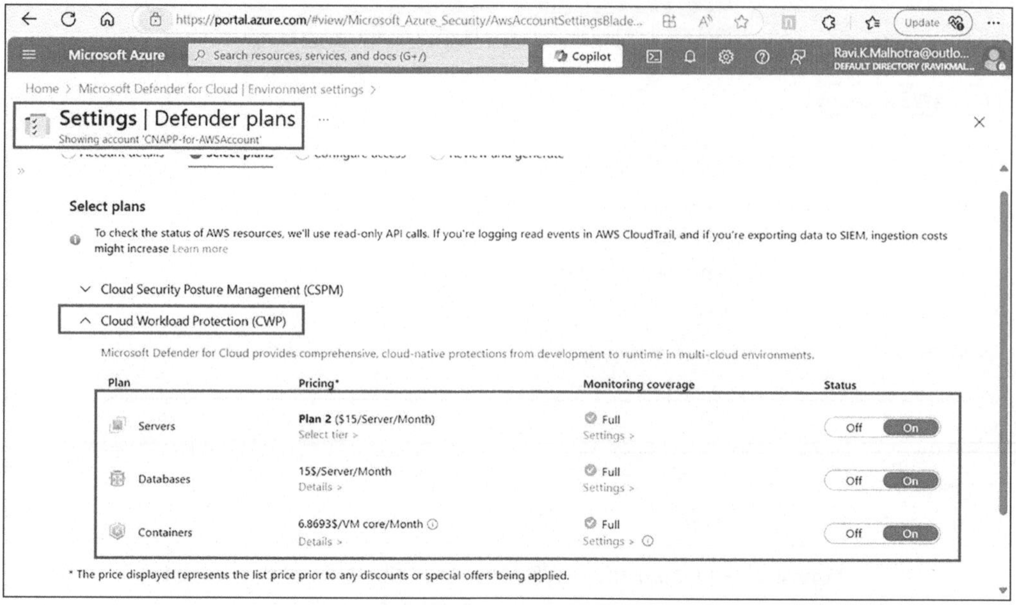

Figure 3.21: *Selecting Defender for Cloud CWP Plan for an AWS Account*

9. Add AWS account.
   a. Select '**Default access**' as the permission type.
   b. Click on the '**Download**' button to download the **CloudFormation** template; the file will be saved to your local computer or laptop.
   c. Next, click on the '**Go to AWS CloudFormation Stacks**' link next to the '**Create stacks in AWS**' option. This action will open a new browser tab with your AWS console already logged in.
   d. Click on **Next: Review and generate**.

Refer to the following screenshot:

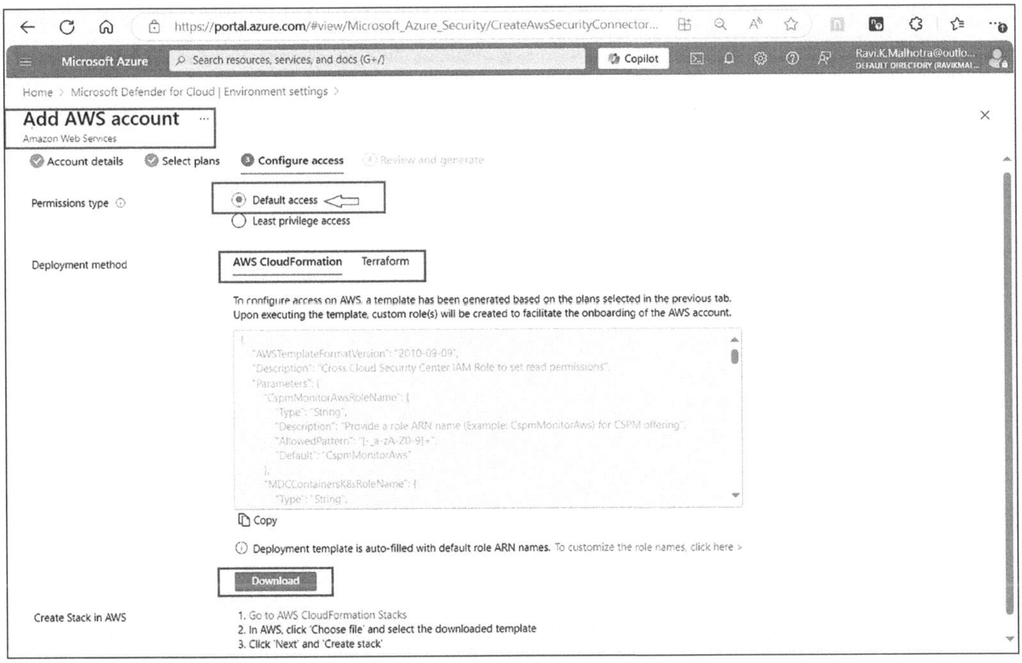

Figure 3.22: *Final Process for Onboarding an AWS Account to Defender for Cloud*

10. Go to **AWS Cloud** console in the parallel tab/browser.

    a. Select '**Choose an existing template**' option.

    b. Select '**Upload a template file**' option.

    c. Click on the '**Choose file**' option, and select the file that you downloaded in the previous step.

    d. Click on **Next**. Refer to the following screenshot:

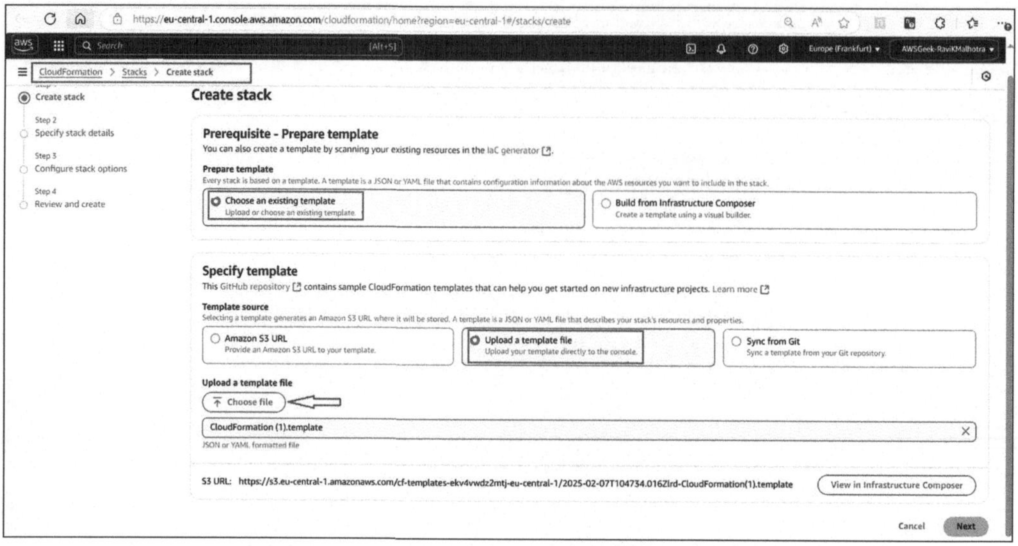

Figure 3.23: *AWS Stack Creation Process for Onboarding an AWS Account*

e. Provide a stack name, I have given it as '**`stack1-cnapp-integration`**'.

f. Click on **`Next`**.

i. Select the option, '**`I acknowledge that AWS CloudFormation might create IAM resources with custom names`**'.

ii. Click on **`Next`** again.

iii. Click on **`Submit`** button.

iv. Wait for some time, and you will see the stack completion status window. Refer to the following screenshot:

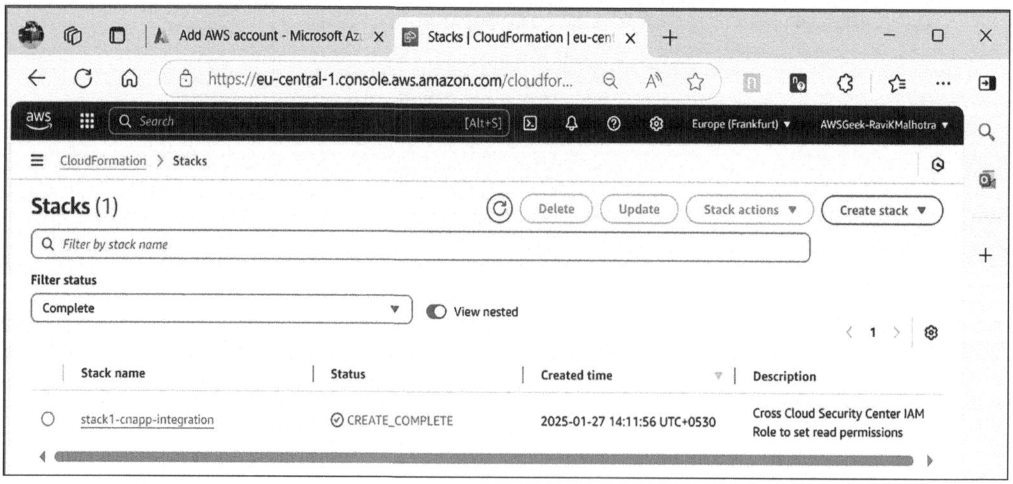

Figure 3.24: *Successfully Created a Stack for Onboarding AWS Accounts*

11. **Review and generate**.
    a. Go back to the Azure portal.
    b. click on the option, '**Next: Review and generate**'.
    c. Click on the **Create** button.
    d. Refer to the following screenshot:

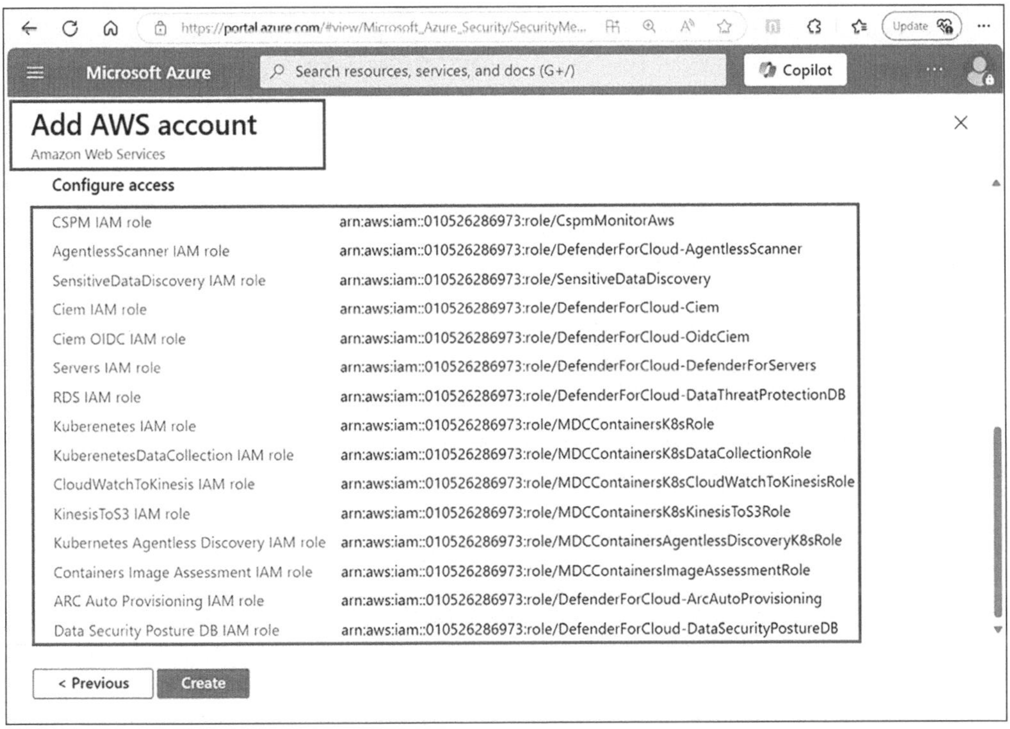

Figure 3.25: *AWS Account Onboarding Validation*

    e. Wait for some time, it will give few notifications. Be careful of notifications, as this onboarding process may fail.

12. Successfully **Onboarded**.

    After completing the onboarding process, you will be directed to the **'Setup'** tab, where you can confirm that one AWS account has been onboarded. In summary, we have successfully enabled all Defender plans for our two Azure subscriptions, and also added one AWS account. Please refer to the following screenshot for more details:

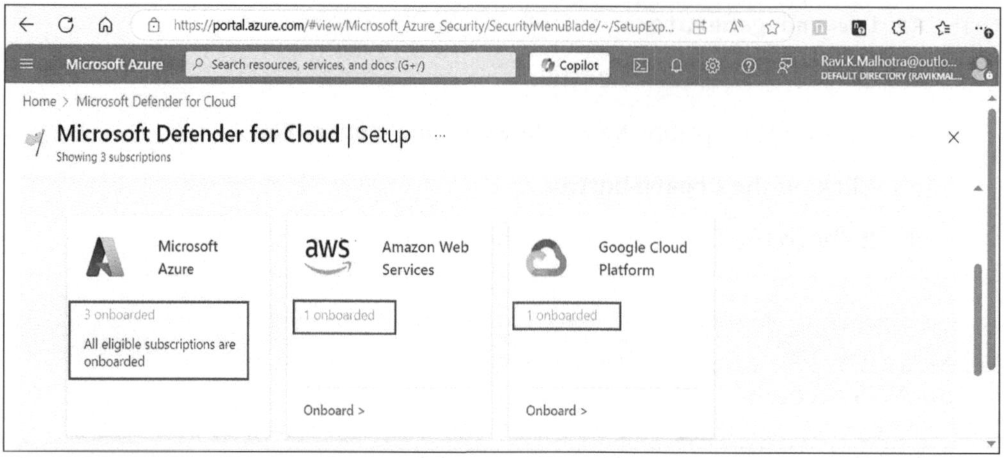

Figure 3.26: *Defender for Cloud Setup Page Showing 2 Azure, and 1 AWS Account Onboarded*

13. Go to the **`Environment Settings`** tab.

    You can see Defender coverage for 2 Azure subscriptions and 1 AWS account. Refer to the following screenshot:

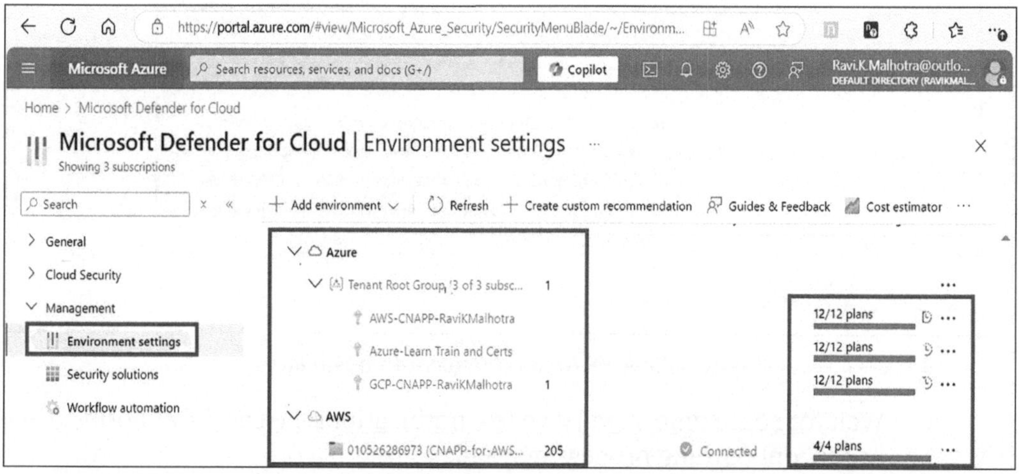

Figure 3.27: *Defender Coverage and Connectivity Status for all Onboarded Accounts*

    From this screenshot, you can see that:

    1. 2 Azure subscriptions are onboarded, and all 12 plans are activated.
    2. 1 AWS account is onboarded, and all 4 plans are activated. The connectivity status with AWS is in 'Connected' state, and a total 188 assets have been discovered.

14. This concludes the lab.

Lab # 6: Onboarding Defender for Cloud to the GCP Cloud Platform

Securing your Google Cloud Platform (GCP) environment with Microsoft Defender for Cloud is a strategic move towards comprehensive cloud security. Here is a detailed guide to help you onboard your GCP account:

1. **Prerequisites: Before you begin, ensure that you have the following:**
    - An active Microsoft Azure subscription.
    - Microsoft Defender for Cloud set up on your Azure account.
    - Access to the GCP project, you want to secure.
    - Contributor level permissions for the relevant Azure subscription.
2. **Connecting Your GCP Account**
    - **Open Defender for Cloud:** Navigate to Defender for Cloud in the Azure portal.
    - **Add GCP Environment:** Go to '`Environment settings`', and select '`Add environment`'. Choose 'Google Cloud Platform (GCP)'.
    - **Authenticate:** Use federated authentication between Microsoft Defender for Cloud and GCP. This involves deploying a GCloud template that sets up a workload identity pool, providers, service accounts, and policy bindings.
3. **Deploying the GCloud Template**
    - **Generate Template:** In the Azure portal, generate the necessary GCloud template.
    - **Deploy Template:** Deploy this template in your GCP project to create the required resources.
    - **Validate Setup:** Ensure that the resources are correctly configured, and that your GCP project is now connected to Defender for Cloud.
4. **Selecting Defender Plans**
    - **Choose Plans:** During the setup, select the Defender for Cloud plans that best suit your GCP resources.
    - **Configure Settings:** Tailor the settings to align with your specific security needs.
5. **Integration and Automation**
    - **CI/CD Integration:** Integrate Defender for Cloud with your CI/CD pipelines to ensure continuous security checks.

- **Terraform Automation:** For those managing multiple GCP projects or seeking streamlined processes, use Terraform templates to automate the onboarding.

6. **Monitoring and Maintenance**

- **Continuous Monitoring:** Regularly monitor your GCP resources through Defender for Cloud to maintain a strong security posture.
- **Update Policies:** Keep your security policies and configurations up to date to counter new threats.

Please perform these steps to onboard your AWS account to the Microsoft Defender for Cloud:

1. **Login into the Azure portal.**
   a. Open your web browser, and navigate to the Azure portal.
   b. Sign in with your Azure account credentials.
2. **Login into the GCP portal.**
   a. Open your web browser, and navigate to the GCP portal.
   b. Sign in with your GCP root account credentials.
3. **Get the GCP project number, and GCP project id.**
   a. If you have multiple projects in your GCP environment, choose the relevant project. There, you will find both the GCP project number and the GCP project ID. Copy both details, as they will be needed in the next step.

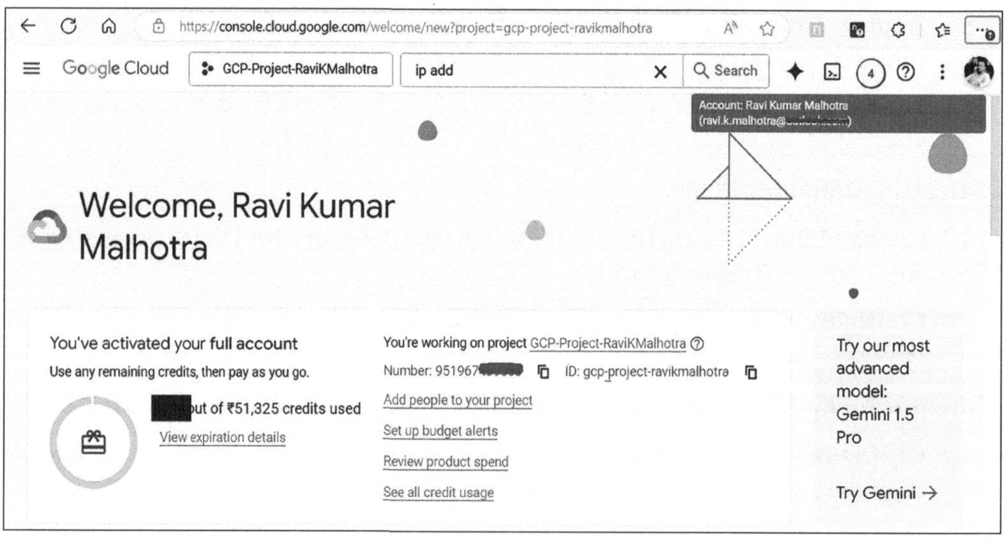

Figure 3.28: *GCP Console Main Page Showing the Current Project Number and Project ID*

4. **Check for active subscriptions in the Azure portal.**
   a. Once logged in, verify if you have any active subscriptions.
   b. If possible, create a new subscription in your Azure account, before onboarding your GCP account to Microsoft Defender for Cloud. I have created an exclusive subscription before onboarding the GCP account, please refer to the following screenshot:

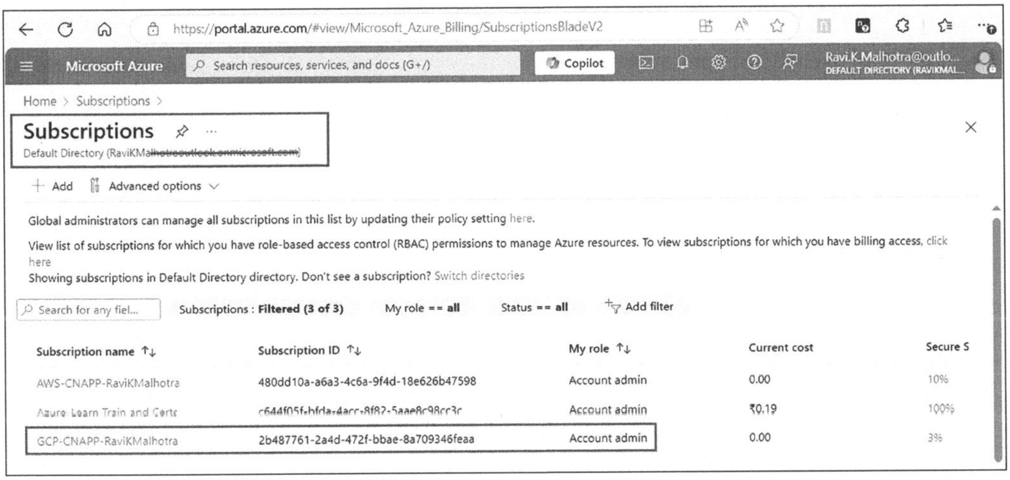

Figure 3.29: *Creating a Dedicated Azure Subscription for Onboarding the GCP Project*

5. **Navigate to Setup Tab in the Microsoft Defender for Cloud in Azure.**
   a. On the left-hand side, click on the **`Setup`** tab.
   b. Click on Onboard in the '**`Google Cloud Platform`**' tile. Fill the Account details as follows:
      - **Connector Name: `CNAPP-for-GCPAccount`.**
      - **Onboard:** Select the Single Account.
      - **Subscription:** Select the subscription that you have created. In my case, I have selected '**`GCP-CNAPP-RaviKMalhotra`**'.
      - **Resource Group:** Click on '**`Create New`**', and create a new Resource Group.
      - **Location:** Select the desired location.
      - **Scan Interval:** Leave it as it is.
      - **GCP Project Number and GCP Project ID:** Provide the GCP project number copied from the previous step here.
      - **GCP Project ID:** Provide the project id copied from the previous step here.

- Click on Next: Select **Plans** >

Refer to the following screenshot:

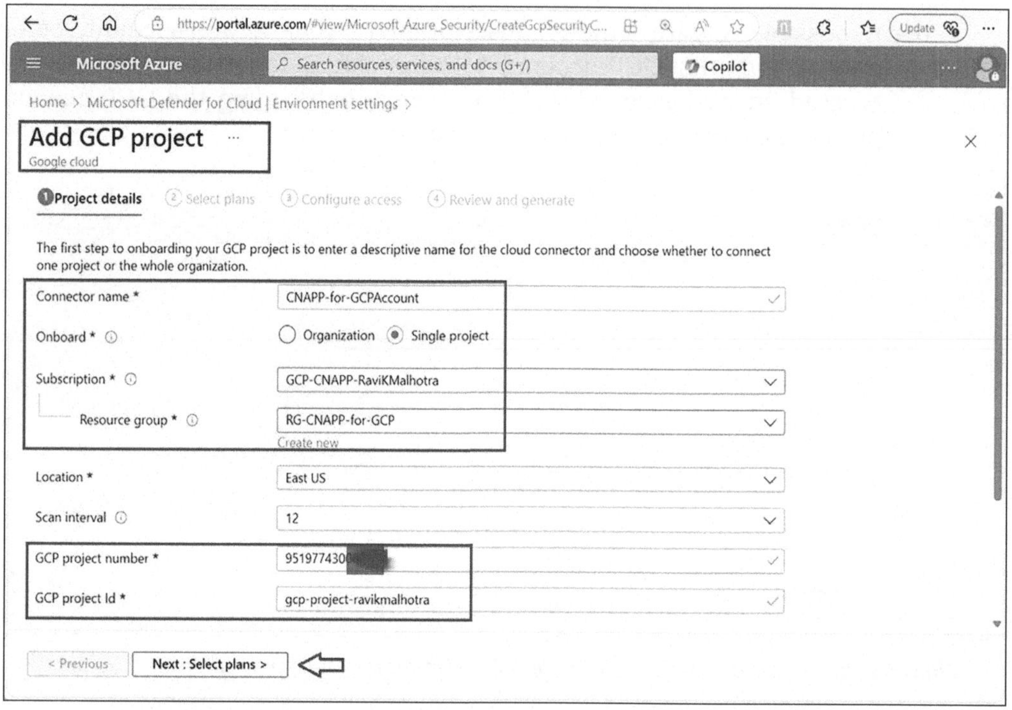

Figure 3.30: *Onboarding the GCP Project to Defender for Cloud*

6. Enable all the options under CSPM and CWPP modules, similar to exactly what we did in the previous lab, while adding an AWS account.
7. Click on **Configure Access**.
    a. Select '**Default access**' option as the permission type.
    b. You will see a template there, click on '**Copy**' button to copy the template. Refer to the following screenshot.

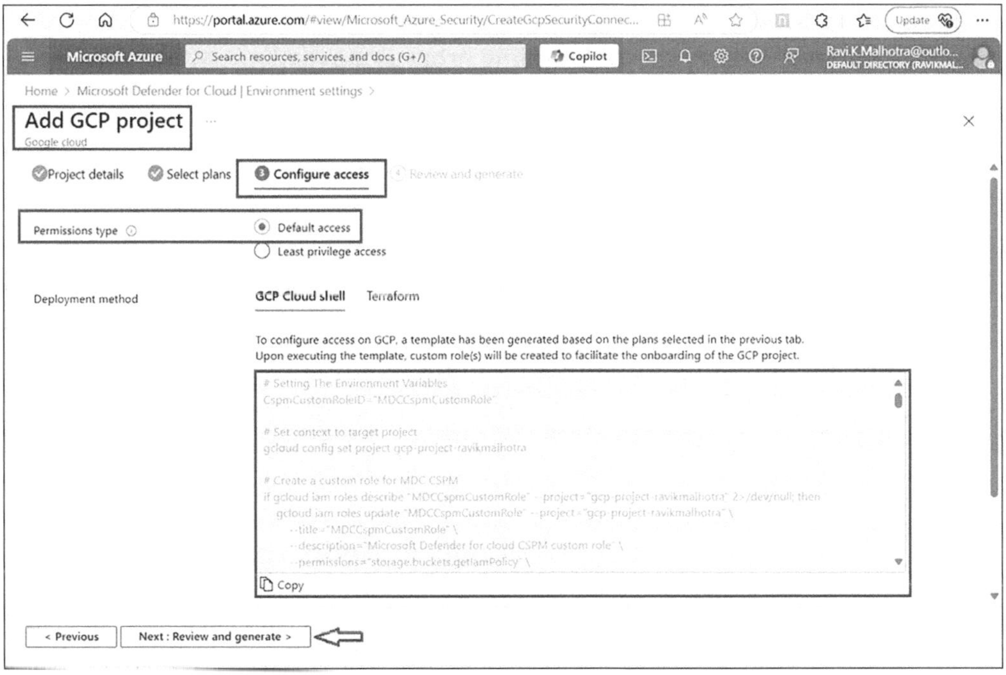

Figure 3.31: *Configuring Access for GCP Onboarding in Defender for Cloud*

   c. Click on **`Next: Review and generate`**.

8. Go to GCP Cloud console in the parallel tab/browser.

   a. Ensure that you are in the desired GCP project.

   b. Go to **`APIs and Services`** → **`Library`**

   c. Search for all these APIs, and enable them one by one.

      - `iam.googleapis.com`
      - `sts.googleapis.com`
      - `cloudresourcemanager.googleapis.com`
      - `iamcredentials.googleapis.com`
      - `compute.googleapis.com`

   d. Now, go to cloud shell, and paste the template copied from the other parallel browser running Microsoft Azure portal.

   e. Click on the '**`Authorize`**' button in the Authorization pop up.

   f. Wait for some time, it may take up to 10 minutes.

   g. Go back to the **`Azure`** portal, and click on the **`Create`** button.

   h. Wait for some time, it will give few notifications. Be careful of the notifications, as this onboarding process may fail.

9. Successfully Onboarded.

   a. After completing the onboarding process, you will be directed to the **'Setup'** tab in Microsoft Defender for Cloud, where you can confirm that one GCP account has been onboarded.

   b. In summary, we have successfully enabled all Defender plans **for our three (3) Azure subscriptions, one (1) AWS account, and now one (1) GCP project as well**. Please refer to the following screenshot for more details:

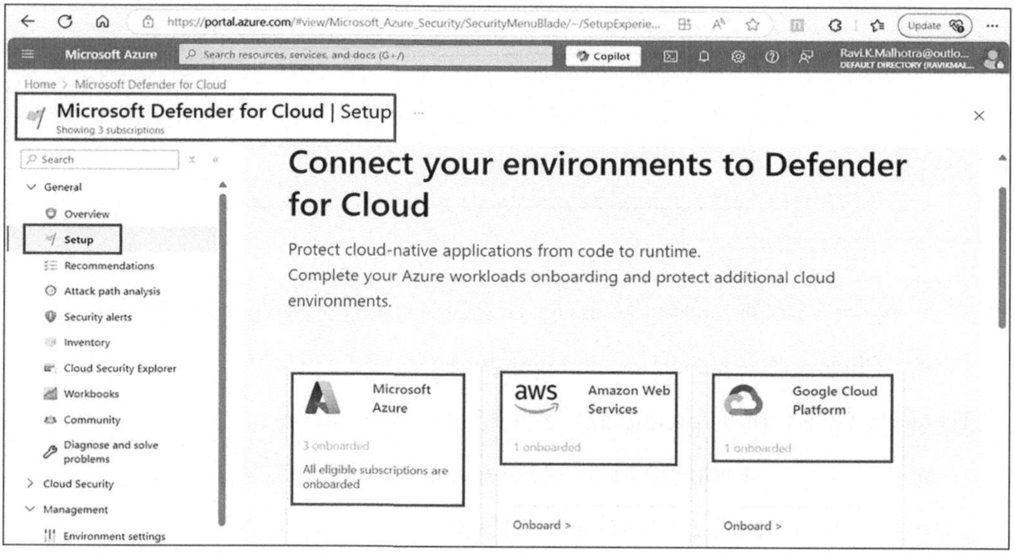

Figure 3.32: *Defender for Cloud Setup Page Showing All Onboarded Accounts*

10. Go to **Environment Settings** tab, there you can see 3 Azure subscriptions and Defender coverage on both Azure subscriptions, 1 AWS account and Defender coverage for an AWS account, as well as 1 recently added GCP account and Defender coverage for GCP account. Refer to the following screenshot:

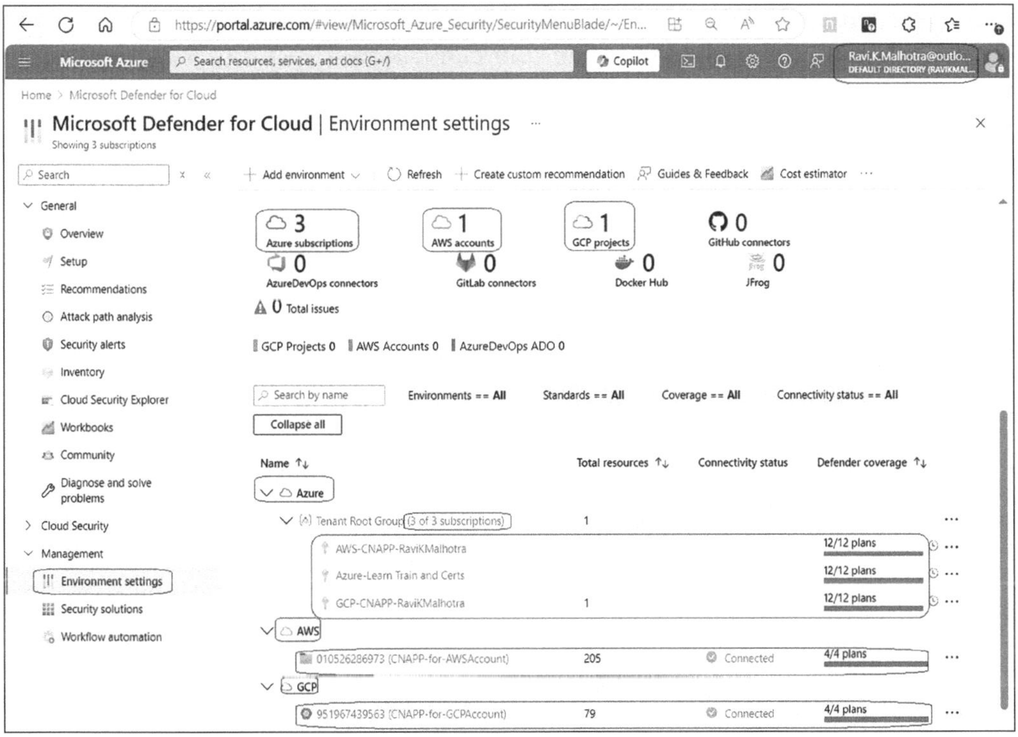

Figure 3.33: *Defender Coverage and Connectivity Status for All Onboarded Accounts*

11. This concludes the lab.

Conclusion

By the end of this chapter, you have gained practical insights into onboarding AWS, Azure, and GCP to Microsoft Defender for Cloud. This hands-on guide has equipped you with the knowledge to enhance your cloud security posture across multiple environments.

As you continue to explore and implement these strategies, remember that securing your cloud infrastructure is an ongoing journey. Stay vigilant, keep learning, and adapt to the evolving landscape of cyber threats. Your proactive efforts today will pave the way for a resilient and secure cloud environment tomorrow.

Points to Remember

- **Onboarding Process:** Follow the step-by-step instructions to successfully onboard AWS, Azure, and GCP to Microsoft Defender for Cloud.
- **Paid Subscriptions:** Ensure that you have paid subscriptions for each cloud platform to complete the onboarding process.

- **Security Features:** Utilize the security features provided by Microsoft Defender for Cloud to enhance your cloud security posture.
- **Screenshots:** Refer to the actual screenshots included in the chapter for visual guidance during the onboarding process.
- **Continuous Learning:** Stay updated with the latest security practices, and continuously monitor your cloud environments for potential threats.

Multiple-Choice Questions

1. What is the primary focus of this chapter?
    a. Understanding cloud pricing plans
    b. Onboarding cloud platforms to Microsoft Defender for Cloud
    c. Configuring network security
    d. Managing cloud storage
2. Which cloud platforms are demonstrated for onboarding in this chapter?
    a. AWS, Azure, and IBM Cloud
    b. Azure, GCP, and Oracle Cloud
    c. AWS, Azure, and GCP
    d. AWS, GCP, and Alibaba Cloud
3. What is required to successfully onboard cloud platforms to Microsoft Defender for Cloud?
    a. Free trial accounts
    b. Paid subscriptions
    c. Basic security knowledge
    d. Third-party security tools
4. What type of guidance is provided in the chapter for the onboarding process?
    a. Theoretical concepts
    b. Step-by-step instructions with screenshots
    c. Video tutorials
    d. Case studies

5. What is the ultimate goal of onboarding cloud platforms to Microsoft Defender for Cloud?
    a. To reduce cloud costs
    b. To enhance cloud security posture
    c. To improve cloud performance
    d. To simplify cloud management

Answers

1. b
2. c
3. b
4. b
5. b

Questions

1. What are the initial steps required to onboard an Azure subscription to Microsoft Defender for Cloud?
2. How do you configure security settings for an AWS account in Microsoft Defender for Cloud?
3. What are the key differences in the onboarding process between Azure and GCP for Microsoft Defender for Cloud?
4. What permissions are needed to successfully onboard a GCP project to Microsoft Defender for Cloud?
5. Describe the role of Azure Policy in the onboarding process for Microsoft Defender for Cloud.
6. How can you verify that an AWS account has been successfully onboarded to Microsoft Defender for Cloud?
7. What are the common challenges faced during the onboarding of cloud platforms to Microsoft Defender for Cloud, and how can they be addressed?
8. Explain the importance of having paid subscriptions for Azure, AWS, and GCP when onboarding to Microsoft Defender for Cloud.

9. What steps should be taken if an error occurs during the onboarding process for a GCP project?
10. How does Microsoft Defender for Cloud enhance the security posture of onboarded cloud platforms?

Key Terms

- **Microsoft Defender for Cloud:** A comprehensive security management solution that provides advanced threat protection across your cloud environments.
- **Onboarding:** The process of integrating cloud accounts and subscriptions into Microsoft Defender for Cloud to enable security monitoring and management.
- **Azure Subscription:** A logical container used to provision resources in Microsoft Azure, which can be onboarded to Microsoft Defender for Cloud.
- **AWS Account:** An Amazon Web Services account that can be integrated with Microsoft Defender for Cloud for enhanced security monitoring.
- **GCP Project:** A Google Cloud Platform project that can be onboarded to Microsoft Defender for Cloud to leverage its security features.
- **Security Posture:** The overall security status of your cloud environments, as assessed by Microsoft Defender for Cloud.
- **Azure Policy:** A service in Azure that you can use to create, assign, and manage policies to enforce rules and effects over your resources.
- **Permissions:** The access rights required to onboard cloud accounts and subscriptions to Microsoft Defender for Cloud.
- **Threat Protection:** The set of features in Microsoft Defender for Cloud designed to detect and respond to security threats.
- **Compliance Assessment:** The process of evaluating your cloud environments against regulatory and organizational compliance requirements, using Microsoft Defender for Cloud.

Chapter 4
Understanding Cloud Security Posture Management (CSPM)

Introduction

In today's rapidly evolving digital landscape, securing cloud environments has become paramount. Enter Cloud Security Posture Management (CSPM) – a revolutionary approach that empowers organizations to continuously monitor, assess, and enhance their cloud security posture. CSPM tools provide unparalleled visibility into cloud resources, automate threat detection, and ensure compliance with industry standards. By **identifying misconfigurations and vulnerabilities in real-time**, CSPM not only **fortifies defenses**, but also streamlines remediation processes, and offers essential hardening guidance. As we delve into the intricacies of CSPM, we will uncover how this indispensable technology is reshaping cloud security, making it more robust, proactive, and resilient than ever before. In this chapter, we are going to cover Microsoft Defender for Cloud as a CNAPP solution to leverage its CSPM capabilities, and help us learn and understand how it improves the security posture of the cloud environment.

A key part of CSPM is **proactive risk identification and attack surface reduction**, which is why `Cloud Security Explorer` and `Attack Path Analysis` play a crucial role in strengthening cloud security.

`Cloud Security Explorer` enables security teams to **`search`, `filter`, and investigate cloud assets** across Azure, AWS, and GCP, helping to discover misconfigurations, security risks, and active recommendations in real-time.

On the other hand, `Attack Path Analysis` provides a **graphical visualization of potential attack paths**, showing how **privilege misconfigurations**, **exposed assets**, **and security gaps** could be exploited by attackers.

Together, these features give organizations deep security insights, allowing them to proactively fix vulnerabilities, before they can be leveraged in real attacks.

To make this chapter more insightful, we have included **Eight (8) hands-on labs**, providing **live demonstrations** using **Microsoft Defender for Cloud**. The following is the list of all hands-on demonstrations covered in this chapter:

- **Lab # 1:** Enabling Foundational and Defender CSPM
- **Lab # 2:** Understanding the Next Steps after Enabling CSPM
- **Lab # 3:** Exploring Inventory in Microsoft Defender for Cloud
- **Lab # 4:** Discovering Hard Disks Using Cloud Security Explorer
- **Lab # 5:** Discover Virtual Machines Using Cloud Security Explorer
- **Lab # 6:** Discover All Recommendations Only for Virtual Machines (VMs) from Recommendations Page
- **Lab # 7:** Exploring Security Posture, and Secure Score
- **Lab # 8:** Explore Attack Path Analysis

These labs are designed to **bridge the gap between theory and real-world applications**, enabling you to **strengthen cloud security posture** across **multi-cloud environments**.

Structure

The following topics will be covered in this chapter:

- Introduction to CSPM
- Key Components of CSPM
- Why CSPM Matters in Real-World Cloud Security
- The Growing Importance of CSPM
- Adoption Trends
- Leading CSPM Solutions in the Industry
- Challenges and Future of CSPM
- Microsoft Defender for Cloud as a CSPM Solution
- Understanding Attack Path Analysis
- Understanding Cloud Security Explorer
- Understanding Attack Path Analysis
- CSPM Labs

Introduction to CSPM

In today's digital age, cloud computing has become the backbone of many organizations. With this shift, ensuring the security of cloud environments is more important than ever. This is where Cloud Security Posture Management (CSPM) comes into play. CSPM is a set of tools and practices designed to continuously monitor and improve the security of cloud infrastructures. It helps organizations to identify and fix security risks, ensuring that their cloud environments are safe and compliant with the industry standards.

CSPM tools provide visibility into cloud resources, detect misconfigurations, and offer recommendations for improving security. They continuously monitor cloud environments to ensure that they meet the security and compliance requirements.

Key Components of CSPM

Cloud Security Posture Management (**CSPM**) is the **backbone** of cloud security, **ensuring** that cloud environments are **configured** correctly, continuously **monitored**, and **compliant** with the security best practices.

As organizations move to the cloud, they often struggle with **misconfigurations**, **excessive permissions**, and evolving threats. CSPM provides a **proactive approach** to identifying risks, enforcing policies, and automating security fixes.

This section breaks down the key components of CSPM in a simple and digestible way, helping you to understand how each plays a role in strengthening cloud security. Now, let us understand each of these CSPM components in detail:

- **Visibility First - Know What is in Your Cloud:** Security starts with knowing what actually exists in your own cloud environments. **Many organizations struggle with shadow IT–resources being deployed, without security oversight**.

  CSPM solves this by providing a real-time, centralized view of all cloud assets such as virtual machines, databases, storage, and network configurations. This allows security teams to track every resource, identify unauthorized deployments, and ensure that nothing is left unmonitored.

  Without visibility, security risks remain hidden, making this the foundation of a strong cloud security strategy.

- **Misconfiguration Guard - Fix Risky Settings Automatically: Cloud misconfigurations are one of the leading causes of security breaches**. A single mistake such as leaving a database open to the public, can lead to data leaks or unauthorized access.

CSPM continuously scans for misconfigurations across cloud services, and alerts teams to these security gaps. Some solutions even provide **automated remediation, fixing issues instantly or offering guided steps** for manual resolution. This ensures that cloud environments stay secure without relying solely on human intervention.

- **Risk Radar - Continuously Assess and Rank Rises:** Not every security issue is urgent, and organizations must prioritize their responses. **CSPM evaluates risks based on severity, and assigns a risk score** to each security finding.

  For example, an exposed database with sensitive customer data will be ranked as high risk, whereas a non-critical test server with a minor misconfiguration may be marked as low risk.

  By using a risk-based approach, security teams can focus their efforts on fixing the most critical threats first, rather than wasting time on low-impact warnings.

- **Compliance Compass - Stay on Track with Security Standards: Most organizations must follow security frameworks like CIS Benchmarks, NIST, PCI-DSS, and ISO 27001 to meet the regulatory and industry standards.** However, manually checking compliance across a cloud environment is nearly impossible.

  CSPM automates compliance checks by continuously comparing cloud configurations against these security standards. If a resource is non-compliant, CSPM provides detailed reports and remediation steps to bring it back in line. This simplifies audits, and ensures organizations to stay compliant effortlessly.

- **Threat Scout - Identify Vulnerabilities Before Attackers Do: Cyber attackers are always searching for weak points in cloud environments.** CSPM helps organizations **stay ahead** by scanning for security vulnerabilities such as unpatched software, weak encryption, and publicly exposed services. By detecting these threats early, organizations can patch vulnerabilities before they are exploited.

  Some CSPM solutions also integrate with threat intelligence feeds to provide real-time updates on newly discovered attack techniques, helping security teams stay proactive.

- **Draft Detector - Spot Unauthorized Changes: Cloud security settings should remain consistent,** but in fast-moving cloud environments, configurations often change–sometimes intentionally, sometimes accidentally. A misconfigured firewall rule, or an unintentional change in access permissions could expose the sensitive data.

  CSPM acts as a drift detector, monitoring configuration changes and immediately flagging any that violate security policies. This prevents accidental security gaps, and ensures that security controls remain intact at all times.

- **Remediation Guide - Automate Fixes and Guided Actions: Security teams often deal with a flood of alerts,** making it difficult to manually fix each and every issue.

  CSPM helps by providing automated remediation for common security problems.

  For example, if a storage bucket is found to be publicly accessible, CSPM can automatically restrict access based on predefined security policies. When automation is not possible, CSPM provides step-by-step guidance, so that teams can quickly fix the issue themselves. This **reduces the workload for security teams,** and ensures faster incident response.

- **Multi-Cloud Lens - Security Across AWS, Azure and GCP: Many businesses use multiple cloud platforms** which introduces complexity in security management. Each cloud provider (AWS, Azure, and GCP) has different security controls, making it challenging to maintain a consistent security posture across all environments.

  CSPM provides a single security dashboard that **aggregates security findings from multiple clouds**, helping organizations enforce uniform security policies, no matter where their workloads run. This ensures that security teams do not have to juggle multiple tools and dashboards to keep their cloud infrastructure safe.

- **Identity Watchover - Guard Against Excessive Permissions: One of the most overlooked security risks in the cloud is excessive user permissions.** Employees, applications, and third-party services are often given more access than they actually need, increasing the risk of insider threats or privilege misuse.

  CSPM continuously audits who has access to what, and **flags over-permissioned accounts.**

  It also recommends the least privilege access policies, ensuring that users and applications only have the permissions necessary to do their jobs. **This reduces the attack surface, and strengthens cloud security.**

- **Incident Anchor - Investigate and Respond to Security Events:** When a security issue arises, understanding what happened, when, and why is crucial for a fast and effective response.

  CSPM integrates with cloud logs and security analytics tools to provide detailed insights into security incidents. For example, if an unauthorized user gains access to a sensitive database, CSPM can trace the event back to its source, **showing how the breach occurred, and what actions were taken**. This helps security teams respond quickly, contain threats, and prevent future incidents.

CSPM is essential for securing cloud environments at scale.

By combining automation, continuous monitoring, risk prioritization, and compliance enforcement, CSPM helps organizations proactively manage cloud security, without overwhelming security teams.

Each of these components works together to reduce misconfigurations, limit attack surfaces, and strengthen the overall security posture–making **CSPM a critical part of any Cloud-Native Application Protection Platform (CNAPP) strategy.**

Importance of CSPM Matters in Real-World Cloud Security

Cloud security misconfigurations are one of the biggest silent threats, organizations face today.

Unlike traditional on-premises environments, cloud platforms introduce a **shared responsibility model**, where cloud providers secure the infrastructure, but customers are responsible for configuring their cloud services correctly. **This is where CSPM plays a crucial role.**

Real-World Cloud Security Incidents

Cloud misconfigurations have been at the heart of some of the largest data breaches in recent history.

Organizations often assume that moving to the cloud means security is automatically handled by the cloud provider. However, the **shared responsibility model** dictates that while cloud providers secure the infrastructure, it is up to the customer to configure security settings correctly.

Unfortunately, simple configuration errors like leaving a database publicly accessible, or failing to enforce multi-factor authentication–have led to devastating breaches, affecting millions of users, and causing financial and reputational damage. Let us dive into some notable real-world security incidents that highlight why CSPM is critical. Some real-world examples include:

- **The Capital One Data Breach (2019) - A Misconfigured AWS S3 Bucket - Impact: 100 million+ customers' personal data leaked**
    - In one of the **biggest cloud security breaches**, an attacker exploited a

server-side request forgery (SSRF) vulnerability in Capital One's web application to gain access to sensitive AWS resources.

- The attacker was able to access misconfigured IAM roles, giving them excessive permissions to retrieve sensitive data from an exposed Amazon S3 bucket.
- The breach resulted in social security numbers, bank account details, and credit scores being leaked.

Key Misconfiguration: Overly permissive IAM roles allowed the attacker to list and retrieve data from the cloud storage bucket.

How CSPM Could Have Helped: CSPM solutions would have **detected excessive IAM permissions** and **flagged them as a high-risk misconfiguration**, before the breach occurred.

- **The Microsoft PowerApps Data Leak (2021) – Misconfigured Permissions - Impact: 38 million sensitive records exposed**
  - Microsoft Power Apps, a low-code development platform, suffered a **massive data exposure** because of a misconfiguration in its **default security settings**.
  - Multiple companies and government agencies used Power Apps to collect the sensitive data, including **COVID-19 test results, employee databases, and social security numbers**.
  - The issue arose because **some Power Apps portals were left publicly accessible**, allowing anyone to extract the sensitive information.

  Key Misconfiguration: Organizations assumed **Power Apps data was private by default**, but instead, it was **publicly accessible, unless manually restricted**.

  How CSPM Could Have Helped: A CSPM solution would have scanned **Power Apps configurations**, and flagged **publicly exposed datasets**, preventing accidental data leaks.

- **The Accenture Ransomware Attack (2021) – Unsecured Cloud Backup - Impact:** 6TB **of confidential corporate data stolen**
  - Accenture, a major IT services provider, suffered a **ransomware attack** that exploited **weak cloud storage security**.
  - The cybercriminal group, **LockBit** managed to access an **unprotected cloud backup server** which stored the sensitive corporate data.
  - Since **cloud backups were not properly secured with encryption and access controls**, attackers were able to **exfiltrate large amounts of confidential client data**.

Key Misconfiguration: Cloud backup storage was not encrypted and lacked strict access controls, making it an easy target.

How CSPM Could Have Helped: A **CSPM tool would have flagged unencrypted storage and weak access controls**, helping Accenture remediate the risks, before the attack.

- **The Facebook (Meta) Cloud Data Exposure (2019) – Publicly Accessible AWS S3 Buckets - Impact: 540 million Facebook user records exposed**
  - Security researchers found **two publicly accessible AWS S3 buckets** containing **Facebook user data** uploaded by third-party app developers.
  - The exposed data included **user IDs, comments, reactions, and account names**, which cybercriminals could use for phishing attacks, or identity theft.
  - These **databases were not owned by Facebook** but by third-party companies using Facebook's platform, showing the risks of **cloud security oversight failures**.

  Key Misconfiguration: Cloud storage was publicly accessible, exposing private user data to anyone with the right URL.

  How CSPM Could Have Helped: A **CSPM tool would have detected publicly exposed storage buckets**, and issued an immediate alert to restrict access.

- **The Tesla Kubernetes Attack (2018) – Exposed Kubernetes Console - Impact: Cryptojacking attack on Tesla's cloud infrastructure**
  - Hackers gained access to **Tesla's AWS cloud infrastructure** by exploiting an **unprotected Kubernetes dashboard** that was publicly accessible.
  - The attackers deployed **cryptojacking malware**, using Tesla's cloud computing power to mine cryptocurrency.
  - Tesla's cloud security monitoring did not immediately detect the attack, allowing the cryptominers to run unnoticed.

  Key Misconfiguration: The Kubernetes console was left open to the Internet with **no authentication required**.

  How CSPM Could Have Helped: CSPM solutions would have detected the publicly exposed Kubernetes dashboard, and flagged it as a critical misconfiguration.

CSPM helps prevent such incidents by **continuously scanning cloud environments** for misconfigurations, compliance violations, and potential risks.

The Growing Importance of CSPM

Organizations are increasingly moving to multi-cloud environments, making manual security oversight nearly impossible. CSPM addresses this by providing:

- **Automated security checks** to detect misconfigurations.
- **Risk-based prioritization** to focus on critical issues first.
- **Remediation recommendations** to fix security gaps quickly.

With cyber threats evolving, **CSPM is no longer just an optional security tool**—it is now a **core requirement for cloud security strategies.**

Adoption Trends

As cloud adoption grows, different industries are incorporating CSPM to strengthen security and compliance. Let us look at how different sectors are leveraging CSPM:

- **Tech and SaaS Companies**
  - Companies operating **fully in the cloud** need **real-time visibility** into their cloud security posture.
  - Many SaaS providers **use CSPM to ensure that customer data is securely stored**, and meets the compliance requirements.
- **Financial and Banking Industry**
  - Financial institutions must comply with strict regulations (PCI-DSS, ISO 27001, SOC 2, and so on).
  - CSPM helps them detect unauthorized access, misconfigured encryption settings, and ensure secure transactions.
- **Healthcare and Life Sciences**
  - Regulations like HIPAA require strong data security for patient records.
  - CSPM ensures that cloud-stored medical data is encrypted and access-controlled.
- **Government and Public Sector**
  - Governments are adopting CSPM to protect the sensitive citizen data, and secure the cloud infrastructure.
  - Compliance with frameworks like FedRAMP and NIST is enforced through automated CSPM compliance checks.
- **Enterprises with Multi-Cloud Strategies**
  - Large enterprises often use AWS, Azure, and Google Cloud simultaneously.

  - CSPM provides a unified security view across multiple cloud platforms, reducing complexity.
- **DevOps and Cloud-Native Companies**
  - Security must be integrated into CI/CD pipelines.
  - CSPM helps by **scanning Infrastructure-as-Code (IaC) templates to prevent misconfigurations** before deployment.

CSPM adoption is growing rapidly because it helps organizations of all sizes secure their cloud environments, without slowing down innovation.

Leading CSPM Solutions in the Industry

Several security vendors offer **CSPM solutions**, either as **standalone products**, or as part of broader **Cloud-Native Application Protection Platform (CNAPP) suites**. Here are some of the most widely used CSPM solutions:

- **Microsoft Defender for Cloud**
  - Offers **built-in CSPM capabilities** with **Azure Security Benchmark assessments.**
  - Supports **multi-cloud security** with AWS and GCP integrations.
  - Provides **compliance tracking, and risk-based prioritization.**
- **Prisma Cloud by Palo Alto Networks**
  - Delivers **agentless and continuous cloud security monitoring.**
  - Provides **compliance enforcement across multiple cloud providers.**
  - Detects **IAM misconfigurations, and excessive permissions.**
- **Wiz**
  - Focuses on **deep cloud workload scanning** for vulnerabilities.
  - Provides **security graph-based risk insights.**
  - Identifies **exposed secrets, misconfigurations, and IAM risks.**
- **Orca Security**
  - Uses **side-scanning technology** to analyze cloud environments, without agents.
  - Provides **risk visualization and automated remediation.**
  - Detects **misconfigured cloud services and identity threats.**
- **Other Notable CSPM Solutions**
  - **Check Point CloudGuard:** Focuses on **compliance enforcement and misconfiguration detection.**

- **Lacework:** Uses **behavioral analytics for risk detection.**
- **Trend Micro Cloud One:** Provides **CSPM with cloud-native threat protection.**

Choosing the right CSPM tool depends on factors like **multi-cloud compatibility, compliance needs, and integration with the existing security workflows.**

Challenges and Future of CSPM

While CSPM provides **critical security benefits**, organizations still face challenges in implementing and managing CSPM solutions effectively.

Current Challenges

- **Too Many Alerts (Alert Fatigue)**
  - Security teams often receive **thousands of alerts**, making it hard to **prioritize real threats.**
  - Solutions with **better risk-based prioritizations** are needed.
- **False Positives and Noisy Findings**
  - CSPM tools sometimes **flag non-critical issues**, causing unnecessary disruptions.
  - AI-driven **context-aware alerting** can help reduce noise.
- **Integration with DevOps and CI/CD Pipelines**
  - Many security teams struggle to **enforce CSPM policies in DevOps workflows.**
  - **Shift-left security** (integrating security checks in early development stages) is becoming a priority.
- **Cloud Complexity and Multi-Cloud Challenges**
  - Organizations using multiple cloud providers need **CSPM solutions that unify security across different platforms.**
  - Cross-cloud policy enforcement is still evolving.

The Future of CSPM

The next evolution of CSPM will focus on **more automation, AI-driven insights, and deeper identity security**. Some future trends include:

- **AI-Powered Risk Assessment:** Using AI to predict **which misconfigurations are most likely to be exploited.**

- **Automated Risk Remediation:** CSPM tools will move toward **fully automated security fixes with minimal human intervention.**
- **Identity-Centric CSPM:** More focus on **detecting excessive permissions, and securing cloud identities.**
- **Stronger DevSecOps Integration: CSPM will be embedded directly into development pipelines to prevent security issues** before deployment.

CSPM is rapidly evolving to meet the needs of **modern cloud security challenges**, and its role in **cloud security strategies will only continue to grow.**

Microsoft Defender for Cloud as a CSPM Solution

Microsoft Defender for Cloud's CSPM offers a holistic approach to safeguarding cloud environments. Microsoft Defender for Cloud continually compares the configuration of your resources with industry standards, regulations, and benchmarks. By continuously evaluating the configuration of cloud resources against industry standards, regulations, and best practices, it helps organizations stay compliant and secure.

This proactive system identifies (i) vulnerabilities and misconfigurations early, (ii) preventing potential security breaches.

With features such as **`tailored security recommendations`**, **`a comprehensive secure score`**, and **`automated remediation processes`**, **`Microsoft Defender for Cloud`** equips organizations with the tools needed to maintain a strong and resilient security posture.

To understand how Security Posture Management evaluates your environment, it is important to grasp the concepts of security policies and initiatives. We will understand the following topics in this section:

- Azure policy
- Security Initiatives
- Security Recommendations
- Secure Score
- Workbooks

Understanding Security Policies

An **Azure Policy definition**, created within **Azure Policy**, establishes rules for specific **security conditions** you want to control.

Built-in definitions include rules like restricting the types of resources that can be deployed or enforcing the use of tags on all resources. Additionally, you have the flexibility to create custom policy definitions tailored to your needs. To implement these policy definitions, whether built-in or custom, you need to assign them. This can be done through the Azure portal, PowerShell, or Azure CLI. **Policies can be easily enabled or disabled from Azure Policy**.

Azure Policy offers different types of policies.

Microsoft Defender for Cloud primarily utilizes **`'Audit'` policies**, which check specific conditions and configurations, then report on compliance.

There are also **'Enforce' policies** that apply secure settings to ensure compliance with the security standards.

Understanding Security Initiative

An Azure Policy initiative is a collection of Azure Policy definitions, or rules, grouped together to achieve a specific goal or purpose.

These initiatives simplify policy management by logically bundling multiple policies into a single entity. A security initiative **outlines the desired configuration** for your workloads, **ensuring compliance with your company's security requirements and regulatory standards.**

Similar to security policies, Defender for Cloud initiatives are created within Azure Policy. You can manage these policies, build initiatives, and assign them to multiple subscriptions or entire management groups using Azure Policy.

The default initiative assigned to every subscription in **`Microsoft Defender for Cloud`** is the **Azure Security Benchmark.** This benchmark, **authored by Microsoft**, provides Azure-specific guidelines for security and compliance best practices based on common frameworks. **It incorporates controls from the Center for Internet Security (CIS) and the National Institute of Standards and Technology (NIST), with a focus on cloud-centric security.**

Defender for Cloud offers several options for working with security initiatives and policies:

- **View and Edit the Built-in Default Initiative:** When you enable Defender for Cloud, the '**`Azure Security Benchmark`**' initiative is automatically assigned to all registered subscriptions. You can customize this initiative by enabling or disabling individual policies within it. Refer to the list of built-in security policies to understand the available options.
- **Add Your Own Custom Initiatives:** If you need to tailor the security initiatives for your subscription, you can create custom initiatives within Defender for Cloud. You will receive recommendations if your resources do not comply

with the policies you create. For guidance on building and assigning custom policies, see the section on using custom security initiatives and policies.

- **Add Regulatory Compliance Standards as Initiatives:** Defender for Cloud's regulatory compliance dashboard displays the status of all assessments within your environment, aligned with specific standards or regulations (such as Azure CIS, NIST SP 800-53 R4, and SWIFT CSP CSCF-v2020).

I hope this version meets your needs! If you need any further adjustments or additional content, feel free to let me know.

Understanding Security Recommendations

Defender for Cloud uses policies to regularly check the compliance status of your resources, identifying any security misconfigurations and weaknesses.

It then provides recommendations on how to fix these issues. These suggestions are based on assessing your resources against relevant policies, and identifying those that do not meet your defined requirements.

Defender for Cloud's recommendations are driven by your chosen initiatives. When a policy from your initiative is compared against your resources, and finds non-compliant ones, it presents a recommendation in the Defender for Cloud.

Each recommendation includes:

- A brief description of the issue.
- Steps to remediate the issue.
- The affected resources.

For example, the **Azure Security Benchmark initiative** includes requirements like restricting network access for Azure Storage accounts to reduce their attack surface. This requirement is enforced by a policy such as "*Storage accounts should restrict network access, using virtual network rules.*"

Defender for Cloud continuously assesses your connected subscriptions. If it finds a resource that does not comply with a policy, it displays a recommendation to fix the issue, and enhance the security of your resources.

In summary, an initiative includes policies that generate environment-specific recommendations. As a Security Operations Analyst, you are responsible for ensuring regulatory compliance of your hybrid-cloud resources, and improving the number of controls that pass the Azure Security Benchmark in Defender for Cloud. Now that you understand Microsoft Defender for Cloud's security policies, initiatives, and recommendations, let us see it in action.

Explore Secure Score

Microsoft Defender for Cloud continuously checks your cross-cloud resources for security issues, and the combines all findings into a single score.

This secure score gives you a quick overview of your current security status: **The higher the score, the lower the risk. On the Microsoft Defender for Cloud Overview page, the secure score is displayed as a percentage, with detailed values clearly shown in the following illustration.**

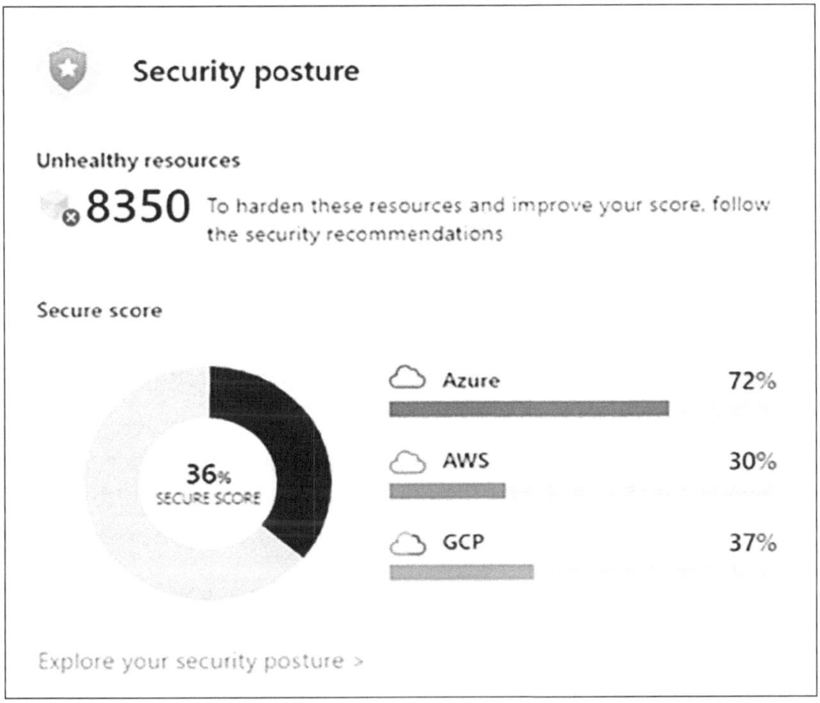

Figure 4.1: *Microsoft Defender for Cloud - Sample Security Posture with Secure Score. (Source: https://learn.microsoft.com/en-us/training/wwl-sci/manage-cloud-security-posture-management/media/single-secure-score.png)*

To boost your security, visit the recommendations page, and follow the remediation steps for each issue. By default, all environments are displayed.

Recommendations are grouped into security controls which are logical collections of related security suggestions.

Your score improves only when you address all the recommendations for a single resource, within a control.

To see how well your organization is protecting each attack surface, review the scores for each security control.

On the **`Security Posture page`**, you can view the **`secure score`** for your entire subscription, and each environment within it.

Figure 4.2: *Microsoft Defender for Cloud - Sample Security Posture. (Source: https://learn.microsoft.com/en-us/training/wwl-sci/manage-cloud-security-posture-management/media/security-posture-page.png#lightbox)*

The lower half of the page lets you manage your individual subscriptions, accounts, and projects by viewing their secure scores, the number of unhealthy resources, and their recommendations.

How is Your Secure Score Calculated

To get all the possible points for a security control, all of your resources must comply with all of the security recommendations within the security control. For example, Defender for Cloud has multiple recommendations regarding how to secure your management ports. You will need to remediate them all to make a difference to your secure score.

Explore Recommendations

Defender for Cloud's recommendations are based on the Azure Security Benchmark Standard which aligns with common compliance frameworks like CIS and NIST, focusing on cloud security. Additional recommendations come from regulatory compliance initiatives.

View Your Recommendations:

1. **`Sign into`** the Azure portal.

2. **Navigate** to **`Microsoft Defender for Cloud`** > **`Recommendations`**.

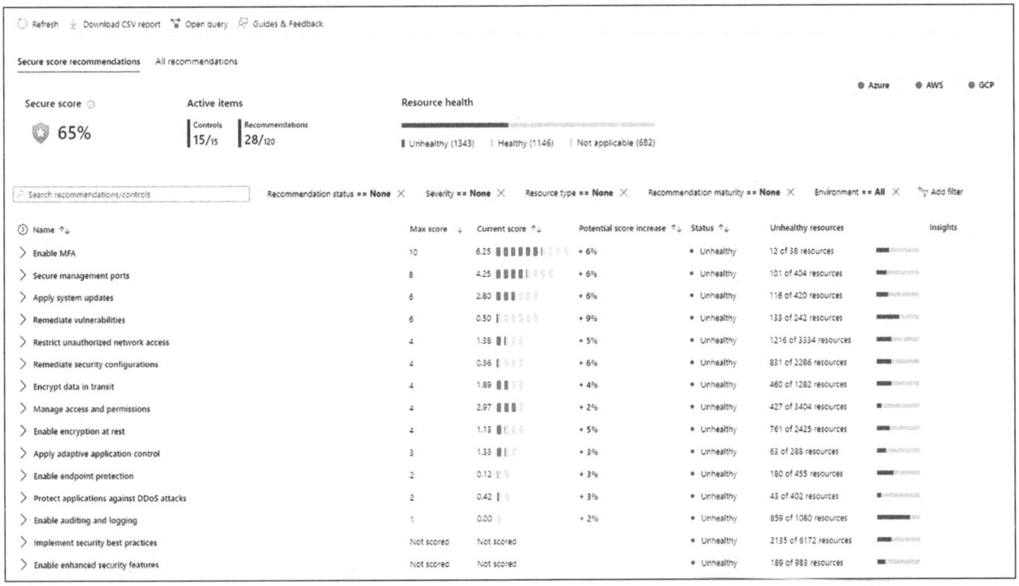

Figure 4.3: *Microsoft Defender for Cloud - Sample Recommendations. (Source: https://learn.microsoft.com/en-us/training/wwl-sci/manage-cloud-security-posture-management/media/recommendations-view.png#lightbox)*

Here, you will find recommendations **`grouped into security controls`**.

`Secure score recommendations` impact your secure score, and are mapped to various security controls.

The "**`All recommendations`**" tab shows all the recommendations, including those from different regulatory standards.

Steps to Follow:

1. **Select** a relevant environment (optional).
2. **Expand** the control to view a list of recommendations.
3. **Select** a specific recommendation to view the details.

For supported recommendations, you may see options such as Enforce, Deny, View policy definition, Open query, and many more. Each suggestion includes a description, severity, freshness interval, and affected resources.

Remediation Steps:

1. **Select** a recommendation.
2. **Follow** the instructions in the Remediation steps section.

3. **Complete** the steps, and check for a notification confirming resolution.

Fix Option:

For recommendations with a Fix option:

1. Select a recommendation with the Fix action icon.
2. Select the resources to remediate, and click Remediate.
3. Confirm the remediation details, and approve.

Once completed, you will receive a notification about the success of the remediation.

Understanding Workbooks

Azure Monitor Workbooks provide a flexible canvas for data analysis, **and the creation of rich visual reports within the Azure portal.**

They allow you to tap into multiple data sources from across Azure, and combine them into unified interactive experiences. Within Microsoft Defender for Cloud, you can access the **built-in workbooks to track your organization's security posture.** You can also build **custom workbooks** to view a wide range of data from Defender for Cloud, or other supported data sources.

With the integrated Azure Workbooks functionality, Microsoft Defender for Cloud makes it straightforward to build your own custom, interactive workbooks.

Defender for Cloud also includes a gallery with the following workbooks, ready for your customization:

- **Secure Score over Time Workbook:** Track your subscriptions' scores and changes to recommendations for your resources.
- **System Updates Workbook:** View the missing system updates by resources, OS, severity, and much more.
- **Vulnerability Assessment Findings Workbook:** View the findings of the vulnerability scans of your Azure resources.
- **Compliance over Time Workbook:** View the status of a subscription's compliance with the regulatory or industry standards, you have selected.
- **Active Alerts Workbook:** View the active alerts by severity, type, tag, MITRE ATT&CK tactics, and location.

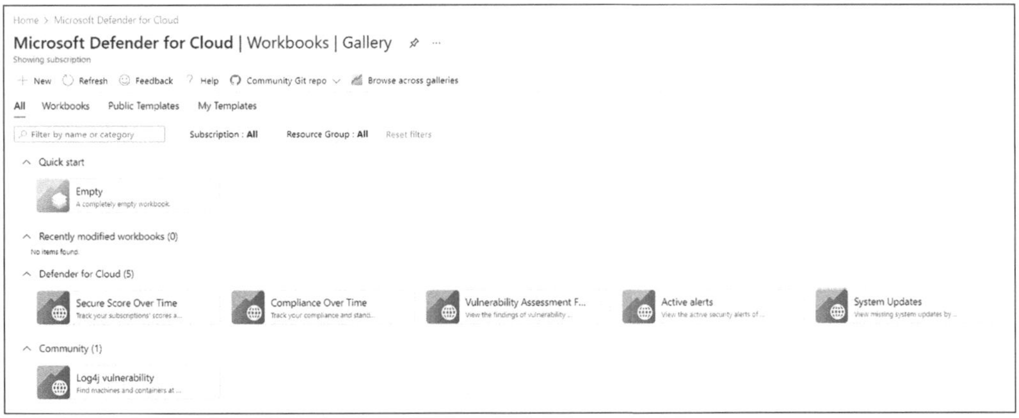

Figure 4.4: *Microsoft Defender for Cloud - Workbook Gallery. (source: https://learn.microsoft.com/en-us/training/wwl-sci/manage-cloud-security-posture-management/media/workbooks-gallery-microsoft-defender-for-cloud.png)*

Understanding Attack Path Analysis

One of the most critical dashboards in **Microsoft Defender for Cloud** is **Attack Path Analysis**, as it provides **deep, context-aware insights** that are invaluable to **CISOs and security leaders**. This feature enables organizations to **proactively assess their cloud security posture**, visualize potential attack chains, and take **strategic, risk-based actions** to mitigate threats before they materialize. By **identifying misconfigurations, excessive permissions, and exploitable vulnerabilities, Attack Path Analysis empowers security teams to break the attack chain, and strengthen cloud defenses against evolving threats.**

The **`Attack Path Analysis`** dashboard offers powerful insights, including:

- **`Total attack paths`** detected
- **`Affected resources`** across cloud environments
- **`Active recommendations`**, categorized by risk level
- **`Risk levels`**, segmented into **`Critical`**, **`High`**, **`Medium`**, and **`Low`**
- **`Entry points`** that attackers could exploit
- **`Potential targets`** within the cloud infrastructure
- **`Cloud environment`** (Azure, AWS, or GCP) associated with the risk
- **`Risk factors`** contributing to security gaps

Refer to the following screenshot for a **`real-world view of the Attack Path Analysis`** **dashboard** from our instance of **`Microsoft Defender for Cloud`**.

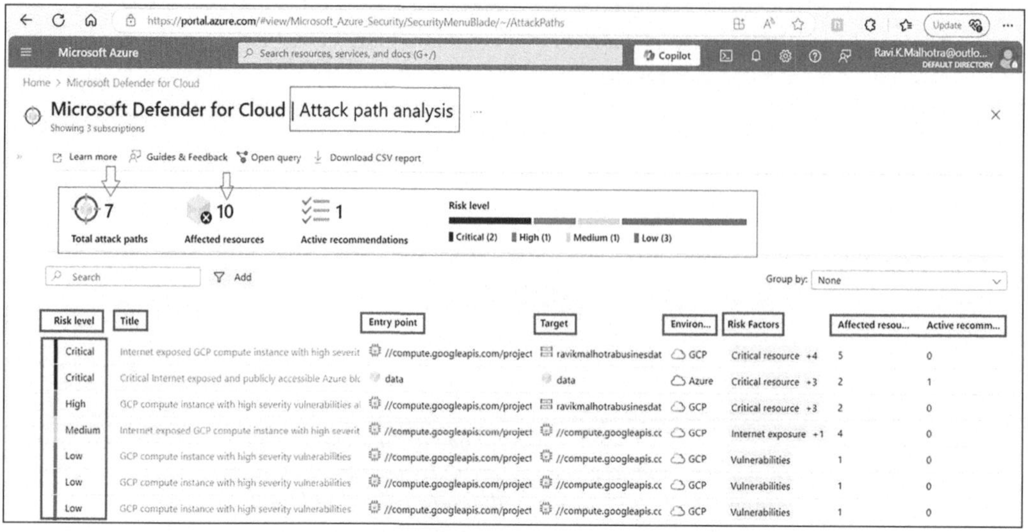

Figure 4.5: Attack Path Analysis Dashboard

The **Attack Path Analysis dashboard** in Microsoft Defender for Cloud presents a comprehensive and visual breakdown of potential attack vectors across cloud environments. At the top of the dashboard, key metrics are summarized, including **7** **`Total attack paths`**, **10** **`Affected resources`**, and **1 Active recommendation**–offering a quick overview of the organization's exposure. The **risk level distribution** is also clearly displayed, with threats categorized as **`Critical`** **(2)**, **`High`** **(1)**, **`Medium`** **(1)**, and **`Low`** **(3)**, helping security teams prioritize mitigation efforts, based on severity.

Following this summary, a detailed table lists each identified attack path, beginning with its **`Risk level`**, followed by the **`Title`** which describes the nature of the exposure or vulnerability–for example, "*Internet exposed* GCP *compute instance with high severity vulnerabilities.*" Each row highlights the **`Entry point`**, showing how the attack could potentially start (example, a GCP compute instance or publicly accessible data), and the **`Target`**, which represents the intended goal of the attacker. The **`Environment`** column helps distinguish between cloud platforms involved such as **GCP** and **Azure**, while **Risk Factors** provide contextual insight, such as whether a resource is deemed "**`Critical`**," exposed to the internet, or vulnerable due to configuration issues. Finally, the columns for **`Affected resources`** and **`Active recommendations`** indicate how many assets are impacted by each attack path, and whether remediation steps have been suggested.

This dashboard serves as a strategic control point, enabling teams to visualize lateral movement paths across cloud environments, and take proactive and risk-informed actions. Hence, whether it is identifying misconfigured virtual machines or detecting excessive exposure to public networks, Attack Path Analysis empowers cloud defenders to break the chain, before a breach occurs.

Understanding Cloud Security Explorer

Cloud Security Explorer is a valuable feature in Microsoft Defender for Cloud, allowing security teams to query cloud assets, identify misconfigurations, and uncover security risks efficiently. Cloud Security Explorer is a **powerful and dynamic security analysis tool within Microsoft Defender for Cloud**.

It enables security teams to **query, search, and investigate cloud resources** across **Azure, AWS, and Google Cloud**, providing deep visibility into cloud security risks. This tool goes beyond static security reports by offering an **interactive and real-time way** to uncover misconfigurations, exposed assets, and compliance violations, before they become serious threats.

One of the **key advantages of `Cloud Security Explorer`** is its ability to **leverage the Defender CSPM security graph**, allowing security teams to conduct **complex security queries** with ease. Whether an organization needs to find **publicly exposed storage accounts**, detect **unrestricted network access**, or identify **unprotected virtual machines**, this tool provides actionable insights instantly. By allowing security professionals to perform **custom queries**, it enables a **proactive approach** to cloud security rather than relying solely on traditional alerts or periodic audits.

Understanding Attack Paths and Risk Propagation

One of the most powerful aspects of Cloud Security Explorer is **its ability to provide deep insights into attack paths** within a cloud environment. **Attackers often exploit misconfigurations, weak security policies, and excessive permissions to move laterally, and escalate privileges.**

With Cloud Security Explorer, security teams can identify potential entry points, privilege escalation routes, and high-risk dependencies, gaining a clear understanding of how threats can spread across their cloud infrastructure. This visibility helps organizations prioritize remediation efforts, allowing security teams to break the attack chain, before it can be exploited.

While Attack Paths and Cloud Security Explorer are closely related, they serve distinct but complementary roles within Microsoft Defender for Cloud. Cloud Security Explorer is designed to query, search, and analyze cloud assets for security risks, including misconfigurations and vulnerabilities, providing deep insights into an organization's cloud security posture. In contrast, Attack Paths focus on visualizing how an attacker could exploit security weaknesses, showing the relationships between misconfigured assets, exposed resources, and identity privileges.

Together, these features create a powerful security strategy–Cloud Security Explorer helps security teams discover and address weaknesses proactively, while Attack Paths reveal how attackers could exploit them.

Leveraging both tools ensures a proactive and defensive approach to cloud security, reducing risk exposure, and improving overall security resilience.

Multi-Cloud Support for Unified Security Governance

As organizations increasingly adopt **multi-cloud strategies**, maintaining **consistent security visibility** across different cloud platforms becomes a challenge. Cloud Security Explorer addresses this issue by offering **cross-cloud security insights**, ensuring that security teams can monitor **Azure, AWS, and Google Cloud** from a **single interface**. This unified approach helps eliminate security blind spots and enforces **consistent security policies** across all cloud environments.

Enabling Proactive Threat Hunting

Unlike traditional security tools that focus on reactive defense, Cloud Security Explorer empowers organizations to take a proactive approach to cloud security.

By continuously scanning and querying cloud assets, security teams can **hunt for vulnerabilities, detect suspicious patterns, and prevent potential breaches before they occur**. This tool is essential for organizations that aim to **enhance their cloud security posture, reduce risk exposure, and adopt a data-driven security strategy**.

Cloud Security Explorer is more than just an asset discovery tool–it's a **critical component** of modern cloud security operations. With its **real-time analysis, attack path visualization, and multi-cloud support**, it equips organizations with the **insights needed to safeguard their cloud environments**. Whether used for **threat detection, compliance monitoring, or risk assessment**, Cloud Security Explorer plays a key role in strengthening **Microsoft Defender for Cloud's CSPM capabilities**, making it an **indispensable tool** for cloud security teams.

CSPM Labs

Thus, to truly understand and implement CSPM, hands-on experience is essential. This section is dedicated to a series of practical labs designed to help security professionals explore and apply CSPM concepts, using Microsoft Defender for Cloud. Each lab builds on the previous one, starting with enabling CSPM, understanding next steps, and exploring cloud inventory. As we progress, we dive into the advanced features like Cloud Security Explorer, attack path analysis, and automation of security best practices. These labs are structured to provide real-world scenarios, ensuring that by the end of this chapter, you not only understand CSPM in theory, but also gain the confidence to navigate and secure cloud environments effectively.

Lab # 1: Enabling Foundational and Defender CSPM

Microsoft Defender for Cloud delivers Cloud Security Posture Management (**CSPM**) through two distinct modules: Foundational CSPM and Defender CSPM, each designed to address different levels of security needs.

Foundational CSPM is automatically enabled for all Azure subscriptions, providing essential security posture visibility, misconfiguration detection, compliance tracking, and security recommendations. This foundational layer ensures that every Azure environment benefits from the basic security assessments, without requiring manual activation.

However, organizations seeking a more advanced, proactive approach to cloud security must manually enable Defender CSPM. This enhanced module introduces context-aware risk analysis, attack path mapping, deep misconfiguration insights, and cloud security graph analytics, offering a broader and more intelligent view of security vulnerabilities.

Unlike the static assessments of Foundational CSPM, **Defender CSPM continuously evaluates security risks in real time, prioritizing threats based on their potential impact, and exposure within the cloud environment.** By leveraging AI-driven security intelligence and automated risk mitigation, Defender CSPM empowers organizations to stay ahead of emerging threats, identify high-risk attack paths, and enforce a more dynamic security strategy.

As modern cloud infrastructures continue to grow in complexity, integrating both Foundational CSPM for baseline security and Defender CSPM for advanced protection is crucial for achieving a resilient and well-governed cloud security posture.

Before starting this lab, you should have completed *Chapter 3, A Practical Guide to Onboarding CNAPP.*

Foundational CSPM (Enabled by Default)

Follow these steps to verify whether Foundational CSPM is enabled for all your Azure subscriptions:

1. Log into the Azure portal. using your administrative credentials.
2. Go to the search bar > type "`Microsoft Defender for Cloud`", and select the service to open the dashboard.

3. Once inside the dashboard, locate the "**`Environment Settings`**" tab on the left-hand menu.

4. Expand **Azure**, and then expand **`Tenant Root Group`**, which is a management group.

5. Here, you will see all your active subscriptions detected by Microsoft Defender for Cloud. It will also display the currently active plans.

6. Here, you will notice that Foundational CSPM is fully operational and enabled by default. This plan cannot be disabled.

7. Additionally, you will observe that the Defender CSPM plan is not enabled by default, but you have the option to enable it manually.

   Refer to the following screenshot for a visual representation.

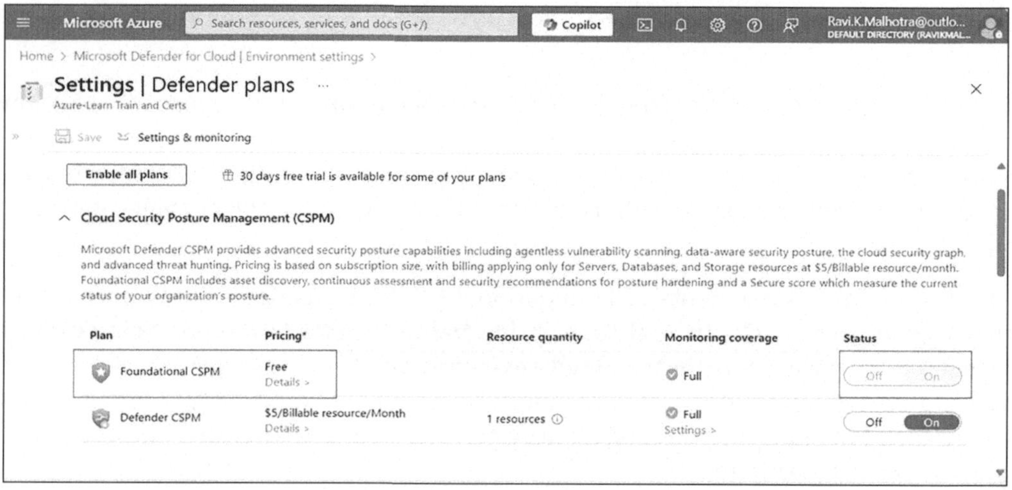

Figure 4.6: *Status of Foundational CSPM and Defender CSPM*

8. As shown in the above-mentioned screenshot, Foundational CSPM is enabled by default. The On switch is grayed out, and cannot be disabled.

9. This concludes the lab.

Defender CSPM (Must be Manually Enabled)

Follow these steps to enable Defender CSPM for all your Azure subscriptions:

1. Now, we will enable the **`Defender CSPM`** feature manually.

2. Enabling this feature '**`Defender CSPM`**' unlocks a comprehensive suite of advanced security capabilities, including:
    a. Agentless VM vulnerability scanning
    b. Agentless VM secrets scanning
    c. Attack path analysis
    d. Risk prioritization
    e. Risk hunting with Security Explorer
    f. Code-to-cloud mapping for containers
    g. Code-to-code mapping for IaC
    h. PR annotations
    i. Internet exposure analysis
    j. **External Attack Surface Management (EASM)**
    k. **Permissions Management (CIEM)**
    l. Regulatory compliance assessments
    m. ServiceNow Integration
    n. Critical assets protection
    o. Governance to drive remediation at-scale
    p. AI Security Posture Management
    q. Data-aware security posture, Sensitive data scanning
    r. K8S API access
    s. Agentless code-to-cloud containers vulnerability assessment
    t. API Security Posture Management
3. Go to **`Environment Settings`** >> Select the **`desired subscription`** >> **`toggle the switch to On against Defender CSPM`**.
4. Click on the '**`Save`**' button on top. Wait for some time.
5. Upon returning to the **`Environment settings`** page, you will observe that 1 out of 12 plans is now activated for your subscription.

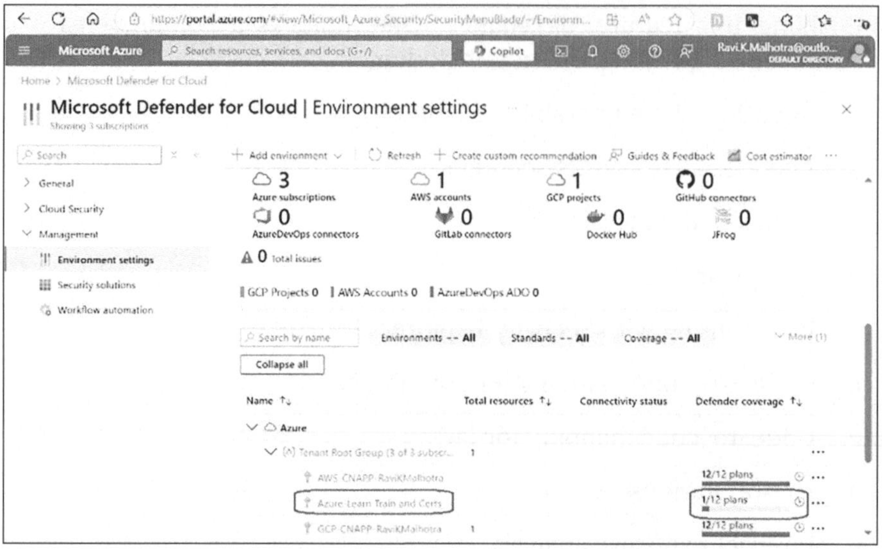

Figure 4.7: *Defender Coverage Status after Enabling Defender CSPM Plan*

6. As shown in the screenshot, Defender CSPM is enabled for the '**`Azure-Learn Train and Certs`**' Azure subscription.

7. This concludes the lab.

Lab # 2: Understanding the Next Steps after Enabling CSPM

Now that CSPM is enabled in Microsoft Defender for Cloud, the next critical step is to leverage its capabilities effectively. Enabling CSPM is just the beginning–your cloud environment must be continuously monitored, assessed, and improved to maintain a strong security posture. This lab will guide you through the essential actions to take after enabling CSPM, ensuring that your cloud infrastructure remains secure, compliant, and resilient against threats.

Steps to Follow After Enabling CSPM:

1. **Review Security Recommendations**

   a. Navigate to **`Microsoft Defender for Cloud`** → **`Recommendations`** page.

   b. Review the list of security recommendations generated based on detected misconfigurations and security risks.

   c. Prioritize critical and high-severity recommendations that pose the greatest security risks.

   d. Implement **suggested fixes** to enhance your cloud security posture.

2. **Analyze Your `Security Score`**
    a. Access the **`Secure Score`** dashboard to get a quantifiable measure of your cloud security posture.
    b. Identify security weaknesses affecting your score, and take action to improve it.
    c. Regularly monitor changes in your **`Secure Score`** to track progress, and address emerging risks.
3. **Enable Continuous Compliance Monitoring**
    a. Go to **`Microsoft Defender for Cloud`** → **`Regulatory Compliance`**.
    b. Select the compliance frameworks relevant to your organization (for example, CIS, NIST, and ISO 27001).
    c. Identify any gaps in compliance, and take corrective actions to align with the industry standards.
    d. Generate compliance reports for audits and governance purposes.
4. **Identify and Remediate Attack Paths**
    a. If Defender CSPM is enabled, navigate to **`Attack Paths`** under **`Microsoft Defender for Cloud`**.
    b. Analyze potential attack paths that adversaries could exploit in your environment.
    c. Prioritize the most exposed and high-risk assets to break the potential attack chains.
5. **Configure Security Alerts and Threat Protection**
    a. Ensure that Defender for Cloud alerts are enabled to notify you of security threats.
    b. Investigate alerts related to misconfigurations, unauthorized access, and suspicious activities.
    c. Set up automated responses to critical security alerts to minimize risks.
6. **Establish a Continuous Monitoring Strategy**
    a. Schedule regular security assessments to ensure your cloud environment remains compliant and well-protected.
    b. Set up Log Analytics and Security Center integration for enhanced visibility into security events.

c. Continuously refine security policies, and update security baselines as new threats emerge.

By following these steps, you ensure that your cloud security posture remains proactive, adaptive, and aligned with the best practices. CSPM is not just about enabling a tool–it is about actively managing risks, improving compliance, and strengthening your overall cloud security strategy.

Lab # X: Exploring the Overview Tab

In a cloud environment, maintaining visibility into all resources is critical for effective security management.xxxx.

Lab # 3: Exploring Inventory in Microsoft Defender for Cloud

In a cloud environment, maintaining visibility into all resources is critical for effective security management. Microsoft Defender for Cloud provides a centralized inventory that helps security teams track, analyze, and monitor cloud assets across Azure, AWS, and Google Cloud. This inventory allows organizations to identify unprotected, misconfigured, or non-compliant resources, ensuring that they meet security and compliance standards. With filtering, searching, and categorization features, security teams can quickly pinpoint high-risk assets and take appropriate action. This lab will guide you through navigating and exploring the inventory within Defender for Cloud, helping you gain a clear understanding of your cloud infrastructure.

Cloud inventory management is a core part of CSPM, as it helps security teams keep track of all cloud resources. Microsoft Defender for Cloud provides detailed visibility into assets across Azure, AWS, and Google Cloud. Security professionals can identify unprotected, misconfigured, or non-compliant resources using inventory data. Understanding inventory allows for better security monitoring, compliance checks, and risk analysis.

This lab, "**Exploring Inventory in Microsoft Defender for Cloud**," is a crucial next step after enabling CSPM. It builds on previous labs to ensure a comprehensive understanding of your cloud security posture:

- **Lab # 1**: You have successfully enabled Foundational and Defender CSPM to activate security monitoring.
- **Lab # 2**: You have explored the next steps after enabling CSPM, setting the foundation for security insights.
- **Now**: It is essential to discover, analyze, and manage your cloud inventory, before diving deeper into security posture management.

Follow these steps to explore the inventory across all your Azure subscriptions, as well as other connected cloud accounts and projects:

1. Log into the Azure portal, using your administrative credentials.
2. Go to the search bar > type "**`Microsoft Defender for Cloud`**", and select the service to open the dashboard.
3. Once inside the dashboard, locate the "**`Inventory`**" button under the General tab.
4. Click on the "**`Inventory`**" to access a list of all cloud assets across your Azure, AWS, and Google Cloud environments. Refer to the following screenshot which showcases the **`default view`** of the **`'Inventory'`** tab. This view provides:
    a. A comprehensive list of all discovered cloud assets, along with their security postures.
    b. It highlights the number of unhealthy resources, and displays security recommendations for each asset, helping you quickly assess and address potential risks.
    c. It also displays cloud assets from all onboarded cloud accounts within your environment.

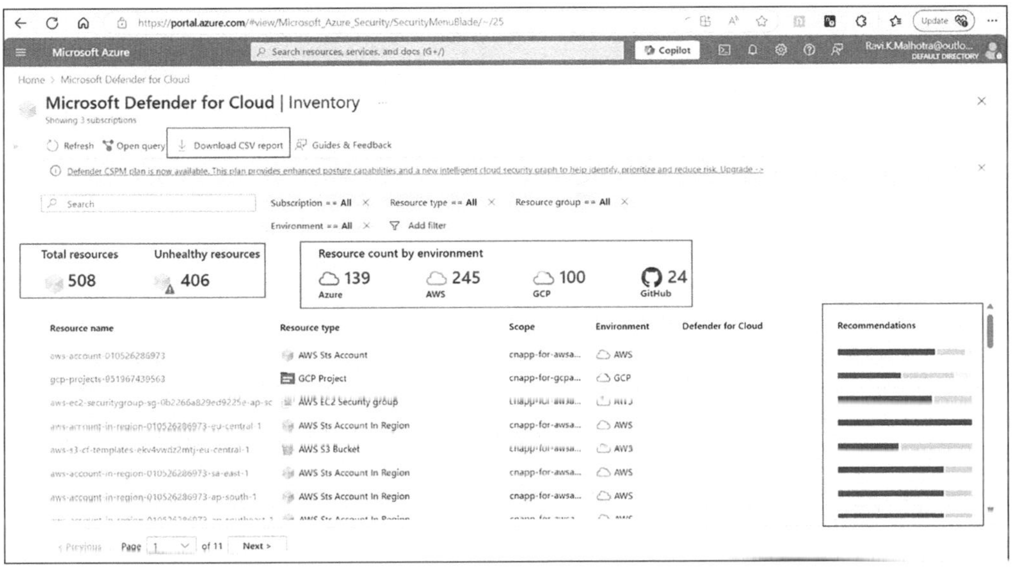

Figure 4.8: *Inventory Default View*

5. Use the search bar at the top to quickly locate specific resources, such as **`Virtual Machines`**, **`Storage Accounts`**, or **`Databases`**. **For instance, if you want to find all cloud assets named `'monika'` across your inventory**, simply type **`'monika'`** in the search bar, and press Enter.

Upon searching, multiple results appeared, revealing a total of seven (7) IAM user accounts with the name '**monika**.' Among them, six (6) belong to AWS, while one (1) is from the GCP cloud platform. Additionally, six (6) out of the seven accounts are **flagged as unhealthy**, with only **one account maintaining a completely healthy status**. Security recommendations are also available for each discovered user account, helping to assess and remediate the potential risks. Refer to the following screenshot for a visual representation:

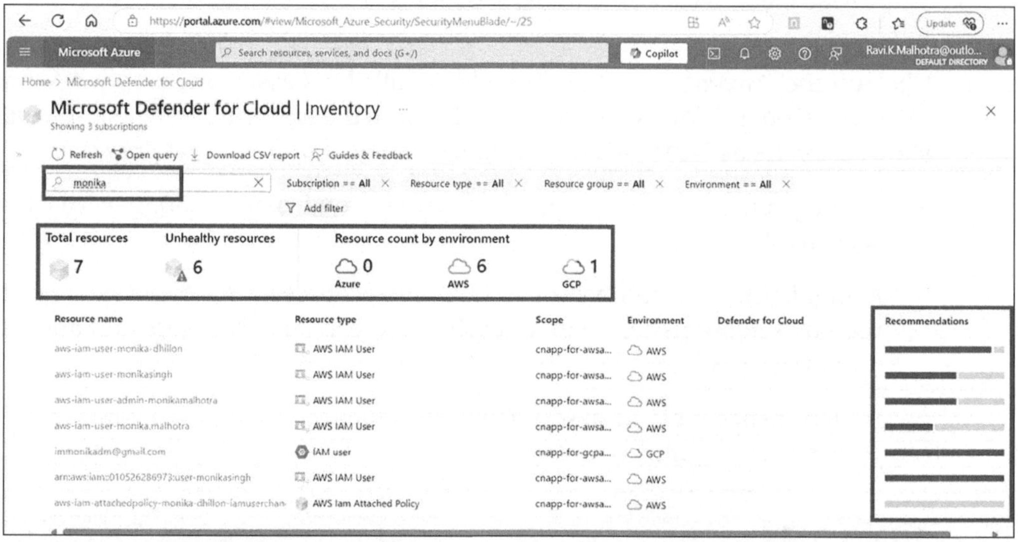

Figure 4.9: *Inventory Default View - Search Bar*

6. Apply filters to narrow down resources based on subscriptions, resource type, and resource group environment.

7. Click on the "**`Download CSV report`**" button to download the inventory data, and all the details in the CSV format for further analysis.

By completing this lab, you have successfully explored your cloud resource inventory within **Microsoft Defender for Cloud**. This knowledge will help you monitor cloud assets, enforce security best practices, and proactively mitigate risks. Continue to the next lab for deeper insights into security recommendations and Secure Score analysis.

Lab # 4: Discover Hard Disks Using `Cloud Security Explorer`

`Cloud Security Explorer` in **`Microsoft Defender for Cloud`** allows security teams to efficiently search and analyze cloud assets for security risks. You can perform searches using custom queries or leverage predefined templates to quickly identify misconfigurations, exposed resources, and compliance violations. This lab will guide you through utilizing *Cloud Security Explorer* to discover cloud assets, and analyze potential security risks.

Follow these steps to explore all the Hard Disks, the inventory across all your Azure subscriptions, as well as other connected cloud accounts and projects:

1. Log into the Azure portal, using your administrative credentials.
2. Go to the search bar > type, "`Microsoft Defender for Cloud`", and select the service to open the dashboard.
3. Click on the "`Cloud Security Explorer`" button. Refer to the following screenshot which showcases the **default view** of the `Cloud Security Explorer` tab.
4. Click on the **search box** → Select "`Compute`" option on the left side → select a checkbox against "`Disks`" → click on the "`Done`" button. Then click on the "`Search`" button in the next screen. Refer to the following screenshot for visual understanding:

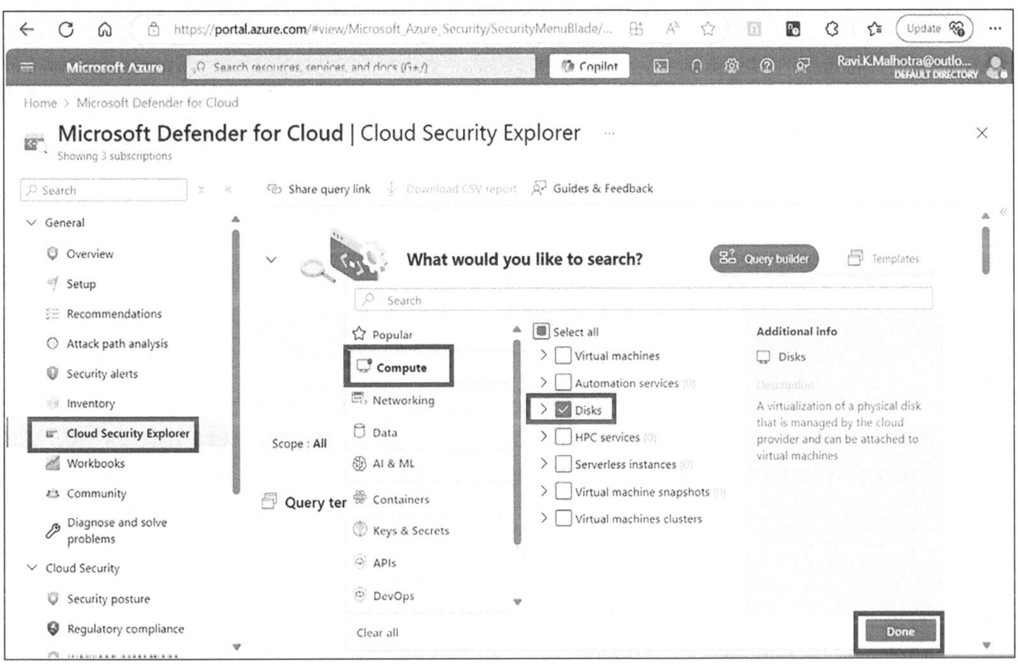

Figure 4.10: *Cloud Security Explorer Page*

5. Cloud Security Explorer will **scan and retrieve all active hard disks** across the **cloud platforms onboarded to `Microsoft Defender for Cloud`**. In this instance, it has identified **a total of five hard disks**. Refer to the following screenshot for a detailed view.

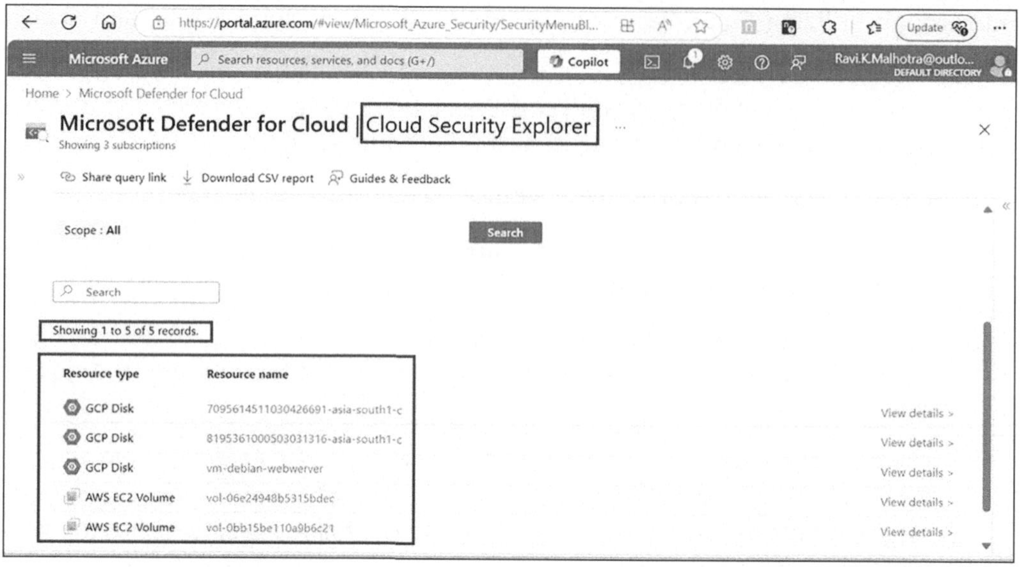

Figure 4.11: *Cloud Security Explorer - Hard Disk Findings*

6. **`Cloud Security Explorer`** is not only useful for discovering cloud assets, but also for identifying **active security recommendations and alerts** associated with specific resources. To explore this further, click on any **hard disk object** from the retrieved list.

   In this instance, I selected the **first hard disk detected from the GCP cloud**. Upon inspection, I found **one active security recommendation** titled: **"`Ensure VM disks for critical VMs are encrypted with a Customer-Supplied Encryption Key`."** Additionally, the **health status** of this disk is marked as **"`Unhealthy`"**, and the **risk level** is categorized as **"`Low`."**

   By leveraging **`Cloud Security Explorer`**, security teams can quickly pinpoint **misconfigurations, compliance issues, and potential vulnerabilities**, allowing for **proactive risk mitigation**. Refer to the following screenshot:

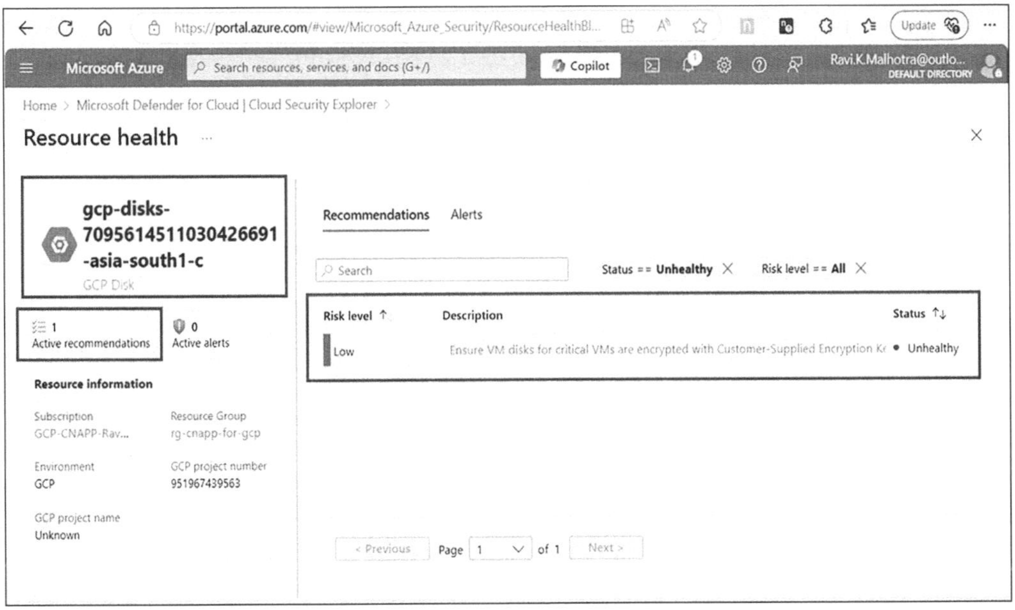

Figure 4.12: *Cloud Security Explorer - Active Recommendation for a Hard Disk*

7. You can also click on this active recommendation which will directly navigate you to its detailed recommendation page. Alternatively, you can go to the "**`Recommendations`**" page, and search for the same recommendation manually. Both methods will lead you to the same destination.

8. This concludes Lab 4.

Lab # 5: Discover Virtual Machines Using Cloud Security Explorer

Follow these steps to explore all the Hard Disks and the inventory across all your Azure subscriptions, as well as other connected cloud accounts and projects:

1. Log into the Azure portal using your administrative credentials.

2. Go to the search bar > type "**`Microsoft Defender for Cloud`**", and select the service to open the dashboard.

3. click on the "**`Cloud Security Explorer`**" button. Refer to the following screenshot which showcases the **default view** of the **`Cloud Security Explorer`** tab.

4. Click on the **search box** → Select "**`Compute`**" option on the left side → select a checkbox against "**`Virtual Machines`**" → click on the "**`Done`**" button. Then click on the "**`Search`**" button in the next screen.

5. **`Cloud Security Explorer`** will **scan and retrieve all active virtual machines** across the **cloud platforms onboarded to `Microsoft Defender for Cloud`**.
6. It will also display active security recommendations and alerts associated with specific virtual machines. You can manage these recommendations either by clicking on them directly, or by navigating to the **`Recommendations`** page.
7. This concludes the lab.

Lab # 6: Discover All Recommendations Only for Virtual Machines from Recommendations Page

In a cloud environment, **Virtual Machines (VMs)** are among the most critical assets, often holding sensitive workloads and data ensuring that their **security posture** is essential for preventing misconfigurations, vulnerabilities, and compliance risks. In this lab, we will use **Cloud Security Explorer** in **Microsoft Defender for Cloud** to **filter and discover security recommendations** that apply **exclusively to virtual machines** across **Azure, AWS, and GCP**. This hands-on approach will help you efficiently identify and address security gaps in your VM infrastructure.

Follow these steps to explore all the recommendations for Virtual Machines:

1. Log in to the Azure portal using your administrative credentials.
2. Navigate to the "**`Recommendations`**" tab in **`Microsoft Defender for Cloud`**.
3. In the search bar, type "**`Virtual Machine`**" and enable the "**`Group by title`**" option.
4. The results will now display **only the recommendations related to Virtual Machines** resources across your cloud environment.
5. Click on any **specific recommendation** to explore its details, remediation steps, and security insights.
6. In our instance, we observed approximately 23 active recommendations across all virtual machines in our environment. The following is a list of the recommendations visible in our setup:
   - Guest Attestation extension should be installed on supported Windows virtual machines.
   - IP forwarding on your virtual machine should be disabled.
   - Machines should have vulnerability findings resolved.

- Virtual Machines' Guest Configuration extension should be deployed with system-assigned managed identity.
- EDR configuration issues should be resolved on Virtual Machines(VMs).
- Machines should have secrets findings resolved.
- Management ports of VMs should be protected with just-in-time network access control.
- Secure Boot should be enabled on supported Windows Virtual Machines.
- EDR solution should be installed on VMs.
- Internet-facing VMs should be protected with network security groups.
- Ensure that IAM users are not assigned the **`Service Account User`** or **`Service Account Token Creator`** roles at the project level.
- vTPM should be enabled on supported virtual machines.
- Azure Backup should be enabled for virtual machines
- Windows virtual machines should enable **`Azure Disk Encryption`** or **`EncryptionAtHost`**.
- Management ports should be closed on your virtual machines.
- All network ports should be restricted on network security groups associated to your virtual machine.
- Virtual machines and virtual machine scale sets should have encryption at host enabled.
- Non-internet-facing virtual machines should be protected with network security groups.
- Virtual machines should be migrated to new Azure Resource Manager resources.

7. This concludes the lab.

Lab # 7: Exploring Security Posture, and Secure Score

Understanding your cloud security posture is necessary for identifying risks, ensuring compliance, and maintaining a strong defense against potential threats. Microsoft Defender for Cloud provides **a comprehensive view of your security posture** across Azure, AWS, and GCP, allowing security teams to monitor vulnerabilities, assess risk levels, and take corrective actions.

In this lab, we will explore **how to analyze the security posture** of your cloud environment, understand the key metrics displayed in **`Microsoft Defender for`**

`Cloud`, and interpret security scores and recommendations. By the end of this lab, you will be able to **assess and improve your organization's cloud security posture** effectively.

Follow these steps to explore the security posture and the Total Secure Score:

1. Log in to the **`Azure portal`** using your administrative credentials.
2. Navigate to the "**`Security Posture`**" option under "**`Cloud Security`**" tab in **`Microsoft Defender for Cloud`**.
3. The results will now display the aggregated **`Secure Score`** as a percentage across all onboarded cloud accounts and environments. It also categorizes recommendations by risk level, including **`Critical`**, **`High`**, **`Medium`**, and **`Low`**. Additionally, it provides individual **`Secure Scores`** for each cloud environment, such as **`AWS`**, **`Azure`**, and **`GCP`**. From this view, you also have the ability to manage and remediate recommendations directly. Refer to the following screenshot for visual understanding:

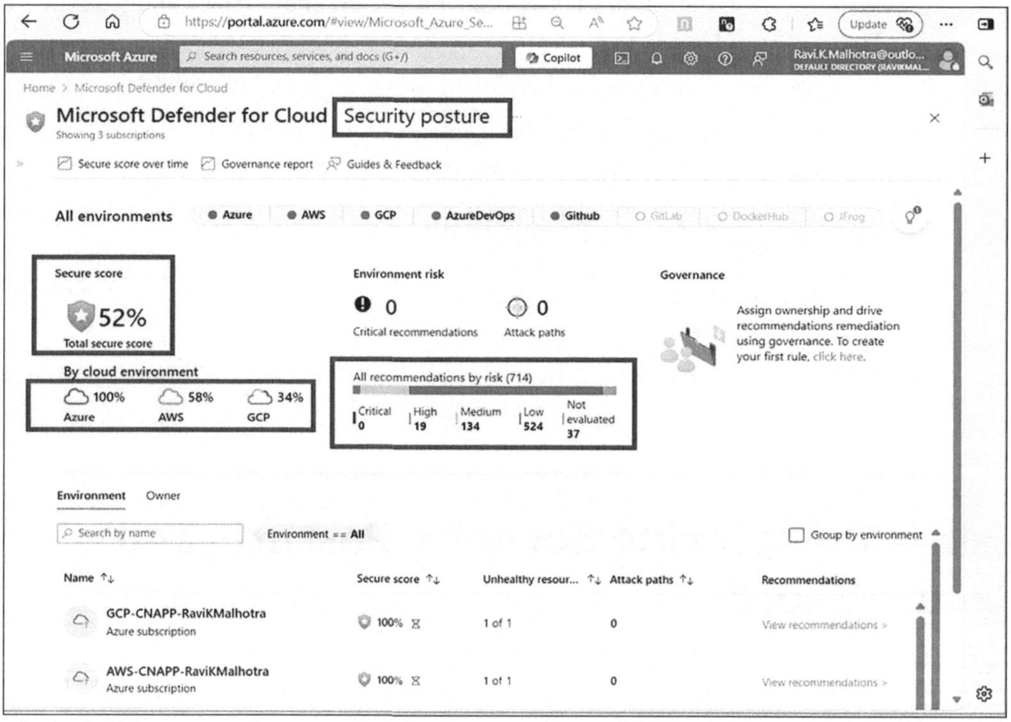

Figure 4.13: *Cloud Security Posture Default View*

4. As you can see, the aggregated **`Secure Score`** is **`52%`**. Additionally, the **`Secure Scores`** for individual cloud environments are displayed: **`Azure`** at **`100%`**, **`AWS`** at **`58%`**, and **`GCP`** at **`34%`**. You can also observe that there are a total of **714 active recommendations** across all cloud environments.

5. This concludes the lab.

Conclusion

In this chapter, we explored the fundamental concepts of Cloud Security Posture Management (CSPM), and its key components, gaining insights into how organizations leverage CSPM to strengthen their cloud security. We examined CSPM's role in the industry and took a deep dive into Microsoft Defender for Cloud as a powerful CSPM solution, highlighting its capabilities in securing multi-cloud environments. Additionally, we explored Cloud Security Explorer as an essential tool for cloud asset discovery, and risk analysis.

To reinforce these concepts, we included hands-on labs demonstrating real-world scenarios in Microsoft Defender for Cloud. By following these labs, you have gained practical experience in enabling CSPM, navigating security recommendations, discovering cloud inventory, analyzing attack paths, and automating security best practices. These skills are vital for securing cloud environments effectively.

In the next chapter, we will dive into **Cloud Workload Protection Platform (CWPP)** which focuses on securing virtual machines, containers, and serverless functions from runtime threats, vulnerabilities, and malware. As cloud workloads become more dynamic and distributed, understanding CWPP is necessary for a comprehensive cloud security strategy. Let us explore how CWPP strengthens workload security, and complements CSPM for end-to-end cloud protection.

Points to Remember

- **CSPM Fundamentals:** Cloud Security Posture Management (CSPM) is necessary for identifying misconfigurations, enforcing compliance, and maintaining cloud security across Azure, AWS, and GCP.
- **Microsoft Defender for Cloud as a CSPM Solution:** Microsoft Defender for Cloud provides both **Foundational CSPM** (default security posture management) and **Defender CSPM** (advanced risk-based security posture management).
- **Cloud Security Explorer:** A powerful tool in Defender for Cloud that enables deep security analysis, asset discovery, and identification of security risks across multi-cloud environments.
- **Attack Path Analysis:** A Defender CSPM feature that visualizes how attackers could exploit vulnerabilities, helping security teams prioritize critical security gaps.
- **Secure Score and Recommendations:** Defender for Cloud provides an aggregated **Secure Score** for all onboarded cloud environments and categorizes

security recommendations based on risk levels: **`Critical`**, **`High`**, **`Medium`**, and **`Low`**.

- **Hands-On Labs for Practical Learning**: The CSPM Labs provide step-by-step guidance on:
    a. Enabling and configuring **Foundational and Defender CSPM.**
    b. Understanding the next steps after enabling CSPM.
    c. Exploring cloud inventory to manage the discovered assets.
    d. Using **Cloud Security Explorer** for asset discovery and security insights.
    e. **Analyzing attack paths** to understand potential lateral movement risks.
    f. **Automating security best practices** to enhance cloud security posture.
    g. **Exploring Secure Score,** and managing security recommendations.
- **Multi-Cloud Visibility: `Microsoft Defender for Cloud`** supports **Azure, AWS, and GCP**, ensuring a unified security posture across different cloud environments.
- **Proactive Risk Mitigation:** CSPM helps security teams stay ahead of potential threats by continuously monitoring, identifying, and remediating security vulnerabilities, before they are exploited.

By mastering these concepts and completing the labs, you will gain hands-on experience in strengthening your cloud security posture, and leveraging CSPM effectively within Microsoft Defender for Cloud.

Multiple-Choice Questions

1. What is the primary role of CSPM in cloud security?
    a. Managing cloud billing
    b. Identifying and remediating cloud misconfigurations
    c. Deploying virtual machines
    d. Automating CI/CD pipelines
2. Which feature in Microsoft Defender for Cloud provides attack path visualization?
    a. Cloud Security Explorer
    b. Foundational CSPM

   c. Defender CSPM

   d. Secure Score

3. What does Secure Score in Microsoft Defender for Cloud represent?

   a. The financial cost of cloud security tools

   b. A metric to assess cloud security posture

   c. Thc numbcr of active subscriptions

   d. The total storage used in the cloud

4. Which CSPM feature allows security teams to search and analyze cloud assets?

   a. Cloud Security Explorer

   b. Defender for Endpoint

   c. Attack Path Analysis

   d. Azure Policy

5. What is the key benefit of using Defender CSPM over Foundational CSPM?

   a. It provides basic security monitoring.

   b. It offers proactive risk insights, and attack path analysis.

   c. It only works for Azure environments.

   d. It reduces cloud service costs.

Answers

1. b
2. c
3. b
4. a
5. b

Questions

1. What is the primary purpose of CSPM in cloud security?
2. How does Microsoft Defender for Cloud enhance CSPM capabilities?

3. What is the difference between Foundational CSPM and Defender CSPM?
4. How can Cloud Security Explorer help in identifying security risks?
5. What does Secure Score represent in Microsoft Defender for Cloud?

Key Terms

- **Cloud Security Posture Management (CSPM):** A set of security tools and practices designed to identify and remediate cloud misconfigurations.
- **Foundational CSPM:** The default, free-tier CSPM feature in Microsoft Defender for Cloud that provides basic security monitoring.
- **Defender CSPM:** The advanced CSPM tier offering proactive attack path analysis, and deeper security insights.
- **Attack Path Analysis:** A feature in Defender CSPM that visualizes how threats can propagate across cloud environments.
- **Security Recommendations:** Actionable security insights provided by Defender for Cloud to help mitigate risks, and enhance compliance.

CHAPTER 5

Understanding Cloud Workload Protection Platform (CWPP)

Introduction

Cloud Workload Protection Platforms (CWPPs) have become a critical component in securing cloud-native applications, providing **runtime** protection, **vulnerability** management, and **compliance** enforcement. Unlike traditional endpoint security solutions, CWPP is built to handle the dynamic nature of cloud computing.

In this chapter, we will explore CWPP concepts, technologies, and industry best practices, followed by hands-on labs, using Microsoft Defender for Cloud to implement both agent-based and agentless security for servers and serverless workloads.

CWPP is a security solution designed to protect workloads running in cloud environments, whether they are VMs, containers, or serverless functions.

To make this chapter more insightful, we have included **four (4) hands-on labs**, providing **live demonstrations**, using the **CWPP** module in **Microsoft Defender for Cloud.** These labs will help you gain **practical experience** in implementing the **Cloud Workload Protection Platform**, and exploring its key capabilities.

Structure

The following topics will be covered in this chapter:

- Concepts and Theories of CWPP
- Core Capabilities of CWPP
- Microsoft Defender for Cloud as a CWPP Solution

- CWPP Deployment Models
- Emerging Trends in CWPP
- Understanding WAAP
- How WAAP Complements CWPP
- Use Cases of WAAP in CWPP Context
- CWPP Labs

Concepts and Theories of CWPP

In today's rapidly evolving digital landscape, organizations are increasingly adopting cloud technologies to enhance scalability, flexibility, and efficiency. However, this shift to the cloud also brings new security challenges, necessitating robust solutions to protect cloud workloads.

Cloud Workload Protection Platforms (CWPP) have emerged as a critical component in the cybersecurity arsenal, designed to safeguard workloads such as **virtual machines**, **containers**, and **serverless functions** across diverse cloud environments.

CWPPs provide comprehensive security by integrating **multiple protective measures**, including **threat detection**, **vulnerability management**, and **compliance monitoring**. For example, a leading e-commerce company utilizing **CWPP** can **ensure the security of its customer data** and transaction processes by continuously monitoring its cloud workloads for potential threats. This proactive approach not only helps in identifying and mitigating risks in real-time, but also enhances customer trust and business reputation.

Another compelling use case is seen in the healthcare sector, where organizations must comply with stringent regulatory standards such as HIPAA. A healthcare provider can leverage CWPP to maintain compliance by automating the enforcement of security policies and conducting regular vulnerability assessments. This ensures that patient data remains secure and confidential while also reducing the administrative burden on IT teams.

CWPPs also offer the flexibility of agent-based and agentless protection, catering to different organizational needs and environments. Agent-based protection involves **deploying security agents** on individual workloads, **providing deep visibility and control**. For instance, a financial institution can use **agent-based CWPP** to monitor and protect its critical banking applications, ensuring that any anomalies are detected and addressed promptly.

On the other hand, **agentless protection leverages cloud-native APIs to secure workloads without the need for agents**, **making it ideal for dynamic and scalable**

environments. A tech startup, for example, can benefit from agentless CWPP by securing its rapidly evolving cloud infrastructure with minimal overhead.

The integration of advanced technologies such as artificial intelligence (AI) and machine learning (ML) further enhances the capabilities of CWPPs. These technologies enable more accurate threat detection and faster response times by analyzing vast amounts of security data and identifying patterns indicative of malicious activity. As organizations continue to embrace digital transformation, the role of CWPPs in ensuring robust cloud security will only become more pivotal.

In summary, Cloud Workload Protection Platforms are indispensable for modern enterprises seeking to secure their cloud environments. By providing comprehensive protection, ensuring compliance, and leveraging advanced technologies, CWPPs empower organizations to confidently navigate the complexities of cloud security. Whether it is an e-commerce giant, a healthcare provider, or a tech startup, CWPPs offer tailored solutions to meet the unique security needs of diverse industries.

Core Capabilities of CWPP

As organizations accelerate their cloud adoption, securing workloads across diverse environments has become a pressing challenge. **Traditional security approaches, designed for static, on-premises infrastructures, often fail to provide the dynamic, context-aware protection required in cloud-native ecosystems.** CWPPs bridge this gap by delivering a unified security framework **tailored for cloud workloads**, ensuring visibility, threat detection, and compliance across hybrid and multi-cloud landscapes.

There are many CWPP providers in the industry, but **Microsoft Defender for Cloud** stands at the forefront of CWPP solutions, leveraging **cutting-edge security analytics**, **automation**, and **AI-driven intelligence** to safeguard cloud resources.

By integrating seamlessly with Azure, AWS, and GCP, Defender for Cloud enables organizations to proactively mitigate threats, enforce security policies, and maintain regulatory compliance.

The following sections explore the **core capabilities** that make **CWPP** indispensable for modern cloud security.

- **Workload Visibility and Discovery:** CWPP solutions provide complete **visibility** into all cloud workloads, including **virtual machines**, **containers**, and **serverless functions**. This visibility **helps security teams identify unmanaged and rogue instances** that could pose security risks.

  By continuously **discovering and monitoring workloads**, organizations can maintain a **clear inventory** of assets. Additionally, **workload classification** based on metadata and labels ensures structured security enforcement. Enhanced visibility also enables tracking the workload lifecycle from deployment to decommissioning, ensuring comprehensive security oversight.

Defender for Cloud CNAPP **continuously scans workloads** across multi-cloud and hybrid environments, providing centralized visibility into all running assets, including virtual machines, Kubernetes clusters, containers, and serverless functions. It **identifies** security gaps, **classifies** resources based on **risk exposure**, and ensures compliance with security best practices. This real-time asset discovery helps organizations understand their attack surface and enforce security policies consistently.

- **Vulnerability Management:** A robust CWPP solution **scans** workloads **for vulnerabilities**, **misconfigurations**, and **outdated software**. By identifying security weaknesses before they can be exploited, organizations can proactively mitigate risks. These solutions often integrate with industry databases such as Common Vulnerabilities and Exposures (CVE) to stay updated on emerging threats. Automated patch management and remediation suggestions further streamline security operations.

  Additionally, vulnerability management extends to containerized workloads, ensuring images are free from known vulnerabilities before deployment. This continuous assessment minimizes security gaps and strengthens cloud defenses.

  Integrated with Microsoft Defender Vulnerability Management, the Defender for Cloud CNAPP solution identifies known vulnerabilities, outdated software, and misconfigurations within cloud workloads. By leveraging security baselines and compliance benchmarks, it prioritizes risks based on severity and exploitability. Automated threat intelligence feeds ensure up-to-date vulnerability detection, reducing the attack surface of critical cloud assets.

- **Runtime Protection:** Runtime protection ensures that workloads are **monitored for suspicious activity in real time. Behavioral analysis and anomaly detection identify deviations from normal operations, helping prevent unauthorized access and malware execution.**

  CWPP solutions often **use machine learning to analyze patterns and detect zero-day attacks.** Threat response mechanisms such as process whitelisting and integrity checks further enhance the security posture. Additionally, runtime protection includes memory scanning to detect in-memory threats that evade traditional detection methods. By continuously safeguarding workloads during execution, CWPP helps prevent sophisticated cyber threats.

  Defender for Cloud utilizes advanced behavioral analytics, machine learning, and anomaly detection to identify suspicious activities at runtime. It monitors process execution, network traffic, and system behaviors, alerting security teams about unauthorized access, privilege escalation, and lateral movement attempts. With deep integration into Microsoft Sentinel and SIEM tools, organizations can quickly correlate threats and respond to incidents in real time.

- **File Integrity Monitoring (FIM):** File Integrity Monitoring **(FIM) ensures that unauthorized changes to critical system files are detected and flagged.** This capability is essential for identifying unauthorized modifications caused by **malware, insider threats, or configuration drift.** FIM solutions monitor file access and changes, generating real-time alerts when anomalies are detected. Additionally, FIM extends to cloud storage services, ensuring data integrity across various environments. By maintaining a historical record of changes, **FIM supports forensic investigations and compliance reporting**.

  Defender for Cloud ensures workload integrity by implementing file integrity monitoring (FIM) and adaptive application controls. It tracks unauthorized modifications to system files, registry entries, and critical configurations, preventing malware execution and unauthorized software deployment. These security controls help organizations maintain a trusted workload environment and prevent unauthorized code execution.

- **Microservices Security and Protection:** Microservices architectures introduce complex security challenges, including increased attack surfaces, API exposure, and **risks associated with service-to-service communication**.

  Microsoft Defender for Cloud addresses these challenges by providing runtime threat detection, network segmentation, and behavioral monitoring to protect microservices workloads. It secures containerized applications and Kubernetes clusters by scanning container images for vulnerabilities, enforcing Zero Trust security policies, and preventing unauthorized API access. Defender for Cloud integrates with Azure Policy, Azure Firewall, and Microsoft Entra ID to ensure fine-grained access control and limit lateral movement between microservices.

  Additionally, its behavioral analytics and anomaly detection help identify compromised services, API abuse, and insider threats in real time. By combining agent-based runtime security with agentless vulnerability scanning, Defender for Cloud ensures comprehensive protection for microservices running across multi-cloud and hybrid environments.

- **Network Segmentation and Micro-Segmentation:** Micro-segmentation restricts workload communication to minimize the attack surface. By implementing fine-grained network segmentation, organizations can prevent lateral movement of threats within cloud environments. CWPP solutions enable policy-based segmentation, ensuring only authorized services communicate with each other. This approach significantly reduces the risk of widespread compromise in case of a breach. Additionally, micro-segmentation enhances zero-trust security by enforcing least privilege access between workloads. Automated policy enforcement and visualization tools help maintain and audit segmentation strategies effectively.

By integrating with Azure Firewall, Azure Policy, and network security groups (NSGs), Defender for Cloud enforces workload isolation and zero-trust network access. It dynamically segments workloads based on security policies, limiting lateral movement and reducing exposure to external threats. These capabilities are crucial for protecting workloads deployed across hybrid and multi-cloud environments.

- **Threat Intelligence Integration:** CWPP solutions leverage threat intelligence feeds to detect and mitigate known and emerging threats. By integrating with global threat databases, organizations gain insights into adversary tactics and techniques. This proactive approach enables security teams to anticipate and block attacks before they escalate. Additionally, CWPP solutions use machine learning models to analyze patterns and enhance threat detection accuracy. Continuous updates to threat intelligence ensure defenses remain effective against evolving cyber threats. Organizations can also customize threat feeds to align with their industry-specific risks, improving targeted threat response.
- **Compliance and Regulatory Assurance:** Ensuring cloud workloads adhere to regulatory standards is a critical aspect of CWPP. These solutions provide continuous compliance monitoring and generate audit-ready reports for frameworks such as CIS, NIST, and ISO 27001. Automated compliance assessments help identify gaps and provide remediation guidance. By enforcing security policies consistently across workloads, organizations reduce the risk of non-compliance penalties. Additionally, CWPP solutions facilitate security benchmarking to measure and improve overall security posture. Customizable compliance templates enable organizations to tailor security controls to their specific regulatory requirements.

  Defender for Cloud continuously assesses workloads against industry standards such as CIS benchmarks, NIST, PCI-DSS, and ISO 27001. It provides built-in compliance reports and security recommendations, allowing organizations to maintain regulatory compliance effortlessly. Automated remediation capabilities streamline security operations, reducing the burden of manual compliance enforcement.
- **Automated Response and Remediation:** Defender for Cloud integrates with Microsoft Defender XDR and Microsoft Sentinel to automate threat response workflows. Security teams can configure playbooks for automatic remediation of detected threats, such as quarantining compromised workloads, blocking malicious IPs, or revoking access permissions. These automated actions enhance security efficiency and minimize response times.

Microsoft Defender for Cloud as a CWPP Solution

After understanding the core capabilities of Microsoft Defender for Cloud as a Cloud Workload Protection Platform (CWPP), the next step is to operationalize these capabilities effectively across your cloud environments. **Defender for Cloud** provides a **modular**, **agent-based**, and **agentless** approach to securing workloads, ensuring organizations can tailor their deployment to fit hybrid and multi-cloud strategies.

Here is how organizations can start using Microsoft Defender for Cloud as a CWPP solution:

1. **Enable Microsoft Defender for Cloud Plans:** Begin by activating Defender for Cloud Plans for your subscription, management group, or organization. The Defender for Servers plan is particularly critical, as it provides vulnerability assessment, file integrity monitoring, Endpoint Detection and Response (EDR), and advanced threat protection features for cloud workloads.

   Similarly, plans such as Defender for Kubernetes, Defender for Containers, and Defender for App Service extend protection to containerized and serverless workloads.

   Tip: *Defender for Cloud offers free trial capabilities for basic posture management. Activating Defender Plans unlocks CWPP capabilities.*

2. **Integrate Multi-Cloud Workloads:** Microsoft Defender for Cloud **natively** supports Azure environments, but you can also onboard **AWS** and **GCP** accounts using built-in connectors. This integration ensures that workloads running outside Azure receive the same level of visibility, threat detection, and compliance assessment.

   AWS and GCP assets are discovered automatically, and Defender for Cloud agents (or agentless scanning) extend protection seamlessly.

3. **Deploy Defender Agents and Extensions:** For deep workload protection, deploy the **Log Analytics agent** (**Azure Monitor Agent** for newer deployments) on **virtual machines** and **servers**. These agents **enable** Defender for Cloud to **collect** security signals, perform vulnerability scanning, enable file integrity monitoring, and apply security baselines.

   Note: *Some lightweight capabilities such as agentless container scanning and vulnerability discovery are also available if agent deployment is not feasible.*

4. **Configure Security Recommendations and Policies**

   Defender for Cloud automatically generates **security recommendations**, based on your workload configurations and detected vulnerabilities. Organizations can customize these recommendations, create **custom policies**, and apply them at scale, using **Azure Policy**.

Defining policies around encryption, network controls, identity configurations, and resource hardening help enforce consistent workload security practices across clouds.

5. **Enable Continuous Vulnerability Assessment**

   Use integrated **vulnerability management** tools such as Microsoft Defender Vulnerability Management or integrated partner solutions to perform ongoing vulnerability assessments.

   Continuous scanning ensures that newly discovered vulnerabilities or misconfigurations are promptly identified and remediated, before they are exploited.

6. **Monitor Runtime Behavior and Threat Detection**

   Runtime protection capabilities such as **behavioral analytics**, **anomaly detection**, **process monitoring**, and **network traffic analysis** are activated, once workloads are onboarded.

   Defender for Cloud continuously monitors workload behavior, and raises alerts for:

   - Unauthorized access attempts
   - Privilege escalations
   - Malware execution
   - Suspicious network traffic
   - File system anomalies

   These insights are natively integrated with Microsoft Sentinel or third-party SIEMs for efficient incident response.

7. **Automate Threat Response and Remediation**

   Defender for Cloud allows you to create **automation rules** and **playbooks** (via Azure Logic Apps) to respond to detected threats automatically. The common actions include:

   - Isolating compromised workloads
   - Quarantining suspicious files
   - Revoking access to sensitive resources
   - Triggering alerts and escalation workflows

Automation minimizes that the time attackers have to exploit vulnerabilities, and reduces the burden on security teams.

8. **Maintain Compliance and Governance**

   Defender for Cloud continuously assesses cloud resources against regulatory standards such as **CIS Benchmarks**, **NIST**, **PCI-DSS**, and many more.

   Built-in compliance dashboards and **audit-ready reports help organizations** prove **compliance during audits, and streamline the ongoing governance activities.**

   Tip: *You can customize compliance initiatives to match your specific regulatory obligations and industry standards.*

Using Microsoft Defender for Cloud as a CWPP involves a combination of smart onboarding, workload protection activation, continuous monitoring, and automation. By leveraging its integrated capabilities, organizations can effectively protect workloads running across Azure, AWS, GCP, and hybrid infrastructures from modern cloud threats.

CWPP Deployment Models

CWPP solutions can be deployed in different ways, and Microsoft Defender for Cloud offers flexible deployment options to cater to various security needs.

- **Agent-Based Deployment with Microsoft Defender for Cloud:** Agent-based CWPP solutions utilize **Microsoft Defender for Cloud's security agents**, which are installed on workloads such as virtual machines, Kubernetes nodes, and containers. These agents provide **deep telemetry**, enabling real-time threat detection, behavioral analytics, and process monitoring. Defender for Cloud's agent-based protection offers features such as adaptive application controls, file integrity monitoring, and Just-in-Time (JIT) access control. While agent-based deployments provide granular visibility and control, they require ongoing management, updates, and resource consumption on protected workloads. This model is **best suited for enterprises needing in-depth security coverage for mission-critical workloads** that handle the sensitive data or are frequently targeted by cyber threats.
- **Agentless Deployment with Microsoft Defender for Cloud:** The **agentless** approach in **Microsoft Defender for Cloud** leverages cloud-native integrations with Azure and multi-cloud environments **to scan and assess** security risks, **without deploying agents**. This model is particularly **useful** for **identifying misconfigurations**, **vulnerabilities**, and **compliance violations** at scale across hybrid and multi-cloud deployments. Defender for Cloud provides security posture management and vulnerability scanning through API-based

integrations, allowing organizations to enforce security policies, without impacting workload performance. However, agentless solutions primarily focus on at-rest scanning, and lack the runtime monitoring capabilities of agent-based deployments. This deployment model is ideal for organizations seeking a low-maintenance approach to cloud security, while ensuring regulatory compliance.

- **Hybrid Deployment with Microsoft Defender for Cloud:** Many organizations adopt a hybrid CWPP deployment strategy, leveraging both agent-based and agentless security features of Microsoft Defender for Cloud. This approach enables security teams to balance performance, visibility, and operational efficiency. For example, enterprises can deploy security agents on high-risk workloads such as production databases and critical application servers while using agentless scanning for broader security posture management. Hybrid deployments are particularly beneficial in multi-cloud environments where different workloads may have varying security requirements. By integrating both models, Defender for Cloud ensures organizations have a comprehensive defense mechanism that adapts to their evolving cloud security landscape.
- **Security for Microservices in Kubernetes and Serverless Environments:** Securing microservices workloads in Kubernetes and serverless environments requires a combination of agent-based and agentless security to provide comprehensive visibility and runtime protection. Agent-based security, as implemented in Microsoft Defender for Cloud, deploys security agents on Kubernetes nodes and containerized workloads to enable deep runtime monitoring, behavioral analytics, and process integrity checks. This approach provides granular telemetry, allowing security teams to detect anomalies, enforce container security policies, and respond to threats in real time. However, for serverless workloads and ephemeral microservices, where deploying an agent may not be feasible, Defender for Cloud's agentless security leverages API-based scanning and continuous configuration assessments. It analyzes function permissions, identifies exposed secrets, and monitors event-driven behavior, without impacting workload performance. By combining agent-based protection for deep runtime security and agentless scanning for broad risk assessments, Defender for Cloud ensures robust microservices security across hybrid and multi-cloud environments.

Emerging Trends in CWPP

As cloud adoption continues to accelerate, Cloud Workload Protection Platforms (**CWPP**) are also **evolving** to meet **new and more complex security needs**. Organizations are no longer just looking for basic workload protection – **they need smarter, faster, and more automated solutions** that can keep up with dynamic cloud environments. To address these challenges, CWPP solutions such as Microsoft Defender for Cloud are **integrating advanced** technologies such as **AI/ML-based threat detection**, **Zero Trust security models**, **CSPM integration**, **automated security orchestration**, and **deeper protections for containers and serverless workloads**.

These trends are shaping the future of cloud security, helping businesses stay ahead of sophisticated threats, while improving operational efficiency. In this section, we will explore the key emerging trends in CWPP, and how they are being applied in real-world scenarios.

- **AI/ML-Based Threat Detection: AI-driven threat detection models** within Microsoft Defender for Cloud **analyze** vast amounts of **workload telemetry** to **identify abnormal patterns**, and **predict attacks** before they occur. These models can detect sophisticated threats such as **fileless malware** and **insider threats** in real time, reducing false positives, and improving response efficiency.

  Use case: Financial institutions can leverage AI-based detection to identify unauthorized transactions or anomalous user behavior in cloud workloads.

- **Zero Trust Security:** Defender for Cloud **incorporates Zero Trust principles** by enforcing **least privilege** access controls, **continuous verification**, and **strict segmentation** policies for cloud workloads. It ensures that only authenticated and authorized identities interact with workloads, minimizing the attack surface.

  Use case: Enterprises hosting multi-tenant SaaS applications can use Zero Trust workload protection to prevent unauthorized access between tenants.

- **Integration with CSPM: Microsoft Defender for Cloud integrates CWPP with CSPM capabilities to provide a holistic security approach.** This allows organizations to continuously monitor cloud configurations, enforce compliance policies, and detect misconfigurations that could lead to breaches.

  Use case: A healthcare organization can ensure HIPAA compliance by automatically identifying and remediating security misconfigurations in cloud workloads.

- **Automated Security Orchestration and Remediation:** Defender for Cloud's integration with Microsoft Sentinel enables automated threat remediation through security playbooks. These playbooks can isolate compromised workloads, block malicious IPs, and revoke unauthorized permissions automatically, reducing response time and manual effort.

  Use case: E-commerce businesses can automatically mitigate DDoS attacks by dynamically adjusting network security policies, when anomalies are detected.

- **Container and Serverless Security Enhancements:** With the rise of microservices, Defender for Cloud extends its capabilities to secure containerized and serverless workloads. It scans container images for vulnerabilities, applies runtime protection, and ensures function-level security for serverless applications.

  Use case: DevOps teams can implement automated security scanning in CI/CD pipelines to ensure only secure container images are deployed.

Understanding WAAP

As organizations move their applications to the cloud, securing these applications becomes just as important as protecting cloud workloads. While Cloud Workload Protection Platforms (CWPP) focus on securing virtual machines, containers, serverless functions, and databases, **there is another essential layer of protection needed for cloud-native applications themselves – this is where WAAP comes into play.**

WAAP stands for **Web Application and API Protection**. It is a modern security solution that protects web applications and APIs from cyberattacks. In today's world, most businesses run critical services through web portals, mobile apps, and exposed APIs. Attackers often target these endpoints to steal data, disrupt services, or gain unauthorized access. A WAAP acts as a front-line defense, ensuring that applications and APIs are not only accessible, but also secure.

When combined with CWPP, WAAP completes the cloud security picture. CWPP secures the backend infrastructure – the workloads and compute resources – while WAAP protects the front-facing services that users interact with. Both are essential for building a truly resilient cloud security architecture.

Importance of WAAP in Cloud Environments

In the past, organizations would install a traditional Web Application Firewall (WAF) in their on-premises data centers to protect their websites. However, cloud-native applications are distributed, elastic, and dynamic. Traditional WAFs cannot keep up with the changing landscape of APIs, serverless functions, and microservices.

WAAP is designed for this modern reality: It does not just block known attack patterns – it uses machine learning to detect unusual behavior, protects against new threats such as API abuse, and automatically adapts as the application changes.

Some of the major attack types WAAP helps to protect against include:

- **SQL Injection** (injecting malicious database commands)
- **Cross-Site Scripting (XSS)** (injecting malicious scripts into websites)
- **API Abuse** (overuse, misuse, or unauthorized access of APIs)

- **Bot Attacks** (automated programs trying to exploit applications)
- **DDoS Attacks** (overwhelming a service to make it crash)

In cloud workloads, securing APIs is particularly critical because microservices heavily depend on APIs to talk to each other. If an API is compromised, an attacker could move deeper into the environment, making the job of CWPP much harder.

WAAP and CWPP: A Unified Defense for Modern Applications

CWPP and WAAP serve different – yet equally important – roles in cloud security. CWPP is responsible for the internal protection of workloads such as virtual machines, containers, serverless functions, and databases. WAAP, on the other hand, protects the surface where users, APIs, and applications interact with the cloud. To achieve full protection in modern cloud-native environments, organizations need both. This section explains how WAAP complements CWPP, and why this combination is necessary.

Internal versus External Security: A Dual Approach

CWPP focuses on safeguarding the internal environment. It ensures that the workloads running inside the cloud are secure, free from vulnerabilities, and protected from malicious behavior. It monitors runtime activities, detects anomalies within workloads, and stops lateral movement between systems, if an attacker gains a foothold.

WAAP, however, is built to protect what is exposed to the world – your web applications, APIs, and traffic entering your cloud from the internet. It ensures only safe, valid, and authorized interactions are allowed to reach your cloud workloads. It defends against common web application threats such as SQL injection, cross-site scripting (XSS), API abuse, and bot attacks.

Together, CWPP and WAAP provide what is known as **defense in depth** – a layered security approach. Think of CWPP as the security guard inside your building, and WAAP as the security system at the entrance gate. They work together to block attackers both at the perimeter and within the system.

Real-Life Analogy: Home Security

Imagine your cloud environment is like a smart home. CWPP secures the rooms, valuables, and devices inside the house. It makes sure everything is running correctly, alerts you if something unusual happens, and locks down internal doors if needed.

WAAP acts like your video doorbell, alarm system, and smart locks on the front door and windows. It ensures only trusted people can come in. It blocks package thieves (bots), keeps track of who entered when (API logs), and alerts you when someone tries to force open the door (attack attempts).

If you only have CWPP, attackers might be able to walk through an unguarded front door (an exposed API). If you only have WAAP, an attacker who has already slipped in could roam freely inside your home. Both are essential for complete safety.

Why Integration Matters

In real-world cloud environments, attackers are constantly targeting web-facing applications and APIs. These applications are often the entry point. WAAP ensures that only sanitized, authorized traffic gets through, stopping attacks before they reach the internal workloads.

CWPP takes over once traffic enters the system. It watches how that traffic behaves inside, catches suspicious patterns, stops malware from spreading, and isolates impacted components. When WAAP and CWPP are integrated into a platform such as Microsoft Defender for Cloud, they share intelligence, giving security teams a unified view of threats and allowing faster, automated responses.

For example:

- **Use Case 1:** A retail company using Azure might expose APIs for its mobile shopping app. WAAP can inspect and block malicious API calls, while CWPP ensures the backend services handling those calls are hardened and safe.
- **Use Case 2:** A finance app may be targeted by credential stuffing bots. WAAP can detect and block the bots. If one slips through, CWPP can catch abnormal behavior inside the VM or container, and stop further damage.
- **Use Case 3:** During a zero-day vulnerability exploit on a popular web framework, WAAP applies virtual patching to block exploit attempts, while CWPP monitors the workloads for any signs of compromise.

A Modern and Unified Security Approach

Today's cloud-native applications use microservices, serverless functions, APIs, and containers – all running in dynamic, distributed environments. No single security layer is enough.

WAAP and CWPP are not competing solutions – they are complementary technologies. When combined, **they close the gaps in cloud security by protecting both what is outside and inside your cloud.** Platforms such as Microsoft Defender for Cloud aim to bring these capabilities under one roof, making it easier for teams to manage, detect, and respond to threats in real time.

As cyber threats continue to evolve, adopting a dual approach to security becomes not just a best practice, but a necessity. Together, WAAP and CWPP help ensure that your cloud environment is secure, resilient, and ready to support business innovation, without compromise.

Use Cases of WAAP in CWPP Context

As organizations move their applications to the cloud, protecting these applications from web-based threats becomes essential. Web Application and API Protection (WAAP) plays a critical role in securing cloud workloads by guarding web apps and APIs against attacks such as SQL injection, cross-site scripting (XSS), and bot abuse. Within the CWPP framework, WAAP extends protection beyond just virtual machines and containers – it adds a vital layer of defense for application-layer workloads. In this section, we will explore practical use cases where WAAP complements CWPP strategies, ensuring cloud applications remain resilient, compliant, and secure in real-world environments.

Here are a few simple real-world scenarios where WAAP and CWPP work hand-in-hand:

- **Protecting a Public-Facing API:** An e-commerce company has its backend workloads (databases, inventory systems) protected by CWPP. But its APIs (for customers to browse products) are publicly exposed. WAAP protects these APIs from abuse, such as credential stuffing or scraping attacks, ensuring attackers cannot compromise the workloads via API vulnerabilities.
- **Blocking Malicious Traffic Before It Reaches Workloads:** A financial services app faces heavy bot traffic attempting to exploit vulnerabilities. WAAP detects and blocks the bots at the edge, before they can even reach the app's workloads. Meanwhile, CWPP continues to monitor internal workloads for anomalies.
- **Securing a Dynamic Microservices Architecture:** A healthcare application uses hundreds of microservices talking over APIs. Defender for Cloud (CWPP) ensures the container workloads are secure and compliant, while WAAP continuously secures API endpoints, ensuring that no broken authentication or injection vulnerabilities are exploited.
- **Handling Zero Day Threats:** When a new web application vulnerability (a zero day) is discovered, WAAP can apply virtual patching – blocking attacks before developers even fix the code – while CWPP ensures that the workloads running the vulnerable applications are isolated and monitored for any suspicious activity.

In a modern cloud security strategy, CWPP and WAAP are not optional – they are essential partners.

CWPP defends what runs inside the cloud (virtual machines, containers, serverless apps), while WAAP defends what is exposed to the outside world (websites, mobile apps, APIs).

Without WAAP, attackers can find easy entry points through exposed apps and APIs, bypassing even the strongest CWPP protections.

Without CWPP, even if WAAP blocks known attacks, misconfigured workloads can still be exploited from inside.

In simple terms, **WAAP guards the gate, CWPP guards the kingdom**. **Together, they provide the full, end-to-end security that cloud-native applications need today.**

CWPP Labs

The best way to understand Cloud Workload Protection Platforms (CWPP) is by putting concepts into practice. This section is dedicated to helping you experience CWPP firsthand using Microsoft Defender for Cloud. Hence, whether you are a cloud security enthusiast, an IT professional, or someone preparing for real-world deployments, these labs are designed to walk you through core protection features in a guided and practical way.

CWPP plays a crucial role in securing workloads such as virtual machines, containers, web applications, and serverless functions across hybrid and multi-cloud environments. But it is not enough to just read about it—getting hands-on is where you will truly see how CWPP identifies risks, protects assets, and responds to threats in real time.

Each lab in this section builds on the previous one, starting from basic enablement of CWPP capabilities, and then gradually moving towards deeper insights such as workload visibility, vulnerability assessments, just-in-time access, and more. You will be guided through the Azure portal step-by-step with screenshots and explanations, using a real or test subscription to explore key features without the need for any advanced setup or local tools.

These labs are based on actual practices followed by cloud security professionals and align closely with how Microsoft Defender for Cloud implements CWPP. They will give you the confidence to explore and secure workloads in a real cloud environment—learning not just what to do, but why it matters.

Let us get started with the hands-on journey into CWPP!

Lab # 1: Setting Up Microsoft Defender for Cloud as a CWPP

Setting up Microsoft Defender for Cloud as a **CWPP** is the **first and most crucial step** in securing your cloud environments. This lab will guide you through **enabling core Defender capabilities** to protect **virtual machines**, **containers**, and **serverless workloads**. Following these simple steps, you will establish a strong security foundation that supports workload protection across hybrid and multi-cloud platforms:

1. Log into the Azure portal, using your administrative credentials.

2. Go to the search bar > type "**Microsoft Defender for Cloud**", and select the service to open the dashboard.

3. Once inside the dashboard, locate the "**Environment Settings**" tab on the left-hand menu.

4. Expand **Azure**, and then expand **Tenant Root Group**, which is a management group.

5. Here, you will see all your active subscriptions detected by **Microsoft Defender for Cloud**, along with the currently active plans.

6. Select the relevant **Azure subscription**.

7. To enable Cloud Workload Protection (CWPP) features, ensure that the following modules, along with their associated submodules, are turned **ON** under the **Cloud Workload Protection (CWP)** section. If any module is not enabled, toggle it ON to activate full protection.

   - **Defender for Servers** (For virtual machines and server workloads)
   - **Defender for App Service** (for web application)
   - **Defender for Containers** (for Kubernetes and container workloads)

8. We have now successfully enabled all the three modules in the desired subscription within our **Microsoft Defender for Cloud** instance. Refer to the following screenshot for confirmation:

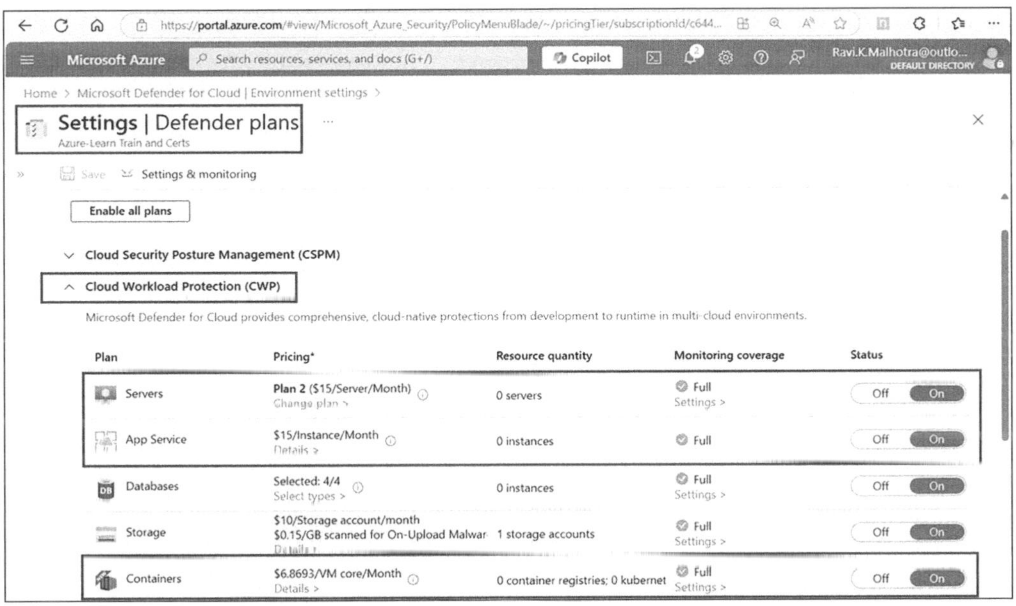

Figure 5.1: *Enabling All Modules to Get the CWPP Protection*

9. After ensuring these modules are active, click on the **`Save`** button.
10. Now, click on the "**`Settings and monitoring`**" option within the same subscription. Refer to the following screenshot for a graphical reference:

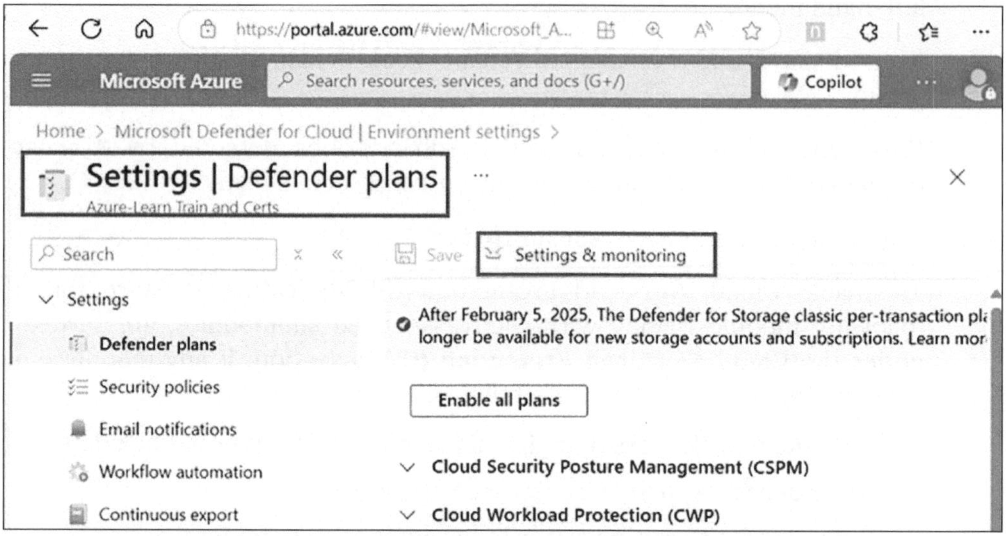

Figure 5.2: *Settings and Monitoring Option*

11. Inside the "**`Settings and monitoring`**" section, ensure that all the following features are shown as **`Enabled`** for the effective functioning of CWPP.
12. In our instance of Microsoft Defender for Cloud, all these features are currently enabled:
    - Vulnerability assessment for machines
    - Guest Configuration Agent (preview)
    - Endpoint protection
    - Agentless scanning for machines
    - Malware scanning
    - Kubernetes API access
    - File Integrity Monitoring
    - API Security Posture Management
13. Once these modules are enabled, Microsoft Defender for Cloud will begin delivering full **Cloud Workload Protection Platform (CWPP)** functionality, providing critical security insights for **Virtual Machines, Containers,** and **Serverless Workloads.**
14. This concludes the lab.

Lab # 2: Exploring Workload Protection

In the previous lab, we focused on enabling key Cloud Workload Protection (CWPP) modules within Microsoft Defender for Cloud to lay the foundation for workload security.

Now that the protection features are active, it is time to see them in action.

In this lab, we will explore how Defender for Cloud monitors and protects different types of workloads in real time. We will create a set of sample resources, including a Windows and Linux virtual machine, a web application, a container instance, and a serverless Azure Function. Then, we will validate how Defender for Cloud detects these workloads, assesses their security posture, and generates useful recommendations.

This hands-on lab will help you experience how CWPP works in a real-world cloud environment, offering continuous visibility and protection for critical business workloads.

1. Log into the Azure portal using your administrative credentials.
2. Go to the search bar > type "**`Microsoft Defender for Cloud`**", and select the service to open the dashboard.
3. Click on the "**`Workload Protection`**" option located under the "**`Cloud Security`**" section on the left-hand side of the screen.
4. As soon as you open **Workload Protection**, you will see a summary view displaying the number and types of workloads detected by the CWPP module. In our instance of **`Microsoft Defender for Cloud`**, a total of **9 workloads** were detected – including **1 storage account**, **2 containers**, **3 Azure virtual machines**, and **3 subscriptions**.
5. The dashboard also highlights the **protection status** across workloads, showing:
    - o The percentage of workloads fully protected by CWPP,
    - o Workloads missing agents,
    - o Workloads not yet covered.
6. In our case, Defender for Cloud reports **100% full CWPP coverage** for all detected workloads. Refer to the following screenshot for visual reference:

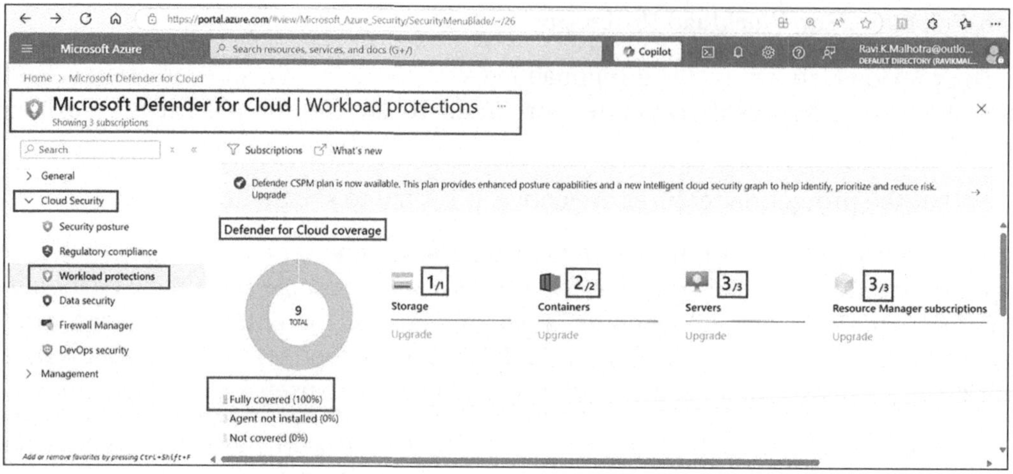

Figure 5.3: *Cloud Workload Protection Screen*

7. This concludes the lab.

Lab # 3: Exploring Workloads Requiring Vulnerability Assessments Panel under CWPP

In the previous labs, we successfully enabled the essential CWPP modules and explored the visibility CWPP provides across different workloads such as virtual machines, containers, storage accounts, and serverless resources.

With full workload protection achieved, we now move deeper into understanding **how CWPP handles vulnerability management**, an important aspect of securing cloud workloads.

In this lab, we will focus on evaluating how Microsoft Defender for Cloud identifies workloads that require a vulnerability assessment solution.

One of CWPP's critical strengths is its native integration of vulnerability management for virtual machines, reducing the need for separate third-party solutions.

In our environment, Defender for Cloud has detected three healthy virtual machines, all of which are already covered without requiring additional vulnerability assessment tools.

This demonstrates **how CWPP simplifies vulnerability management by offering built-in protection, ensuring workloads are secure and compliant**, without extra configuration efforts. Please follow these steps to explore how Microsoft Defender for Cloud identifies workloads for vulnerability assessments:

1. Log into the Azure portal, using your administrative credentials.
2. Go to the search bar > type "`Microsoft Defender for Cloud`", and select the service to open the dashboard.

3. Click on the "**Workload Protection**" option located under the "**Cloud Security**" section on the left-hand side of the screen.
4. Once you open **Workload Protection**, scroll down to the bottom of the page and locate the "**Advanced Protection**" section. Refer to the following screenshot:

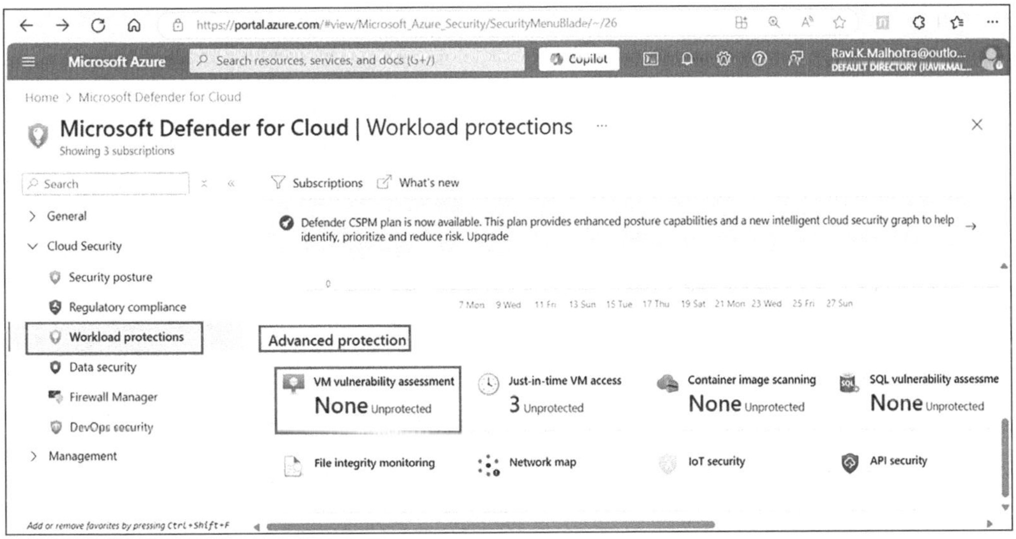

Figure 5.4: *Advanced Protection Section under Workload Protection*

5. Under **Advanced Protection**, find the subsection named "**VM vulnerability assessment**" and click on it. This will take you to a new screen where you can view any related recommendations, their severity levels, the number of affected resources, and the suggested remediation steps.
6. In our instance of Microsoft Defender for Cloud, the "**VM vulnerability assessment**" section shows "**None**", meaning no virtual machines currently require an external vulnerability assessment solution. All virtual machines are natively protected by CWPP features.
7. If you click on **Healthy resources** under the **Affected resources** tab, you will see **three (3) virtual machines** listed, confirming that Defender for Cloud's native protection is fully active. Refer to the following screenshot:

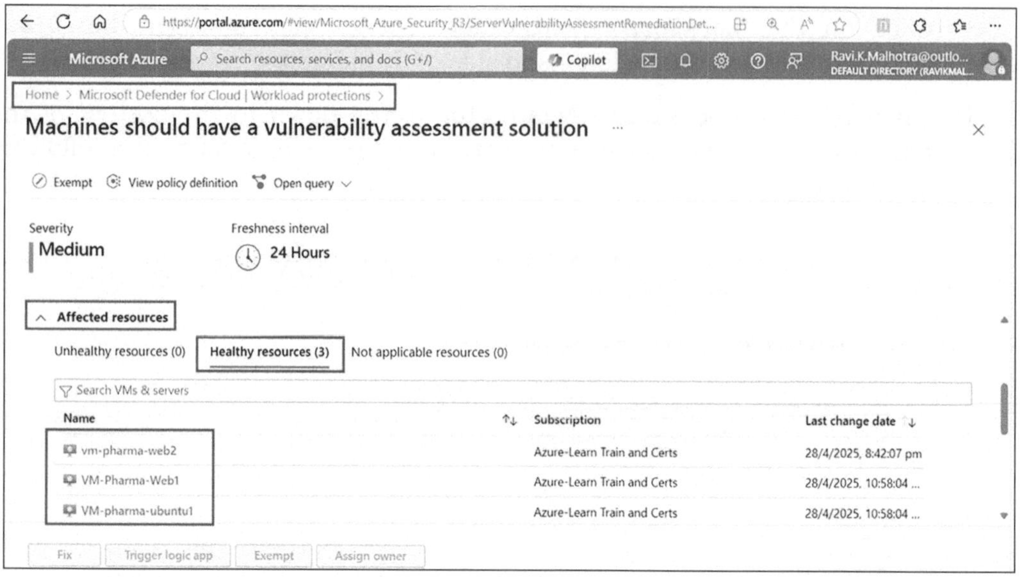

Figure 5.5: *Vulnerability Assessment Panel under CWPP Advanced Protection*

8. **This clearly dictates that the CWPP modules simplify vulnerability management** by offering **built-in protection**, **ensuring workloads are secure and compliant**, without extra configuration efforts.
9. This concludes the lab.

Lab # 4: Exploring Just-In-Time VM AccessPanel under CWPP

In the previous labs, we explored **how Cloud Workload Protection (CWPP) detects and secures various workloads** and **ensures native vulnerability protection** for virtual machines, **without requiring additional solutions**.

Now, in this lab, we will focus on another important CWPP capability – **Just-In-Time (JIT) Access** for virtual machines.

JIT access enhances security by **reducing the exposure of your VMs to the Internet**.

Instead of leaving management ports such as SSH (port 22) or RDP (port 3389) open all the time, JIT access locks these ports, and opens them only for a limited time when an authorized user requests it.

This **minimizes the attack surface**, and helps **protect against threats such as brute-force attacks**. In our instance of Microsoft Defender for Cloud, **CWPP has detected three virtual machines eligible for JIT configuration**.

In this lab, we will explore how JIT access works, check the list of VMs where it can be enabled, and understand its importance in protecting cloud workloads.

1. Log into the Azure portal, using your administrative credentials.

2. Go to the search bar > type "**`Microsoft Defender for Cloud`**", and select the service to open the dashboard.

3. Click on the "**`Workload Protection`**" option located under the "**`Cloud Security`**" section on the left-hand side of the screen.

4. Once you open **`Workload Protection`**, scroll down to the bottom of the page, and locate the "**`Advanced Protection`**" section. Refer to the following screenshot:

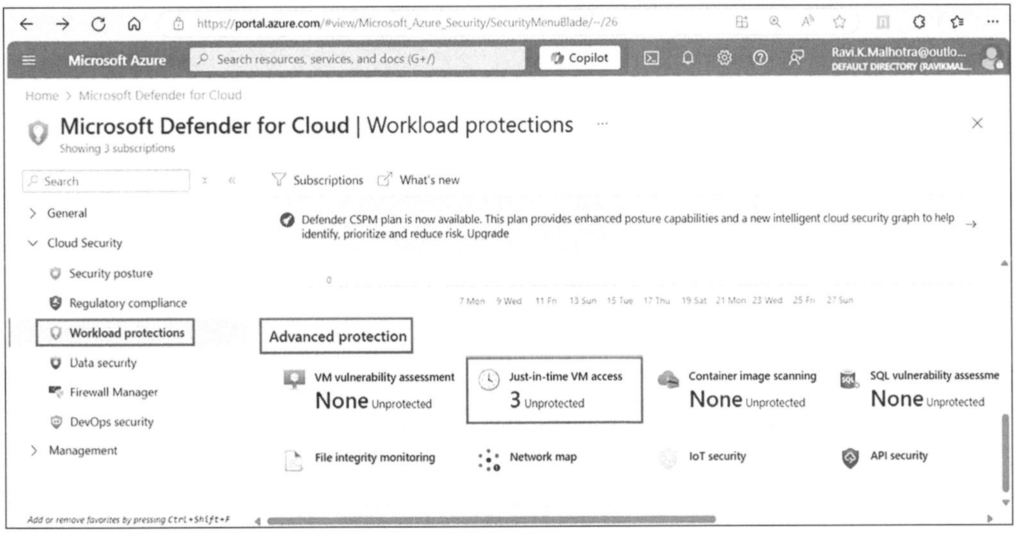

***Figure 5.6**: Advanced Protection Section under Workload Protection - Just-In-Time VM Access*

5. Under the **`Advanced Protection`** section, locate the subsection labeled "**`Just-In-Time VM access`**." This panel displays the number of workloads that are currently **not protected using JIT access**. When you click on it, you will be redirected to a detailed view that shows which virtual machines are configured with JIT access, and which ones are not.

6. To examine the unprotected VMs, go to the "**`Not Configured`**" tab. This section provides comprehensive details such as the **hostnames** of the virtual machines, their respective **resource groups**, **subscription names**, and the **reasons** why JIT access is not yet applied.

7. In our instance of **`Microsoft Defender for Cloud`**, the **Just-in-Time VM access section indicates a total of three (3) virtual machines** that are currently not configured with JIT protection. By selecting the "**`Not Configured`**" tab, we can clearly see the list of these machines.

8. Enabling **Just-in-Time access for virtual machines is a crucial security control** that significantly reduces exposure to brute force and unauthorized

access attacks by allowing access only when needed, and only for a limited time.

9. **This not only enhances security posture, but also aligns with Zero Trust principles by ensuring least privilege and Just-in-Time access control for sensitive cloud workloads.**

Refer to the following screenshot for a visual walkthrough:

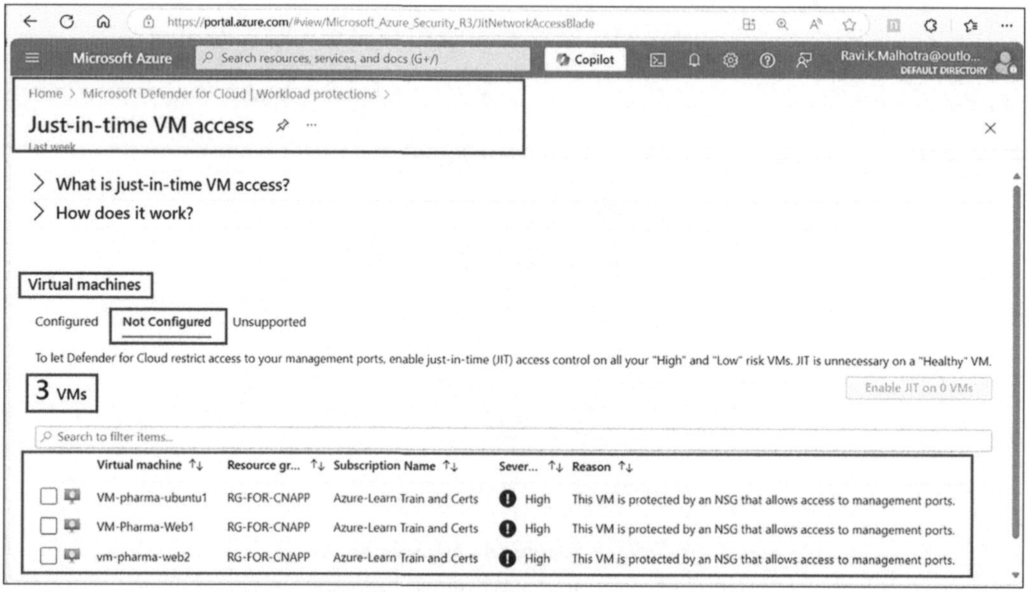

***Figure 5.7:** Just-in-Time VM Access Advanced Protection under CWPP*

10. This concludes the lab.

Conclusion

Cloud Workload Protection Platforms (CWPPs) have become a cornerstone of modern cloud security strategies. As organizations continue to adopt multi-cloud, hybrid, and serverless architectures, the need for unified workload protection has never been more critical. Throughout this chapter, we explored how CWPP solutions – particularly Microsoft Defender for Cloud – provide comprehensive visibility, advanced threat protection, and continuous monitoring for a wide range of workloads, including virtual machines, containers, App Services, and serverless functions.

We began by understanding the key concepts behind CWPP: Securing workloads across different environments, without relying on traditional network boundaries. We then explored how Microsoft Defender for Cloud enables CWPP capabilities by offering agent-based and agentless protections, native vulnerability management, workload detection, Just-in-Time access controls, and integration with threat intelligence as well as automation systems.

Through our practical labs, we saw how easy it is to enable CWPP features, monitor the protection status of workloads, review vulnerability assessments, and implement security best practices such as Just-in-Time access. Each lab reinforced the idea that CWPP is not just about deploying tools – it is about maintaining continuous visibility, reducing the attack surface, and enabling intelligent, proactive security actions.

Emerging trends such as AI/ML-based threat detection, Zero Trust principles for workloads, integration with Cloud Security Posture Management (CSPM), and automated security orchestration show that CWPP solutions are rapidly evolving. Microsoft Defender for Cloud stands at the forefront of these innovations, helping organizations simplify and strengthen their cloud security posture.

To close, CWPP is no longer optional for businesses operating in the cloud. It is a must-have layer that ensures that cloud-native applications, legacy systems, and serverless services are secure, resilient, and compliant.

By understanding and implementing CWPP effectively, security teams can confidently manage risks, defend against advanced threats, and support business growth in the dynamic world of cloud computing.

As we conclude our deep dive into Cloud Workload Protection Platforms (CWPP), and their practical implementation using Microsoft Defender for Cloud, it is evident how crucial workload security is in today's cloud-native environments. From protecting virtual machines to securing serverless functions and containers, CWPP provides the foundational defense layer for cloud workloads. However, securing workloads alone is not enough–controlling who has access to what, and ensuring that access follows the principle of least privilege, is equally critical. In the next chapter, we shift our focus to **Cloud Infrastructure Entitlement Management (CIEM)**. This emerging domain helps organizations manage and govern cloud identities and permissions at scale, reducing the risks of over-permissioned accounts, and potential insider threats. Get ready to explore how CIEM solutions–especially within Microsoft Defender for Cloud–enhance your cloud security posture by tightening access controls across multi-cloud environments.

Points to Remember

Here are some **key points to remember** from this chapter on **Understanding Cloud Workload Protection Platform (CWPP)**:

- **Cloud Workload Protection Platform (CWPP)** protects workloads such as virtual machines, containers, serverless applications, and more, across cloud and hybrid environments.

- **Microsoft Defender for Cloud** acts as a CWPP solution by providing threat detection, vulnerability management, and security recommendations for a wide range of workloads.
- **Enabling CWPP features requires turning on key modules** such as **Defender for Servers**, **Defender for App Services**, and **Defender for Containers** under the Cloud Workload Protection (CWP) section.
- **Workload visibility is crucial:** CWPP automatically discovers and categorizes all workloads, whether they are servers, containers, or serverless resources.
- **Agent-based and agentless protections** are both supported. Auto-provisioning ensures that workloads get protected without manual agent installation in many cases.
- **Vulnerability assessments** are natively integrated for supported VMs, minimizing the need for third-party tools, unless specifically recommended.
- **Just-in-Time (JIT) access can be enabled to protect virtual machines** by allowing access only when needed, thereby reducing exposure to attacks.
- **Emerging trends such as AI/ML-driven detection**, **Zero Trust security**, and **automated security orchestration** are shaping the future of CWPP.
- **Integration with Cloud Security Posture Management (CSPM)** offers a more complete security posture for cloud resources.
- **CWPP capabilities extend beyond just servers** – it also includes **containers**, **serverless functions**, **web applications**, and **APIs**.

Multiple-Choice Questions

1. What is the primary goal of Cloud Workload Protection Platform (CWPP)?
    a. To manage billing and subscriptions in the cloud
    b. To protect cloud-based workloads such as VMs, containers, and serverless apps
    c. To create cloud storage accounts
    d. To monitor network traffic
2. In Microsoft Defender for Cloud, which module provides protection for virtual machines?
    a. Defender for Storage
    b. Defender for Servers

c. Defender for Containers

d. Defender for Databases

3. What does enabling Just-in-Time access on a virtual machine help to achieve?

a. Faster scaling of VMs

b. Immediate deletion of VMs

c. Reducing unnecessary exposure to attacks by limiting access windows

d. Allowing permanent open access to VMs

4. Which of the following is an emerging trend in CWPP?

a. Manual patch management

b. Zero-trust security models

c. Traditional perimeter-based firewalls

d. Manual user provisioning

5. If a VM is showing under "**`Healthy Resources`**" in the Vulnerability Assessment panel of Defender for Cloud, what does it mean?

a. The VM needs a new OS installed.

b. The VM requires a third-party security tool.

c. The VM is protected, and does not require any additional vulnerability assessment installation.

d. The VM is offline.

Answers

1. b
2. b
3. c
4. b
5. c

Questions

1. What does CWPP stand for in cloud security architecture?
2. Which Microsoft Defender for Cloud module provides protection for container workloads?
3. What is the primary benefit of enabling Just-in-Time VM access?
4. Which CWPP capability helps detect vulnerabilities in virtual machines, without installing agents?
5. How does CWPP help in applying the principle of least privilege?
6. What is the role of workload visibility in CWPP?
7. Which cloud-native resource can be used to demonstrate serverless protection in CWPP?
8. Which section in Defender for Cloud provides the percentage of workloads covered by CWPP?
9. Which type of malware can CWPP detect, using AI-based threat models?
10. How does CWPP integrate with CSPM to enhance the overall cloud security?

Key Terms

- **Cloud Workload Protection Platform (CWPP):** A security solution that protects workloads across virtual machines, containers, serverless, and more.
- **Microsoft Defender for Cloud:** A comprehensive CNAPP solution by Microsoft that includes CWPP and CSPM capabilities.
- **Workload Protection:** The process of securing cloud-hosted workloads such as VMs, containers, and serverless applications.
- **Agent-Based Protection:** A method of protection where a lightweight agent is installed on workloads to collect telemetry, and enforce security.
- **Agentless Scanning:** Security scanning performed without installing an agent, ideal for compliance and visibility.
- **Just-in-Time (JIT) VM Access:** A security feature that locks down ports on VMs, and allows access only for a limited time and approved users.
- **Vulnerability Assessment:** The process of identifying and evaluating vulnerabilities in workloads to mitigate risks.
- **File Integrity Monitoring (FIM):** Tracks changes to files and alerts on unauthorized or suspicious modifications.

- **Zero Trust Security Model:** A security framework that assumes a breach, and enforces least privilege access continuously.
- **Container Security:** The protection of containerized environments, including image scanning and runtime protection.
- **Serverless Workload Protection:** Securing functions and APIs in serverless platforms such as Azure Functions.
- **Workload Visibility:** The ability to see and monitor all workload resources within a cloud environment.
- **Advanced Protection:** Additional capabilities provided by Defender for Cloud such as malware scanning, endpoint protection, and API security.
- **Recommendation Engine:** A feature in Defender for Cloud that provides actionable security recommendations for workloads.
- **Resource Health:** An indicator of whether workloads are secured, partially secured, or not covered by CWPP.

CHAPTER 6

Understanding Cloud Infrastructure Entitlement Management (CIEM)

Introduction

As cloud technology continues to transform how organizations operate, securing cloud environments has become more crucial than ever. This chapter takes you on a journey into Cloud Infrastructure Entitlement Management (CIEM), a key component of modern cloud security. We will start by covering the basics of Identity and Access Management (IAM), setting the stage for a deeper dive into CIEM. Our aim is to help you understand how to effectively manage and secure cloud entitlements. Combining theory with practical labs, this chapter provides a comprehensive look at IAM and CIEM. We will begin by breaking down the core concepts of IAM, focusing on its role in controlling access to cloud resources, and ensuring proper permission assignments. Then, we will explore CIEM, showcasing its advanced features for granular control and visibility over cloud entitlements. This chapter is designed to be both educational and interactive, with hands-on labs that let you apply the concepts in real-world scenarios.

Hence, whether you are a seasoned security professional or new to cloud security, the insights and exercises here will equip you with the tools to protect your cloud assets from unauthorized access and potential threats. By the end of this chapter, you will have a solid understanding of IAM and CIEM, empowering you to implement these critical security measures in your own cloud environments.

To make this chapter more insightful, we have included a total of **nine (9) hands-on labs**, providing **live demonstrations** using **Microsoft Defender for Cloud** across **Azure, AWS, and GCP**. These labs will help you gain **practical experience** in implementing

CIEM, and exploring its key capabilities. The following is the list of **all hands-on demonstrations covered in this chapter:**

- **IAM Lab # 1:** Creating a Group and User Accounts, and assigning a Policy in AWS, Azure and GCP
- **IAM Lab # 2:** Enable Multi-Factor Authentication (MFA) in AWS, Azure and GCP
- **CIEM Lab # 1:** Enabling the CIEM Module in Microsoft Defender for Cloud for the Azure Environment
- **CIEM Lab # 2:** Enabling the CIEM Module in Microsoft Defender for Cloud for the AWS Environment
- **CIEM Lab # 3:** Enabling the CIEM Module in Microsoft Defender for Cloud for the GCP Environment
- **CIEM Lab # 4:** Navigating Inventory to Discover IAM related Resources from Azure, AWS and GCP cloud platforms
- **CIEM Lab # 5:** Navigating Recommendations Page for CIEM related Insights
- **CIEM Lab # 6:** Explore all Recommendations and List Down all for CIEM Entities (Users/Groups and Roles)
- **CIEM Lab # 7:** Explore the Recommendation - "MFA *should be enabled for all* IAM *users*"

These labs are designed to **bridge the gap between theory and real-world application**, enabling you to **strengthen cloud security posture** across **multi-cloud environments**.

Structure

In this chapter, the following topics will be covered:

- Understanding Identity and Access Management (IAM)
- IAM Services in the Cloud
- IAM Best Security Practices across AWS, Azure, and GCP
- Future Trends in IAM
- IAM Labs (2 Labs)
- Understanding CIEM
- Compliances and Governance in CIEM
- CIEM Labs (7 Labs)
- CIEM – SIEM – SOAR: Enhancing Cloud Security

Understanding Identity and Access Management (IAM)

Identity and Access Management (IAM) is essential for securing digital identities, and controlling access to resources. It helps organizations to protect the sensitive data, comply with regulations, and improve operational efficiency. This section explores IAM's core components, technologies, and best practices.

IAM is a comprehensive framework of policies, processes, and technologies that facilitates the management of digital identities, and regulates access to resources. IAM is pivotal in safeguarding sensitive information, ensuring regulatory compliance, and streamlining operational workflows.

By implementing robust IAM practices, organizations can mitigate security risks, prevent unauthorized access, and enhance user productivity. The concept of IAM has undergone significant transformation over the decades. Initially, IAM systems were designed to manage user identities within the confines of an organization, primarily focusing on employee access to internal systems.

With the proliferation of cloud computing, mobile devices, and remote work, **IAM has expanded its scope to encompass external users such as partners and customers, as well as a diverse array of devices.**

This evolution has made IAM an indispensable element of modern cybersecurity strategies, addressing the complexities of today's digital landscape.

Core Components of IAM

Identity and Access Management (IAM) ensures that the right individuals access the right resources securely.

Its core components–Identity Lifecycle Management, Access Control, Authentication and Authorization, as well as Identity Governance–work together to protect organizational assets and maintain compliance.

1. **Identity Lifecycle Management:** This encompasses the entire journey of a digital identity within an organization, from creation to deactivation. This process includes onboarding new users, managing changes to their roles, access privileges, and securely deactivating accounts when users depart.
2. **Access Control:** Access control is a critical component of IAM that defines who can access the specific resources, and under what conditions. It includes various models such as **Role-Based Access Control (RBAC)** which assigns permissions based on user roles, and **Attribute-Based Access Control (ABAC)** which uses user attributes to determine access rights.

Implementing stringent access control policies helps protect sensitive information, and ensures compliance with regulatory standards.

3. **Authentication and Authorization:** Authentication is the process of verifying a user's identity, while authorization determines the resources a verified user can access. Authentication methods range from traditional passwords to advanced biometrics, and Multi-factor Authentication (MFA). Authorization mechanisms ensure that users can only access resources they are permitted to, based on their roles and permissions, thereby safeguarding organizational assets.

IAM Technologies and Tools

Identity and Access Management (IAM) is a critical framework that ensures secure and efficient access to technology resources. By managing digital identities, and controlling their access, IAM helps organizations protect the sensitive data, comply with regulations, and streamline operations.

This section delves into the **essential components**, **technologies, and best practices of IAM** to provide a comprehensive understanding of its significance.

- **Directory Services:** These are the **backbone of IAM**, providing a **centralized repository** for storing and managing information about users, devices, and other resources. These services enable efficient management, and retrieval of the identity data.

  For example, **Microsoft Active Directory (AD)** is widely used in enterprises to manage user accounts, computers, and security policies. AD allows administrators to create and manage domains, users, and objects within a network, ensuring that only authorized users can access the specific resources.

  Another example is **LDAP (Lightweight Directory Access Protocol)** which is an open, vendor-neutral protocol for accessing and maintaining distributed directory information services over an IP network.

  Azure Active Directory (Azure AD) extends these capabilities to the cloud, offering identity management and access control for cloud-based applications. Here is a list of top Directory Services providers in the industry.

- **Single Sign-On (SSO):** The SSO enhances the user experience by allowing users to **authenticate once, and gain access to multiple applications and systems, without needing to log in again**. This not only simplifies the login process, but also improves security by reducing the number of password users need to remember and manage. For instance, a company using SSO can enable employees to access email, CRM systems, and other business applications with a single set of credentials.

- **Multi-Factor Authentication (MFA):** The MFA adds an extra layer of security by **requiring users to provide two or more verification factors to gain access to a resource**. These factors can include something the user knows (a password), something the user has (a security token or smartphone), and something the user is? (Biometric verification such as a fingerprint or facial recognition.
- **Privileged Access Management (PAM):** The PAM focuses on controlling and monitoring access to critical systems and sensitive information by privileged users, such as system administrators and IT staff. The PAM solutions help organizations enforce the principle of least privilege, ensuring that users have the minimum level of access necessary to perform their tasks.

IAM Processes and Best Practices

Effective Identity and Access Management (IAM) is necessary for keeping an organization's digital assets secure. By setting up strong procedures for giving and taking away access, using role-based access controls and managing policies well, organizations can make sure that access rights are correctly assigned and maintained.

Regular reviews and audits of access rights help to find and fix any potential security issues. In this section, we will look at the key processes and best practices that are the foundation of a strong IAM strategy.

- **User Provisioning and De-provisioning:** User provisioning is the process of creating user accounts and granting access to resources, based on their roles and responsibilities within the organization. This involves setting up new accounts, assigning appropriate permissions, and ensuring that users have access to the tools and information, they need to perform their duties. Automated provisioning systems can streamline this process, reducing the time and effort required to onboard new employees.

  De-provisioning, on the other hand, involves revoking access and disabling accounts, when users leave the organization or change roles. This is a critical step in maintaining security, as it ensures that former employees or those who no longer require certain access cannot exploit their previous permissions. Automated de-provisioning systems can quickly and efficiently remove access, reducing the risk of unauthorized access and potential data breaches.
- **Role-Based Access Control (RBAC):** The RBAC is a method of managing access to resources by assigning permissions based on user roles within the organization. This approach simplifies access management by grouping users with similar responsibilities and granting them the same access rights. For example, all members of the IT department might have access to network management tools, while marketing personnel have access to Customer Relationship Management (CRM) systems.

- **Policy Management:** This involves defining, implementing, and enforcing access policies that govern how identities are managed and how access is granted within the organization. These policies should align with organizational goals, security requirements, and regulatory standards. Effective policy management ensures that security measures are consistently applied, and that access controls are aligned with business objectives.

  For example, an organization might implement a policy requiring Multi-factor Authentication (MFA) for accessing the sensitive data. This policy would mandate that users provide two or more verification factors such as a password and a fingerprint scan, to gain access. Another policy might require regular password changes, and enforce complexity requirements to enhance security. By clearly defining and communicating these policies, organizations can ensure that all users understand and adhere to security protocols.

- **Access Reviews and Audits:** Regular access reviews and audits are essential for maintaining the integrity of IAM systems. Access reviews involve periodically checking user access rights to ensure they are still appropriate based on current roles and responsibilities. This process helps identify and address any discrepancies such as users retaining access to resources, they no longer need.

  Audits, on the other hand, involve examining access logs and other records to detect any anomalies or unauthorized access attempts. Conducting regular audits helps organizations identify potential security issues, and take corrective actions.

IAM Services in The Cloud

Cloud Infrastructure Entitlement Management (CIEM) has emerged as a cornerstone of modern cloud security, addressing the challenges posed by identity sprawl, and permission over-provisioning.

In the cloud, where identities and permissions scale rapidly, traditional manual approaches to managing access become impractical and error-prone. CIEM provides the tools to automate entitlement discovery, enforce least privilege principles, and monitor access patterns in real-time.

By bridging the gap between security teams and cloud operations, CIEM not only reduces risk but also ensures compliance with evolving regulatory standards. It is the glue that holds secure identity management together in the dynamic cloud ecosystem.

Managing digital identities and their corresponding entitlements has become a cornerstone of securing cloud environments. With the vast array of services, tools, and technologies available across major cloud platforms, organizations face both opportunities and challenges in maintaining control over access.

Each cloud provider–AWS, Azure, and GCP–offers robust IAM services tailored to address these needs, ensuring secure, efficient, and compliant operations. In this section, we will explore the essential IAM services offered by these leading platforms, shedding light on how they enable organizations to safeguard their digital ecosystems.

Practical Knowledge: IAM Services Offered in AWS

Amazon Web Services (**AWS) Identity and Access Management (IAM) is a powerful tool that enables organizations to securely manage access to AWS services and resources.** AWS IAM allows administrators to create and manage AWS users and groups, and to set permissions that control which AWS resource users and applications can access.

This section will provide a practical guide to using AWS IAM, highlighting its key features and best practices for effective implementation. Here is a list of IAM tools and services available in AWS:

S. No.	AWS IAM Services	Description
1	**AWS Identity and Access Management**	Core service for managing access to AWS resources, including user and group management, roles, and policies.
2	**AWS Single Sign-On (SSO)**	Centrally manages SSO access to multiple AWS accounts and business applications.
3	**AWS Directory Service**	Provides multiple ways to use Microsoft Active Directory with other AWS services, including AWS Managed Microsoft AD, AD Connector, and Simple AD.
4	**AWS Organizations**	Centrally manages and governs your environment as you grow and scale your AWS resources.
5	**AWS Resource Access Manager (RAM)**	Enables you to share your resources with any AWS account or within your AWS Organization.
6	**AWS Secrets Manager**	Protects access to your applications, services, and IT resources by managing secrets.
7	**AWS Key Management Service (KMS)**	Creates and controls cryptographic keys used to encrypt your data.
8	**AWS Cognito**	Provides user sign-up, sign-in, and access control to web and mobile apps.

9	**AWS Control Tower**	Sets up and governs a secure, multi-account AWS environment based on AWS best practices.
10	**AWS CloudTrail**	Enables governance, compliance, and operational and risk auditing of your AWS account.
11	**AWS Config**	Provides AWS resource inventory, configuration history, and configuration change notifications.
12	**AWS Security Hub**	Provides a comprehensive view of your high-priority security alerts and compliance status across AWS accounts.

Table 6.1: *IAM Tools and Services Offered by AWS*

These tools and services help you manage identities, control access, and ensure security and compliance within your AWS environment.

Practical Knowledge: IAM Services Offered in Azure

In the realm of cloud computing, Microsoft Azure stands out with its comprehensive suite of Identity and Access Management (IAM) services. Azure IAM provides robust tools to manage user identities, control access to resources, and ensure compliance with regulatory requirements. By leveraging services like Azure Active Directory, Role-Based Access Control, and Multi-Factor Authentication, organizations can secure their cloud environments, and streamline access management processes.

This section delves into the practical aspects of implementing IAM in Azure, highlighting the key features and best practices. Here is a table listing IAM-specific services for Azure:

S. No.	Azure IAM Services	Description
1	**Azure Active Directory (Azure AD)**	Comprehensive identity and access management service with SSO, MFA, and conditional access.
2	**Azure Role-Based Access Control (RBAC)**	Fine-grained access management of Azure resources based on user roles.
3	**Azure Multi-Factor Authentication (MFA)**	Adds an extra layer of security by requiring multiple forms of verification.
4	**Azure Privileged Identity Management**	Manages, controls, and monitors access to important resources within Azure.
5	**Azure AD B2C**	Identity management for consumer-facing applications.

6	**Azure AD B2B**	Facilitates collaboration with external partners using their own credentials.
7	**Azure Managed Identities**	Simplifies identity management for applications running on Azure.
8	**Azure Key Vault**	Safeguards cryptographic keys and secrets used by cloud applications and services.
9	**Azure AD Identity Protection**	Detects and responds to potential identity risks using adaptive machine learning.
10	**Azure AD Conditional Access**	Enforces access controls based on specific conditions like user location or device compliance.

Table 6.2: *IAM Tools and Services Offered by Azure*

These tools and services help you manage identities, control access, and ensure security and compliance within your AWS environment.

Practical Knowledge: IAM Services Offered in GCP

Google Cloud Platform (GCP) offers a powerful set of Identity and Access Management (IAM) services designed to provide fine-grained control over access to cloud resources. GCP IAM enables administrators to define who can do what on which resources, ensuring secure and efficient access management. This section explores the practical implementation of IAM in GCP, focusing on its unique features and best practices. Here is a table listing IAM-specific services for GCP:

S. No.	GCP IAM Services	Description
1	**Google Cloud Identity**	Central identity management service with SSO, MFA, and user lifecycle management.
2	**GCP IAM Roles and Policies**	Manages access to resources using predefined and custom roles and policies.
3	**GCP Multi-Factor Authentication (MFA)**	Enhances account security by requiring additional verification factors.
4	**GCP Cloud Identity-Aware Proxy**	Secures access to applications by verifying user identity and context.
5	**GCP Service Accounts**	Provides identities for applications and services to interact with GCP resources securely.
6	**GCP Organization Policy Service**	Defines and enforces policies for GCP resources.

7	**GCP Access Transparency**	Provides visibility into actions taken by Google staff when accessing your data.
8	**GCP Access Context Manager**	Defines fine-grained access control policies based on attributes like device security status and IP address.
9	**GCP Cloud Key Management Service**	Manages cryptographic keys for cloud services.
10	**GCP Cloud Audit Logs**	Tracks and logs all administrative activities and access to GCP resources for compliance and security monitoring.

Table 6.3: *IAM Tools and Services Offered by GCP*

These tools and services help you manage identities, control access, and ensure security and compliance within your AWS environment.

IAM Best Security Practices Across AWS, Azure and GCP

As organizations increasingly move to the cloud, ensuring secure and efficient management of identities and access is more important than ever. Whether operating within AWS, Azure, or Google Cloud Platform, a well-implemented Identity and Access Management (IAM) strategy is necessary to protecting cloud-based resources. Each cloud provider has its own IAM framework, yet the overarching goal remains the same: To control and restrict access to resources based on user roles and privileges. In this section, we will dive into the security best practices for IAM across AWS, Azure, and GCP, offering actionable insights on how to enforce least privilege, secure user authentication, and maintain a vigilant approach to monitoring and auditing access to critical cloud environments.

Embrace the Principle of Least Privilege (PoLP)

- **AWS:** Equip your IAM users and roles with only the permissions they need to complete their tasks.
- **Azure:** Implement Azure Role-Based Access Control (RBAC) with narrowly scoped roles.
- **GCP:** Apply predefined roles or create custom roles with granular permissions, steering clear of overly permissive roles like "`Owner`."

Practice	AWS	Azure	GCP
Use least privilege permissions	☑	☑	☑
Audit roles and assignments	☑	☑	☑

Table 6.4: *Principle of Least Privilege across Azure, AWS and GCP*

The Multi-Factor Authentication (MFA) Mandate

- **AWS:** Enforce MFA for all users, including root accounts. Set up hardware-based MFA devices for extra security.
- **Azure:** Use Conditional Access policies to enforce MFA, ensuring all privileged accounts are protected.
- **GCP:** Mandate MFA via Identity Platform or Security Keys, especially for administrators.

Practice	AWS	Azure	GCP
Enforce MFA for all users	☑	☑	☑
Use hardware-based MFA	☑	☑	☑

Table 6.5: *MFA Policies across Azure, AWS and GCP*

Rotate, Rotate, Rotate

- **AWS:** Automate access key rotation using AWS Secrets Manager or Lambda functions.
- **Azure:** Use Azure Key Vault to manage and rotate secrets, certificates, and keys.
- **GCP:** Rotate service account keys regularly using Cloud IAM API, and limit their usage.

Practice	AWS	Azure	GCP
Automate key rotation	☑	☑	☑
Use secret management service	☑	☑	☑

Table 6.6: *Key Rotation Policies across Azure, AWS and GCP*

The "`No Hardcoding`" Commandment

- **AWS:** Replace hardcoded credentials with AWS SDKs and IAM roles for EC2.
- **Azure:** Use Managed Identities to authenticate resources, without storing credentials in code.
- **GCP:** Leverage Application Default Credentials (ADC) for seamless authentication.

Practice	AWS	Azure	GCP
Replace hard coded credentials	☑	☑	☑
Use managed identities	☑	☑	☑

Table 6.7: *Managed Identities Settings across Azure, AWS and GCP*

Centralized Identity Management

- **AWS:** Integrate AWS IAM with AWS Single Sign-On (SSO) and Active Directory.
- **Azure:** Use Azure Active Directory (AAD) to unify access and streamline governance.
- **GCP:** Federate identities, using Google Workspace or third-party IdPs for centralized control.

Practice	AWS	Azure	GCP
Integrate with central directory	☑	☑	☑
Use SSO for unified access	☑	☑	☑

Table 6.8: *Centralized Identity Management across Azure, AWS and GCP*

Log and Audit Everything

- **AWS:** Enable CloudTrail and configure it to send logs to an S3 bucket for centralized analysis.
- **Azure:** Use Azure Monitor and Azure Activity Logs to track identity-related events.
- **GCP:** Turn on Cloud Audit Logs, and export them to BigQuery for deeper insights.

Practice	AWS	Azure	GCP
Enable activity logging	☑	☑	☑
Centralize log analysis	☑	☑	☑

Table 6.9: *Logging Policies across Azure, AWS and GCP*

Prepare for the Worst

- **AWS:** Designate an emergency account with MFA and strict access controls for disaster recovery.
- **Azure:** Implement a "`break glass`" global administrator account with secure access procedures.
- **GCP:** Keep a secure emergency access group and document its usage.

Practice	AWS	Azure	GCP
Create emergency accounts	☑	☑	☑
Secure break-glass procedures	☑	☑	☑

Table 6.10: *Emergency Access Policies across Azure, AWS and GCP*

Policy Guardrails are a Must

- **AWS:** Leverage Service Control Policies (SCPs) in AWS Organizations to enforce compliance.
- **Azure:** Use Azure Policy to restrict resource creation, and enforce identity standards.
- **GCP:** Employ Organization Policies to enforce IAM and security constraints.

Practice	AWS	Azure	GCP
Enforce policies to restrict access	☑	☑	☑
Use governance frameworks	☑	☑	☑

Table 6.11: *Organization Level Policies across Azure, AWS and GCP*

Automate Remediation

- **AWS:** Use Config rules and Lambda functions to auto-remediate non-compliant IAM configurations.
- **Azure:** Set up Azure Security Center workflows for automatic remediation.
- **GCP:** Deploy Cloud Functions to fix misconfigurations in real-time.

Practice	AWS	Azure	GCP
Auto-remediate non-compliance	☑	☑	☑
Use cloud-native workflows	☑	☑	☑

Table 6.12: *Automated Remediation Policies across Azure, AWS and GCP*

1. **Test Like a Hacker**
    - **AWS:** Run IAM Access Analyzer to uncover over-permissioned roles and resources.
    - **Azure:** Use tools like Azure AD Identity Secure Score to assess, and enhance security.
    - **GCP:** Analyze IAM policies with the Policy Troubleshooter, and simulate attacks with IAM Recommender.

Practice	AWS	Azure	GCP
Analyze permissions with tools	☑	☑	☑
Simulate attacks to validate security	☑	☑	☑

Table 6.13: *IAM Analyzer Policies across Azure, AWS and GCP*

IAM security is not a one-time endeavor; it is a living and breathing entity. The key is to keep learning, adapting, and improving. With these best practices, your cloud realms across AWS, Azure, and GCP will remain fortified and resilient—ready to fend off the most cunning adversaries.

Future Trends in IAM

The landscape of Identity and Access Management (IAM) is rapidly evolving, driven by advancements in technology, and the increasing complexity of security threats. As organizations strive to protect their digital assets, and ensure seamless access for users, emerging trends such as AI and machine learning, decentralized identity, and Zero Trust Architecture are reshaping the IAM landscape.

This section explores these future trends, highlighting their potential impact on IAM strategies, and the ways they can enhance security as well as efficiency in the digital age.

- **AI and Machine Learning in IAM:** Artificial Intelligence (AI) and Machine Learning (ML) are revolutionizing IAM by enhancing security, and automating complex processes. AI and ML can analyze vast amounts of data to detect anomalies, and predict potential security threats. For example, AI-driven IAM solutions can identify unusual login patterns or access behaviors, triggering alerts or automated responses to mitigate risks.

  Machine learning algorithms can also optimize access controls by continuously learning from user behavior, and adapting policies accordingly.

- **Decentralized Identity (Blockchain):** Decentralized identity is an emerging trend that aims to give individuals more control over their digital identities. **Unlike traditional IAM systems, which rely on centralized authorities to manage identities, decentralized identity uses blockchain technology to create a secure, and tamper-proof identity framework.**

  Users can store their identity information in a digital wallet and share it with service providers as needed, without relying on a central authority. This approach enhances privacy and security by reducing the risk of identity theft and data breaches.

- **Zero Trust Architecture:** The ZTA is a security model **that assumes no user or device, whether inside or outside the network, should be trusted by default. Instead, every access request must be verified and authenticated before granting access to resources.**

- **Identity as a Service (IDaaS): The IDaaS is a cloud-based IAM solution that provides identity management and access control as a subscription service.**

  IDaaS solutions offer a range of features, including Single Sign-on (SSO), Multi-factor Authentication (MFA), and user lifecycle management, without the need for on-premises infrastructure.

- **Biometric Authentication:** This is becoming increasingly popular as a secure and convenient method of verifying user identities. Biometric methods such as fingerprint scanning, facial recognition, and voice recognition, offer a higher level of security compared to traditional passwords.

IAM Labs

Welcome to the IAM Labs section! In this series of hands-on labs, you will gain practical experience with key IAM tasks across three major cloud platforms: AWS, Azure, and GCP. These labs are designed to help you master the essential IAM skills, from creating user accounts and groups to enabling multi-factor authentication (MFA), and automating key rotation. Each lab provides step-by-step instructions to guide you through the processes, ensuring you can apply these critical security measures in real-world scenarios.

By the end of this section, you will be well-equipped to manage and secure your cloud environments effectively. Let us get started.

IAM Lab # 1: Creating a Group and User Account, and Assigning a Policy in AWS, Azure, and GCP

In this lab, you will learn how to create a group and user account, and assign a policy in three major cloud platforms: AWS, Azure, and GCP. We will guide you step-by-step through the process, ensuring that you understand how to manage user access and permissions effectively. By the end of this lab, you will have hands-on experience with IAM in each platform, empowering you to secure your cloud environments with confidence. Let us get started!

Follow these high level steps to first create a group, assign the appropriate policy to the group, and then create a new user in **AWS**. Once the user is added to the group, they will inherit the group's policy, ensuring consistent and streamlined permission management.

1. Login into the `AWS` cloud portal.
2. Navigate to `IAM` > `Select Groups` > `Create New Group`
3. Name the group (for example, "`Developers`")
4. Attach any desired policy, let us say, "`AmazonS3ReadOnlyAccess`".
5. Click on `Create Group`.
6. Go to `Users` > `Add User`.

7. Enter the username, and select the access type.
8. Click Next: **Permission**, then add the user to the "**Developers**" group.
9. Review the summary, and click **Create User**.
10. Download the user's access keys or credentials.
11. Use the credentials to log in or access AWS services, and verify permissions.

Follow these high level steps to first create a group, assign the appropriate policy to the group, and then create a new user in **Azure**. Once the user is added to the group. They will inherit the group's policy, ensuring consistent and streamlined permission management.

1. Login into the **Azure** cloud portal.
2. Go to **Azure Active Directory** > **Groups** > click **+ New Group**.
3. Choose a group type (for example, **Security**), and enter a name (for example, "**Developers**").
4. Click Create.
5. Now, navigate to **Users** > **New User**.
6. Choose Create user, and fill in details like name, username and password.
7. Assign the user to the "**Developers**" group by selecting **Groups** > **Add Membership**.
8. Now, go to the resource (for example, a Storage Account).
9. Click **Access Control (IAM)** > **Add Role Assignment**.
10. Assign the **Developers** group to a role (for example, "**Reader**") and save.
11. Log in as the user, and verify access to the assigned resource.

Follow these high-level steps to first create a group, assign the appropriate policy to the group, and then create a new user in **GCP**. Once the user is added to the group, they will inherit the group's policy, ensuring consistent and streamlined permission management.

1. First, create a member user account, using the **@gmail.com** domain.
2. Login into the GCP portal, search for IAM service, and click on that.
3. Go to the **IAM service**.
4. Click on **Grant Access**.
5. Add the member account that you created.

6. Select the desired role, and click on the **Save** button.
7. This concludes the lab.

IAM Lab # 2: Enable MFA in AWS, Azure and GCP

Enabling Multi-Factor Authentication (MFA) adds an extra layer of security to your cloud environment (AWS/Azure/GCP). MFA requires users to provide a second form of authentication such as a code from a mobile device, in addition to their password. Perform these steps to enable MFA for a user account.

Use Case: Enforce and verify MFA for administrators in AWS, Azure, and GCP.

Perform these high-level steps to enable MFA in **AWS** using IAM.

1. Login into the AWS cloud portal
2. Go to **`IAM`** > **`Users`**
3. Select a user and click, "**`Security Credentials`**".
4. Assign a virtual MFA device or hardware MFA.
5. Test by logging in with and without MFA.

Perform these high-level steps to enable MFA in **Azure,** using Conditional Access.

1. Login into the Azure cloud portal.
2. Open **`Azure Active Directory`** > **`Security`** > **`Conditional Access`**.
3. Create a new policy to require MFA for specific roles.
4. Assign the policy to the Administrator account.
5. Test the policy by signing in with an Admin account.

Perform these high-level steps to enable MFA in **GCP,** using Identity Platform MFA.

1. Login into the GCP cloud portal.
2. Navigate to **`Identity Platform`** > **`MFA`**.
3. Enable MFA for specific groups or users.
4. Test the configuration by logging in with an account requiring MFA.

With MFA implemented, your privileged accounts are now shielded by a dual layer of security, making unauthorized access nearly impossible.

Understanding CIEM

Cloud Infrastructure Entitlement Management (CIEM) solutions orchestrate, and streamline the automation of managing user entitlements and privileges across cloud and multi-cloud environments. Often known as Cloud Entitlements Management or Cloud Permissions Management solutions, CIEM systems strictly apply the Principle of Least Privilege. These solutions are pivotal to an organization's Identity and Access Management (IAM) and Cloud Security Posture Management (CSPM) frameworks.

By leveraging CIEM, organizations can more efficiently tackle the complexities of enforcing consistent access controls and zero trust policies across multi-cloud deployments. This strategic approach ensures minimal access necessary to perform tasks, thereby fortifying defenses against data breaches, malicious intrusions, and the myriad risks associated with excessive cloud permissions. This process helps to identify and avoid risks resulting from privileges being higher or broader than they should.

Understanding Entitlements in CIEM

In the realm of CIEM, entitlements refer to the effective permissions granted to users, workloads, and data. These permissions define what actions a cloud identity–such as human users, connected devices, or artificial intelligence acting on behalf of a human–can perform within cloud and multi-cloud environments. Entitlements also dictate how these identities interact with access credentials, and undergo authentication for privileged tasks. Essentially, an entitlement sets the boundaries for what a cloud identity is authorized to do, and which resources it can access.

Difference Between IAM, PAM, IGA and CIEM

While fundamentally similar, Identity Access Management (IAM) and Cloud Infrastructure Entitlement Management (CIEM) serve distinct purposes. IAM is concerned with managing user identities, authentication, and access controls across an organization's entire IT infrastructure, encompassing both on-premises and cloud environments.

In contrast, CIEM is a specialized subset of IAM that focuses specifically on managing user identities and entitlements within multiple cloud services. While IAM addresses access management broadly, **CIEM hones in on the unique challenges of cloud computing and multi-cloud environments**, ensuring precise control and visibility over cloud entitlements.

Difference Between PAM and CIEM

Privileged Access Management (PAM) and Cloud Infrastructure Entitlement Management (CIEM) serve distinct yet complementary roles in access management. PAM focuses on controlling access to administrative, super user, and other high-privilege accounts typically associated with internal IT resources. It is a broad methodology, akin to Identity Access Management (IAM), that spans across all IT systems and infrastructures, including both on-premises and cloud environments.

In contrast, CIEM is specifically tailored to managing entitlements within cloud infrastructures. Despite their different focuses, PAM and CIEM are often deployed together to provide a comprehensive access management solution. PAM ensures the secure management of highly privileged accounts, while CIEM extends this control into multi-cloud environments.

By integrating CIEM with PAM, organizations can maintain centralized visibility, continuous monitoring of entitlements, and robust threat response for privileged accounts and beyond. This synergy ensures that even the most sensitive access points are managed securely and efficiently across diverse IT landscapes.

Difference between CSPM and CIEM

Cloud Infrastructure Entitlement Management (CIEM) is dedicated to governing cloud identities and managing the privileges of users and services within cloud environments. It plays a crucial role in identifying and mitigating over-privileged access, excessive permissions, and unused entitlements, thereby reducing the risk of security breaches. As a component of privileged access management, CIEM ensures that only authorized individuals have access to critical resources.

Conversely, Cloud Security Posture Management (CSPM) focuses on compliance and risk management. It involves detecting and addressing risks related to IAM misconfigurations, such as weak or default passwords, hardcoded secrets, wildcard permissions, and the absence of Multi-factor Authentication (MFA).

While both CIEM and CSPM are vital for maintaining cloud security, they target different aspects. CIEM governs the actions that users and services can perform, whereas CSPM evaluates the configuration of cloud services against established frameworks and best practices. Together, they form a comprehensive strategy for securing cloud environments.

Importance of CIEM

In recent years, the adoption of cloud technology has surged dramatically. Organizations are increasingly migrating their data and applications to cloud-based infrastructures, often spanning multiple cloud platforms.

As these cloud deployments expand and become more intricate, **the number of entitlements necessary to enforce access control across these platforms also increases.**

The principle of least privilege dictates that users, applications, and systems should possess only the minimal permissions required to perform their functions.

This principle is a cornerstone of the zero trust security model, crucial for reducing the attack surface of corporate cloud environments, and limiting an attacker's ability to move laterally as well as achieve their objectives within an organization's cloud infrastructure.

Implementing least privilege involves precisely calibrating the entitlements of all identities, resources, and services across all cloud platforms.

Manually managing these entitlements across diverse cloud infrastructures, and thousands of permissions, actors, and resources is impractical as well as unscalable.

Traditional tools such as Privileged Access Management (PAM) and Identity Governance Administration (IGA) solutions lack the granularity needed to secure access at the resource level. While native tools provided by cloud service providers are beneficial, they often fall short in terms of maturity, granularity, and scalability, and do not offer comprehensive support across multiple providers' platforms.

Envision a cloud environment bustling with numerous users and automated software, collectively known as identities. Within this environment, you also have various resources such as data and services. Now, consider the necessity to restrict access to certain resources, or establish an identity hierarchy to assign privileges appropriately.

An Identity and Access Management (IAM) service can effectively manage these privileges for your cloud environment identities. However, what if one of your identities starts behaving unexpectedly? An entity is performing actions, it should not. There is an underlying reason you are unaware of.

While IAM services manage and log these privileges, they do not verify if any are misconfigured or excessively permissive.

This is where CIEM steps in, continuously monitoring, and adjusting privileges as necessary to ensure optimal security.

Identifying the precise benefits of CIEM for your organization is a crucial first step in selecting the optimal security solution. As threats to cloud infrastructures escalate, the demand for robust access security and stringent compliance measures increases dramatically. CIEM has emerged as an indispensable component of the cybersecurity toolkit, ensuring that cloud access is meticulously regulated, and fully aligned with the evolving regulatory standards.

Working of CIEM

Cloud Infrastructure Entitlement Management (CIEM) is a crucial tool for managing user permissions in cloud environments. It helps organizations identify, analyze, and optimize permissions to ensure security and compliance.

It begins by identifying all the permissions assigned to users and services across the cloud infrastructure. This comprehensive scan helps in understanding the current access landscape.

Next, CIEM tools analyze the usage patterns of these permissions, identifying any that are unused or excessive. This analysis is crucial for pinpointing potential security risks, and ensuring that permissions are aligned with actual needs.

Based on the insights gained, CIEM tools recommend optimizations to permissions. These recommendations often involve removing unnecessary permissions or adjusting them to adhere to the principle of least privilege, ensuring that users have only the access, they require.

CIEM also enforces security policies and compliance requirements by continuously monitoring and adjusting permissions. This ongoing process helps maintain a secure and compliant cloud environment.

Finally, CIEM provides detailed reports and audit logs which are essential for tracking changes, and ensuring accountability. These reports support regulatory compliance, and facilitate security audits.

By automating these processes, CIEM makes it easier to control access and maintain a secure cloud infrastructure. Cloud Infrastructure Entitlement Management (CIEM) helps manage and control user permissions in cloud environments.

Best Scenarios for Using CIEM

Organizations leverage CIEM solutions to bolster their security posture, ensure compliance, and efficiently manage access within cloud environments.

The following real-world scenarios underscore the critical importance of CIEM:

- **Over-Privileged Access and Firewall Misconfigurations:** In 2019, Capital One experienced a breach impacting over 100 million individuals due to a misconfigured Web Application Firewall (WAF), and an overly permissive role that enabled unauthorized access. This breach was executed via a Server-Side Request Forgery (SSRF) attack, where the attacker manipulated the server into making requests on their behalf, exploiting the over-privileged WAF role to access and extract sensitive customer data from cloud storage. This incident underscores the necessity of strictly limiting access privileges to essential operational functions. Properly constrained access privileges could have significantly mitigated the breach's impact. CIEM solutions, with their continuous monitoring and validation of configurations, are invaluable in preventing such breaches.

- **Excessive Cloud Permissions:** In large global corporations, employees often accumulate unnecessary cloud access privileges over time. According to the "*State of Cloud Permission Risk Report*," over 40% of cloud identities are inactive, and active identities utilize only about 5% of their assigned permissions. This over-provisioning of privileges can lead to severe security incidents such as the 2017 Verizon breach, where an unauthorized party accessed a publicly accessible cloud-based data repository, exposing 6 million customer records. CIEM enables companies to proactively identify and revoke excessive permissions automatically, based on criteria such as unused admin privileges for over 90 days, or access to sensitive data not utilized within the last six months. This aligns access rights with the principle of least privilege, preventing similar incidents.
- **Cloud Configuration Errors:** Between 2015 and 2023, Toyota Motor suffered a significant data breach due to cloud misconfiguration, affecting approximately 260,000 customers across Japan, Asia, and Oceania. This prolonged exposure of sensitive data, including vehicle and personal customer information, resulted from a misconfigured cloud environment that went undetected for over eight years. Had Toyota employed a CIEM solution, it could have continuously monitored cloud configurations, detected the misconfiguration early, and prevented unauthorized access. CIEM solutions are necessary for enforcing strict data handling rules, and ensuring securely configured cloud environments, mitigating the risk of similar breaches.
- **Unrotated AWS Keys:** In February 2021, Sendtech experienced a data breach caused by an unrotated AWS access key created in 2015. AWS keys are credentials that allow access to AWS services, and leaving them unchanged for extended periods makes it easier for attackers to gain unauthorized access. This security lapse allowed an attacker to gain admin privileges, and access the sensitive data on over 67,000 individuals, including contact information, partial financial information, and copies of identification documents. The breach exposed critical weaknesses in credential management and broader security gaps, prompting Sendtech to respond swiftly, and pay the subsequent regulatory fine. A robust CIEM solution could have prevented this breach by enforcing the principle of least privilege, and implementing strong policies for credential rotation, and secure access practices.

Compliances and Governance in CIEM

Cloud Infrastructure Entitlement Management (CIEM) is vital for ensuring security and compliance in cloud environments. It provides detailed visibility and control over user permissions, ensuring only authorized access to critical resources. This strengthens security, and helps meet regulatory standards.

Key Compliance Frameworks and Standards

- **NIST:** CIEM helps implement controls for access, identification, and auditing, supporting frameworks like **NIST SP 800-53** and **NIST SP 800-171**.
- **ISO/IEC 27001:** CIEM manages access controls, and monitors entitlements, ensuring compliance with this international standard.
- **GDPR:** CIEM enforces data access policies and maintains audit trails, helping organizations comply with GDPR requirements.
- **HIPAA:** CIEM implements access controls, and monitors ePHI, ensuring compliance with HIPAA's security rules.
- **PCI DSS:** CIEM manages access to cardholder data, enforces least privilege, and maintains audit logs for PCI DSS compliance.

CIEM Compliance Capabilities

- **Visibility**: CIEM provides clear visibility into who has access to what, ensuring appropriate access to the sensitive data.
- **Automated Audits**: CIEM automates audits, generating reports to demonstrate compliance with regulatory requirements.
- **Continuous Monitoring**: CIEM continuously monitors entitlements, detecting and correcting deviations from compliance policies.
- **Least Privilege**: CIEM enforces the principle of least privilege, minimizing the attack surface, and maintaining security standards.
- **Incident Response**: CIEM provides detailed logs and audit trails for forensic investigations, and compliance with incident response requirements.

Integrating CIEM into your security strategy enhances cloud security, ensures compliance, and simplifies management. CIEM offers continuous monitoring, automated remediation, and detailed reporting, making it an essential tool for modern cloud environments.

CIEM Labs

Welcome to the CIEM Labs section! In this series of hands-on labs, you will gain practical experience with Cloud Infrastructure Entitlement Management (CIEM) across various cloud platforms. These labs are designed to help you understand and implement CIEM modules in Microsoft Defender for Cloud for Azure, AWS, and GCP environments. You will also learn how to navigate inventory to discover IAM-related resources, explore CIEM recommendations, and ensure the best practices like enabling Multi-Factor Authentication (MFA) for all IAM users. Each lab provides step-by-step instructions to guide you through the processes, ensuring that you can apply these critical security measures in real-world scenarios. Let us dive in, and enhance your CIEM skills.

CIEM Lab # 1: Enabling the CIEM Module in Microsoft Defender for Cloud for the Azure Environment

Managing identities and their respective permissions in these ever-dynamic cloud environments requires precision, visibility, and automation. **Microsoft Defender for Cloud** introduces a powerful **CIEM** (Cloud Infrastructure Entitlement Management) module that bridges the gap between excessive permissions and secure access governance.

As cloud adoption accelerates, CIEM is the linchpin for securing digital access in a scalable and sustainable manner.

This lab will guide you through the steps to enable and configure the CIEM module for your Azure cloud environments, ensuring that your organization can proactively detect, analyze, and remediate identity risks in Azure cloud platform.

Follow these steps to enable the CIEM module in Microsoft Defender for Cloud:

1. Log into the Azure portal, using your administrative credentials.
2. Go to the search bar > type "**`Microsoft Defender for Cloud`**", and select the service to open the dashboard.
3. Once inside the dashboard, locate the "**`Environment Settings`**" tab on the left-hand menu.
4. Now, select the desired **`subscription`** where you want to enable the CIEM.

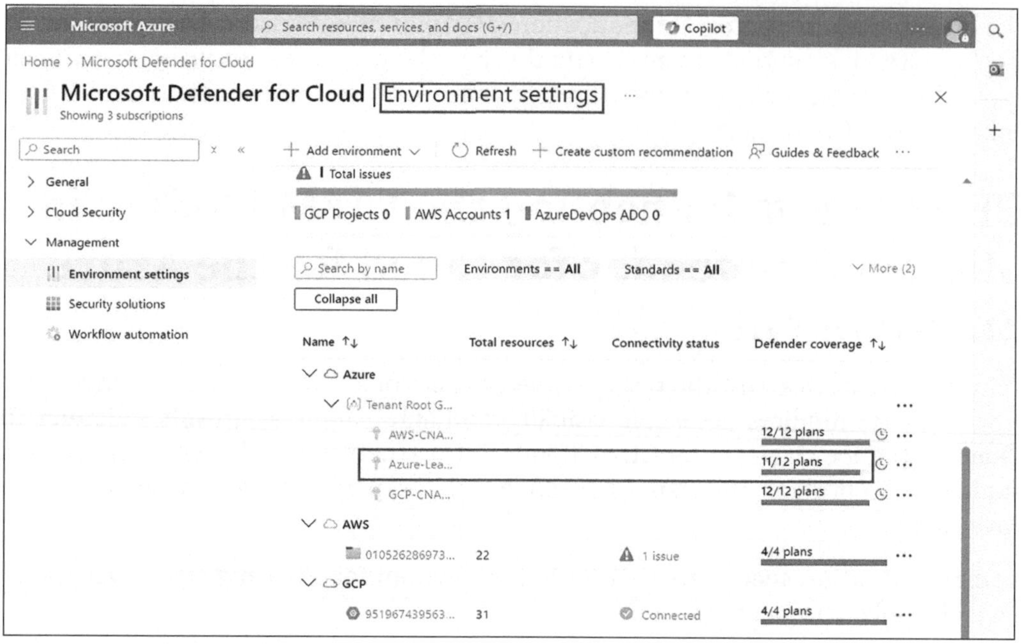

Figure 6.1: *Selecting the Desired Subscriptions for Enabling the CIEM Module*

5. Go to **`Defender Plans` > Click on `Settings`**

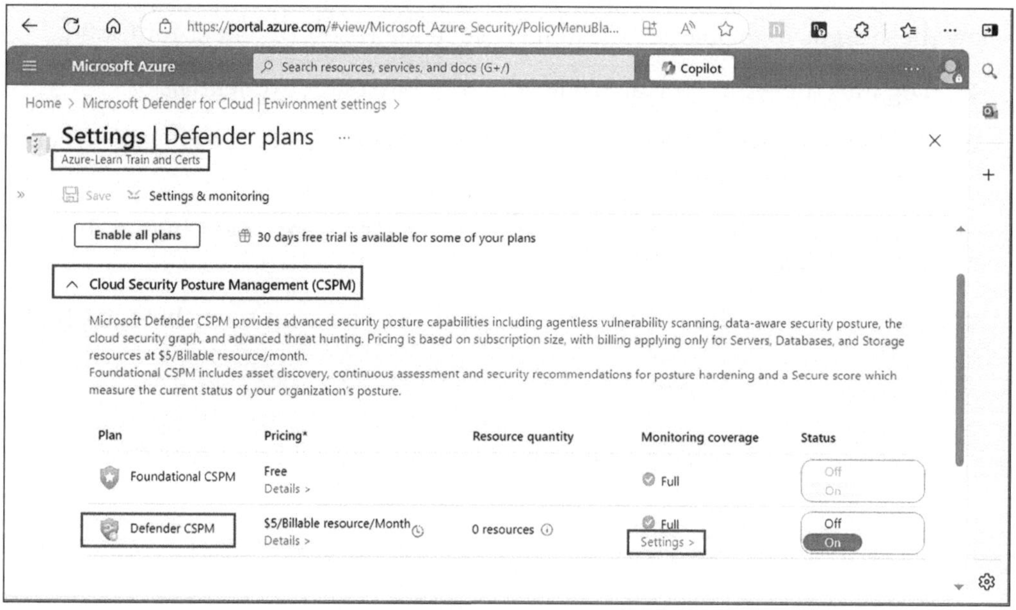

Figure 6.2: *Defender Plan Settings*

6. Toggle on the "**`Permission Management`**" component, if not already toggled on.

7. Select **Continue > Save.**
8. Refer to the following screenshot:

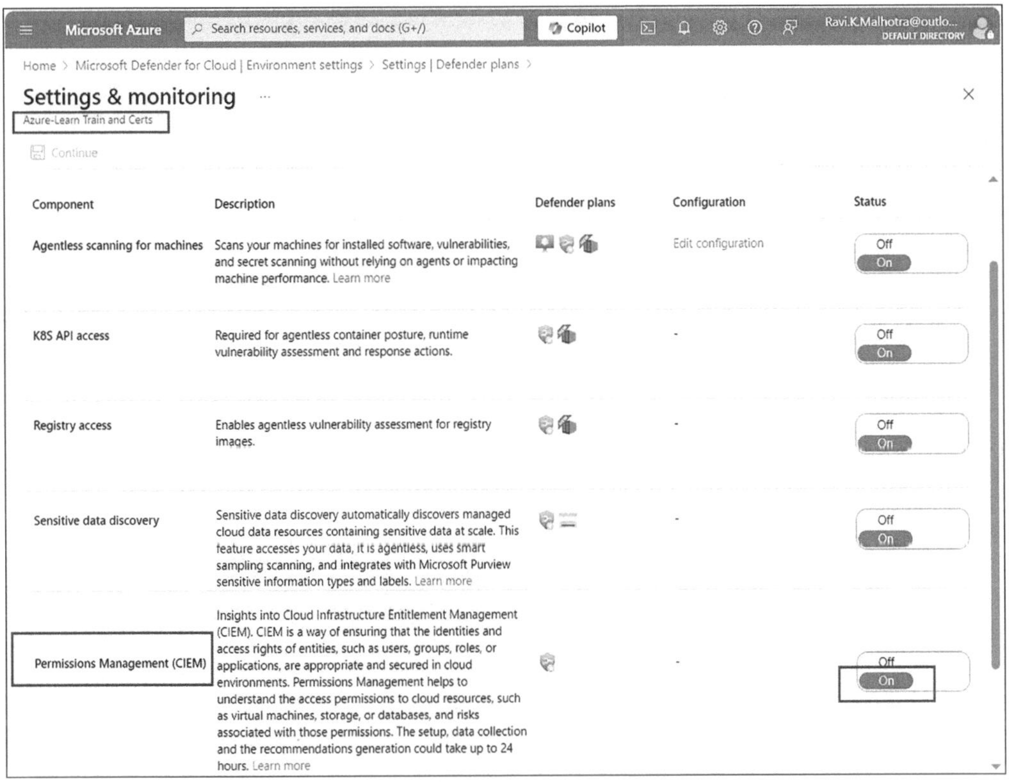

Figure 6.3: *Enabling the CIEM Module in the Desired Subscription*

9. Once the module is enabled, allow time for data collection.
10. The applicable Permissions Management recommendations will appear on your subscriptions within a few hours.
11. Navigate to the Inventory page under the General tab, in Defender for Cloud to view CIEM-related resources.
12. Navigate to the Recommendations page in Defender for Cloud to view CIEM-related insights.
13. With this, you have ensured that the CIEM module is enabled for your desired Azure subscription in the Azure account.
14. This concludes the lab.

By enabling the CIEM module in **Microsoft Defender for Cloud**, organizations can **transform their approach to identity security in Azure**. This proactive stance ensures not only compliance with security standards, but also a **fortified cloud environment where identities are tightly governed**.

CIEM Lab # 2: Enabling the CIEM Module in Microsoft Defender for Cloud for the AWS Environment

In today's multi-cloud world, managing permissions across platforms such as AWS is critical for maintaining a secure and efficient cloud environment. CIEM empowers organizations to identify and address over-permissioned roles, ensuring that users and resources operate with only the access, they need. This lab will guide you step-by-step to enable CIEM capabilities for AWS within Microsoft Defender for Cloud, setting the stage for robust identity, and access governance.

Follow these steps to enable the CIEM module in Microsoft Defender for Cloud:

1. Log into the Azure portal, using your administrative credentials.
2. Go to the search bar > type "**`Microsoft Defender for Cloud`**", and select the service to open the dashboard.
3. Once inside the dashboard, locate the "**`Environment Settings`**" tab on the left-hand menu.
4. Ensure that you see the desired AWS account there. If not, you need to onboard the AWS account as per the instructions in *Chapter* 3, *Onboard* CNAPP: A *Practical Guide*. In our case, we see the AWS account already onboarded to Microsoft Defender for Cloud, so click on this account.
5. Go to **`Defender Plans`** **> Click on** **`Settings`**.
6. Toggle on the "**`Permission Management`**" component, if not already toggled on.
7. Select **`Continue`** **>** **`Save`**.
8. Once the module is enabled, allow time for data collection. Then, refer to the Inventory page and the Recommendations page to see the discovered items, and their respective insights.
9. This concludes the lab.

CIEM Lab # 3: Enabling the CIEM Module in Microsoft Defender for Cloud for the GCP Environment

In this lab, we will guide you through the process of enabling Microsoft Defender for Cloud on a Google Cloud Platform (GCP) account. This involves configuring the necessary settings to ensure comprehensive security and compliance monitoring. By the end of this lab, you will have a secure and well-monitored GCP environment integrated with Microsoft Defender for Cloud. The steps are identical to those in the previous two labs. Follow these steps to enable the CIEM module in Microsoft Defender for Cloud:

1. Log into the Azure portal, using your administrative credentials.
2. Go to the search bar > type "**`Microsoft Defender for Cloud`**", and select the service to open the dashboard.
3. Once inside the dashboard, locate the "**`Environment Settings`**" tab on the left-hand menu.
4. Ensure that you see the desired GCP account there. If not, you need to onboard the GCP account as per the instructions in *Chapter* 3, *Onboard* CNAPP: A *Practical Guide*. In our case, we see the GCP account already onboarded to Microsoft Defender for Cloud, so click on this account.
5. Go to **`Defender Plans`** **> Click on `Settings`.**
6. Toggle on the "**`Permission Management`**" component, if not already toggled on.
7. Select **`Continue`** **> `Save`.**
8. Once the module is enabled, allow time for data collection. Then, refer to the Inventory page and the Recommendations page to see the discovered items, and their respective insights.
9. This concludes the lab.

CIEM Lab # 4: Navigating Inventory to Discover IAM Related Resources from Azure, AWS and GCP Cloud Platforms

In this lab, we will explore how to navigate the inventory within CIEM to discover Identity and Access Management (IAM) related resources across Azure, AWS, and GCP cloud platforms. This hands-on exercise will guide you through the process of identifying and managing IAM resources, ensuring that you have a comprehensive understanding of how to maintain secure and compliant cloud environments. By the end of this lab, you will be proficient in using CIEM tools to monitor and control IAM permissions across multiple cloud platforms.

Use Case: Explore inventory within CIEM to discover IAM related resources across Azure, AWS and GCP cloud platform.

To effectively explore the inventory within CIEM, and discover IAM-related resources across Azure, AWS, and GCP cloud platforms, please follow these steps:

1. Log into the Azure portal, using your administrative credentials.
2. Go to the search bar > type "`Microsoft Defender for Cloud`", and select the service to open the dashboard.
3. Navigate to the "`Inventory`" page under the "`General`" tab. Here, you will find the following items:
    - **Total Resources:** The count of total resources discovered across all cloud platforms.
    - **Unhealthy Resources:** The count of unhealthy resources according to CNAPP policies.
    - **Resource Count by Environment:** The exact resource count for each cloud platform.
4. In our case, you can see that we have a total of 485 resources discovered, and out of which, 391 resources are unhealthy. Out of 485 resources, 141 resources discovered from the Azure subscriptions, 251 are from the AWS account, and 93 resources from the GCP account. Refer to the following screenshot:

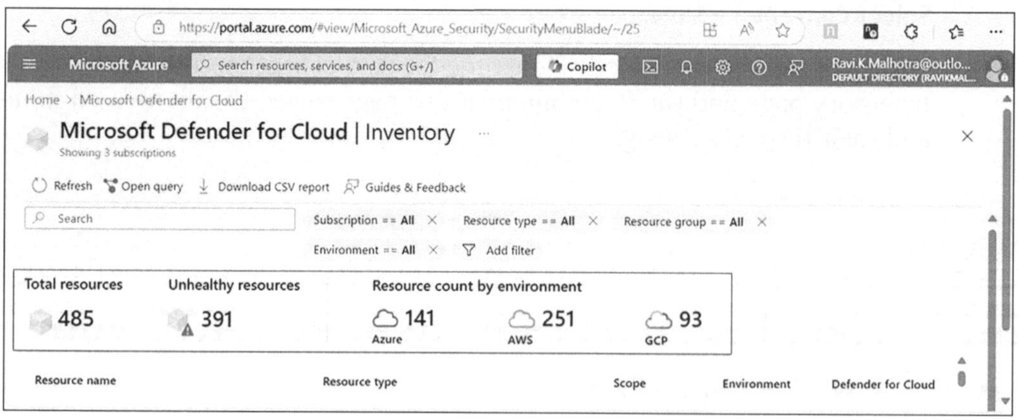

Figure 6.4: *Inventory Resource Count*

5. You can perform the following operation in the `Inventory` page:

- **Open Query:** A query generator to write the detailed queries for fetching data.
- **Download CSV Report:** An option to download all resources in a CSV format report.

6. At the bottom of the Inventory page, you will find a detailed inventory of cloud assets discovered from all onboarded cloud environments. You will find these details:
    - **`Resource Name`:** The exact name of each resource.
    - **`Resource Type`:** The exact type of each resource such as computer or IAM.
    - **`Scope`:** Subscription or account level details.
    - **`Environment`:** Details of the environment such as Azure, AWS, or GCP account.
    - **`Defender for Cloud`:** Indicates if Defender for Cloud is enabled (Yes/No).
    - **`Recommendations`:** All the recommendations according to CNAPP policies.
7. Refer to the screenshot from my Defender for the **`Cloud Inventory`** overview page:

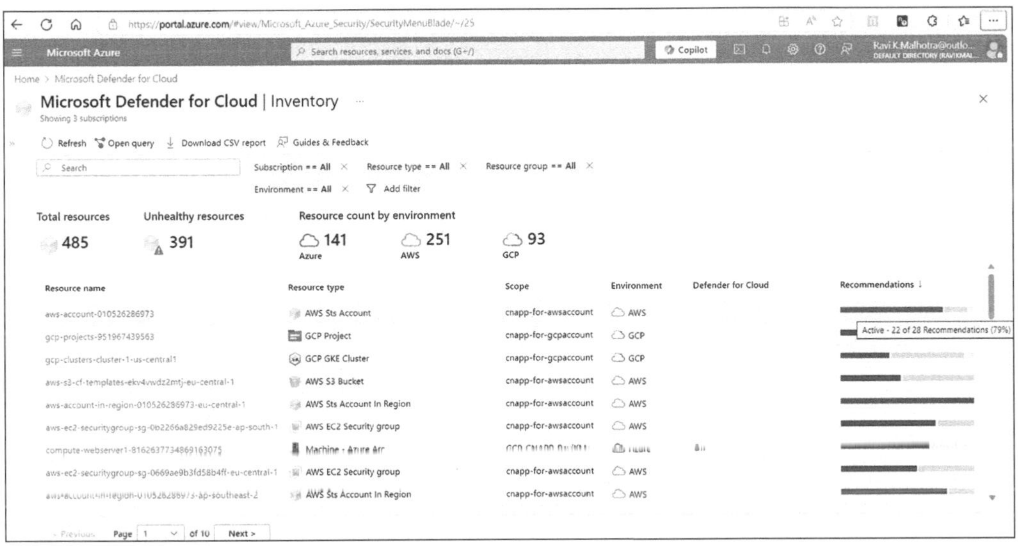

Figure 6.5: *Inventory Resource Details*

8. In the above-mentioned screenshot, you can see the recommendations for each discovered cloud asset in the inventory.
9. Hover your mouse over any recommendation to view the number of active and

completed recommendations. As shown, out of 28 recommendations for the AWS environment, 22 are active, and 6 have been completed.

10. To view these recommendations in detail, navigate to the "**Recommendations**" page. We will cover this in our next lab.
11. This concludes the lab.

CIEM Lab # 5: Navigating Recommendations Page for CIEM Related Insights

In this lab, we will explore how to navigate the "Recommendations" page within CIEM to manage and optimize CIEM entities. This exercise will guide you through the process of reviewing and implementing recommendations to enhance security and compliance. By the end of this lab, you will be proficient in using CIEM tools to address potential issues, and improve the overall security posture of your cloud environment.

Prerequisite for this Lab: For this lab to work, it is important to create some users and groups, and assign them permissions and roles in your respective cloud environments. If you have yet not created, please create them first.

Follow these steps to explore the Recommendations Page:

1. Log into the Azure portal, using your administrative credentials.
2. Go to the search bar > type "**Microsoft Defender for Cloud**", and select the service to open the dashboard.
3. Click on the **Recommendations** page under the General tab. This page is very informative, and provides a wealth of details such as:
    a. You can toggle specific cloud environments on or off to view their recommendations. Available scope options include Azure subscriptions, AWS accounts, GCP projects, GitHub connections, and Azure DevOps connections.
    b. You can see risk-based recommendations, categorized as **Critical**, **High**, **Medium**, or **Low** risks.
    c. It provides other useful details such as **Recommendation Title**, **Affected Resource**, **Risk Level**, **Risk Factors**, **Attack Path**, **Owner**, **Status**, and **Insights**.
4. Refer to the following screenshot to see all the environments connected to Microsoft Defender for Cloud for recommendations. You can see that we have 3 Azure subscriptions, 1 AWS account, 1 GCP project, 1 GitHub connector, and

1 Azure DevOps connector attached to Microsoft Defender for Cloud.

Figure 6.6: *Scope Section in a Recommendations Page*

5. Refer to the following screenshot to see `Risk based recommendations`. You can see that we have zero (0) critical risk-based recommendations, 19 High risk-based recommendations, 54 Medium risk-based recommendations, and 603 as Low risk-based recommendations. You can also see zero (0) Active Attack paths, and zero (0) Overdue Recommendations.

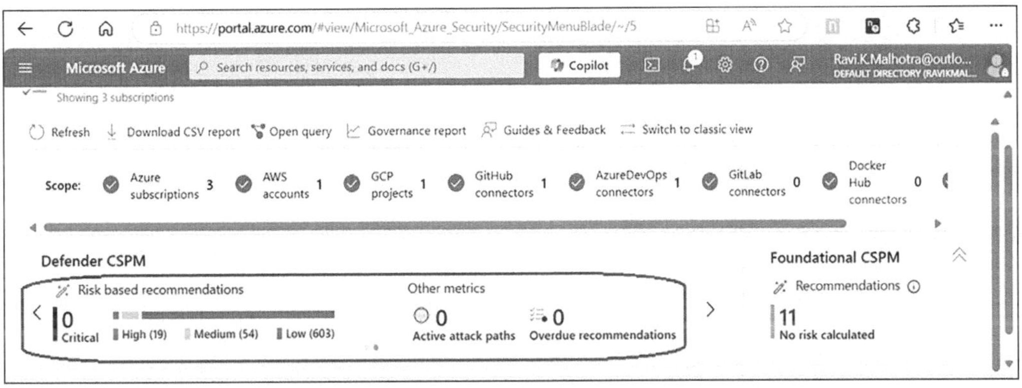

Figure 6.7: *Risk-Based Recommendations*

6. Refer to the following screenshot to see all the recommendations grouped by title, spanned across four (4) pages. Here in this screenshot, please focus on the Recommendation Title, count of Affected Resources, Risk Factor, Resources by Risk Level and Insights.

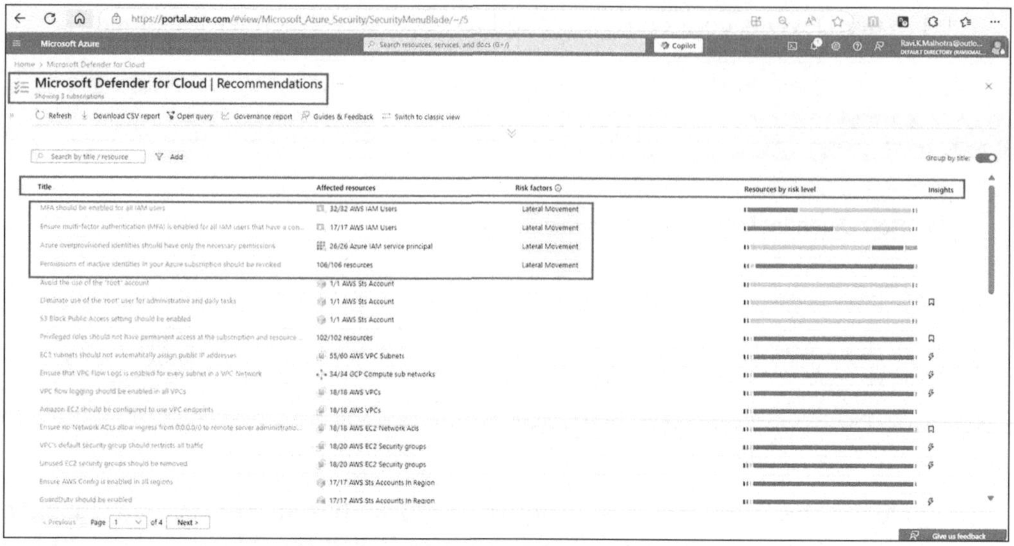

Figure 6.8: *Detailed Recommendations*

7. You can click on the actual recommendation bar to see the recommendation in detail.

8. This concludes the lab.

CIEM Lab # 6: Explore all Recommendations and List Down all for CIEM Entities (Users/ Groups and Roles)

In this lab, we will delve into the recommendations provided by CIEM for various entities such as users, groups, and roles. This exercise will help you gain a comprehensive understanding of the security posture of your cloud environments, and ensure that appropriate measures are taken to mitigate the potential risks.

Use Case: List down all the recommendations for either Users/Groups/Permissions/ Roles.

Follow these steps to explore the Recommendations Page:

1. Log into the Azure portal, using your administrative credentials.

2. Go to the search bar > type "**`Microsoft Defender for Cloud`**", and select the service to open the dashboard.

3. Click on the **`Recommendations`** page under the General tab. This page is very informative, and provides a wealth of details.

4. After reviewing all the suggestions, I am listing down the following relevant recommendations related to the CIEM module:
    a. MFA should be enabled for all IAM users.
    b. Ensure that MFA is enabled for all IAM users that have a console Password.
    c. Azure Overprovisioned identities should have only the necessary permissions.
    d. AWS Overprovisioned identities should have only the necessary permissions.
    e. Eliminate use of the `'root'` user for administrative and daily tasks.
    f. Permissions of inactive identities in your Azure subscription should be revoked.
    g. Permissions of inactive identities in your AWS Account should be revoked.
    h. Permissions of inactive identities in your GCP project should be revoked.
    i. Avoid the use of the `'root'` account.
    j. IAM Access Analyzer should be configured.
    k. IAM policies should be attached only to the group or roles.
    l. Privileged roles should not have permanent access at the subscription and resource group level.
    m. Users should have least privilege access with granular IAM roles.
5. The following is a table of affected resources (users/groups/roles) across all the onboarded accounts:

Recommendation	Count of Affected resources
MFA should be enabled for all IAM users.	**32/32** AWS IAM Users
Ensure MFA is enabled for all IAM users that have a console Password.	**17/17** AWS IAM Users
Azure Overprovisioned identities should have only the necessary permissions.	**26/26** Azure IAM service principal
AWS Overprovisioned identities should have only the necessary permissions.	**12/12** resources
Eliminate use of the 'root' user for administrative and daily tasks	**1/1** AWS sts Account
Permissions of inactive identities in your Azure subscription should be revoked.	**106/106** resources
Permissions of inactive identities in your AWS Account should be revoked.	**17/17** resources
Permissions of inactive identities in your GCP project should be revoked.	**13/13** resources
Avoid the use of the 'root' account.	**1/1** AWS sts Account
IAM Access Analyzer should be configured.	**17/17** AWS sts Accounts in Region
IAM policies should be attached only to the group or roles.	**32/32** AWS IAM Users
Privileged roles should not have permanent access at the subscription and resource group level.	**102/102** resourcs
Users should have least privilege access with granular IAM roles.	**1/1 GCP** Project

Figure 6.9: *Count of the Affected Resources in all CIEM Related Recommendations*

6. From the given table, you can see that all the users, groups, and roles created in the onboarded accounts are shown as affected. This highlights the true power of CIEM. Without CIEM, obtaining such comprehensive insights from native cloud identity tools would be nearly impossible. CIEM provides a centralized view of identity and access management across multiple cloud environments, enabling you to identify and address potential security issues more effectively. This level of visibility is crucial for maintaining a robust security posture, and ensuring compliance with organizational policies.
7. You may receive different recommendations, and varying counts of affected resources based on the configurations, you have set up in your cloud environments.
8. This concludes the lab.

CIEM Lab # 7: Explore the Recommendation - "MFA *should be enabled for all* IAM *users*"

In this lab, we will focus on the critical security recommendation to enable Multi-Factor Authentication (MFA) for all Identity and Access Management (IAM) users. Enabling MFA is a vital security measure that adds an extra layer of protection to user accounts, significantly reducing the risk of unauthorized access. We will explore the details of this recommendation, understand its importance, and learn how to implement it effectively across your cloud environments.

Use Case: Explore the recommendation, "MFA *should be enabled for all* IAM *users*", and see what all actions you can perform as a CNAPP Administrator.

Follow these steps to explore the Recommendations Page:

1. Log into the Azure portal, using your administrative credentials.
2. Go to the search bar > type "**`Microsoft Defender for Cloud`**", and select the service to open the dashboard.
3. Click on the **`Recommendations`** page under the General tab, search for the recommendation "MFA *should be enabled for all* IAM *users*," and click on the recommendation. Refer to the following screenshot:

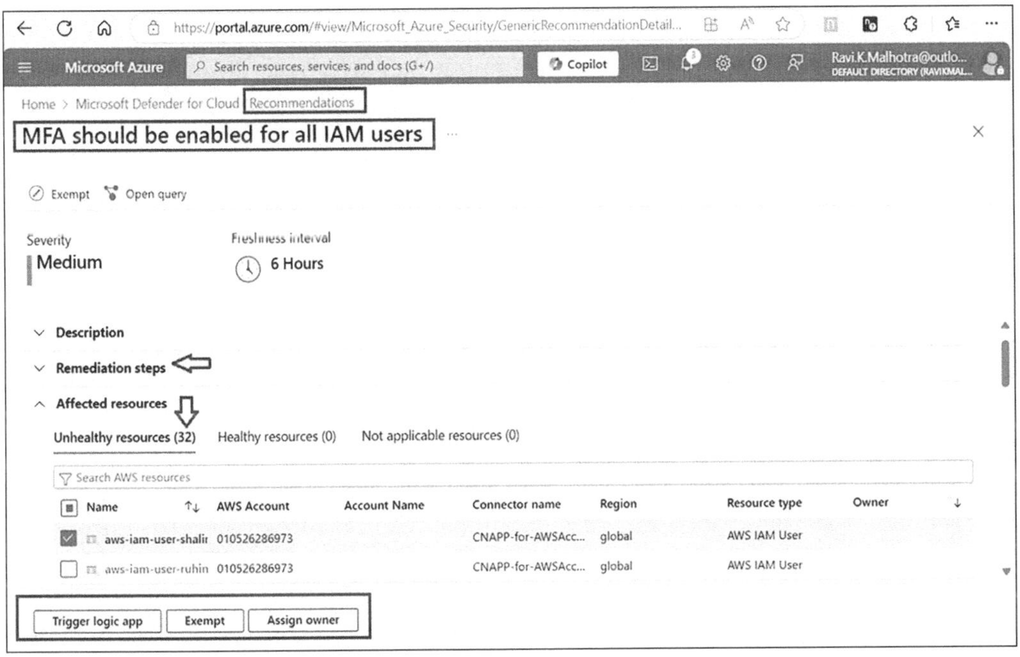

Figure 6.10: *Recommendation - "MFA Should be Enabled for all IAM Users"*

4. You can observe the following items from the above-mentioned screenshot:
   a. You can see that this recommendation was refreshed and updated 6 hours ago.
   b. You can also see that you have 32 unhealthy resources, specifically IAM users, highlighted for this recommendation. It also provides the exact names of the AWS IAM users. For example, in our case, we see 2 users out of 32 in this screenshot: (1) aws-iam-user-shalu and (2) aws-iam-user-ruhin.

c. You can also exempt any specific single resource (IAM user) or account from this recommendation.

d. You can remediate this recommendation manually by following the steps under "**Remediation steps**," or use automated techniques with the "**Trigger Logic App**" feature.

e. The "**Trigger Logic App**" option in **Microsoft Defender for Cloud** is used to automate responses to security alerts, recommendations, and changes in regulatory compliance. By triggering a Logic App, you can create automated workflows that perform specific actions, when certain conditions are met. For example, you might set up a Logic App to send an email notification to a security team, when a critical alert is generated, or to automatically remediate a security issue by applying a predefined fix. This feature helps to streamline security operations, ensuring that responses are quick, consistent, and aligned with your organization's security policies.

f. You can also assign ownership to either single or multiple affected resources.

5. This concludes the lab.

CIEM – SIEM – SOAR: Enhancing Cloud Security

In the rapidly evolving landscape of cloud security, three critical components have emerged as essential tools for organizations: Cloud Infrastructure Entitlement Management (CIEM), Security Information and Event Management (SIEM), and Security Orchestration, Automation, and Response (SOAR). Each of these solutions plays a unique role in fortifying an organization's security posture, and together, they provide a comprehensive approach to managing and mitigating security risks.

Cloud Infrastructure Entitlement Management (CIEM)

CIEM focuses on managing and securing cloud entitlements, ensuring that users and applications have the appropriate level of access to cloud resources. As organizations increasingly adopt multi-cloud environments, the complexity of managing permissions and entitlements grows exponentially. CIEM solutions automate the process of discovering, right-sizing, and continuously monitoring permissions, enforcing the principle of least privilege.

Key Benefits of CIEM:

- **Enhanced Security:** By ensuring that access is limited to what is necessary, CIEM reduces the attack surface, and minimizes the risk of unauthorized access.
- **Compliance Assurance:** CIEM helps organizations meet regulatory requirements by providing detailed visibility into access controls, and generating compliance reports.
- **Operational Efficiency:** Automating the management of cloud entitlements reduces the administrative burden on IT and security teams, allowing them to focus on more strategic tasks.

Security Information and Event Management (SIEM)

SIEM solutions are designed to collect, analyze, and correlate security data from various sources to detect and respond to security incidents in real-time. By aggregating data from servers, applications, network devices, and other security tools, SIEM provides a centralized view of an organization's security posture.

Key Benefits of SIEM:

- **Threat Detection:** SIEM solutions use advanced analytics and correlation techniques to identify potential security threats, and generate alerts.
- **Incident Response:** By providing real-time visibility into security events, SIEM enables security teams to quickly investigate, and respond to incidents.
- **Compliance Reporting:** SIEM helps organizations to meet the regulatory requirements by maintaining detailed logs of security events, and generating audit reports.

Security Orchestration, Automation, and Response (SOAR)

SOAR platforms extend the capabilities of SIEM by automating and orchestrating the response to security incidents. SOAR solutions integrate with various security tools and technologies, enabling the execution of predefined workflows and playbooks to respond to incidents efficiently.

Key Benefits of SOAR:

- **Automation:** SOAR automates repetitive tasks, reducing the workload on security teams, and allowing them to focus on more complex threats.

- **Orchestration:** By integrating with multiple security tools, SOAR ensures seamless communication and coordination between different security solutions.
- **Incident Response:** SOAR provides a collaborative environment for incident investigation and response, reducing the Mean Time to Resolution (MTTR), and improving the overall security posture.

Integrating CIEM, SIEM, and SOAR

While each of these solutions offers distinct benefits, their true power lies in their integration. By combining CIEM, SIEM, and SOAR, organizations can achieve a holistic approach to cloud security:

- **Comprehensive Visibility:** CIEM provides detailed insights into cloud entitlements, while SIEM aggregates and analyzes security data from various sources. Together, they offer a complete view of an organization's security posture.
- **Proactive Security:** CIEM ensures that access controls are properly configured, reducing the risk of unauthorized access. SIEM detects potential threats in real-time, and SOAR automates the response, ensuring swift and effective mitigation.
- **Streamlined Operations:** The integration of these solutions reduces the administrative burden on security teams, allowing them to focus on strategic initiatives, and improving the overall operational efficiency.

In conclusion, CIEM, SIEM, and SOAR are indispensable components of a robust cloud security strategy. By leveraging the strengths of each solution, and integrating them effectively, organizations can enhance their security posture, ensure compliance, and efficiently manage and respond to security incidents.

Conclusion

In this chapter, we have explored the critical role of Cloud Infrastructure Entitlement Management (CIEM) in securing cloud environments. By understanding and implementing CIEM, organizations can gain granular control over cloud entitlements, ensuring that access rights are properly managed and monitored. We have covered the foundational principles of Identity and Access Management (IAM), and delved into the advanced capabilities of CIEM, highlighting its importance in modern cloud security.

Through theoretical discussions and practical labs, we have provided you with the knowledge and tools needed to effectively manage cloud entitlements. Whether you are a seasoned security professional, or new to the field, the insights gained from this chapter will empower you to protect your cloud assets from unauthorized access, and potential threats.

In the next chapter, we will explore **Kubernetes Security Posture Management (KSPM)**–a specialized approach to identifying misconfigurations, enforcing security policies, and strengthening the security posture of Kubernetes clusters. With Kubernetes becoming the backbone of modern cloud-native applications, understanding KSPM is essential for ensuring robust container security and compliance. Let us dive into KSPM, and uncover how it helps organizations safeguard their containerized environments.

Multiple-Choice Questions

1. What is the primary goal of CIEM?
    a. Managing cloud costs
    b. Preventing malware attacks
    c. Ensuring least privilege access to cloud resources
    d. Automating cloud resource creation
2. Which of the following practices aligns with CIEM principles?
    a. Using default admin roles for all users
    b. Granting permissions based on job requirements
    c. Disabling logging for sensitive resources
    d. Hard coding credentials in application code
3. How does CIEM improve security posture in cloud environments?
    a. By enforcing policy guardrails and monitoring access
    b. By automating deployment pipelines
    c. By providing detailed cost analysis
    d. By disabling all external network access
4. Which tool in AWS can help identify over-permissioned roles as part of CIEM practices?
    a. CloudWatch
    b. IAM Access Analyzer

   c. Trusted Advisor

   d. AWS Lambda

5. Which of the following is a key feature of CIEM in multi-cloud environments?

   a. Centralized management of permissions across platforms

   b. Automated database scaling

   c. Load balancing for web applications

   d. Continuous software deployment

Answers

1. c
2. b
3. a
4. b
5. a

Points to Remember

1. **Importance of CIEM:** CIEM is essential for managing and securing cloud entitlements, providing granular control and visibility over access rights.
2. **IAM Fundamentals:** A strong understanding of IAM principles is crucial for implementing effective CIEM strategies.
3. **Role-Based Access Controls:** Implementing role-based access controls helps ensure that permissions are appropriately assigned and maintained.
4. **Regular Reviews and Audits:** Conducting regular access reviews and audits helps identify and address potential security vulnerabilities.
5. **Hands-On Practice:** Practical labs and real-world scenarios are invaluable for gaining hands-on experience with IAM and CIEM.
6. **Continuous Learning:** Cloud security is an evolving field, and staying updated with the latest best practices and technologies is essential for maintaining robust security measures.

By keeping these points in mind, you will be well-equipped to implement and manage CIEM effectively, ensuring the security and integrity of your cloud environments.

Questions

1. What does CIEM stand for?
2. Which principle is fundamental to CIEM: Least privilege or default admin access?
3. What is the primary goal of CIEM in cloud environments?
4. Which cloud providers offer native CIEM tools?
5. How does CIEM help manage over-permissioned roles?
6. What is a common CIEM practice for mitigating insider threats?
7. Name one AWS service that supports CIEM practices.
8. How does CIEM enhance compliance in multi-cloud environments?
9. Which CIEM feature is crucial for detecting permission misuse?
10. What role does automated remediation play in CIEM?

Key Terms

- **IAM:** Identity and Access Management
- **SSO:** Single Sign-On
- **MFA:** Multi-Factor Authentication
- **RBAC:** Role-Based Access Control
- **User, Group, Role and Permissions:** Software or hardware that provides certain functionality for other programs or devices (clients).
- **CIEM:** Cloud Identity Entitlement Management
- **PAM:** Privileged Access Management

CHAPTER 7
Understanding Kubernetes Security Posture Management (KSPM)

Introduction

Kubernetes is everywhere–from startups to enterprises–powering modern apps in the cloud. But with all that flexibility and scale comes a big challenge: **security**. That is where **Kubernetes Security Posture Management (KSPM)** comes in.

KSPM helps you **find and fix misconfigurations**, **identify risks before attackers do**, and **monitor your cluster setup** against security best practices. Think of it as a **security health check** for your Kubernetes clusters–constantly checking how they are configured, what they are running, and whether they follow the compliance standards.

In this chapter, you will explore how **KSPM fits into a CNAPP strategy**, and learn how to use **Microsoft Defender for Cloud** to secure your **GKE (Google Kubernetes Engine)** clusters with confidence.

Structure

The following topics will be covered in this chapter:

- Introduction to Kubernetes and Security Posture
- Understanding Fundamentals of Containers
- Understanding Fundamentals of Dockers
- Understanding Fundamentals of Kubernetes

- Containers vs Dockers vs Kubernetes
- Kubernetes Security Risks and Challenges
- Key Components of Kubernetes Security
- Understanding KSPM Tools and Solutions
- Microsoft Defender for Cloud as a KSPM Solution
- Integrating KSPM with CI/CD Pipeline
- KSPM Best Practices: A Mindset, Not Just a Checklist
- Configuring KSPM for Kubernetes Security
- KSPM Labs

Introduction to Kubernetes and Security Posture

Before delving into Kubernetes Security Posture Management (KSPM), it is crucial to have a foundational understanding of **Containers and Kubernetes**.

Containers are lightweight, portable units **that package an application and its dependencies**, enabling consistent execution across different environments. The concept of containers in computing is inspired by the shipping industry. Just as shipping containers revolutionized global trade by standardizing the transportation of goods, software containers standardize the deployment of applications across different environments.

Kubernetes, on the other hand, is an open-source platform **designed to automate the deployment, scaling, and management of containerized applications**. Kubernetes was originally developed by Google, and released as an open-source project in 2014. The name "*Kubernetes*" comes from the Greek word for "*Helmsman*" or "*pilot*," symbolizing its role in guiding containerized applications. Kubernetes is often abbreviated as **"K8s"** because there are eight letters between the "K" and the "s." This numeronym makes it easier to reference in conversations and documentation.

Understanding these core concepts will provide the necessary context for comprehending the intricacies of KSPM which focuses on securing and maintaining the integrity of Kubernetes environments.

In a cloud-native world, where Kubernetes has become the de facto standard for container orchestration, **security posture** becomes a critical concern. Kubernetes environments are highly dynamic, and often consist of many moving parts–clusters, nodes, pods, and services–that need to be monitored and secured continuously. Misconfigurations, overly permissive access controls, and lack of visibility into cluster activity can all introduce vulnerabilities, if not addressed. This is where **Kubernetes**

Security Posture Management (KSPM) comes into play. KSPM is not just about threat detection; it is about ensuring that your Kubernetes clusters are configured according to the security best practices, continuously monitored for risk, and aligned with compliance standards. Whether running on a single cloud, or across multiple platforms like GCP, AWS, or Azure, having a robust KSPM strategy helps organizations maintain a strong defense against emerging cloud-native threats.

Understanding Fundamentals of Containers

Containers used in cloud computing are **lightweight**, **standalone**, and **executable software packages** that **include everything** needed to **run** a piece of software, such as an application code, runtime, system tools, libraries, and settings. Here are some key points to understand about containers. Let us explore some of the interesting facts about containers:

- **Isolation:** Containers isolate applications from the underlying system, ensuring that they run consistently across different environments. This isolation helps prevent conflicts between applications, and their dependencies.
- **Efficiency:** Containers **share the host system's kernel**, making them more efficient than traditional Virtual Machines (VMs). This efficiency allows for **faster startup times** and better resource utilization.
- **Scalability:** Containers can be easily **scaled up or down to handle the varying loads**. This makes them **ideal for cloud environments** where resources can be **dynamically allocated, based on demand**.
- **Consistency:** By packaging all **dependencies with the application**, containers **ensure** that the **software runs the same way, regardless of where it is deployed**.
- **Microservices Architecture:** Containers are **well-suited for microservices architecture**, where applications are **broken** down into **smaller**, **independent services**. Each service can be developed, deployed, and scaled independently, enhancing agility and resilience.

Understanding Containerization Techniques in AWS

Now, let us look at some of the container techniques offered by **AWS cloud computing platform:**

- **Amazon Elastic Container Service (ECS):** This is a **fully managed container**

orchestration service that supports **Docker containers**. ECS allows you to run and scale containerized applications easily on AWS.

- **Amazon Elastic Kubernetes Service (EKS):** This is a **fully managed Kubernetes service** that makes it easy to run **Kubernetes on AWS**, without needing to install and operate your own Kubernetes control plane or nodes.
- **AWS Fargate:** Fargate is an **AWS serverless compute engine for containers** that works with **both ECS and EKS**. It allows you to run containers, without having to manage the underlying infrastructure.

Understanding Containerization Techniques in Azure

Now, let us look at some of the container techniques used and offered by **Azure cloud computing platform**:

- **Azure Kubernetes Service (AKS):** A **managed Kubernetes service** that simplifies deploying, managing, and operating Kubernetes clusters. AKS provides **serverless Kubernetes**, **integrated CI/CD**, and **enterprise-grade security and governance**.
- **Azure Container Instance (ACI):** A service that allows you to **run containers without managing servers**. ACI is ideal for scenarios that can operate in isolated containers, such as simple applications, task automation, and build jobs.
- **Azure Container Apps:** A **fully managed serverless container service** that enables you to run microservices and containerized applications on a serverless platform.

Understanding Containerization Techniques in GCP

Now, let us look at some of the container techniques offered by **GCP cloud computing platform**:

- **Google Kubernetes Engine (GKE):** A managed Kubernetes service that provides a powerful and flexible way to run Kubernetes clusters on Google Cloud infrastructure. **GKE offers advanced features like `auto-scaling`, `auto-upgrades`, and `integrated logging` as well as `monitoring`.**
- **Cloud Run:** A fully managed compute platform that automatically scales your stateless containers. **Cloud Run abstracts away all infrastructure management, allowing you to focus on writing codes.**
- **Google Cloud Functions:** While not a traditional container service, **Cloud**

Functions can run containerized workloads, providing a serverless execution environment for building and connecting cloud services.

These services and techniques enable developers to deploy, manage, and scale containerized applications efficiently across different cloud environments, leveraging the unique strengths of each platform.

Understanding Fundamentals of Docker

Docker is a powerful and widely used **containerization platform** that allows developers, **DevOps engineers**, and **IT teams** to **package applications, along with all their dependencies** into **lightweight, portable containers**. This approach ensures that applications run consistently across different environments—whether on a developer's laptop, a test server, or in a production cloud environment.

Unlike traditional virtualization, which relies on hypervisors and full-blown guest operating systems, **Docker uses OS-level virtualization**. Containers share the host system's kernel, but remain isolated from one another. **This results in faster startup times**, **smaller resource footprints**, and **greater efficiency compared to virtual machines.**

You can install Docker on desktops and laptops for development and testing. The **Docker Desktop application** supports **Linux**, **Windows**, and **macOS**, making it accessible to developers working on different platforms. For production use, Docker runs seamlessly on server environments, including major **Linux distributions** and **Windows Server 2016 and above.**

One of the key strengths of Docker is its portability. Once you build a container image, you can run it on any system that supports Docker. This "*build once, run anywhere*" model eliminates the classic "*it works on my machine*" problem, which is especially useful in **CI/CD pipelines**, **DevOps practices**, and **microservices architecture**.

The Docker platform consists of several core components that are crucial to understand:

- **Docker Engine:** The underlying runtime that builds and runs containers.
- **Docker Images:** Immutable templates used to create containers. Images are often based on official images from **Docker Hub** or custom-built using **Dockerfiles.**
- **Docker Containers:** Running instances of Docker images, isolated and lightweight.
- **Docker CLI and Docker Compose:** Command-line tools that help you manage containers and define multi-container applications with ease.

- **Docker Hub:** A cloud-based registry service for sharing container images publicly or privately.

In practice, Docker enables a variety of workflows and use cases:

- **Local Development:** Developers can spin up full application stacks locally, using containers, test their code, and debug issues quickly.
- **Testing and QA:** Automated test suites can run inside containers to replicate production conditions.
- **Continuous Integration/Continuous Deployment (CI/CD):** Docker integrates well with tools such as GitHub Actions, Jenkins, GitLab CI, and Azure DevOps for automated builds and deployments.
- **Scalable Production Deployments:** Docker containers can be orchestrated using platforms like **Kubernetes** to support enterprise-grade workloads across multiple cloud and on-premises environments.

Docker also encourages a **modular approach to application design**. Rather than building monolithic applications, developers can create loosely coupled microservices that communicate through APIs. This leads to better scalability, flexibility, and ease of maintenance.

In summary, Docker has fundamentally changed how we develop, ship, and run applications. It offers **speed, consistency, and scalability**, making it an essential tool in the modern software development lifecycle. Whether you are just getting started or working in advanced cloud environments, **understanding Docker is a foundational skill that will empower you to build better and more reliable software.**

Understanding Fundamentals of Kubernetes

Kubernetes is like the backstage crew of a live concert. While the audience (users) enjoys the music (apps), Kubernetes makes sure everything runs smoothly behind the scenes. It sets up the stage (containers), moves the right instruments (resources) into place, replaces broken strings (restarts failed apps), and even makes sure everyone is in sync. You do not see the crew, but without them, the show can't go on. In the same way, Kubernetes helps developers manage and organize their applications—especially when they grow big or complex. It takes care of the boring, repetitive tasks, so that your app stays healthy, performs well, and is always ready, when someone presses "**play**."

- **Pod Concept:** In Kubernetes, the smallest deployable unit is called a "**pod**." A pod can contain one or more containers that share the same network namespace and storage, allowing them to communicate easily and work together.

- **Self-Healing:** One of the standout features of Kubernetes is its self-healing capability. If a container fails, Kubernetes automatically restarts it, ensuring that your application remains available and resilient.
- **Scalability:** Kubernetes can automatically scale your applications up or down, based on demand. This horizontal scaling ensures that your application can handle the varying loads efficiently, without manual intervention.
- **Security-Features:** Kubernetes includes robust security features such as Role-Based Access Control (RBAC), network policies, and secrets management. These features help protect your applications and data from unauthorized access and breaches.
- **Multi-Cloud Support:** Kubernetes is designed to run on various environments, including on-premises, public clouds, and hybrid clouds. This flexibility allows organizations to deploy their applications, wherever it makes the most sense for their business.
- **Declarative Configuration:** Kubernetes uses a declarative approach to configuration. You define the desired state of your application in YAML or JSON files, and Kubernetes takes care of maintaining that state, simplifying the management of complex applications.
- **Extensive Ecosystem:** The Kubernetes ecosystem is vast, with numerous tools and projects that extend its functionality. **For example, Helm is a package manager for Kubernetes that simplifies the deployment of applications, and Prometheus is a popular monitoring tool.**
- **Community and Contribution:** Kubernetes has a vibrant and active community. It is one of the most contributed-to projects on GitHub, with thousands of developers and companies contributing to its development and improvement.

Containers vs Docker vs Kubernetes

Containers, Docker, and Kubernetes have revolutionized how we develop, deploy, and manage applications, each contributing unique capabilities that, when combined, create a powerful and efficient ecosystem. Let us explore how these three components work together, and what sets them apart in the world of cloud computing.

- **The Common Ground:** Containers, Docker, and Kubernetes all share a common mission: to streamline the development, deployment, and management of applications. They are the pillars of modern cloud-native architecture, each playing a distinct yet complementary role.
- **Containers (The Building Blocks):** Containers are like the fundamental building blocks of modern applications. They encapsulate everything an application needs to run: the code, runtime, system tools, libraries, and settings. This

encapsulation ensures that the application runs consistently across different environments, from a developer's laptop to a production server.

- **Docker (The Master Builder):** Docker is the master builder that crafts these containers. It provides the tools and platform to create, manage, and distribute containers. Docker simplifies the process of packaging applications into containers, making it easy to share and deploy them. Think of Docker as the skilled artisan who ensures that each container is perfectly crafted, and ready for deployment.
- **Kubernetes (The Orchestrator):** Kubernetes is the orchestrator that manages and scales these containers across a cluster of machines. It automates the deployment, scaling, and operations of application containers. Kubernetes ensures that the right containers are running in the right places, balancing loads, and maintaining the desired state of the application. Imagine Kubernetes as the conductor of an orchestra, ensuring that every container plays its part in harmony.
- **Technical Similarities:** These are the technical similarities between Containers, Dockers and Kubernetes:
    - **Isolation:** Both containers and Docker provide isolated environments for applications, ensuring consistency across different systems.
    - **Portability:** Containers, whether managed by Docker or Kubernetes, can run consistently across various environments, enhancing portability.
    - **Efficiency:** Containers share the host system's kernel, making them more efficient than traditional virtual machines. Docker and Kubernetes leverage this efficiency to optimize resource usage.
- **Technical Differences:** These are the technical differences between Containers, Dockers and Kubernetes:

	Containers	**Docker**	**Kubernetes**
Scope	The basic units that encapsulate an application, and its dependencies	A platform and set of tools for creating, managing, and running containers.	A system for orchestrating and managing clusters of containers.
Functionality	Provide the runtime environment for applications	Facilitates the creation, packaging, and distribution of containers.	Manages the deployment, scaling, and operations of containers across multiple hosts.
Management	Focus on running applications in isolated environments	Provides a comprehensive toolkit for container lifecycle management	Adds a layer of orchestration, and handling complex tasks like load balancing, scaling, and self-healing.

Complexity	Simple and lightweight, ideal for individual applications.	Adds the ease of use and management capabilities to containers.	Introduces advanced features for managing large-scale, distributed applications, but with added complexity

***Table* 7.1**: *Containers vs Docker vs Kubernetes*

- **The Symphony of Cloud-Native Applications:** In the grand symphony of cloud-native applications, containers are the instruments, Docker is the luthier crafting and tuning these instruments, and Kubernetes is the maestro conducting the performance. Together, they create a harmonious environment where applications can thrive, scale, and perform at their best.

This unique interplay between Containers, Docker, and Kubernetes forms the backbone of modern cloud-native architectures, enabling developers to build resilient, scalable, and efficient applications.

Kubernetes Security Risks and Challenges

As **Kubernetes adoption continues to surge across industries**, **so does its attractiveness as a target for attackers.**

The flexibility and power of Kubernetes can also become its Achilles' heel, when not properly secured.

Understanding the security risks and operational challenges associated with Kubernetes is the first step **toward building a resilient Kubernetes environment. Some of the most common Kubernetes security risks include:**

- **Misconfigurations:** One of the most prevalent risks. A simple misconfigured pod or service can expose your cluster to the internet or grant unnecessary privileges to a container.
- **Over-permissive RBAC Roles:** Role-Based Access Control (RBAC) governs who can do what inside a cluster. Granting admin-level access too broadly can result in unintentional exposure or privilege escalation.
- **Unrestricted Network Access:** Without proper network policies, services and workloads may communicate freely, increasing the blast radius in case of compromise.
- **Container Image Vulnerabilities:** Containers often pull from public image repositories that may contain known vulnerabilities or malicious code if not properly vetted.
- **Lack of Visibility and Monitoring:** Security blind spots within the cluster—such as unmonitored namespaces or unaudited API access—can delay detection and response to breaches.

Additionally, the **fast-paced and decentralized nature of DevOps pipelines makes it difficult to enforce consistent security standards across teams.** Developers often deploy services rapidly, and without the right guardrails in place, clusters can drift from their secure state.

To address these challenges, a **KSPM solution** continuously scans the Kubernetes environment, highlights risks, and recommends remediations, based on security benchmarks such as **CIS Kubernetes Benchmark** and **compliance frameworks like NIST, PCI-DSS, or HIPAA**. With KSPM, organizations can shift from reactive to proactive security, ensuring that configurations and access controls stay in check as environments evolve.

Key Components of Kubernetes Security

Kubernetes security involves several core components that work together to protect containerized workloads and ensure a secure environment. These components form the foundation of what KSPM solutions aim to automate and enhance. These components include:

- **Configuration Management:** One of the foundational aspects of KSPM is the ability to manage and enforce secure configurations for Kubernetes clusters. This involves continuously scanning cluster configurations to identify misconfigurations and deviations from security best practices. Configuration management ensures that clusters are configured securely from the outset, and remain compliant with security policies over time.
- **Access Control and Identity Management:** Effective access control is critical for securing Kubernetes environments. KSPM solutions provide tools for managing access controls and identities within Kubernetes clusters. This includes implementing Role-Based Access Control (RBAC), managing service accounts, and enforcing the principle of least privilege. By ensuring that only authorized users and services have access to sensitive resources, KSPM reduces the risk of unauthorized access and potential breaches.
- **Runtime Security:** Protecting Kubernetes workloads during runtime is a key function of KSPM. This involves monitoring the behavior of containers and pods to detect and respond to suspicious activities. Runtime security includes capabilities such as anomaly detection, intrusion detection and prevention, and behavioral analysis. By continuously monitoring runtime activities, KSPM can detect and mitigate threats in real-time, minimizing the impact of security incidents.
- **Network Security:** Kubernetes environments rely on complex networking configurations to facilitate communication between containers, pods, and external services. KSPM solutions provide tools for securing these network communications, including network segmentation, encryption, and network

policy enforcement. By securing network traffic, KSPM helps prevent lateral movement of threats within the cluster, and protects data in transit.

- **Compliance and Governance:** KSPM helps organizations maintain compliance with regulatory requirements and industry standards. This includes automated compliance checks, policy enforcement, and audit reporting. By ensuring that Kubernetes clusters adhere to security policies and compliance frameworks, KSPM reduces the risk of non-compliance and associated penalties.
- **Threat Intelligence and Response:** Integrating threat intelligence into KSPM enhances the ability to detect and respond to the emerging threats. This involves leveraging threat intelligence feeds to stay informed about the latest threats and vulnerabilities. KSPM solutions use this information to enhance threat detection capabilities, and orchestrate automated responses to neutralize threats, before they can cause harm.

Understanding KSPM Tools and Solution

Kubernetes Security Posture Management (KSPM) is the process of putting into place a system for ensuring the defenses of Kubernetes – also referred to as K8s. Securing the management of containerized workloads across environments include practices such as leveraging role-based access control (RBAC), limiting API access, ensuring kubernetes itself is up-to-date, and performing proactive scanning and monitoring.

As organizations increasingly adopt Kubernetes for orchestrating their containerized applications, ensuring the security of these environments has become a critical concern. KSPM is an emerging discipline that focuses on securing Kubernetes clusters by continuously monitoring and managing their security posture. This chapter delves into the intricacies of KSPM, exploring its significance, core components, and the benefits it offers to organizations striving to secure their Kubernetes environments.

The Significance of KSPM

Kubernetes has become the de facto standard for container orchestration, enabling organizations to deploy, scale, and manage containerized applications efficiently. However, the complexity and dynamic nature of Kubernetes environments introduce unique security challenges.

Misconfigurations, inadequate access controls, and lack of visibility can **lead to vulnerabilities** that are easily exploitable by malicious actors.

KSPM addresses these challenges by providing a comprehensive framework for managing and improving the security posture of Kubernetes clusters. By continuously monitoring configurations, access controls, and runtime activities, KSPM helps organizations identify and mitigate security risks, ensuring that their Kubernetes environments remain secure and compliant. Implementing KSPM offers numerous benefits to organizations, enhancing their ability to secure Kubernetes environments and achieve operational resilience. Key benefits include:

- **Improved Security Posture:** KSPM provides continuous monitoring and automated remediation, ensuring that Kubernetes clusters remain secure and compliant. By proactively identifying and addressing security risks, KSPM helps organizations maintain a strong security posture and reduce the likelihood of security incidents.
- **Enhanced Visibility:** KSPM solutions offer comprehensive visibility into Kubernetes environments, enabling security teams to identify and address potential security risks. Enhanced visibility ensures that organizations have a clear understanding of their security posture, and can take proactive measures to mitigate risks.
- **Operational Efficiency:** Automation is a key feature of KSPM, reducing the manual effort required to manage Kubernetes security. Automated configuration management, compliance checks, and threat response enhance operational efficiency, as well as allow security teams to focus on strategic initiatives.
- **Improved Compliance:** KSPM helps organizations maintain compliance with regulatory requirements and industry standards. Automated compliance checks and detailed reports simplify the process of demonstrating adherence to security policies and frameworks.
- **Reduced Risk:** By continuously monitoring Kubernetes environments, and implementing proactive security measures, KSPM reduces the risk of data breaches and other security incidents. This proactive approach to security ensures that vulnerabilities are addressed before they can be exploited by malicious actors.
- **Scalability:** KSPM solutions are designed to scale with the needs of the organization, providing consistent security coverage regardless of the size or complexity of the Kubernetes environment. This scalability ensures that organizations can secure their Kubernetes clusters as they grow and evolve.

KSPM is an essential solution for organizations seeking to secure their Kubernetes environments, and maintain a robust security posture. By providing comprehensive visibility, automated remediation, compliance management, and enhanced security, KSPM addresses the unique challenges of managing Kubernetes security. Implementing KSPM offers numerous benefits, including improved security posture, enhanced visibility, operational efficiency, improved compliance, reduced risk, and scalability. As Kubernetes adoption continues to grow, the importance of KSPM in ensuring Kubernetes security will only become more critical.

As illustrated in the pie chart above in the previous section, "*Introduction to CSPM*", you can see that the KSPM module alone accounts for 10% of the utilization within the CNAPP suite. This significant adoption underscores the critical role KSPM plays in enhancing cloud security and compliance.

This section served as an introductory overview of the "*Kubernetes Security Posture Management* (KSPM)" module. In the upcoming dedicated chapter, "*Understanding Kubernetes Security Posture Management* (KSPM)," we will delve deeper into various concepts, explore advanced topics, and engage in hands-on labs and exercises to enhance our understanding of KSPM.

KSPM Tools and Solutions

As Kubernetes adoption grows across industries, so does the need to secure it effectively. Kubernetes Security Posture Management (KSPM) tools are designed to help organizations continuously monitor and improve the security health of their Kubernetes environments. These tools automate the discovery of risks, enforce best practices, and simplify compliance—making it easier for teams to focus on building and deploying applications securely.

At their core, **KSPM tools provide visibility, policy enforcement, misconfiguration detection**, and **security benchmarking** across Kubernetes clusters. Whether clusters are hosted in the cloud or on-premises, these tools act as a watchdog for your container orchestration platform.

Several KSPM solutions are available today, each offering different capabilities. Some are standalone tools, while others are part of broader Cloud-Native Application Protection Platform (CNAPP) offerings. Let us look at a few common types of tools:

- **Open-source tools** like **Kubescape**, **Kube-bench**, and **Kube-hunter** are widely used for quick scans and compliance checks. These are ideal for developers and small teams getting started with Kubernetes security.
- **Cloud-native security platforms** such as **`Microsoft Defender for Cloud`**, **`Palo Alto Prisma Cloud`**, and **`Sysdig Secure`** offer enterprise-grade KSPM as part of their CNAPP solutions. These tools integrate seamlessly with cloud platforms like Azure, AWS, and GCP, delivering continuous security assessments and advanced features such as alerting, automation, and reporting.
- **Built-in security features** provided by managed Kubernetes services (like GKE, EKS, and AKS) can also contribute to posture management. Though not comprehensive KSPM tools by themselves, they offer controls such as role-based access, network policies, and audit logs that work in conjunction with dedicated KSPM solutions.

When choosing a KSPM solution, organizations typically look for:

- **Ease of integration with their existing cloud and DevOps environments.**
- Support for multi-cloud and hybrid deployments.
- Automated remediation and alerting.
- Compliance mapping to standards like CIS, NIST, and PCI-DSS.

Ultimately, **the goal of any KSPM tool is to reduce Kubernetes attack surface**, enforce consistent security policies, and **support secure, scalable growth** of containerized workloads. In the next section, we will explore how Microsoft Defender for Cloud offers a powerful, integrated KSPM solution–especially when managing Kubernetes clusters across GCP, Azure, and beyond.

Microsoft Defender for Cloud as a KSPM Solution

With the growing adoption of Kubernetes to run cloud-native applications at scale, ensuring the security of these containerized environments has become a crucial priority for organizations. Kubernetes Security Posture Management (KSPM) introduces a systematic approach to securing and managing Kubernetes environments. **Microsoft Defender for Cloud plays a pivotal role in this process, offering an automated, integrated, and multi-cloud solution designed to continuously assess, monitor, and secure Kubernetes clusters** across various cloud platforms, including **Azure**, **AWS**, and **Google Cloud**.

Microsoft Defender for Cloud's KSPM solution provides a centralized security dashboard, enabling organizations to gain visibility into the health and security of their Kubernetes clusters, regardless of where they are deployed. This is vital in today's **multi-cloud** and **hybrid cloud environments**, where businesses typically use multiple cloud providers to host their workloads. Defender for Cloud integrates seamlessly with **Azure Kubernetes Service (AKS)**, **Amazon Elastic Kubernetes Service (EKS)**, and **Google Kubernetes Engine (GKE)**, providing consistent security and governance across all Kubernetes clusters.

One of the core strengths of Microsoft Defender for Cloud is its **policy-driven approach to security**, which is built on widely adopted industry standards such as the **CIS Kubernetes Benchmarks**. Defender for Cloud evaluates clusters against these benchmarks, identifying misconfigurations, vulnerabilities, and non-compliance issues. The key risks detected include:

- **Privileged containers** that allow excessive privileges to workloads, increasing the attack surface.

- **Unrestricted network access** which exposes sensitive services to potential attackers.
- **Containers running with root access** which could enable a breach to escalate privileges in the event of a compromise.
- **Inadequate secrets management**, where sensitive credentials and keys are improperly stored, potentially exposing critical assets.

Each of these findings is tagged with **risk levels, detailed explanations, and remediation guidance** that outlines the necessary steps to mitigate the risks. Additionally, each recommendation is tracked, allowing security teams to prioritize tasks, and monitor progress over time. **This proactive approach ensures that security teams are not reactive**, but rather continuously optimizing security practices, and minimizing vulnerabilities in real time.

Defender for Cloud's KSPM capabilities are not isolated. **Instead, they are tightly integrated into the broader cloud security posture management ecosystem of Microsoft Defender for Cloud.** This means Kubernetes security is embedded into the overall security fabric which includes:

- **Secure Score:** A metric that measures the overall security posture, and provides actionable recommendations to improve it.
- **Regulatory Compliance:** Automated assessments and built-in compliance frameworks to help organizations adhere to global standards such as **GDPR**, **HIPAA**, and **PCI DSS**.
- **Threat Protection:** Advanced capabilities for detecting and responding to potential threats, including real-time alerts for suspicious activity.
- **Attack Path Analysis:** An advanced feature that allows teams to visualize how threats might move across the environment, helping to predict and prevent potential attack paths, before they are exploited.

This integration ensures that Kubernetes security is not seen as a standalone function, but as a critical part of the broader cloud security framework. It helps organizations understand the entire security landscape, enabling them to make more informed decisions regarding their security posture.

One of the most significant advantages of Microsoft Defender for Cloud is its automation capabilities. The solution integrates with other Microsoft services such as **Microsoft Sentinel**, **Logic Apps**, and **Azure Automation**, allowing security teams to automate responses and remediation workflows. This **automation** enables organizations to scale their security operations efficiently, ensuring that security measures are taken promptly, without manual intervention. For example, when a security issue is detected, Defender for Cloud can automatically trigger actions such as deploying patches, altering configurations, or even isolating compromised workloads.

In addition to automation, **Defender for Cloud's KSPM solution** helps organizations stay on top of new and evolving threats by **integrating threat intelligence**. Defender for Cloud continuously updates its threat detection capabilities based on real-time intelligence feeds, enabling it to stay ahead of the latest vulnerabilities and attack tactics. By **combining threat intelligence** with **real-time monitoring** and **risk categorization**, Defender for Cloud ensures that security teams are always aware of the current threat landscape, and can take swift action to neutralize emerging risks.

Furthermore, **Microsoft Defender for Cloud provides detailed insights** into the **overall security health of Kubernetes workloads** through its **security recommendations** and **detailed reporting**. These reports provide security teams with an in-depth view of their Kubernetes environments, allowing them to track changes, evaluate risks, and ensure compliance with security policies. Whether managing production-grade clusters or early-stage development workloads, Defender for Cloud provides the tools needed to maintain a **secure, compliant**, and **resilient Kubernetes environment**.

The solution also allows for **continuous monitoring** which means security teams do not need to wait for an audit or manual review to understand their security posture. Defender for Cloud provides constant surveillance of Kubernetes environments, alerting administrators in real-time about potential threats, policy violations, or misconfigurations.

In conclusion, **Microsoft Defender for Cloud as a KSPM solution empowers organizations to effectively secure their Kubernetes environments by offering comprehensive risk assessments**, automated remediation, and integration into a unified cloud security platform. Hence, whether you are running a large-scale, mission-critical application, or just starting with containerized workloads, Microsoft Defender for Cloud provides the tools and capabilities necessary to secure your Kubernetes clusters, reduce risks, and ensure compliance across the cloud.

Integrating KSPM with CI/CD Pipeline

In today's fast-paced software development landscape, integrating **Kubernetes Security Posture Management (KSPM)** with the **Continuous Integration and Continuous Deployment (CI/CD) pipeline is essential for ensuring security throughout the entire application lifecycle.**

As developers push updates to production at an increasing rate, **security must shift left–meaning it should be considered and enforced early in the development cycle**, rather than after deployment.

The **CI/CD pipeline is designed to automate the stages of software delivery**, from code integration to deployment, and security needs to be seamlessly woven into this pipeline.

By integrating KSPM into your CI/CD pipeline, you ensure that security is not only maintained in runtime but is also **enforced during code development and before deployment.**

Why Integrate KSPM with CI/CD?

1. **Continuous Security Checks:** Traditional security measures often focus on runtime security, meaning they only protect applications, once they are already running in production. With CI/CD pipeline integration, security checks can be applied as soon as the code is written, and before it is deployed.
2. **Automated Security:** Automation is at the heart of CI/CD pipelines, and security should be no exception. Integrating KSPM into the CI/CD pipeline allows automated security checks for every change made to the code or configuration.
3. **Faster Remediation:** By continuously assessing code and Kubernetes cluster configurations for security issues, KSPM integration in the CI/CD pipeline allows security teams to identify and fix vulnerabilities faster.
4. **Consistency and Compliance:** Ensuring that every deployment adheres to the security best practices and organizational compliance standards is easier with an integrated pipeline. KSPM solutions typically provide policy-driven assessments, making it simple to check that every new release complies with industry standards like CIS Benchmarks, GDPR, HIPAA, and more. By integrating these checks into the CI/CD process, you ensure that all the codes are consistently validated before being deployed.

How to Integrate KSPM with Your CI/CD Pipeline?

To integrate KSPM into your CI/CD pipeline, you can follow these steps:

1. **Set Up Kubernetes Security Tools:** First, ensure that you are using a comprehensive KSPM solution like **Microsoft Defender for Cloud**, or any other cloud-native security tool that supports integration with Kubernetes and CI/CD pipelines. **These tools will have pre-built connectors and APIs that facilitate easy integration.**
2. **Integrate with CI/CD Platforms:** Modern CI/CD platforms such as **Jenkins**, **GitLab CI**, **CircleCI**, **GitHub Actions**, and **Azure DevOps** provide the flexibility to integrate third-party security tools. For example, you can **configure your pipeline to call the Defender for Cloud APIs, which will automatically scan container images,** Kubernetes configurations, and deployments for potential vulnerabilities or misconfigurations.
3. **Automate Security Scanning:** Use pre-deployment security scanning to check for vulnerabilities in container images, configuration files, and Helm

charts before they are pushed to your Kubernetes cluster. **Enforce Security Gates**: Integrating KSPM with the CI/CD pipeline allows you to create security gates. These gates can halt the deployment if certain critical vulnerabilities or misconfigurations are detected.

4. **Monitor and Audit:** As part of the CI/CD pipeline, enable continuous monitoring of security issues. KSPM integration will allow you to get real-time visibility of your deployments and continuously assess risk levels. **Enable logging and auditing capabilities to track all security-related actions,** providing a complete history of the changes and the actions taken to remediate vulnerabilities.

5. **Automated Remediation:** Once the security issues are identified during the CI/CD process, automated remediation can be set up through tools like **Microsoft Sentinel**, **Azure Logic Apps**, or **GitHub Actions**. Remediation can include automatically updating misconfigurations, patching container images, or applying security policies to Kubernetes deployments without manual intervention.

Integrating KSPM into your CI/CD pipeline is no longer a luxury–it is a necessity for maintaining a secure Kubernetes environment.

By automating security checks, enforcing policy-driven assessments, and enabling faster remediation, organizations can ensure that their Kubernetes clusters are secure throughout the entire application lifecycle. With KSPM integration, security becomes an integral part of the development process, reducing the risk of vulnerabilities being introduced into production, and allowing security teams to stay one step ahead in the fight against cyber threats.

KSPM Best Practices: A Mindset, Not Just A Checklist

Securing Kubernetes is not just about installing tools and running audits–**it is about embedding a proactive security culture into every stage of the cluster lifecycle.** Kubernetes Security Posture Management (KSPM) becomes most effective when it is treated as an ongoing discipline, rather than a one-time setup. **The following are some best practices that reflect a mature, real-world approach to KSPM:**

1. **Treat the Cluster as Code:** Start by adopting an **Infrastructure-as-Code (IaC)** approach. Your cluster configurations (RBAC roles, network policies, and so on.) should be version-controlled and reviewed like application code. This enables:

    - Reusability and peer review of security controls.

- Detection of misconfigurations, before they reach production.
- Easier rollbacks, and change tracking.

2. **Build Posture Checks into CI/CD Pipelines:** Security posture should not be something you check after deployment. Instead, **embed KSPM policies into your CI/CD workflows to catch drift or insecure settings**, before they go live. Use tools like policy-as-code engines (for example, Open Policy Agent or Contest) to shift posture checks left.
3. **Harden by Default, Not by Remediation:** Do not wait for alerts to tell you what is wrong. Build hardened base configurations into your node images, container templates, and Helm charts. Secure defaults mean fewer surprises later.
4. **Monitor Behavior, Not Just Configuration:** Configuration scanning is essential, but KSPM goes beyond that. **Observe runtime behavior** to **spot anomalies, lateral movement, or unexpected network traffic.** Integrate behavior analytics into your KSPM strategy for real-time insights.
5. **Keep Developer Feedback Loops Tight:** Developers are often the ones defining Kubernetes manifests. If they are not looped into security findings, risks will repeat. **Ensure that your KSPM tooling integrates with collaboration platforms (Slack, Teams, Jira) to keep devs informed without waiting for a security ticket.**
6. **Segment Workloads with Purpose: Use Kubernetes namespaces, network policies, and RBAC to logically isolate workloads**, based on trust levels or teams. Do not treat segmentation as optional–it limits blast radius, and simplifies audit trails.
7. **Sync with Cloud-Native Threat Intel:** Static policies are great, but threats evolve. **Leverage cloud threat intelligence to update your posture checks**, based on the latest attack vectors, CVEs, or zero-days targeting Kubernetes environments.
8. **Prioritize with Context:** Every misconfiguration is not equally risky. Use KSPM tools that offer **context-aware prioritization**–for example, distinguishing a publicly exposed dashboard in production from one in staging.
9. **Enforce with Gentle Automation:** Do not jump to auto-remediation everywhere–especially in production. **Instead, implement graduated automation:**
    - Alert in dev
    - Block in staging
    - Auto-remediate in lower-risk clusters

This helps teams to adapt without the fear of breakage.

10. **Review, Refactor, Repeat:** Security posture is never "*done*." Set up regular posture reviews, track drift trends, and use findings to refine your cluster designs and DevOps workflows. **Security is a journey–make it iterative.**

Configuring KSPM for Kubernetes Security

Setting up Kubernetes Security Posture Management (KSPM) is not just about turning on a tool–it is about designing visibility, accountability, and control into your Kubernetes clusters from day one.

Think of it like setting up a home security system: You do not just install cameras; you position them carefully, configure alerts, and define who gets notified, when something is off.

Here is a breakdown of how to **thoughtfully configure KSPM to truly secure your Kubernetes environment:**

1. **Start with Inventory Awareness:** Before securing anything, you need to know what you have. KSPM solutions should be configured to **auto-discover all Kubernetes clusters**, regardless of whether they are in Azure (AKS), AWS (EKS), GCP (GKE), or on-prem.
   a. Ensure all clusters are onboarded into the KSPM tool.
   b. Group clusters by environment (for example, dev, staging, and prod) for better policy targeting.
2. **Define Baseline Security Policies:** KSPM becomes powerful, when aligned with **real-world security policies**. Configure your solution to evaluate clusters, using industry benchmarks like:
   - CIS Kubernetes Benchmarks
   - **Pod Security Standards (PSS)**
   - Your internal security guidelines

Most KSPM tools come with pre-defined policies, but **customizing them to your environment** is key to avoiding noise and focusing on what matters.

3. **Map Roles and Access:** Mismanaged access is one of the top attack vectors. **As part of configuring KSPM, integrate with your identity provider** (for example, Azure AD, Google IAM) and:
   a. Review Role-Based Access Control (RBAC) settings.

   b. Highlight over-permissioned users or service accounts.

   c. Identify privilege escalations.

4. **Enable Runtime Monitoring (Where Supported):** Configuration drift happens. A secure cluster today can become vulnerable tomorrow. **Enable KSPM's runtime and drift detection features to:**

   a. Spot changes in deployed workloads.

   b. Detect containers that suddenly run in privileged mode.

   c. Alert on risky behavior such as network sniffing, or access to sensitive APIs.

5. **Integrate with Notifications and DevOps Tools:** Make sure that your KSPM tool is not a silo. Configure it to **send alerts** to your team's communication channels or ticketing tools (Slack, Teams, and Jira).

   You can also:

   a. Add KSPM checks to your CI/CD pipeline.

   b. Use webhook or API integrations to trigger automated remediations, or policy enforcement.

6. **Establish Secure Score and Reporting: Many KSPM solutions** (like Microsoft Defender for Cloud) **offer a secure score or posture dashboard**. Set this up to reflect:

   - The overall health of your clusters.
   - Remediation trends over time.
   - Compliance status against regulatory frameworks (for example, PCI, HIPAA, and SOC 2)

   This gives you a measurable way to track progress, and justify security investments.

7. **Review and Refine Regularly:** Security posture is not static. Schedule regular reviews of:

   - Policy coverage
   - Alert noise vs. true positives
   - User access and drift findings

This helps you **tune your KSPM configuration to remain relevant** as your clusters grow and evolve.

Configuring KSPM for Kubernetes is about more than just enabling a feature–**it is about embedding security into the DNA of your infrastructure.** With the right configuration, KSPM does not just protect your environment–it empowers your team with clarity, confidence, and control.

KSPM Labs

Kubernetes Security Posture Management (KSPM) is necessary for maintaining a secure and compliant Kubernetes environment, regardless of where it is deployed.

Lab # 1: Enabling the KSPM Module in Microsoft Defender for Cloud

Organizations use **Kubernetes** across different cloud providers such as **Google Kubernetes Engine (GKE) on Google Cloud, Azure Kubernetes Service (AKS) on Microsoft Azure, and Amazon Elastic Kubernetes Service (EKS) on AWS**, as well as in **on-premises and hybrid environments**. Securing these clusters is critical to prevent misconfigurations, unauthorized access, and compliance violations.

Microsoft Defender for Cloud provides **KSPM capabilities** to help detect security risks, enforce best practices, and align with compliance standards like **CIS Kubernetes Benchmark**.

In this lab, we will **enable the KSPM module in Microsoft Defender for Cloud** to monitor and secure **GKE clusters running on Google Cloud Platform (GCP),** Azure Kubernetes Service (AKS) running on Azure Cloud Platform, and AWS EKS running on AWS Cloud Platform.

By completing this lab, you will take the first step toward **integrating KSPM into a CNAPP strategy**, ensuring continuous security monitoring for your Kubernetes workloads, whether in the cloud or hybrid environments.

Prerequisite: Ensure that you have completed *Chapter 3, Onboarding* CNAPP: A *Practical Guide and have successfully onboarded your Azure*, AWS and GCP accounts to Microsoft Defender for Cloud, before proceeding with this lab.

Follow these steps to enable the KSPM module in Microsoft Defender for Cloud:

1. Log into the Azure portal using your administrative credentials.
2. Go to the search bar > type "`Microsoft Defender for Cloud`", and select the service to open the dashboard.
3. Once inside the dashboard, locate the "`Environment Settings`" tab on the left-hand menu.

4. Now, select the subscription where you want to enable the KSPM module. In our case, we are selecting the subscription that was linked to the Google Cloud project during the initial onboarding process. Refer to the following screenshot, which displays all available subscriptions in our Microsoft Defender for Cloud instance:

Figure 7.1: *Selecting the Subscription Linked to the GCP Project*

5. Click on **Settings, in front of Defender CSPM under the `Cloud Security Posture Management`** section. Refer to the following screenshot:

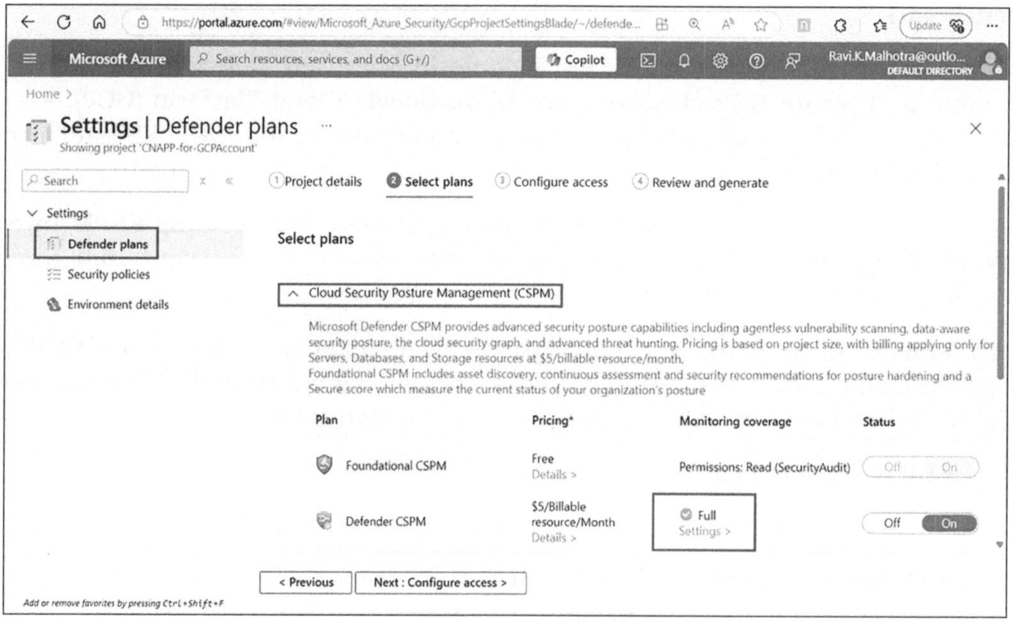

Figure 7.2: *Settings Panel for Defender CSPM*

6. Toggle on the "**`Kubernetes API access`**" component, if not already toggled on.

7. Click on **Save** button.
8. Go to **Containers > Settings** under **Cloud Workload Protection** section.

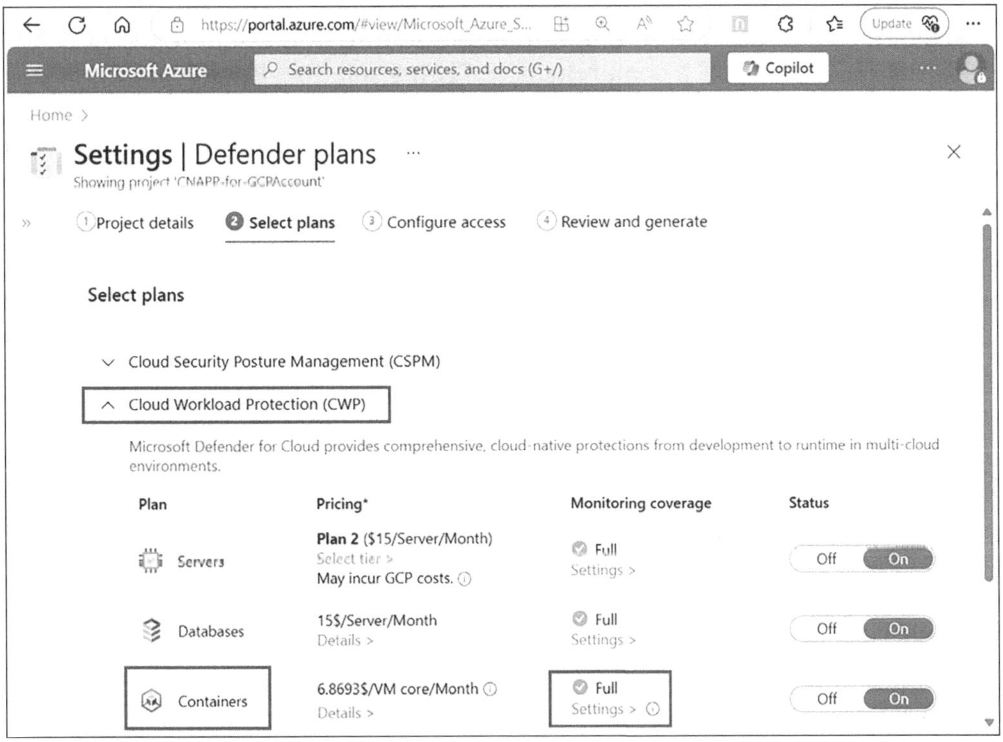

Figure 7.3: *Settings Panel for Containers under CWP*

9. Toggle on the "**Kubernetes API access**" component, if not already toggled on.
10. With the KSPM module now enabled in **Microsoft Defender for Cloud**, your associated GCP project is successfully onboarded for Kubernetes security posture monitoring.
11. This concludes the lab.

Conclusion

Securing modern cloud-native applications demands a deep understanding of how infrastructure components behave, interact, and scale. Among these, **Kubernetes has emerged as the cornerstone of container orchestration**, powering everything from microservices architectures to enterprise grade deployments. While its capabilities bring unmatched agility and scalability, they also introduce a wide range of security risks–from misconfigurations and overly permissive access to lack of network segmentation and insecure workloads.

This is where **Kubernetes Security Posture Management (KSPM)** plays a vital role. Throughout this chapter, we explored how **Microsoft Defender for Cloud** delivers KSPM as an integral part of a comprehensive CNAPP solution. By onboarding a **Google Cloud Platform (GCP)** project and deploying a **Google Kubernetes Engine (GKE)** cluster, we demonstrated how cloud practitioners can gain deep visibility into the security posture of their Kubernetes environments–even in a multi-cloud setting.

We enabled KSPM, reviewed meaningful security recommendations, mapped them to the **CIS Kubernetes Benchmark**, and understood how remediation steps directly contribute to improving the overall cluster health. We also walked through how Defender for Cloud detects potential threats in real time and raises contextual alerts, empowering teams to proactively respond before vulnerabilities are exploited.

The labs in this chapter were not just tasks–they were designed to mirror real-world workflows of modern DevSecOps and cloud security teams. The objective was to build both **confidence and competence** in using Microsoft Defender for Cloud as a **cross-cloud KSPM solution**, specifically leveraging the GCP ecosystem. Whether you are a cloud architect, a security engineer, or a learner preparing for industry roles, these hands-on examples lay the foundation for Kubernetes-native security practices in your environment.

In essence, securing Kubernetes is no longer a reactive task–it must be **continuous, policy-driven, and integrated** into your broader CNAPP strategy. KSPM enables exactly that: providing context-rich, cloud-aware insights and recommendations that help shift security left, reduce risk, and simplify compliance.

As we move from workload-specific posture management into broader cloud protection mechanisms, the next chapter focuses on an equally critical area–**Cloud Service Network Security (CSNS). While Kubernetes posture deals with workload configuration and runtime risks, network security underpins how services communicate, how access is controlled, and how traffic is monitored across your cloud environments.** In the upcoming chapter, we will explore how CNAPP addresses network visibility, segmentation, Zero Trust principles, and how Microsoft Defender for Cloud supports these through native and integrated capabilities across public clouds like GCP.

Points to Remember

Here are some **key points to remember** from this chapter on **Understanding Kubernetes Security Posture Management (KSPM):**

- **KSPM (Kubernetes Security Posture Management)** focuses on identifying and fixing misconfigurations and security risks in Kubernetes environments.

- **Microsoft Defender for Cloud** offers KSPM capabilities that work across **multi-cloud Kubernetes clusters**, including **Google Kubernetes Engine (GKE)** on **GCP**.
- You must **onboard your GCP project to Microsoft Defender for Cloud** before enabling KSPM.
- **Security recommendations** provided by Defender for Cloud align with standards like the **CIS Kubernetes Benchmark**.
- **Remediation actions** (like RBAC tightening, disabling privileged containers, and so on) directly improve your **secure score** and cluster posture.
- **Defender for Cloud not only offers preventive insights**, but also provides **real-time threat detection and alerts** for suspicious Kubernetes activity.
- These **labs lay the foundation for integrating KSPM** as a key component of the **CNAPP (Cloud-Native Application Protection Platform)** strategy.

Multiple-Choice Questions

1. What is the primary goal of Kubernetes Security Posture Management?
   a. Automating application deployment
   b. Enhancing container image performance
   c. Identifying and remediating misconfigurations in Kubernetes clusters
   d. Managing billing in multi-cloud environments
2. Before enabling the KSPM module in Microsoft Defender for Cloud for a GCP cluster, what must be done first?
   a. Setup a custom VPC.
   b. Create a GCP cluster.
   c. Onboard the GCP project to Defender for Cloud.
   d. Enable billing alerts.
3. Which Kubernetes service was used in this chapter for hands-on KSPM labs on GCP?
   a. Cloud Run
   b. Cloud Functions
   c. Google Kubernetes Engine
   d. App Engine

4. Which benchmark does Microsoft Defender for Cloud align with for Kubernetes security best practices?
    a. ISO 27001
    b. CIS Kubernetes Benchmark
    c. SOC 2
    d. PCI-DSS
5. What type of insights does KSPM provide, once enabled in Microsoft Defender for Cloud?
    a. CBilling cost trends
    b. Network latency reports
    c. Security misconfigurations and posture recommendations
    d. Backup status of cloud VMs

Answers

1. c
2. c
3. c
4. b
5. c

Questions

1. What does KSPM stand for?
2. Which Microsoft service provides KSPM capabilities?
3. What GCP service is used to deploy Kubernetes clusters?
4. What is the first step before enabling KSPM in Microsoft Defender for Cloud for GCP?
5. Which security benchmark does Defender for Cloud use for Kubernetes posture checks?
6. What kind of misconfigurations does KSPM help identify?

7. Does KSPM provide security recommendations in real time or after a manual scan?
8. Can Microsoft Defender for Cloud perform KSPM on GKE clusters hosted in GCP?
9. What type of alerts does KSPM generate in Defender for Cloud?
10. How does enabling KSPM help in improving Kubernetes cluster security?

Key Terms

- **Kubernetes Security Posture Management (KSPM):** A security approach that focuses on identifying, managing, and remediating misconfigurations in Kubernetes clusters to improve security posture.
- **Google Kubernetes Engine (GKE):** A managed Kubernetes service on Google Cloud Platform (GCP) that allows users to run containerized applications.
- **Microsoft Defender for Cloud (MDC):** A cloud-native security solution that provides KSPM capabilities across multi-cloud environments, including Kubernetes security management.
- **CIS Kubernetes Benchmark:** A set of best practices and security guidelines used to secure Kubernetes clusters, and align them with industry standards.
- **Kubernetes Misconfigurations:** Incorrect configurations or vulnerabilities in Kubernetes clusters such as exposed dashboards, insecure access controls, and improperly configured network policies.
- **Cluster Security Posture:** The overall security configuration and settings of a Kubernetes cluster, including the configuration of nodes, containers, and network policies.
- **Continuous Security Monitoring:** Ongoing assessment and real-time monitoring of security risks within Kubernetes clusters to ensure posture management is always up-to-date.
- **Security Alerts:** Notifications generated by Microsoft Defender for Cloud, when potential security risks such as misconfigurations or vulnerabilities are detected in the Kubernetes environment.
- **Cross-Cloud Security Posture:** The ability to manage security across multiple cloud platforms, including GCP, using tools like Microsoft Defender for Cloud for Kubernetes security management.
- **Kubernetes Compliance:** The process of ensuring that Kubernetes clusters meet industry and organizational security standards and regulations such as the CIS Kubernetes Benchmark.

Chapter 8
Understanding DevSecOps with CNAPP

Introduction

In today's fast-moving digital era, **where businesses are deploying code hundreds of times a day and scaling across multi-cloud environments**, traditional approaches to application security no longer hold ground. **Security can no longer be an afterthought or a final step before deployment – it must be embedded from day one**.

This is where **DevSecOps comes in** – a **modern cultural and technical shift** that **integrates security practices directly into DevOps** workflows. It is not about slowing teams down; it is about **building secure, scalable, and resilient systems, without sacrificing speed or innovation**.

This chapter introduces the principles and practices of DevSecOps in the context of cloud-native development, breaking down how security is automated, enforced, and monitored at every phase of the software lifecycle.

From **secure code and CI/CD pipelines to runtime protection** and **feedback loops**, we will explore how tools like **Microsoft Defender for Cloud empower organizations to operationalize security at cloud scale – turning DevSecOps from a buzzword into a business advantage**.

Structure

The following topics will be covered in this chapter:

- Modern DevOps Buzzwords Explained
- Understanding DevSecOps in Action
- Integrating Microsoft Defender for Cloud in a DevSecOps Workflow

- Real-World Use Cases and Best Practices
- Popular IaC Languages Used by Industry Experts
- Understanding JSON Language
- Understanding YAML Language
- Understanding Terraform Language
- The Fundamentals of IaC Scanning
- Tools and Technologies for IaC Scanning
- Challenges in IaC Scanning

Modern DevOps Buzzwords Explained

The world of DevSecOps has exploded with new terminology, and for someone trying to make sense of it all, it can feel overwhelming. But the truth is – all these buzzwords are just simplified ways to explain how security fits into modern cloud-based software development. In this section, we will break down the most talked-about DevSecOps concepts in plain language. Whether you are a security engineer, developer, or cloud enthusiast, this guide will help you understand how these ideas come together inside any CNAPP solution like Microsoft Defender for Cloud.

Let us begin with **Shift Left Security** – a concept that essentially means bringing security earlier into the software development lifecycle. Traditionally, security checks were done at the end of development, right before releasing code into production. But with shift left, the idea is to catch issues early when code is still being written, tested, and reviewed. This saves time, reduces cost, and helps fix problems, before they grow big. Microsoft Defender for Cloud enables this shift by integrating directly with developer tools like GitHub and Azure Repos to scan code and infrastructure templates, before they are ever deployed.

Another term you will frequently come across is **CI/CD Security**. This refers to embedding security checks directly into Continuous Integration and Continuous Deployment (CI/CD) pipelines. These are automated systems that developers use to push code, run tests, and deploy applications. With DevSecOps, tools like Defender for DevOps scan for misconfigurations, hardcoded secrets, exposed credentials, and insecure settings every time the code passes through the pipeline. This makes sure security doesn't slow down automation it flows with it.

You will also hear about **Secrets Detection**, a powerful but often overlooked DevSecOps feature. Secrets like API keys, passwords, and database credentials are sometimes mistakenly left in code. When this happens, it becomes a massive risk – anyone who sees that code can misuse these secrets. Defender for DevOps continuously scans your repositories to catch hardcoded secrets and alerts you before they go public.

A closely related idea is **Policy-as-Code**, which means writing security policies (what should and should not be allowed) in a programmable way, often using JSON or YAML files. These policies can be enforced automatically through tools like Azure Policy or GitHub Actions. For instance, you can create a policy that says, "*No resource should be deployed without encryption*," and the pipeline will fail, if someone violates it.

Another rising concept is **Runtime Security** – security that protects your application after it's deployed and running live in the cloud. Defender for Cloud provides real-time monitoring, behavioral analytics, and threat detection for virtual machines, containers, databases, and serverless apps across Azure, AWS, and GCP. This helps identify things like privilege escalation, malware, unusual logins, or data exfiltration attempts.

Also gaining attention is **Supply Chain Security**. Today's applications depend on external libraries, APIs, and container images pulled from public sources. If any of these components are compromised, your entire application becomes vulnerable. Defender helps detect known vulnerabilities in packages and images used in your pipeline, offering early visibility into supply chain risks.

Lastly, **DevSecOps Automation** is the thread that ties all of this together. It means automating security actions wherever possible – from blocking risky deployments to automatically opening tickets in Jira or triggering alerts when something suspicious happens. With Defender for Cloud, you can automate threat response, send alerts to SIEM systems, or even auto-remediate some issues using Logic Apps or playbooks.

Then comes **Infrastructure as Code (IaC) Scanning** – an essential buzzword today. Infrastructure as Code means you write cloud infrastructure (like virtual machines, networks, storage, and databases) in code files using formats like Terraform, Bicep, or ARM templates. Since these are just code files, they can also have bugs and insecure defaults. Defender for Cloud offers built-in scanning for these IaC templates, allowing you to identify misconfigurations such as public access to storage buckets or missing encryption settings – all before deploying them.

Let us say you are setting up your cloud environment – not by clicking buttons on a portal, but by writing everything as code (called Infrastructure as Code, or IaC). This includes things such as:

- Which servers to create
- What storage to use
- Who gets access to what

Now imagine if there is a small mistake in that code – like a public-facing server or an open database. **IaC Scanning automatically reviews this code before it goes live**, flags risky configurations, and helps fix them fast.

Why it matters: It is like proofreading a recipe before cooking, so you do not add salt instead of sugar.

Where Defender for Cloud fits in: It scans your Bicep, ARM, Terraform, or other IaC templates for security risks, and suggests the best practices.

Here is a complete list of modern buzzwords used on a day-to-day basis:

- Shift-left security
- Security as Code (SaC)
- AI-Drive Threat Detection
- Continuous Compliance
- Infrastructure as Code (IaC) Security
- DevSecOps Automation
- Zero Trust Architecture
- Secure Software Supply Chain
- Secure Orchestration, Automation and Response (SOAR)
- Policy as Code (PaC)
- Runtime Application Self-Protection (RASP)
- Cloud-Native Security
- Security Observability
- Immutable Infrastructure
- Compliance as Code
- Micro segmentation
- Security Champions Program
- DevSecOps Maturity Model
- Security Posture Management
- Automated Penetration Testing

In summary, these modern DevSecOps buzzwords are not just trends – they represent a smarter, automated, and developer-friendly way to build secure cloud-native apps. And Microsoft Defender for Cloud, acting as a CNAPP solution, brings all these capabilities under one roof, helping organizations adopt these practices, without slowing down innovation.

Understanding DevSecOps in Action

In today's dynamic cloud-native development landscape, security is no longer an afterthought, but a fundamental component woven throughout the software development lifecycle. DevSecOps embodies this paradigm shift by integrating security practices seamlessly into every phase of the DevOps pipeline–from initial code creation to deployment and ongoing operations. This approach ensures that security is continuous, automated, and collaborative, aligning with the agility and scalability demands of modern cloud environments.

By embedding security tools and practices into development workflows, organizations can proactively identify vulnerabilities, enforce compliance policies, and respond swiftly to threats, without hindering innovation. This section delves into the core components of a functional DevSecOps pipeline, illustrating how each stage–from secure coding and version control integration to infrastructure as code (IaC) security and runtime protection–contributes to building robust and secure applications at scale. Through this exploration, we aim to provide a comprehensive understanding of how DevSecOps operates in practice, fostering a culture, where security is a shared responsibility, and an enabler of innovation.

- **Secure Code Practices:** The journey begins with developers writing secure code. This means following secure coding guidelines, avoiding known coding flaws (like SQL injection or insecure deserialization), and performing static analysis using tools integrated directly into the development environment.

  Microsoft Defender for DevOps can connect with code repositories such as GitHub and Azure Repos to scan for vulnerabilities, secrets, and misconfigurations, even before the code is committed.

- **Version Control Integration**: DevSecOps extends into version control systems like Git, where code is stored and reviewed. Automated security checks can be triggered during pull requests, flagging issues like hardcoded secrets or insecure dependencies. Security reviews become part of the normal code review process, creating collaboration between developers and security teams.
- **Build Pipeline Security**: As the code is pushed through Continuous Integration (CI) pipelines, it passes through automated checks. These include Software Composition Analysis (SCA) to detect vulnerabilities in third-party libraries and dependency chains. Defender for Cloud integrates with these CI pipelines to scan both code and infrastructure templates, ensuring that security is not bypassed during builds.
- **Infrastructure as Code (IaC) Security**: Infrastructure is now deployed using code – Terraform, ARM, Bicep, and so on. These IaC templates can introduce risks, if misconfigured. Defender for Cloud scans these templates for known issues such as open security groups, missing encryption settings, or public access to sensitive resources. This step is crucial to prevent insecure infrastructure from ever being deployed.
- **Policy Enforcement and Gates**: Once security scans are complete, DevSecOps enforces *security gates* – automated policies that block deployments if high-severity issues are found. These gates can be customized to match your

organization's risk appetite and compliance needs. For example, you might block any deployment with an unencrypted storage account, or allow only approved container images.

- **Deployment and Runtime Protection**: Even after applications are deployed, security does not stop. DevSecOps ensures that cloud workloads are monitored continuously. Defender for Cloud offers runtime protections such as workload vulnerability assessment, anomaly detection, endpoint protection, and even container runtime insights. If a new vulnerability is discovered in a running app, teams can be alerted in real time.
- **Threat Detection and Automated Response**: A key DevSecOps principle is speed – not just in building software, but also in responding to threats. Defender for Cloud can trigger alerts to SIEM systems like Microsoft Sentinel, and even automate responses using Logic Apps. This allows teams to quarantine affected VMs, rotate secrets, or trigger incident workflows within minutes of detection.
- **Continuous Feedback and Improvement**: Lastly, every incident, vulnerability, or failed policy check creates a learning loop. DevSecOps thrives on feedback – it helps teams understand root causes, update security baselines, refine IaC templates, and improve future builds. Microsoft Defender for Cloud supports this feedback loop with dashboards, scorecards, and detailed recommendations that guide future action.

DevSecOps in action is about weaving security into every thread of your cloud fabric. It empowers developers to take ownership of security, without slowing them down, while giving security teams the visibility and control they need. Tools like Microsoft Defender for Cloud make this process scalable, multi-cloud-ready, and aligned with real-world threats. Whether you are working in Azure, AWS, or GCP, the core ideas remain the same: Automate, integrate, and continuously secure everything.

Integrating Microsoft Defender for Cloud in a DevSecOps Workflow

In the rapidly evolving landscape of cloud-native development, **organizations are increasingly embracing DevSecOps to embed security throughout the software development lifecycle.**

Microsoft Defender for Cloud emerges as a pivotal tool in this paradigm, offering a suite of capabilities that **seamlessly integrate security into DevOps workflows**. By providing **comprehensive visibility**, **continuous monitoring**, and **automated threat protection across multicloud environments**–including **Azure**, **AWS**, and **GCP**–Defender for Cloud ensures that security is not an afterthought but a continuous, integrated process. It enables security teams to **protect applications and resources**

from code to cloud across multi-pipeline environments, including Azure DevOps, GitHub, and GitLab.

This integration allows for early detection of vulnerabilities, misconfigurations, and compliance issues, thereby reducing the risk of security breaches, and ensuring that **only secure code is promoted to production**.

Moreover, Defender for Cloud's ability to correlate DevOps security recommendations with other contextual cloud security insights helps prioritize remediation efforts effectively.

By embedding security checks into CI/CD pipelines, scanning Infrastructure as Code (IaC) templates, and enforcing security policies automatically, organizations can maintain agility without compromising on security.

This approach not only strengthens the security posture but also fosters a culture of shared responsibility among development, security, and operations teams.

In the following sections, we will delve deeper into how Microsoft Defender for Cloud facilitates this integration, enabling organizations to build, deploy, and manage applications securely and efficiently in a DevSecOps framework.

Microsoft Defender for Cloud **offers robust integration capabilities with leading DevOps platforms**, notably **Azure DevOps** and **GitHub**. By onboarding these platforms, organizations can seamlessly incorporate security assessments, policy enforcement, and compliance checks into their DevSecOps workflows. This section provides a step-by-step guide on **how to connect both Azure DevOps and GitHub to Microsoft Defender for Cloud**, ensuring a unified and secure development pipeline.

Incorporating Microsoft Defender for Cloud into your DevSecOps workflow ensures that security is embedded throughout the software development lifecycle. Here is how you can achieve this:

1. **Onboard Your DevOps Environment**: Integrating your DevOps platforms with `Microsoft Defender for Cloud` is the foundational step in embedding security into your development lifecycle. For Azure DevOps, this involves connecting your organization through the Azure portal, enabling Defender for Cloud to access and monitor your repositories and pipelines. Similarly, for GitHub, establishing this connection allows for continuous security assessments of your codebase. By onboarding these environments, you set the stage for proactive security management across your development processes.

Azure DevOps:

a. **Navigate to:** `Azure Portal > Microsoft Defender for Cloud >` Environment settings.

b. **Select:** '`Add environment`' and choose '`Azure DevOps`'.

c. **Provide Details:** Enter a name, subscription, resource group, and region.

d. **Authorize:** Click `'Authorize'` to grant Defender for Cloud access to your Azure DevOps organization.

e. **Permissions Required:** Ensure that you have `Project Collection Administrator` permissions, and `Basic Access Level` for the Azure DevOps organization.

GitHub:

a. **Navigate to:** `Azure Portal` > `Microsoft Defender for Cloud` > `Environment` settings.

b. **Select:** '`Add environment`' and choose `'GitHub'`.

c. **Authenticate:** Sign in to GitHub and authorize `Defender for Cloud` to access your repositories.

d. **Set Permissions:** Ensure that workflow permissions are set to '`Read and Write`' on the GitHub repository.

2. **Integrate Security Scanning into CI/CD Pipelines**: Embedding security scans into your Continuous Integration and Continuous Deployment (CI/CD) pipelines ensures that vulnerabilities are identified and addressed early in the development process. Microsoft Defender for Cloud facilitates this by integrating with your existing CI/CD tools, allowing automated scanning of code, dependencies, and configurations. This proactive approach helps maintain code quality and security standards, before deployment.

Azure DevOps:

a. **Install Extension:** Add the Microsoft Security DevOps (MSDO) extension to your Azure DevOps organization.

b. **Configure Pipeline:** In your YAML pipeline, add a task to run the MSDO CLI, which executes security analyzers and outputs results in SARIF format.

c. **Publish Results:** Use the '`PublishBuildArtifacts@1`' task to publish the SARIF file to the `'CodeAnalysisLogs'` artifact.

d. **Defender for Cloud Integration:** Defender for Cloud automatically ingests these artifacts and provides security recommendations.

GitHub:

a. **Create Workflow:** In your GitHub repository, navigate to the `'Actions'` tab and set up a new workflow.

b. **Add MSDO Action:** Use the '`microsoft/security-devops-action`' in your workflow YAML file to run security analyzers.

c. **Set Permissions:** Ensure '`id-token: write`' permissions are set in the GitHub Workflow for federation with Defender for Cloud.

3. **Configure Policy Enforcement and Compliance**: Establishing and enforcing security policies is crucial for maintaining compliance and governance across your cloud environments. Microsoft Defender for Cloud allows you to define security standards, and apply them to your resources, ensuring adherence to organizational and regulatory requirements. Through continuous assessment, Defender for Cloud identifies non-compliant resources, and provides recommendations for remediation.

    a. **Navigate to:** `Azure Portal` > `Microsoft Defender for Cloud` > `Environment settings`.

    b. **Select Subscription:** Choose the subscription you want to configure.

    c. **Enable Defender Plans:** Turn on relevant Defender plans (for example, Defender for Servers, and Defender for App Service) to enforce security policies.

    d. **Set Policies:** Use Azure Policy to define and assign policies that enforce compliance requirements across your resources.

4. **Implement Workflow Automation**: Automating responses to security alerts and recommendations streamlines your incident management process. With Microsoft Defender for Cloud, you can set up workflow automations using Logic Apps that trigger actions such as sending notifications, creating tickets, or initiating remediation steps, when specific security events occur. This automation enhances your organization's ability to respond swiftly to potential threats.

    a. **Navigate to:** `Azure Portal` > `Microsoft Defender for Cloud` > `Workflow` automation.

    b. **Create Logic App:** Define a Logic App that triggers on specific Defender for Cloud alerts or recommendations.

    c. **Configure Actions:** Set actions such as sending notifications, creating tickets, or initiating remediation steps.

   d. **Save and Enable:** Once configured, save and enable the workflow automation to respond to security events automatically.

5. **Monitor and Respond to Security Findings**: Continuous monitoring of your cloud resources is essential for maintaining a strong security posture. Microsoft Defender for Cloud provides tools to visualize security findings, track compliance status, and analyze trends over time. By leveraging these insights, your security teams can prioritize remediation efforts, address vulnerabilities promptly, and ensure ongoing protection of your cloud environments.
   - **Use Security Explorer:** In Defender for Cloud, utilize the Security Explorer to view and analyze security findings across your DevOps environments.
   - **Prioritize Remediation:** Leverage the contextual insights provided to prioritize remediation efforts effectively.
   - **Collaborate Across Teams:** Integrate findings into tools like Microsoft Teams or Jira to facilitate collaboration between development and security teams.

By following these steps, you can effectively integrate Microsoft Defender for Cloud into your DevSecOps workflow, ensuring continuous security and compliance throughout your software development lifecycle.

Real-World Use Cases and Best Practices

Integrating Microsoft Defender for Cloud into your DevSecOps workflow is not just about adopting a tool–it is about transforming your development and operations processes to prioritize security at every stage. By examining real-world scenarios, and adhering to best practices, organizations can enhance their security posture, ensure compliance, and streamline their development processes.

Use Case 1: Early Detection of Vulnerabilities in CI/CD Pipelines

Incorporating security scans into Continuous Integration and Continuous Deployment (CI/CD) pipelines allows for the early detection of vulnerabilities. For instance, a development team integrating Defender for Cloud with Azure DevOps can automatically scan Infrastructure as Code (IaC) templates and container images for misconfigurations, before deployment. This proactive approach ensures that security issues are addressed promptly, reducing the risk of breaches in production environments.

Best Practices:

- **Automate Security Scans:** Integrate security scanning tools within your CI/CD pipelines to automatically detect vulnerabilities during the build process.
- **Implement Shift-Left Security:** Encourage developers to consider security from the initial stages of development, fostering a culture of proactive security awareness.

Use Case 2: Enhancing Compliance through Continuous Monitoring

Organizations operating in regulated industries must adhere to strict compliance standards. By leveraging Defender for Cloud's continuous monitoring capabilities, a financial institution can ensure that its cloud resources comply with frameworks like PCI-DSS or ISO 27001. The platform provides real-time insights and recommendations, enabling the organization to maintain compliance, and avoid potential penalties.

Best Practices:

- **Define Compliance Policies:** Establish clear compliance policies within Defender for Cloud to monitor adherence to relevant standards.
- **Regularly Review Compliance Reports:** Utilize the platform's reporting features to assess compliance status, and identify areas for improvement.

Use Case 3: Responding to Security Incidents with Automated Workflows

In the event of a security incident, rapid response is crucial. Consider a scenario where an organization detects unusual activity indicating a potential breach. By configuring automated workflows in Defender for Cloud, the organization can initiate predefined responses such as isolating affected resources or notifying security teams, thereby minimizing the impact of the incident.

Best Practices:

- **Establish Incident Response Playbooks:** Develop and implement automated response strategies for various security scenarios.`TECHCOMMUNITY.MICROSOFT.COM`
- **Integrate with Communication Tools:** Ensure that alerts and notifications are seamlessly integrated with communication platforms to facilitate prompt action.

Use Case 4: Managing Shadow IT and Unauthorized Applications

Shadow IT poses significant risks as unauthorized applications may bypass security controls. An enterprise utilizing Defender for Cloud can identify and monitor unsanctioned applications within its network. By gaining visibility into these applications, the organization can enforce policies to restrict access, and ensure that only approved tools are used.

Best Practices:

- **Conduct Regular Application Discovery:** Use Defender for Cloud to continuously scan for, and identify unauthorized applications.
- **Implement Access Controls:** Enforce strict access policies to prevent the use of unapproved applications, and mitigate associated risks.

Use Case 5: Securing Multi-Cloud Environments

Organizations often operate across multiple cloud platforms, each with its own security challenges. By deploying Defender for Cloud across Azure, AWS, and GCP environments, a company can achieve unified visibility and control over its entire cloud infrastructure. This centralized approach simplifies security management, and ensures consistent policy enforcement across all platforms.

Best Practices:

- **Standardize Security Policies:** Develop uniform security policies applicable across all cloud environments to maintain consistency.
- **Utilize Centralized Dashboards:** Leverage Defender for Cloud's centralized dashboards to monitor and manage security across multiple platforms effectively.

The Fundamentals of Infrastructure as Code (IaC)

In the past, setting up and managing IT systems was a labor-intensive, manual task. Teams would designate an engineer to provision a server for a new application, database, or file storage. This process often included lengthy discussions about naming the new server, and many more low-level configuration tasks such as IP addresses, roles, and permissions.

Today, those days are behind us. With the advent of distributed architectures, ephemeral cloud resources, and global scalability, modern development teams rely on code and automation to configure their systems. **This approach, known as Infrastructure as Code (IaC), accelerates infrastructure setup, and minimizes errors.** For organizations managing complex systems, IaC is a significant advantage.

In a very simple definition, IaC is a modern approach to managing and provisioning computing infrastructure through machine-readable scripts, rather than through manual processes.

Imagine you could set up your entire computer network, including servers, databases, and networking equipment, just by writing a few lines of code. That's essentially what IaC allows you to do.

By defining your infrastructure in code, you can automate the setup, configuration, and management of your IT resources, making it faster, more reliable, and less prone to human errors.

Think of IaC as creating a blueprint for your infrastructure. Just like an architect designs a building with detailed plans, you write scripts that describe how your infrastructure should look and behave. These scripts can be version-controlled, shared, and reused, ensuring consistency across different environments (like development, testing, and production).

In this modern era of cloud computing and DevOps, IaC has revolutionized the way organizations manage and deploy their IT infrastructure. By treating the infrastructure configuration as code, IaC enables automation, consistency, and scalability.

This approach not only saves time, but also enhances collaboration among teams, as everyone can see and modify the infrastructure code. In essence, IaC transforms infrastructure management into a software engineering practice, bringing the benefits of automation, scalability, and repeatability to the world of IT operations.

However, this shift also introduces new security challenges that require specialized solutions.

Popular IaC Languages Used by Industry Experts

Infrastructure as Code (IaC) has revolutionized the way organizations manage and provision their IT infrastructure. **By treating infrastructure configurations as code, IaC enables automation, consistency, and scalability, significantly reducing the time and effort required for manual setup and management.**

AWS CloudFormation and Azure Resource Manager are two of the most renowned IaC techniques widely adopted by cloud experts across the industry. However, the landscape of IaC tools and technologies is vast, offering numerous options for automating and managing cloud IT infrastructure.

Industry experts rely on a variety of IaC languages and tools to streamline their workflows, and ensure reliable, repeatable infrastructure deployments. The following is a list of some of the most commonly used IaC languages and tools in the industry. This is a list of IaC tools and technologies commonly used by industry professionals:

- **Terraform:** Developed by **HashiCorp**, **Terraform** is a widely used open-source tool that allows you to define and provision infrastructure across multiple cloud providers using a simple, declarative language.
- **AWS CloudFormation (JSON/YAML):** This is Amazon Web Services' **(AWS)** native IaC tool, which enables you to model and set up your AWS resources using JSON or YAML templates. It integrates seamlessly with other AWS services.
- **Azure Resource Manager (ARM):** Microsoft's **(Azure)** IaC solution for managing Azure resources. ARM templates are written in JSON and allow you to deploy, manage, and monitor resources as a group.
- **Google Cloud Deployment Manager (JSON/YAML): Google's** IaC tool that uses YAML, Python, or Jinja2 templates to define and deploy Google Cloud resources.
- **Pulumi (Multiple Languages):** A modern IaC tool that supports multiple programming languages like JavaScript, TypeScript, Python, Go, and C#. Pulumi allows you to use familiar languages to define and manage cloud infrastructure.
- **Ansible (YAML):** An **open-source automation tool** that can be used for configuration management, application deployment, and IaC. Ansible uses YAML to define automation jobs, making it easy to read and write.
- **Chef (Ruby):** A powerful configuration management tool that uses Ruby-based DSL for writing configuration "*recipes*." Chef is used to automate infrastructure provisioning and management.
- **Puppet (DSL):** Similar to Chef, Puppet is a configuration management tool that uses its own declarative language to manage infrastructure. It is known for its robust reporting and compliance features.
- **SaltStack:** An open-source configuration management and orchestration tool that uses Python to define infrastructure states. SaltStack is known for its speed and scalability.

- **Vagrant:** A tool for building and managing virtualized development environments. Vagrant provides easy-to-configure, reproducible, and portable work environments.
- **Kubernetes Operators:** These are custom controllers that extend the Kubernetes API to manage complex applications and their dependencies using custom resources.
- **Crossplane:** An open-source project that extends Kubernetes to manage infrastructure across multiple cloud providers using Kubernetes-native APIs.
- **AWS CDK (Cloud Development Kit):** Allows you to define cloud infrastructure using familiar programming languages like TypeScript, JavaScript, Python, Java, and C#.
- **Spacelift:** A management platform that supports multi-IaC workflows, integrating with tools such as Terraform, Pulumi, and Kubernetes to provide a unified management experience.

In summary, the adoption of IaC languages and tools has become essential for modern IT operations. By leveraging these powerful IaC solutions, organizations can achieve greater efficiency, consistency, and scalability in their infrastructure management. Embracing these tools not only streamlines operations, but also paves the way for innovation and agility in the ever-evolving landscape of cloud computing.

Understanding JSON Language

As we delve into the topic of IaC, it is essential to understand JSON, one of the most widely used languages for creating IaC templates used in cloud computing platforms like AWS, Azure, GCP and many more.

JSON plays a crucial role in IaC by providing a structured and human-readable format for defining and managing infrastructure configurations. Many IaC tools such as AWS CloudFormation and Azure Resource Manager, use JSON to describe the desired state of cloud resources. These JSON templates specify the configuration of resources like virtual machines, storage accounts, and networking components, allowing for automated and repeatable deployments.

By leveraging JSON, IaC enables developers and operations teams to **version control their infrastructure, apply consistent configurations across environments**, and **reduce the risk of manual errors. These JSON templates are repeatable, and can be used multiple times.**

JSON is built on **two structures: A collection of key-value pairs** (often referred to as an object) and an **ordered list of values** (known as an array). **Each key in a JSON object must be a string enclosed in double quotes**, and the values can be strings, numbers, booleans, arrays, objects, or null. JSON's simplicity and flexibility make it a popular choice for data exchange in web development, APIs, and configuration files. Its language-independent nature means it can be used across various programming languages, including JavaScript, Python, Java, and many others.

JSON, which stands for JavaScript Object Notation, is a lightweight data interchange format that is easy for humans to read and write, and easy for machines to parse and generate. It is primarily used to transmit data between a server and a web application as text.

Here is a basic syntax overview with short examples:

- **Objects:** Represented as key-value pairs enclosed in curly braces {}.
- **Arrays:** Ordered lists of values enclosed in square brackets [].
- **Values:** Can be strings, numbers, objects, arrays, true, false, or null.

1. **JSON Object:**

```
{
  "name": "John Doe",
  "age": 30,
  "isStudent": false
}
```

Understanding JSON is essential for anyone working in modern software development, as it plays a crucial role in data serialization and communication between systems. Unlike XML, another data interchange format, JSON is less verbose and more straightforward, making it quicker to write and easier to read. This efficiency is particularly beneficial in web development, where JSON is often used to send data between a client and a server.

One of the key advantages of JSON is its compatibility with many programming languages. Most modern languages have built-in functions or libraries for parsing and generating JSON data. The interoperability of JSON with various programming languages and tools further enhances its utility in IaC, making it a foundational element in modern cloud infrastructure management.

In JavaScript, for instance, the **`JSON.parse()` method** converts a JSON string into a JavaScript object, while `JSON.stringify()` does the reverse, converting a JavaScript object into a JSON string. **This interoperability makes JSON an ideal choice for APIs (Application Programming Interfaces), where different systems need to communicate and exchange data efficiently.**

Another important aspect of JSON is its role in configuration files. Many software applications use JSON to store configuration settings, which can be easily read and modified by both humans and machines. This flexibility allows developers to customize application behavior, without altering the underlying code. **For example, a web application might use a JSON file to store settings for database connections,**

API keys, or user preferences. By simply editing the JSON file, developers can adjust these settings as needed, making JSON a powerful tool for managing application configurations.

2. **JSON Array:**

```
[
  "apple",
  "banana",
  "cherry"
]
```

3. **JSON Array of Objects:**

```
[
  {
    "name": "Alice",
    "age": 28
  },
  {
    "name": "Bob",
    "age": 32
  }
]
```

JSON's structure also supports **nested data**, allowing for complex data representations. An object **can contain other objects or arrays**, enabling the modeling of hierarchical data. For instance, a JSON object representing a user might include nested objects for the user's address and contact information. This ability to nest data makes JSON highly versatile, suitable for a wide range of applications from simple data storage to complex data modeling.

4. **Nested JSON Object:**

```
{
  "person": {
    "name": "Jane Doe",
    "age": 25,
    "address": {
      "street": "123 Main St",
      "city": "Anytown"
    }
  }
}
```

These examples cover the basic syntax and structure of JSON, demonstrating how to represent different types of data. JSON's simplicity and flexibility make it a popular choice for data interchange in web applications and APIs.

Understanding YAML Language

YAML, short form "YAML *Ain't Markup Language*," is a versatile and human-readable data serialization standard that is widely used for configuration files and data exchange between programming languages.

YAML serves as a foundational element in the implementation of Infrastructure as Code (IaC) across leading cloud platforms such as AWS, Azure, and Google Cloud Platform (GCP). By leveraging YAML's straightforward and human-readable syntax, developers and IT professionals can define and manage cloud infrastructure in a consistent and efficient manner.

In AWS, YAML is integral to **`AWS CloudFormation`**, enabling users to describe and automate the provisioning of resources. Azure utilizes YAML in its **`Resource Manager`** **(ARM)** templates, streamlining the deployment and configuration of services. Similarly, GCP's **`Deployment Manager`** employs YAML to specify and manage cloud resources. **This uniformity in using YAML across different cloud environments not only simplifies the process of infrastructure management but also enhances collaboration and version control, ensuring that infrastructure definitions are clear, maintainable, scalable, and repeatable.**

Mastering YAML is thus essential for anyone looking to effectively implement IaC and achieve seamless operations across diverse cloud ecosystems. Its simplicity and readability make it an excellent choice for students and professionals alike.

YAML's structure is defined by **indentation**, which represents the hierarchy of data, making it easy to understand at a glance.

Key-value pairs, sequences (lists), and mappings (dictionaries) are the fundamental building blocks of YAML, allowing it to represent complex data structures in a straightforward manner. Additionally, YAML supports comments, denoted by the # symbol, which are useful for adding explanations or notes within the file. Advanced features like anchors and aliases enable the reuse and referencing of data, enhancing the efficiency of your configurations.

Commonly used in tools like Ansible, Kubernetes, and various software applications, YAML's flexibility and ease of use make it an essential skill for anyone involved in software development, system administration, or DevOps. Understanding YAML not only simplifies the management of configuration files but also fosters better collaboration and reduces the likelihood of errors in your projects.

Here is a basic syntax overview with short examples:

- YAML uses **indentation** to represent the structure of data, similar to Python.
- Each level of indentation represents a level of **hierarchy**.
- **Key-value pairs are separated by a colon and a space**.

1. **Simple Key-value pair:**

```
name: John Doe
age: 30
```

2. **Lists are represented by dashes:**

```
hobbies:
  - reading
  - hiking
  - coding
```

YAML supports several data types, including scalars (strings, numbers, booleans), sequences (lists), and mappings (dictionaries). Scalars are simple values like strings or numbers. Sequences are ordered collections of items, and mappings are collections of key-value pairs. This flexibility allows YAML to represent complex data structures in a straightforward manner.

Comments in YAML are denoted by the # symbol, and can be placed anywhere in the file. They are useful for adding explanations or notes. YAML also supports anchors and aliases which allow you to reuse and reference data within the document. Anchors are defined with & and referenced with *.

Examples

```
defaults: &defaults
  adapter: postgres
  host: localhost

development:
  <<: *defaults
  database: dev_db
```

YAML is widely used in various applications, including configuration files for software applications, data exchange between different programming languages, and defining infrastructure as code in tools like Ansible and Kubernetes.

Its readability and simplicity make it an excellent choice for these purposes, helping to reduce errors, and improve maintainability.

Understanding Terraform Language

Terraform, developed by HashiCorp, is a powerful open-source tool that enables users to define and provision infrastructure, using a high-level configuration language known as **HashiCorp Configuration Language (HCL)**.

As a cornerstone of Infrastructure as Code (IaC), Terraform allows you to manage and automate the lifecycle of your infrastructure across various cloud providers, including AWS, Azure, and Google Cloud Platform (GCP). By writing declarative configuration files, you can specify the desired state of your infrastructure, and Terraform will handle the creation, modification, and deletion of resources to match that state.

This approach not only ensures consistency and repeatability, but also enhances collaboration and version control, as infrastructure configurations can be stored in source control systems like Git.

The syntax of Terraform is designed to be both human-readable and machine-friendly. **A basic Terraform configuration file, typically with a `.tf` extension, consists of blocks that define resources, providers, and variables.** For example, a simple configuration to create an AWS EC2 instance might look like this:

Create an AWS EC2 instance:

```
provider "aws"
{
  region = "us-west-2"
}
resource "aws_instance" "example"
{
  ami           = "ami-0c55b159cbfafe1f0"
  instance_type = "t2.micro"
  tags =
{
    Name = "example-instance"
}
}
```

In this example, the provider block specifies the **AWS region**, and the **resource block defines an EC2 instance** with a specific **Amazon Machine Image (AMI)** and **instance type**.

Terraform's ability to manage **infrastructure as code (IaC)**, combined with its extensive support for various cloud providers and services, makes it an indispensable tool for modern DevOps practices.

By mastering Terraform, you can streamline your infrastructure management, reduce manual errors, and achieve greater agility and scalability in your cloud operations.

In addition to its core functionality, Terraform offers several advanced features that are essential for cloud admins to understand. **One such feature is the concept of state management. Terraform maintains a state file that tracks the current state of your infrastructure.** This state file is crucial for planning and applying changes, as it allows Terraform to determine what actions are necessary to achieve the desired state defined in your configuration files. It is important to manage this state file carefully, often by storing it in a remote backend like AWS S3 or HashiCorp's Terraform

Cloud, to ensure consistency and collaboration across teams. Understanding how Terraform's state management works is key to effectively using the tool in real-world scenarios.

Another important aspect of Terraform is its support for modules which are reusable configurations that can be shared and versioned. Modules enable you to encapsulate and abstract complex infrastructure components, making your configurations more modular and maintainable.

For example, you can create a module for a standard VPC setup and reuse it across multiple projects. This not only saves time but also ensures best practices are consistently applied. Additionally, Terraform's rich ecosystem of community-contributed modules available on the Terraform Registry provides a wealth of pre-built solutions that can accelerate your infrastructure development.

By mastering modules, you can write more efficient, scalable, and maintainable Terraform configurations, making them well-prepared for professional DevOps.

The Fundamentals of IaC Scanning

However, simply declaring and codifying the desired state of infrastructure does not ensure that it is free from errors, or security vulnerabilities.

This is where IaC scanning becomes essential. **IaC scanning examines the code for security risks and rule violations before deployment.**

Infrastructure as Code (IaC) Scanning is a crucial practice in modern cloud computing that ensures the security and correctness of your infrastructure configurations. **IaC is a method of managing and provisioning computing infrastructure through machine-readable configuration files, rather than physical hardware configuration or interactive configuration tools.**

These are the Benefits of using IaC Scanning:

- **Early Detection of Issues:** By scanning IaC code early in the development process, teams can catch and fix problems, before they affect live environments.
- **Enhanced Security:** IaC Scanning helps maintain a secure infrastructure by identifying vulnerabilities, and ensuring compliance with security standards.
- **Consistency and Reliability:** Automated scanning ensures that infrastructure configurations are consistent and reliable across different environments.

Key Processes in IaC Scanning

IaC scanning encompasses several critical steps that work together to ensure your infrastructure remains secure and compliant:

- **Establishing policies:** Defining the security and compliance benchmarks that the IaC must meet.
- **Integrating with CI/CD for automation:** Embedding IaC scanning within Continuous Integration/Continuous Delivery (CI/CD) pipelines to automate the scanning process.
- **Scanning:** Employing scanning tools to review all IaC, and verify compliance with policies.
- **Reviewing results:** Analyzing scan results to identify and prioritize issues for remediation.
- **Addressing identified issues:** Fixing the vulnerabilities or compliance issues found during scanning.
- **Refining IaC scanning policies and processes:** Continuously improving the scanning policies and processes, based on feedback and the evolving security landscape.

Tools and Technologies for IaC Scanning

As the adoption of IaC has grown in the software industry, various tools and technologies have emerged to enhance the process of checking infrastructure code for vulnerabilities and compliance issues. IaC scanning tools can be loosely categorized, based on their primary focus and functionality.

- **Static code analyzers:** Evaluate IaC code against a set of predefined rules to identify potential security issues and misconfigurations. They help in enforcing best practices and compliance with security standards. Examples include `Checkov` and `Tfsec` which are popular for `Terraform` code.
- **Compliance scanners:** Focus on ensuring that IaC configurations comply with regulatory standards and internal policies. These tools are crucial for maintaining compliance in highly regulated industries. One example is `Terrascan` which checks for compliance with the security best practices.
- **Dependency scanners:** Search for vulnerabilities within the libraries and modules your IaC code depends on. They are important for catching security issues introduced by third-party dependencies.
- **Security and vulnerability scanners:** Specifically identify a wide range of security vulnerabilities – from simple misconfigurations to critical security flaws – within IaC files.

IaC Scanning involves using automated tools to validate IaC configuration files.

The primary goal is to detect potential errors, security vulnerabilities, and compliance issues in the code before it is deployed. IaC Scanning tools analyze the IaC code to ensure that it adheres to best practices and security policies. These tools can identify misconfigurations, insecure settings, and other issues that could compromise the infrastructure. Some popular IaC Scanning tools include Checkov, TFLint, and KICS. These tools provide comprehensive scanning capabilities for various IaC platforms, and help enforce security and compliance policies. The following is a list of common IaC Scanning tools used by industry experts to enforce security and compliance policies:

- **Checkov:** Widely used for scanning Terraform, CloudFormation, Kubernetes, and ARM templates. It checks for misconfigurations and security issues.
- **TFLint:** Primarily used for linting Terraform code. It helps in identifying errors, and enforcing best practices.
- **KICS (Keeping Infrastructure as Code Secure):** Usage: Scans various IaC frameworks such as Terraform, CloudFormation, and Kubernetes for security vulnerabilities and compliance issues.
- **Terrascan:** Focuses on scanning Terraform code for security and compliance violations. It integrates well with CI/CD pipelines.
- **Bridgecrew:** Provides comprehensive IaC security scanning and policy enforcement for Terraform, CloudFormation, and Kubernetes.
- **Snyk IaC:** Part of the Snyk platform, it scans IaC files for security vulnerabilities, and integrates with development workflows.
- **Prowler:** Primarily used for AWS security best practices and compliance checks, including IaC scanning.
- **CloudFormation Guard:** A tool for validating CloudFormation templates against custom rules to ensure security and compliance.
- **Sentinel:** Used with HashiCorp products such as Terraform to enforce policies and governance in IaC code.
- **Conftest:** A versatile tool for testing configuration files, including IaC, using Open Policy Agent (OPA) policies.

Challenges in IaC Scanning

Implementing IaC scanning effectively introduces several challenges. One of the primary hurdles – especially for large enterprises running complex applications with a large compliance footprint – is in managing complex security policies. As your infrastructure requirements grow more complicated, so does the task of drafting comprehensive policies that accurately reflect the security needs of every component.

This complexity demands not just initial thoroughness, but ongoing adjustments to accommodate evolving infrastructure demands.

Next, organizations struggle to integrate IaC scanning with the existing workflows. For many organizations, introducing IaC scanning into their CI/CD pipelines can lead to a significant overhaul of established processes. Without proper planning and preparation, this kind of disruption can derail development rhythms and impede productivity. Because the cybersecurity landscape is ever-changing, many organizations struggle to keep up with the evolving threat landscape. New vulnerabilities and attack vectors emerge regularly. To protect against the latest threats, organizations need constant vigilance and regular updates to scanning tools and policies.

Lastly, dealing with false positives and noise are common issues. The precision of IaC scanning tools varies, and they can sometimes flag issues that are not genuine threats. This leads to wasting resources on unnecessary fixes and investigations. Balancing the sensitivity of these tools – to minimize false alarms, while still catching real issues – is a delicate task. Organizations need to take a strategic approach to IaC scanning which highlights the importance of selecting the right tools.

Conclusion

In this chapter, we have explored the integration of Microsoft Defender for Cloud into DevSecOps workflows, emphasizing the importance of embedding security throughout the software development lifecycle. By adopting practices such as Infrastructure as Code (IaC), scanning and leveraging tools like Azure DevOps and GitHub, organizations can proactively identify and remediate vulnerabilities, ensuring robust security posture management. This approach not only enhances compliance and governance, but also fosters a culture of continuous improvement and collaboration between development and security teams.

Looking ahead, our next chapter delves into Cloud Service Network Security (CSNS), where we will examine the mechanisms and strategies for securing network infrastructures in cloud environments. We shall also discuss how to implement network segmentation, manage access controls, and monitor traffic to protect against threats, ensuring that your cloud networks are resilient and secure.

Points to Remember

- **Integrate Security Early:** Embedding Microsoft Defender for Cloud into your DevOps workflow enables early detection of vulnerabilities, ensuring that issues are addressed before deployment.
- **Automate IaC Scanning:** Utilize Defender for Cloud's tools to automatically scan Infrastructure as Code (IaC) templates, identifying misconfigurations prior to provisioning.

- **Enforce Security Gates:** Implement security gates in your CI/CD pipelines to prevent the progression of code that does not meet the security standards.
- **Foster Team Collaboration:** Encourage collaboration between development and security teams by providing shared visibility into security issues through Defender for Cloud.
- **Maintain Continuous Compliance:** Leverage Defender for Cloud's continuous compliance monitoring to ensure adherence to regulatory standards, and reduce risks.

Multiple-Choice Questions

1. What does '`Shift Left`' mean in DevSecOps?
   a. Delaying security checks until post-deployment
   b. Integrating security early in the development lifecycle
   c. Moving the development team to a new location
   d. Ignoring security in the development process
2. Which tool is commonly used for Infrastructure as Code (IaC)?
   a. EC2 Compute
   b. Azure Storage
   c. Terraform
   d. GCP Analytics
3. What is the primary benefit of using IaC?
   a. Manual configuration of servers
   b. Faster and consistent infrastructure provisioning
   c. Increased physical hardware usage
   d. Reduced need for coding skills
4. Which language is known for its human-readable syntax in IaC?
   a. Binary
   b. YAML
   c. Assembly
   d. Machine code

5. What is the purpose of integrating security scans into CI/CD pipelines?
    a. To delay deployments
    b. To identify vulnerabilities early
    c. To increase manual testing
    d. To reduce collaboration

Answers

1. b
2. c
3. b
4. b
5. b

Questions

1. What does **`'DevSecOps'`** stand for?
2. Which tool is commonly used for Infrastructure as Code (IaC)?
3. What is the primary benefit of using IaC?
4. Which language is known for its human-readable syntax in IaC?
5. What is the purpose of integrating security scans into CI/CD pipelines?
6. What does 'Shift Left' mean in DevSecOps?
7. Which tool is known for its "*Infrastructure as Code*" capabilities and agentless architecture?
8. What is the main benefit of IaC?
9. Which term describes a method where developers merge their changes back to the main branch, multiple times a day?
10. What is the process of describing the desired infrastructure state called?

Key Terms

- **Security as Code (SaC):** The practice of embedding security policies and controls directly into code, enabling automated and consistent security enforcement throughout the development lifecycle.
- **Immutable Infrastructure:** An approach where infrastructure components are replaced rather than modified, ensuring consistency, and reducing configuration drift.
- **Policy as Code (PaC):** The concept of defining and managing policies through code, allowing for automated compliance checks, and enforcement in infrastructure deployments.
- **Infrastructure Drift:** The phenomenon where the actual state of infrastructure diverges from the defined configuration, often due to manual changes, leading to inconsistencies.
- **Ephemeral Environments:** Temporary infrastructure environments that are created for specific tasks or tests, and destroyed afterward, promoting efficiency and cost savings.
- **Blue-Green Deployment:** A release management strategy that involves running two identical production environments (blue and green) to minimize downtime and risk during deployments.
- **Canary Release:** A deployment strategy that gradually rolls out changes to a small subset of users before a full-scale release, allowing for monitoring and rollback, if issues arise.
- **Configuration Drift:** Similar to infrastructure drift, it refers to the gradual deviation of system configurations from the desired state, often due to untracked changes.
- **Continuous Compliance:** The ongoing process of ensuring that systems and processes adhere to regulatory and organizational standards through automated checks and validations.
- **Security Champions:** Team members who advocate for security best practices within development teams, bridging the gap between security and development.

CHAPTER 9
Understanding Cloud Service Network Security (CSNS)

Introduction

Within a CNAPP framework, Cloud Service Network Security (CSNS) functions as a foundational layer focused on securing network-level communications. It ensures protected traffic flows, enforces controlled access paths, and safeguards infrastructure across multi-cloud and hybrid environments. Unlike traditional perimeter-based firewalls and segmentation tools, CSNS is identity-aware, policy-driven, and natively integrated with cloud-native architectures.

As a core security capability within CNAPP, CSNS plays a critical role in protecting applications and workloads at the network layer. It does so by **reducing the attack surface** through tight control over network exposure, thereby limiting unauthorized access. **CSNS also monitors and inspects traffic** flowing between services, workloads, and external sources, offering continuous visibility and threat detection. It **prevents lateral movement of malicious actors within cloud environments** by segmenting workloads and enforcing strict network policies. In addition, CSNS **helps enforce least privilege access** across services and communication pathways to minimize risks. Finally, **it enables micro-segmentation**, and **aligns with zero trust networking models**, ensuring that access is continuously validated and restricted to only what is necessary.

Structure

The following topics will be covered in this chapter:

- Introduction to Cloud Service Network Security (CSNS) Module in CNAPP
- Core Components and Capabilities of CSNS

- CSNS in Action: Use Cases and Real-World Scenarios
- Microsoft Defender for Cloud as a CSNS Solution

Introduction to Cloud Service Network Security (CSNS) Module in CNAPP

As organizations rapidly adopt cloud-native technologies, **the traditional concept of network security has been fundamentally reshaped**. In modern architectures, where applications are distributed across containers, serverless functions, and Virtual Machines (VMs)–often spanning multiple cloud providers–**network security must evolve beyond static firewalls and perimeter-based controls.**

This is where **CSNS** comes into play.

CSNS is a **crucial component of Cloud-Native Application Protection Platforms (CNAPPs)**, offering organizations the tools and intelligence needed **to secure network traffic**, **manage connectivity**, and **prevent lateral movement of threats** across cloud environments.

Understanding CSNS

At its core, **Cloud Service Network Security (CSNS)** refers to a **set of cloud-native capabilities designed to protect workloads, applications, and data by securing the network paths they use–whether internal (east-west) or external (north-south).**

It ensures that only authorized traffic flows between resources, services, and external users, regardless of where they are deployed.

Unlike legacy models where firewalls were placed at the network boundary, CSNS is **deeply embedded within the cloud fabric**. It integrates with cloud-native services, identity systems, policies, and telemetry, allowing for **context-aware and dynamic enforcement of network security rules.**

Why CSNS Matters in CNAPP

In a CNAPP framework, multiple security layers work together to protect cloud-native applications throughout their lifecycle. **CSNS plays a foundational role by:**

- **Securing the communication layer** between services, APIs, workloads, and end-users.
- **Enforcing zero trust principles** by default-deny access and least privilege communication.

- **Reducing risk exposure** by detecting misconfigurations, exposed services, or anomalous traffic.
- **Supporting compliance** by validating that network policies align with industry standards and frameworks.

In short, **CSNS ensures that the network remains a secure and resilient foundation** for all other cloud-native operations.

Evolution from Traditional Network Security

In traditional IT environments, network security was often hardware-based and perimeter-centric. Firewalls, Intrusion Prevention Systems (IPS), and VLAN segmentation were used to isolate environments, and control traffic.

But cloud-native environments demand something entirely different. Here are some reasons why:

- **No fixed perimeter:** Resources are ephemeral, and often publicly reachable unless properly configured.
- **Dynamic scaling:** Services scale in and out automatically, requiring security policies that adapt in real-time.
- **Multi-cloud reality:** Organizations use multiple cloud platforms, each with its own networking model.
- **Service-to-service communication:** Microservices, containers, and APIs communicate internally at high speed and scale.

These shifts require **software-defined, identity-aware, and API-integrated network security solutions**—the hallmarks of CSNS.

Modern Capabilities of CSNS

CSNS is not just a rebranded firewall in the cloud, it is an **intelligent, multi-layered security approach** that aligns with today's DevOps and cloud-native practices. The key capabilities include:

- **Micro-segmentation:** Fine grained network segmentation at the workload or application level to isolate environments, and reduce attack surfaces.
- **Identity-aware access:** Policies based on the identity of services, users, or devices—not just IPs and ports.
- **Threat detection and anomaly alerts:** Continuous monitoring of traffic patterns to flag unusual or suspicious behavior.
- **Just-in-Time (JIT) access:** Temporarily opening network ports for authorized users, and closing them automatically.

- **Network recommendation engines:** AI-powered insights that analyze configuration risks, and suggest policy improvements.
- **Native integration with CSPs:** Deep hooks into AWS, Azure, and GCP for controlling cloud-specific network configurations such as security groups, VPCs, subnets, and firewalls.

The Role of CSNS in Zero Trust Architectures

A Zero Trust strategy assumes that every network request–internal or external–is untrusted until proven otherwise. CSNS enables this model by:

- Validating traffic based on identity, location, and device posture.
- **Continuously verifying trust** as network conditions change.
- **Applying least-privilege rules** to every service-to-service interaction.
- **Logging and auditing all network activities** for forensics and compliance.

Zero Trust is not a feature–it is a philosophy, and **CSNS is the enforcement engine behind it at the network level.**

Challenges Addressed by CSNS

Organizations face many challenges in securing cloud networks:

- **Misconfigured public endpoints** exposing services to the Internet.
- **Lack of visibility into east-west traffic** between containers or services.
- **Flat network topologies** that allow threats to spread quickly.
- **Manual and error-prone firewall rule management.**
- **Inconsistent security controls** across multi-cloud environments.

CSNS solutions tackle these issues by offering **centralized policy management, automation, visibility, and context** which traditional tools simply cannot match in cloud environments.

Core Components and Capabilities of CSNS

As organizations accelerate their cloud adoption journeys, the underlying network infrastructure has evolved from static and centralized to dynamic, distributed, and software-defined. **Traditional security models–rooted in data center thinking and hardware-based firewalls–struggle to cope with the elastic, API-driven, and highly interconnected nature of cloud-native environments**. This is where **Cloud Service Network Security (CSNS)** becomes crucial.

CSNS is not just about securing the perimeter; it is about embedding security within the very fabric of cloud communication.

In today's architectures, workloads are no longer confined to fixed IPs or static VLANs. Instead, they interact across cloud regions, containers, microservices, and serverless functions–each potentially representing a new attack surface. To defend against modern threats, security must follow the workload, operate at machine speed, and be **deeply integrated into every layer of the cloud network stack**.

This section breaks down the **core components and modern capabilities** that define CSNS in the context of a Cloud-Native Application Protection Platform (CNAPP).

These capabilities are not just theoretical–they represent **real-world practices adopted by leading cloud security teams** to enforce the least privilege, stop lateral movement, monitor traffic patterns, and build zero-trust architectures that scale.

Micro-Segmentation

Micro-segmentation is like setting up digital walls between workloads, applications, or environments–even when they live in the same cloud account or virtual network. Instead of relying on broad network zones (such as "**`prod`**" and "**`dev`**"), CSNS allows you to control exactly **which services can talk to each other**, **and how**. This reduces the risk of lateral movement–where attackers try to hop from one compromised resource to another.

Cloud providers now support micro-segmentation using native features such as Azure NSGs, GCP firewall rules, or Kubernetes network policies. CNAPP platforms integrate with these to simplify and automate the process.

Identity-Aware Network Controls

In the past, access was based on IP addresses and ports. Now, **access decisions are based on who or what is making the request**–not just where it is coming from. This brings a huge security upgrade. Hence, whether it is a user, service, or automated script, the network layer can now evaluate:

- The requestor's identity
- Their role or group membership
- Device health or trust score
- Context, like location or time

A microservice with a "**`read-only`**" identity will not be able to access another service's write APIs–even if it is on the same subnet. This enforces the least privilege at the network level.

Network Visibility and Traffic Analytics

You cannot protect what you cannot see. CSNS tools provide **deep visibility into all network flows**—between services, containers, users, and external systems. You gain insights like:

- Who is talking to what?
- Is that communication normal?
- Are there unexpected outbound connections to the Internet?
- Is sensitive data moving through risky paths?

Cloud-native platforms now offer **traffic flow logs, threat maps, and connection graphs** out of the box. Defender for Cloud, for example, highlights insecure paths and public exposure risks directly in its network recommendations.

Lateral Movement Prevention

Even after an initial breach, CSNS is built to stop attackers from moving across your environment. Most attacks today do not stop at one server. Once in, attackers try to **explore your internal landscape**—looking for secrets, credentials, and valuable assets. CSNS breaks that chain by:

- Limiting internal communication paths
- Monitoring east-west traffic
- Triggering alerts on suspicious pivots

This capability is critical for ransomware protection in cloud workloads. It is like having invisible tripwires between every service.

Threat Detection and Behavioral Anomaly Monitoring

CSNS tools do not just block traffic—they analyze it. With machine learning and rule-based logic, they detect strange or malicious activity in real time. Cloud threats move fast. Behavioral anomaly detection can surface attacks like:

- Command-and-control communication
- Data exfiltration via obscure ports
- Port scanning within your environment
- Tunneling or obfuscated traffic

Integrated insights: Platforms like Defender for Cloud integrate with Microsoft Threat Intelligence to **correlate traffic anomalies with known attack techniques**, making detection even more powerful.

Policy Automation and Continuous Validation

Manually writing firewall rules or managing hundreds of access policies does not scale. **CSNS enables automation and real-time validation of security policies.** Automation ensures that:

- Misconfigurations are caught quickly.
- Policies stay in sync with infrastructure changes.
- Recommendations are actionable and prioritized.

Many CNAPP tools now provide **policy-as-code**, meaning you define network security rules in files, version them in Git, and automatically deploy them using CI/CD tools. This is how DevSecOps teams secure networks at the speed of cloud.

Just-in-Time (JIT) Access Control

JIT access allows users or administrators to **open network ports only when needed, and only for a limited time.** Permanently open management ports (like SSH or RDP) are one of the most common cloud attack vectors. JIT prevents this by:

- Requiring explicit requests and approvals
- Enabling temporary access
- Automatically revoking it after the session ends

Microsoft Defender for Cloud lets you enable JIT for VMs so that **RDP/SSH ports are closed by default**, and opened only when needed–with full audit logging.

Cloud-Native Integration across Multi-Cloud

CSNS is not limited to one cloud provider. It needs to support AWS, Azure, GCP, and hybrid environments consistently. Today's organizations are rarely on a single cloud. CSNS tools offer:

- A unified view of all network exposure.
- Centralized policy controls.
- Standardized threat detection across clouds.

CNAPP platforms now act as a **single-pane-of-glass** for multi-cloud security teams, ensuring policies are consistent, compliant, and always up to date. **CSNS brings together visibility, enforcement, automation, and intelligence** to secure cloud-native network communication at scale. It does not replace traditional network security–it evolves and extends it for the distributed, dynamic, and highly interconnected nature of modern cloud systems.

Thus, whether you are protecting a single microservice or managing a multi-region hybrid architecture, CSNS ensures that your network traffic is:

- Controlled
- Auditable
- Context-aware
- Adaptive to threats

In the next section, we will explore how these capabilities are applied in **real-world cloud environments**, **solving practical problems that security teams face every day**.

CSNS in Action: Real-World Scenarios

Cloud Service Network Security (CSNS) goes far beyond theory–it is the backbone of how modern organizations enforce network-level protection across increasingly complex, hybrid, and cloud-native environments. In this section, we explore how CSNS works in real-world settings, and why it is a critical piece in today's cloud security architecture. These scenarios are based on actual industry challenges and best practices, making them relatable and immediately useful for readers.

Use Case # 1: Securing Multi-Tier Cloud Applications

Scenario: A company is running a multi-tier web application in Microsoft Azure, with the front-end in Azure App Services, the middleware in Kubernetes (AKS), and the backend database in Azure SQL. Each tier resides in separate subnets with different access requirements.

CSNS Solution:

- **Micro-segmentation** is used to enforce communication rules between tiers, preventing any lateral movement beyond what is necessary.
- **NSGs (Network Security Groups)** and **Azure Firewall** policies define allowed traffic, based on IP, port, and protocol.
- **Identity-aware policies** further refine access, allowing only specific service principals or managed identities to communicate across tiers.

This reduces the attack surface, and enforces least privilege at the network level, ensuring that one compromised tier does not expose the entire system.

Use Case # 2: Enabling Zero Trust Networking in a Hybrid Cloud

Scenario: A global enterprise uses Azure for new workloads but retains sensitive legacy systems in an on-premises data center connected via VPN and ExpressRoute. They want to enforce Zero Trust principles across the hybrid environment.

CSNS Solution:

- Implement **Azure Network Security with Private Endpoints** to access PaaS services, without exposing them publicly.
- Use **Azure Policy and Defender for Cloud** to ensure that only authorized traffic flows across the hybrid boundary.
- **Just-in-Time VM access** is configured to reduce persistent exposure to administrative ports.

Even across hybrid environments, the enterprise can restrict, monitor, and enforce secure communications, without relying on static, perimeter-based defenses.

Use Case # 3: Blocking Suspicious East-West Traffic in Kubernetes

Scenario: A containerized microservices architecture runs on Azure Kubernetes Service (AKS). A lateral movement attack is attempted via compromised pods trying to reach internal services.

CSNS Solution:

- **Azure CNI with Network Policies** is enabled to control pod-to-pod traffic.
- **Microsoft Defender for Containers** continuously inspects traffic, and alerts on anomalous or unauthorized communication attempts.
- **Integration with Sentinel SIEM** enables real-time response workflows (for example, blocking traffic, isolating nodes, and so on).

CSNS tools proactively identify, and stop lateral movement, a key weakness in most Kubernetes environments, when left unsecured.

Use Case # 4: Regulatory Compliance and Traffic Logging

Scenario: A healthcare company must comply with HIPAA, and wants to ensure that all data flow and access across its Azure network are auditable and secure.

CSNS Solution:

- **Enable Traffic Analytics and Flow Logs in Azure Network Watcher** to collect and visualize network behavior.
- **Azure Firewall and NSGs** enforce inbound and outbound rules to restrict non-compliant access.
- **Logs are sent to Log Analytics and Microsoft Sentinel** for compliance reporting and incident response.

Benefits: The organization gains full visibility into network flows, and can demonstrate compliance with enforced and monitored security controls.

Use Case # 5: Internet-Exposed Services with Limited Access

Scenario: A DevOps team needs to expose a REST API for third-party integration, but wants to ensure that it is only accessible from specific IPs or identities.

CSNS Solution:

- Use **Application Gateway with Web Application Firewall (WAF)** to protect against OWASP Top 10 vulnerabilities.
- Configure **IP whitelisting** and **geo-blocking rules** to restrict access.
- Integrate with **Azure Front Door** to provide global entry point protection with DDoS mitigation.

Benefits: The exposed API remains resilient and tightly controlled, reducing the likelihood of exploitation, while still being accessible to trusted users.

These examples show how **CSNS is not a single tool, but a collection of tightly integrated services and policies.** In a CNAPP approach, CSNS plays a continuous and dynamic role in protecting workloads as they scale, shift, and evolve. Whether enforcing Zero Trust, enabling secure DevOps, or meeting compliance, CSNS is where network-level security meets cloud-native agility.

Configuring Microsoft Defender for Cloud as a CSNS Solution

In modern cloud environments, traditional perimeter-based security is no longer sufficient to protect applications and workloads from advanced threats. Organizations need visibility, control, and threat prevention embedded into the fabric of their cloud networks. This is where Microsoft Defender for Cloud emerges as a powerful CSNS (Cloud Service Network Security) solution.

It provides native, identity-aware, and context-rich protection across network layers by combining adaptive threat detection, micro-segmentation, traffic analytics, and policy enforcement.

When properly configured, **Microsoft Defender for Cloud enables organizations to monitor**, **analyze**, and **control traffic flows within and across virtual networks**, enforce **least privilege access**, **reduce lateral movement risks**, and **implement Zero Trust principles** – all without relying heavily on third-party tools. Yes, the key here is without relying on any third-party tools.

This section will walk you through a step-by-step approach to configure Microsoft Defender for Cloud as a CSNS solution, ensuring that your cloud-native environments are secure, visible, and resilient against evolving cyber threats.

Prerequisites

Before you begin, ensure the following:

- You have an **Owner** or **Security Admin** access to the subscription(s).
- Microsoft Defender for Cloud is already onboarded to your environment.
- **You have Defender plans enabled (especially for servers, PaaS, and networks).**
- Azure Policy is available to enforce network rules.
- Azure Firewall or third-party Network Virtual Appliances (NVAs) are configured (optional for advanced scenarios).

Enable Network Layer Threat Protection

Follow these steps to enable network layer threat protection:

- Navigate to `Microsoft Defender for Cloud › Environment Settings → Select Subscription → Defender Plans.`
- Enable `Microsoft Defender for App Services`, **Storage**, **Key Vault**, and **Resource Manager**.

- Most importantly, **Enable Microsoft Defender for Network** to activate capabilities, such as **Just-in-Time (JIT) VM access**, **NSG flow logs**, and **Adaptive Network Hardening**.

Configure Just-in-Time (JIT) VM Access

JIT reduces exposure to brute force and lateral movement attacks by limiting VM port access. Follow these steps to configure Just-in-Time access:

1. Go to **`Microsoft Defender for Cloud → Workload Protections → Just-In-Time VM Access`**
2. Go to **`Not Configured`** panel.
3. Select the VMs, you want to protect.
4. Click **`Enable JIT`**.
5. Define the ports, allowed IP ranges, and time windows for access.
6. Click **`Save`**.

Best Practice: Allow only specific Ips, and apply tight time controls (for example, 1 hour).

Implement Adaptive Network Hardening

Adaptive Network Hardening recommends **tighter inbound rules** based on **observed traffic**. **Adaptive Network Hardening** is a **security feature** in Microsoft Defender for Cloud that helps **protect your virtual machines** by **recommending tighter inbound network rules**.

It works by analyzing real-time traffic patterns, and comparing them with Microsoft's threat intelligence to identify unnecessary open ports or risky IP addresses.

Based on this analysis, **it suggests changes to your Network Security Groups** (NSGs) – **such as removing overly broad access or restricting exposure to only trusted sources.**

This helps **reduce the attack surface**, and **prevent threats like brute-force attacks or lateral movement.**

Adaptive Network Hardening is especially useful in enforcing the least privilege access, and aligning with Zero Trust network strategies, without requiring manual rule creation.

1. Navigate to **`Microsoft Defender for Cloud → Recommendations → Adaptive Network Hardening.`**

2. **Select a VM with an active NSG.**
3. Review suggested inbound rules and security groups.
4. Apply recommendations after validation.

   This aligns with `Zero Trust` by enforcing least-privilege network access.

Enable NSG Flow Logs and Traffic Analytics

In a cloud environment, understanding **how network traffic moves in and out of your virtual machines** is **necessary for identifying misconfigurations**, **detecting threats**, and **maintaining compliance**.

One of the most effective ways to achieve this visibility in Microsoft Azure is by enabling **NSG Flow Logs** and **Traffic Analytics**.

Network Security Group (NSG) Flow Logs provide **detailed records of network traffic allowed or denied by NSG rules**, capturing information such as source/destination IP, port, protocol, and traffic direction. These logs are stored in Azure Storage, and can be analyzed to track suspicious activities, open exposure points, or unusual access behavior.

When paired with Traffic Analytics, these logs become even more powerful. Traffic Analytics uses Azure Monitor and Microsoft's built-in intelligence to transform raw flow data into interactive visual reports.

This helps security teams **spot anomalies**, **prioritize threats**, and **make informed decisions quickly.**

Enabling NSG Flow Logs and Traffic Analytics is a foundational step in **building a strong Cloud Service Network Security (CSNS) posture–offering both historical insight and real-time awareness** into the traffic patterns inside your Azure networks.

This provides visibility into all network flows, enabling detection of anomalies and policy violations.

1. Go to `Azure Network Watcher → NSG flow logs`.
2. Choose the NSGs, you want to monitor.
3. Set `Retention`, `Storage Account`, and `Traffic Analytics`.
4. Optionally, integrate with `Log Analytics Workspace` for deeper SIEM integration.

   Use this for auditing east-west and north-south traffic.

Configure Alerts and Workflow Automation

Proactive security requires more than just monitoring – it demands timely response.

In Microsoft Defender for Cloud, **configuring alerts and workflow automation allows security teams to act on threats,** the moment they are detected. **Defender for Cloud continuously analyzes your environment, and generates alerts, when suspicious behavior, misconfigurations, or threats are identified.**

These alerts can be customized based on severity levels, affected resources, or specific policies, helping teams prioritize what truly matters.

To reduce manual effort, and ensure rapid containment, **workflow automation can be set up to automatically respond to certain alerts.**

For example, when an alert is raised for unauthorized access, Defender for Cloud can trigger a Logic App that disables the affected user, isolates a virtual machine, or sends a detailed notification to your security team.

This integration with Azure Logic Apps provides a low-code, flexible way to define, and automate actions, improving both response time and consistency.

Configuring alerts with automated workflows empowers organizations to detect, respond, and recover faster – making it a key pillar of cloud-native network defense.

Perform these steps to react to suspicious traffic in real-time:

1. Go to: `Defender for Cloud → Alerts`
2. Set up:
    - Severity filters
    - Notifications (email, webhook)
    - Logic Apps for automated response

    You can auto-isolate a VM, or trigger firewall changes through automation.

Enforce Network Security via Azure Policy

In cloud environments, consistent enforcement of security standards across subscriptions and resources is a major challenge – and that is where **Azure Policy** plays a critical role.

Azure Policy allows organizations to define and apply rules that govern resource configurations, ensuring that network security best practices are followed automatically. For example, you can enforce policies that deny the creation of NSGs with overly permissive rules, require traffic logging to be enabled, or mandate the use of approved IP address ranges.

By using built-in or custom Azure Policies, you can prevent non-compliant resources from being deployed in the first place, or flag them for remediation, if they already exist. This proactive governance ensures that security settings are not left to chance or individual discretion. Combined with initiatives and policy assignments, Azure Policy helps implement **guardrails** – not just guidance – across your entire cloud environment. For Cloud Service Network Security (CSNS), this means tighter control, less risk of misconfiguration, and a more automated approach to network-level compliance.

Perform these steps to scale and standardize your CSNS posture:

1. Navigate to: **`Azure Policy → Definitions`**
2. **Assign built-in policies such as:**
    - **"Only approved IP ranges should be allowed via NSG."**
    - **"JIT access should be enabled on all VMs."**
    - **"Subnet should be associated with an NSG."**

    Regularly audit policy compliance from the Compliance tab in Azure Policy.

By following the above-mentioned steps, you can transform Microsoft Defender for Cloud into a full-fledged **Cloud Service Network Security** platform. This ensures visibility, control, and response capabilities for cloud-native traffic across VMs, containers, and PaaS resources – vital for Zero Trust, least privilege, and micro-segmentation strategies.

Conclusion

Cloud Service Network Security (CSNS) is no longer a supporting element in cloud security – it is a foundational force. As cloud-native applications scale and operate across complex, distributed environments, the ability to monitor, control, and secure network traffic becomes essential. Through this chapter, we explored how CSNS forms a critical layer within CNAPP by enabling secure traffic flows, reducing lateral movement risks, and supporting zero trust architectures. Tools such as **NSG Flow Logs**, **Traffic Analytics**, and **Azure Policy** help visualize, enforce, and automate network security. Additionally, **adaptive network hardening** and **workflow automation** make the environment smarter – not just secure.

We also examined how **Microsoft Defender for Cloud** plays a pivotal role in bringing CSNS to life by offering integrated visibility, actionable alerts, and intelligent policy enforcement at scale. From configuring alerts to implementing guardrails using Azure Policy, the platform enables security teams to maintain a proactive stance against evolving threats.

While network-level protection is necessary, true cloud-native security does not stop at traffic control. It must extend to managing compliance across services, subscriptions, and entire organizations. This is where **Centralized Compliance Management** becomes the next strategic priority. In the upcoming chapter, we will explore how CNAPP solutions – especially Microsoft Defender for Cloud – helps organizations achieve and maintain compliance with global standards, industry frameworks, and internal governance policies. We will also dive into compliance score management, policy assignments, audit readiness, and how centralized dashboards bring it all together.

CSNS may secure the pathways, but compliance secures the mission. Together, they form the pillars of trust and control in the cloud. Let us now move forward to building that trust at scale.

Points to Remember

Here are some **key points to remember** from this chapter on **CSNS**:

- **CSNS is a Core CNAPP Component:** It provides foundational protection for network-level traffic, enabling zero trust principles, and secure cloud-native architecture.
- **Traditional vs. Cloud-Native Network Security:** Unlike traditional firewalls, CSNS is identity-aware, policy-driven, and integrated with cloud-native resources and services.
- **Key Capabilities of CSNS:** Includes traffic monitoring, micro-segmentation, least privilege access, adaptive hardening, and lateral movement prevention.
- **NSG Flow Logs and Traffic Analytics:** These tools provide deep visibility into network behavior, supporting threat detection and forensic analysis.
- **Workflow Automation for Response:** Integration with Azure Logic Apps allows automated actions (for example, VM isolation and alert notifications) in response to network threats.
- **Azure Policy for Network Governance:** Helps enforce consistent security configurations across resources such as disallowing open ports or requiring traffic logging.
- **Microsoft Defender for Cloud as a CSNS Solution:** Offers a centralized platform for configuring, monitoring, and automating network security controls with real-time alerts.
- **CSNS Enables Zero Trust:** Identity-based policies and micro-segmentation help build zero trust across cloud workloads and services.
- **Security Must Be Continuous and Adaptive:** Static rules are not enough – CSNS must evolve with workloads, users, and threat landscapes.

- **Compliance is the Next Step:** CSNS helps meet network security requirements, but centralized compliance management ensures broader alignment with regulatory and internal standards.

Multiple-Choice Questions

1. What is the primary goal of Cloud Service Network Security (CSNS) within a CNAPP framework (CWPP)?
   a. Managing cloud billing and cost optimization
   b. Protecting application code from injection attacks
   c. Securing network-level communication in cloud environments
   d. Automating DevOps pipelines
2. Which of the following features in Azure provides visibility into network traffic patterns for security analysis?
   a. Azure DevOps Pipelines
   b. NSG Flow Logs and Traffic Analytics
   c. Azure Cosmos DB
   d. Azure Active Directory
3. Adaptive Network Hardening in Microsoft Defender for Cloud primarily helps to:
   a. Automatically patch operating systems
   b. Recommend and apply just-in-time access
   c. Suggest security rules, based on traffic patterns
   d. Manage storage account encryption
4. Which of the following best aligns with Zero Trust principles in CSNS?
   a. Allowing open ports for all users
   b. Using perimeter firewalls only
   c. Applying least privilege access and micro-segmentation
   d. Hosting applications on a single virtual machine

5. What role does Azure Policy play in enforcing CSNS?
    a. Managing application code quality
    b. Enforcing network security rules across cloud resources
    c. Controlling cost allocation
    d. Provisioning virtual machines

Answers

1. c
2. b
3. c
4. c
5. b

Questions

1. What is Cloud Service Network Security (CSNS) in the context of CNAPP?
2. How does CSNS differ from traditional perimeter-based firewalls?
3. What is the purpose of NSG (Network Security Group) Flow Logs in Azure?
4. How does Adaptive Network Hardening improve cloud network security?
5. What role does micro-segmentation play in CSNS?
6. How does CSNS support Zero Trust architecture in cloud environments?
7. What are some real-world use cases of CSNS in multi-cloud environments?
8. How does Microsoft Defender for Cloud implement CSNS features?
9. What types of alerts can be configured in CSNS, using Azure Defender?
10. How can Azure Policy be used to enforce secure network configurations?

Key Terms

- **Cloud Service Network Security (CSNS):** A CNAPP pillar that focuses on securing traffic flows and connectivity within and across cloud environments.
- **Defense-in-Depth:** A layered security approach where multiple security controls are implemented to protect cloud networks.

- **Inbound/Outbound Rules:** Network rules that control the flow of traffic to and from cloud-based resources.
- **Lateral Movement Prevention:** Techniques to stop threat actors from moving between systems after breaching one resource.
- **Service Endpoints:** Private network connections used to securely link Azure services to virtual networks, without using public IPs.
- **Just-in-Time (JIT) VM Access:** A security feature that restricts unnecessary open ports by providing time-bound access to virtual machines.
- **Flow Logging:** The process of tracking network traffic patterns for security visibility and troubleshooting.
- **Network Behavior Anomaly Detection (NBAD):** Using machine learning to detect abnormal network behavior indicating potential threats.
- **Distributed Denial of Service (DDoS) Protection:** Automated defense mechanisms that protect cloud applications from volumetric attacks.
- **Network Hardening Recommendations:** AI/ML-driven suggestions by Defender for Cloud to minimize exposure by restricting unnecessary ports and IPs.

CHAPTER 10
Centralized Compliance Management Using CNAPP

Introduction

As cloud environments grow in scale and complexity, **maintaining regulatory compliance across services, workloads, and subscriptions becomes a critical challenge** for modern enterprises.

This section is dedicated to providing hands-on experience in managing compliance centrally, using **Microsoft Defender for Cloud**.

Through a series of structured labs, readers will gain practical insights into enabling globally recognized standards like **NIST SP 800-53**, understanding how compliance scores are generated, and learning how to interpret these scores across cloud environments.

These labs are designed to simplify a typically complex process, giving security teams the confidence and clarity they need to uphold compliance requirements at scale.

Thus, whether you are a beginner exploring compliance frameworks or a seasoned cloud professional refining your skills, these labs will equip you with the tools, and understanding to approach compliance management with greater control and visibility.

Structure

The following topics will be covered in this chapter:

- Demystifying Compliance Buzzwords
- Understanding Importance of Compliance Management
- Understanding Popular Compliance: AWS Well Architected Framework
- Understanding Popular Compliance: CIS Microsoft Foundations Benchmark
- Understanding Popular Compliance: NIST Cybersecurity Framework (NIST CSF)
- Microsoft Defender for Cloud: Your Single Hub for Compliance Management
- How to Configure Centralized Compliance Management in Microsoft Defender for Cloud
- Centralized Compliance Management Labs
- Lab # 1: Exploring Regulatory Compliance Section in Defender for Cloud
- Lab # 2: Managing Compliance Standards: Enabling NIST SP 800-53 Standard
- Lab # 3: Exploring Compliance Secure Score Generated by All Standards

Demystifying Compliance Buzzwords

In the world of cloud security, **compliance is not just a checkbox–it is a continuous journey guided by a web of policies, standards, and best practices.**

Whether you are a cloud architect, security analyst, or compliance officer, you are likely come across terms like **`security policies`**, **`recommendations`**, **`custom standards`**, and **`vulnerability assessments`**. These buzzwords are everywhere, but what do they really mean in practice? And more importantly, **how do they fit into a CNAPP's mission** to secure modern cloud-native environments?

This section breaks down these essential concepts in plain English, helping you **connect the dots between compliance theory and real world application.**

Let us strip away the jargon, and explore these terms in a way **that is practical, clear, and directly relevant** to your cloud security journey.

- **Security Policies:** Security policies are a **set of rules** that **define how cloud resources should behave to stay secure**.

  Think of them as **guardrails** that **ensure your infrastructure follows the best practices**. These can include rules such as "**`all storage must be encrypted`**" or "**`public access to databases is not allowed`**."

In CNAPP tools, policies are enforced automatically, using tools like Azure Policy or AWS Config.

- **Standards:** Standards are **predefined security and compliance frameworks** created by **industry** or **regulatory bodies** to ensure that systems are protected, and are consistent.

  Common standards include **CIS Benchmarks**, **NIST 800-53**, **PCI-DSS**, and **ISO 27001.**

  CNAPP tools align your environment with these standards, and continuously monitor for violations.

- **Recommendations: Recommendations are security tips or actions provided by the CNAPP** platform to improve your cloud posture.

  For example, you might get a recommendation to **enable multi-factor authentication or close unused ports.** These are **typically prioritized, based on risk impact**, and can be linked to compliance requirements.

- **Custom Standards:** Custom standards allow organizations to **create their own compliance rules tailored to business-specific needs.**

  Instead of only **relying on predefined frameworks**, you can **mix and match controls to align with internal policies, legal requirements, or regional regulations**. CNAPPs help to define and apply these standards across multiple environments.

- **Custom Recommendations: Custom recommendations are user-defined security suggestions** built into the compliance framework. You might use these to enforce organization-specific practices such as naming conventions, tagging standards, or restricting resource types.

  CNAPP tools allow these to be added and tracked alongside built-in recommendations.

- **Compliances:** Compliance refers to the state of adhering to a specific set of rules, laws, or policies.

  In CNAPP, compliance is tracked continuously through assessments that check whether cloud resources align with the selected standards or policies.

  It helps ensure that you are always audit-ready and secure.

- **Vulnerability Assessment:** Vulnerability assessment is the process of **scanning your cloud assets** like VMs, containers, and databases for known security flaws. CNAPP tools perform these scans automatically, and **provide detailed reports highlighting risky components, misconfigurations, or missing patches.**

- **Control Mapping:** Control mapping links CNAPP security policies and recommendations to specific requirements in regulatory standards.

  It ensures that every technical action you take like encrypting a disk or configuring a firewall, maps back to a compliance control such as "*data confidentiality*."

- **Regulatory Compliance Dashboard:** This is a visual **dashboard** that shows how your **environment scores against selected compliance standards.**

  It typically **shows passed, failed, and non-applicable controls**–helping security teams quickly **identify where to focus their efforts.**

- **Secure Score: Secure Score is a numerical representation of your cloud security posture.**

  It reflects how many security best practices and recommendations are being followed.

  A **higher score** indicates **better compliance and lower risk.**

- **Auto Remediation:** Auto-remediation refers to the **automated fixing of compliance violations.**

  For example, if a storage bucket is found to be publicly accessible, **CNAPP tools can automatically make it private again without human intervention**– saving time and reducing risks.

- **Drift Detection:** Drift detection **identifies changes** in your cloud configuration **that move resources away from their intended secure or compliant state.**

  CNAPP platforms **track this continuously and alert teams**, when something changes unexpectedly.

Now that you understand these common buzzwords, cloud compliance will not feel like a puzzle anymore.

These terms such as policies, standards, recommendations, and vulnerabilities might sound technical, but they are really just ways to stay organized, stay safe, and stay in line with rules that matter. Knowing what each one means helps you to take the right steps at the right time, whether you are fixing a security issue or preparing for an audit.

As we go further into centralized compliance tools like Microsoft Defender for Cloud, keep these terms in mind–they will help you understand what is going on, what to fix, and how to keep things running smoothly.

Understanding Importance of Compliance Management

Compliance management in cloud environments means checking if your cloud resources are following the rules–whether those rules come from the government (like GDPR), industry groups (like PCI-DSS for payment systems), or your own company's internal standards.

In simpler words:

> It is making sure your cloud setup is not breaking any important rules–and fixing it fast if it is.

Cloud-native platforms, especially CNAPPs (Cloud-Native Application Protection Platforms), **help by checking your setup automatically, and sending alerts** when something is out of line.

Why is Compliance a Big Deal in the Industry?

In today's fast-moving digital world, no business can afford to ignore compliance.

Whether you are running a small startup or managing a large enterprise, **following security and privacy rules is not just about avoiding trouble–it is about protecting your reputation**, building customer trust, and staying competitive.

With increasing threats, tighter regulations, and growing customer awareness, companies are now treating compliance as a key part of their overall business strategy. It is no longer a one-time task–it is a daily responsibility that helps businesses run safely, and grow confidently in the cloud.

Here are some key reasons why compliance plays such a crucial role across industries today:

- **Avoiding Fines and Penalties:** In many industries such as healthcare, finance, or government services, **following strict rules is not optional–it is mandatory.** These rules, also called regulations or standards (like HIPAA, PCI-DSS, or GDPR), are designed to **protect the sensitive data,** and ensure that systems are secure. **If a company ignores these requirements or slips up**, **it can face serious consequences.**

  This includes large fines, legal trouble, or even losing the license to do business. For example, a healthcare provider that leaks patient records due to weak security could be hit with massive penalties.

  That is why compliance is such a big deal–**it is not just about being safe, it is also about staying in business** without getting into legal or financial trouble.

Good compliance practices, supported by CNAPP tools, help avoid these issues by keeping everything in check from the start.

- **Building Customer Trust**: **In today's digital world, customers care deeply about how their personal data is handled.** Whether it is an email address, a credit card number, or health records, **people expect companies to keep that information private and secure.** When a business follows well-known compliance standards, and shows they take security seriously, it builds confidence.

  Customers are more likely to stay loyal to a company that proves it respects their privacy and follows the rules. **On the other hand, even one public data breach can destroy trust–and that's hard to rebuild.**

  By using CNAPP solutions to maintain strong security and compliance, companies send a clear message: "*We care about your safety, and we have got your back.*"

- **Preparing for Audits Made Easy**: **Audits can be stressful–especially when you are not ready.** But with proper compliance management, audits do not have to be scary or time-consuming.

  CNAPP tools continuously monitor your environment, and keep everything organized behind the scenes. They track configurations, log changes, and flag anything that might cause trouble during an audit. This means that when auditors come knocking, all the necessary reports, evidence, and history are already in place–no scrambling needed.

  Instead of doing last-minute fixes or digging through logs, teams can simply pull up their dashboard, and show proof that they have been compliant all along.

  It saves time, reduces panic, and makes the audit process much smoother.

- **Reducing Risk with Automation**: One of the best things about **using CNAPP tools is that they bring automation into compliance** management.

  In the past, security checks were manual slow, easy to miss, and often done too late. Now, compliance can happen in real-time.

  For example, if someone accidentally exposes a storage bucket to the public, **the system can spot it instantly, and either alert the team or fix it automatically.** This early detection prevents issues from becoming serious security incidents.

  Automation also means that common problems such as missing encryption, misconfigured permissions, or open ports are caught before attackers or auditors find them.

In short, automation turns compliance from a one-time event into a constant, protective process.

- **Supporting DevSecOps:** Modern cloud teams do not wait until the end of a project to worry about compliance.

  With DevSecOps, security and compliance are built right into the development process–from day one.

  This means that every piece of code, every configuration, and every deployment is checked automatically for policy violations and risks. **If something does not meet the compliance standards, it is flagged or fixed before it goes live**. This approach not only makes apps safer, but also saves time and money.

  Developers do not have to go back and fix things later, and security teams do not have to constantly chase issues after the fact.

  CNAPP tools make this smooth by plugging directly into CI/CD pipelines, helping teams ship secure and compliant software faster.

What Does Compliance Management Involve?

Keeping up with compliance might sound tricky, but it really just means making sure your cloud setup follows the right rules and stays secure. It is a mix of simple steps like checking settings, watching for risks, and following company or government rules.

These steps help you avoid problems, fix issues early, and stay ready for audits. In this section, we will break down what compliance work usually includes, so that it is easy to understand what happens behind the scenes.

In real-world cloud security, compliance teams concentrate on several key areas to keep their environments safe and rule-abiding.

- **Security Policy Enforcement** ensures that only approved actions happen within the cloud. For example, this means blocking public access to databases, or restricting who can make changes.
- **Regulatory Mapping** is the process of checking every cloud service against recognized standards and frameworks such as NIST, HIPAA, or CIS to make sure that the setup meets the required rules.
- **Real-Time Monitoring** involves continuous scanning of the environment to spot any violations or misconfigurations as soon as they occur, enabling quick response.
- **Secure Score Tracking** provides a simple number or score that reflects how secure and compliant your cloud setup is, along with practical advice on how to improve.

- **Alerting and Reporting** means teams get immediate notifications about any compliance issues, and comprehensive reports are generated to help with audits or management reviews.
- **Auto-Remediation** refers to the automatic fixing of common problems such as disabling public access or turning on encryption—without manual intervention, saving time and reducing risks.

Lastly, **Multi-Cloud Compliance** makes sure that these rules and checks apply consistently across different cloud providers such as AWS, Azure, and GCP, eliminating any blind spots in security.

How is It Practiced in the Industry?

Compliance is not just a checklist anymore—it is a daily part of how cloud teams work.

In the real world, **companies use smart tools and clear processes** to stay on top of rules and risks.

Whether **it is mapping cloud resources to standards**, **tracking secure scores**, or **setting up alerts**, everything is built to be fast, clear, and automated. **The goal is to catch problems early, fix them quickly, and prove to regulators and customers that the environment is safe**.

Let us now explore how modern businesses actually practice compliance in their day-to-day cloud operations.

- **Big Tech Companies**: They use **custom compliance frameworks** that go beyond standard rules.

  These are applied across hundreds of teams, using CNAPP tools that integrate into their pipelines and dashboards.

- **Fintech and Banking**: These firms follow **PCI-DSS and ISO 27001** strictly.

  Their CNAPP tools are configured to detect and fix issues like open ports, unencrypted databases, or weak passwords in real-time.

- **Healthcare**: They need **HIPAA compliance.**

  CNAPPs are used to classify sensitive patient data, and enforce controls such as encryption and access logging.

- **Startups**: Even **small teams use CNAPP tools to apply CIS Benchmarks,** and track a **compliance score**. This helps them **prove to investors and partners that they take security seriously.**

  Compliance management helps teams stay one step ahead.

It is not only about following rules, but also about being ready– **ready for threats, ready for audits, and ready to grow securely.**

With **tools like Microsoft Defender for Cloud, businesses can centralize this process**, **gain full visibility**, and **automate their response to violations**—making cloud compliance simpler, faster, and smarter.

Understanding Popular Compliance: AWS Well Architected Framework

The **AWS Well-Architected Framework is a practical guide** created by Amazon Web Services to **help cloud users build better, safer, and more reliable systems.**

Think of it as a cloud "health check" that teaches teams how to design, build, and maintain cloud environments, the right way. **It does not just help with compliance—it helps avoid common mistakes and keeps cloud projects healthy from day one.**

This framework is made up of five core pillars.

Each pillar covers a specific area that matters in the real world of cloud operations:

🧱 The 5 Pillars of AWS Well-Architected Framework

At the heart of the AWS Well-Architected Framework are five powerful pillars.

These pillars are like **building blocks** that help teams create cloud systems that are secure, reliable, efficient, and cost-effective. **Each one focuses on a key area that matters for running workloads in the cloud, the right way.**

When used together, they guide teams to make smart, safe, and scalable decisions—without cutting corners.

1. **Operational Excellence**
    - This is all about running systems smoothly.
    - It includes monitoring, automating tasks, tracking problems, and learning from mistakes.
    - **Companies use this pillar to make sure their systems are always improving, and working efficiently.**
2. **Security**
    - This pillar focuses on protecting data and systems.

- It includes Identity and Access Management (IAM), data encryption, threat detection, and regular security reviews.
- **Following this pillar helps businesses meet compliance requirements, and reduce risks.**

3. **Reliability**
   - Here, the focus is on keeping systems available and recoverable.
   - It covers backup planning, disaster recovery, and designing for failover.
   - **The goal is to keep services running, even if something breaks.**
4. **Performance Efficiency**
   - This pillar is about using cloud resources wisely.
   - It helps teams choose the right services, scale automatically, and get the best performance, without wasting money or efforts.
5. **Cost Optimization**
   - Spending money smartly is the focus here.
   - This includes **turning off unused resources**, using pricing models efficiently, and **regularly reviewing costs to save more** over time.

How It Helps with Compliance

Even though the **AWS Well-Architected Framework is not a compliance standard itself**, it supports many compliance goals. For example:

- **Security pillar** helps meet rules from frameworks such as **CIS, ISO 27001, and NIST**.
- **Operational excellence** helps with documentation and incident response which are important in **SOC 2** and **HIPAA**.
- **Cost and performance tracking** supports audits by showing that systems are well-managed and efficient.

AWS also provides the Well-Architected Tool which lets you review your workload against these pillars.

It gives a report showing where you are doing well, and where you need improvement. This tool helps organizations catch problems early and **improve before a real audit or security incident** happens.

Many startups, enterprises, and even regulated industries use the AWS Well-Architected Framework regularly–some quarterly, some yearly.

It is a part of their cloud hygiene routine.

Cloud architects use it to guide design, while compliance teams use it to validate that systems are safe, and ready for audits. And when combined with tools like **Microsoft Defender for Cloud**, teams can continuously monitor how well they are aligned with security best practices—even outside AWS.

Understanding Popular Compliance: CIS Microsoft Foundations Benchmark

The **CIS Microsoft Foundations Benchmark** is a popular security guideline designed to help secure Microsoft cloud environments, especially Microsoft Azure.

Created by the **Center for Internet Security (CIS)**, this benchmark **acts like a trusted checklist** of best practices that **cloud teams can follow to make sure their Microsoft Cloud setup is safe, secure, and well-structured.**

CIS Benchmarks are detailed, step-by-step recommendations that focus on hardening your cloud settings.

For Microsoft environments, this means checking things like:

- **Who** has access to your cloud?
- **Are** your audit logs turned on?
- **Are** risky settings like public access or outdated protocols disabled?

The **Microsoft Foundations Benchmark** gives clear guidance on how to configure these settings the right way, **so that you do not leave doors open for attackers.**

This benchmark is widely adopted in the industry because:

- It is **vendor-neutral and community-driven**—created by experts, and regularly updated.
- It **maps well with other standards like ISO 27001, NIST, and SOC 2.**
- It **helps organizations pass audits faster** by proving that their setup follows industry best practices.
- **Tools such as Microsoft Defender for Cloud can automatically assess your Azure environment** against CIS benchmarks, and show where you fall short.

Why is It So Widely Used?

This benchmark is widely adopted in the industry because:

- It is **vendor-neutral and community-driven**—created by experts, and regularly updated.

- It **maps well with other standards** such as **ISO 27001, NIST, and SOC 2**.
- It **helps organizations pass audits faster** by proving that their setup follows industry best practices.
- **Tools like Microsoft Defender for Cloud** can **automatically assess your Azure environment** against CIS benchmarks, and show where you fall short.

In a real-world setup, cloud security teams scan their Azure environment, using tools that support CIS Benchmarks. These tools generate a compliance score, and point out risky settings like:

- **Admin accounts** without Multi-factor Authentication (MFA)
- Disabled security logging
- Publicly exposed virtual machines

From there, teams can **fix issues manually or set up auto-remediation**, using policies and scripts. This creates a security-first environment that is compliant, even at scale.

The CIS Microsoft Foundations Benchmark is like a security GPS–it tells you if you are on the right track or heading into danger. It is beginner-friendly, widely accepted, and works hand-in-hand with tools such as Microsoft Defender for Cloud.

If your CNAPP strategy includes Microsoft environments, this benchmark should be one of your go-to frameworks.

Understanding Popular Compliance: NIST Cybersecurity Framework (NIST CSF)

When we talk about keeping things secure in the cloud, many people feel lost or unsure about where to even begin.

That is where the **NIST Cybersecurity Framework (NIST CSF)** comes in.

It is not just another heavy document full of technical words. Instead, **it is a very practical and easy-to-follow guide** created by the **National Institute of Standards and Technology (NIST)**.

The idea behind this framework is simple: Help organizations understand their cybersecurity risks and manage them in a smart, organized way. It gives security teams, IT admins, and even business leaders **a common language to talk about cyber threats and protection.**

Whether you are a small startup running everything on the cloud, or a large company with thousands of cloud assets, NIST CSF offers a simple structure that you can follow to improve your security.

It is like having a ready-made checklist to make sure that you are not missing anything important, when it comes to protecting your data and services.

How NIST CSF Fits into Cloud Security

In real-world cloud setups, **security teams use CNAPP solutions** like Microsoft Defender for Cloud to apply the NIST framework, without starting from scratch.

These tools help automate each of the **five steps**:

1. **Identify:** They scan your entire cloud, and show you what resources you have, what is for the public, and where sensitive data lives.
2. **Protect:** They apply security policies, block risky settings, and check that things like encryption and access controls are in place.
3. **Detect:** They monitor all the time, and alert you to misconfigurations, malware, or unusual user activity.
4. **Respond:** They help trigger alerts, open tickets, or even run automated scripts to fix problems as soon as they are found.
5. **Recover:** They keep track of incidents, and give clear guidance to close security gaps as well as avoid future attacks.

Why NIST CSF is Trusted by the Industry

One big reason companies prefer NIST CSF is that it is **simple, flexible, and not tied to any specific technology or platform**.

Whether your data lives in AWS, Azure, GCP, or across all the three, **this framework still applies.**

It also maps easily to other standards such as **CIS Benchmarks, ISO 27001, GDPR, and HIPAA**, making life easier during audits. Even better, **it is focused on continuous improvement**–which means your cloud security setup keeps getting stronger over time, not just once a year during audit season.

Think of NIST CSF as a security GPS for your cloud journey. It does not matter if you are just starting or already running hundreds of services–it shows you where you stand, and how to move forward safely.

For teams using CNAPP tools such as Microsoft Defender for Cloud, following the NIST framework becomes much easier, more automated, and way less stressful. In short, it is one of the smartest, most widely used frameworks to keep your cloud secure and compliant–without the headaches.

`Microsoft Defender for Cloud`: Your Single Hub for Compliance Management

In today's multi-cloud world, where **services are spread across Azure, AWS, and GCP**, keeping up with different compliance rules can be a real challenge. This is where `Microsoft Defender for Cloud` steps in as a **centralized compliance management solution**.

It brings everything under one roof, helping cloud security teams stay compliant, stay organized, and respond quickly to security gaps.

Defender for Cloud acts like a **smart control room**, continuously checking if your cloud resources meet industry standards such as **CIS, NIST CSF, PCI DSS, HIPAA, and more**—not just for Azure, but also for **AWS and GCP**.

At the heart of this system is the `Regulatory Compliance Blade` which gives you a clear, dashboard-style view of how well your cloud environment is meeting the selected compliance frameworks.

Each framework is broken down into **control families**, and each control shows exactly which resources are compliant, non-compliant, or missing data. This makes audits easier, and shows you where to focus next.

`Defender for Cloud` supports **built-in regulatory standards** like:

- `Azure Security Benchmark (ASB)`
- `CIS Microsoft Azure Foundations Benchmark`
- `NIST SP 800-53`
- `PCI DSS`
- `ISO 27001`
- `SOC TSP`
- And many others

You can also **add your own custom initiatives**, allowing your security team to track internal policies or region-specific regulations.

Some of the **key features** that make **Defender a true centralized compliance tool includes**:

- **Secure Score Tracking:** Gives a real-time security score, based on posture and compliance gaps.
- **Cross-cloud Standards Mapping:** Applies the same compliance controls to Azure, AWS, and GCP resources.

- **Custom Compliance Initiatives:** Create your own policy sets, using Azure Policy and assign them for tracking.
- **Alerting and Recommendations:** Shows you what is wrong (for example, missing encryption) and how to fix it.
- **Auto-remediation Scripts:** Suggests or applies fixes automatically to bring resources back into compliance.
- **Resource-level Reporting:** Drill down into each VM, database, or storage account to see what is compliant or not.
- **Role-based Access and Exemptions:** Let the right teams manage policies, while allowing valid exceptions (like for dev environments).
- **Workbook Integration:** Build visual compliance dashboards and reports, using Defender Data in Azure Workbooks.
- **APIs and Export:** Pull compliance results via APIs for external SIEMs, audit logs, or Power BI dashboards.

With all this packed into one place, **Defender for Cloud turns the messy job of compliance tracking into a clean, automated, and continuous process**.

You do not have to hop across cloud portals or worry about different standards manually–it is all done in one view, with full control and clarity.

How to Configure Centralized Compliance Management in Microsoft Defender for Cloud

Setting up Centralized Compliance Management in Microsoft Defender for Cloud may sound complex–but in reality, it is a **guided** and **easy-to-follow process**.

You do not need to be a compliance expert to get started.

Defender for Cloud is designed to help both security professionals and IT teams create a one-stop system that monitors compliance across **Azure**, **AWS**, and **Google Cloud (GCP)**.

This section walks you through all the key steps and options to configure it the right way.

Step 1: Enable `Microsoft Defender for Cloud`

The first thing you need to do is **turn on `Microsoft Defender for Cloud`** in the **`Azure portal`**:

1. Go to the **`Azure Portal`**, and search for **`Microsoft Defender for Cloud`** in the top search bar.
2. Click on **`Environment settings`**, and select your subscription(s).
3. Click **`Enable all Microsoft Defender plans`**, or choose specific plans such as Defender for Servers, SQL, Storage, and so on.

This step makes sure all cloud workloads are covered for security and compliance checks.

Step 2: Connect Multi-Cloud Accounts (AWS/GCP)

To centralize compliance, you need to bring other cloud accounts into Defender for Cloud:

- **For AWS:**
  a. Go to **`Environment Settings`** > **`Add Environment`** > Select **`Amazon Web Services (AWS)`**.
  b. Use the **`CloudFormation template`** that Defender provides to link your AWS account securely.
  c. Choose the compliance standards, you want to be applied (like CIS AWS Foundations).

Note: *Please refer to the Chapter 3, Onboarding* CNAPP: A *Practical Guide for Learning Onboarding* AWS Accounts.

- **For GCP:**
  a. Go to **`Environment Settings`** > **`Add Environment`**. Select **`Google Cloud Platform (GCP)`**.
  b. Follow the guided steps to link your GCP project.
  c. Defender will then start assessing those resources for compliance issues.

Note: *Please refer to the Chapter 3, Onboarding* CNAPP: A *Practical Guide for Learning Onboarding* GCP Accounts.

Step 3: Select Built-in Regulatory Standards

`Microsoft Defender for Cloud` includes **many pre-built compliance standards**. You can choose which ones you want to apply:

a. In the **`Regulatory Compliance blade`**, click **`Add a standard`**.

b. Select from options like:

   - `CIS Microsoft Azure Foundations Benchmark`

- `NIST SP 800-53`
- `ISO 27001`
- `SOC TSP`
- `HIPAA HITRUST`
- `PCI DSS 3.2.1`

c. Click **`Assign`** to apply the selected standard to your subscriptions.

Each standard includes a collection of **security controls**, broken down into what your resources should or should not be doing.

Step 4: Use Custom Compliance Initiatives (Optional)

Want to track your own internal rules or specific country-level compliance? You can create **custom compliance initiatives**:

1. Go to **`Azure Policy`** > **`Definitions`**.
2. Create a **`new initiative`**, and add policies you care about (like requiring encryption at rest).
3. Assign this initiative to a **`subscription`** or **`management group`**.
4. Once assigned, it will show up in your **`Defender for Cloud regulatory compliance dashboard`**, just like any built-in framework.

This allows your security team to track *exactly what matters to your business*, beyond industry templates.

Step 5: View Compliance Dashboard and Reports

Once everything is configured, **`Defender for Cloud`** starts doing real-time assessments. Here is what you will see:

- **Secure Score:** A numerical score that tells you how secure and compliant your environment is.
- **Compliance Dashboard:** A visual board with each standard, showing passed and failed controls.
- **Control-Level Drilldown:** Click on a control (like "**`Ensure encryption is enabled`**") to see which resources pass or fail.
- **Recommendations:** Defender tells you exactly how to fix the issue—step-by-step.

This dashboard acts like your compliance command center.

Step 6: Set Up Alerts, Exemptions, and Auto-Remediation

You can take actions on findings in these ways:

- **Enable Alerts:** Get notified, when a control is violated (for example, a storage account is made public).
- **Set Exemptions:** Mark certain resources as "`excluded`" from policies, if they are a part of testing or dev environments.
- **Auto-Remediation:** Use Azure Policy's `DeployIfNotExists` or `Remediation tasks` to automatically fix issues (like applying encryption or turning off public access).

This reduces manual work, and makes compliance proactive, not reactive.

Step 7: Export and Share Reports

Need to show compliance status to auditors or management?

- Use **Azure Workbooks** to create beautiful visual reports.
- Export data in **CSV or JSON formats** for offline analysis.
- Integrate with **SIEMs (like Microsoft Sentinel)** or **Power BI** for advanced dashboards.

Centralized Compliance Management Labs

In today's multi-standard, multi-cloud environments, managing regulatory compliance can be overwhelming without the right tools and visibility. That is where Microsoft Defender for Cloud shines–by offering a centralized hub for organizations to assess, manage, and monitor their compliance posture against a wide range of industry-recognized standards. Whether you are aligning with NIST SP 800-53, CIS Benchmarks, or cloud-native best practices, Defender for Cloud empowers security teams to stay ahead of compliance requirements with real-time insights and secure score metrics.

This hands-on lab series walks you through how centralized compliance is not just a checkbox activity, but a dynamic process integrated within Defender for Cloud's ecosystem. The labs start with enabling key regulatory standards like NIST SP 800-53 at the subscription level, followed by understanding how the platform evaluates your cloud environment against these controls. You'll then explore how secure scores are generated–offering a quantitative measure of how well your environment adheres to each framework.

Each lab is crafted to help you build practical skills, from toggling compliance standards to interpreting detailed secure score breakdowns. You will see firsthand how Microsoft Defender for Cloud becomes your compliance command center–helping you reduce risk, maintain audit readiness, and establish confidence across your cloud footprint. Whether you're a security engineer or a compliance analyst, these labs serve as a vital foundation for mastering compliance management in cloud-native environments.

Lab # 1: Exploring Regulatory Compliance Section in Defender for Cloud

The regulatory compliance section provides valuable insights. When you are managing security in the cloud, it is easy to feel overwhelmed by rules, standards, and frameworks.

Every industry–from banking to healthcare–has its own checklist of what "**`secure`**" looks like. That is where the **`Regulatory Compliance` section in `Microsoft Defender for Cloud` becomes your best friend**!

Instead of jumping between documents and policies, this section brings all the **major compliance frameworks such as CIS**, **NIST**, and **ISO–right into your Azure dashboard.**

It gives you a clear, visual view of how well your cloud environment stacks up against these standards. More than just showing what is wrong, it also explains how to fix things, and what matters most.

This way, your team can stay audit-ready, reduce risk, and focus efforts on what really needs attention–without guesswork.

To explore Regulatory Compliance section on Defender for Cloud, follow these steps:

1. Log in to the Azure portal, using your administrative credentials.
2. Go to the search bar > type "**`Microsoft Defender for Cloud`**", and select the service to open the dashboard.
3. Once inside the dashboard, locate the "**`Regulatory Compliance`**" tab on the left-hand menu under '**`Cloud Security`**' section.
4. This is the initial view of the '**`Regulatory Compliance`**' dashboard as it appears in my instance of **`Microsoft Defender for Cloud environment`**.

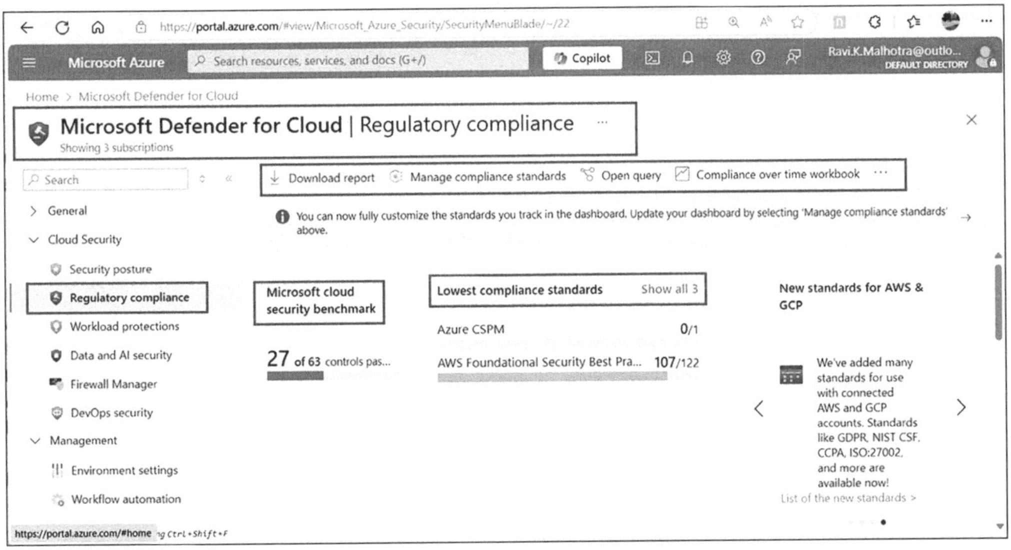

Figure 10.1: *Regulatory Compliance Initial View - Part 1*

5. This screen is your starting point to see how well your cloud setup meets different security rules. It is a part of Microsoft Defender for Cloud, and gives a clear, one-page view of your current compliance status.

   In the middle, you will see progress bars for different standards. For example:

   - **Microsoft Cloud Security Benchmark:** You have **passed 27 out of 63 controls**–good, but there is work to do.
   - **AWS Foundational Security Best Practices:** You have done well here with **107 out of 122 controls passed**.
   - **Azure CSPM:** Currently showing **`0/1`** which means it needs attention.

   At the top, you will find helpful tools such as **Download report**, **`Manage compliance standards`**, and **`Open query`**, making it easy to customize, share, or explore your compliance data.

   On the right, you will see a note about **new standards for AWS and GCP** like GDPR, NIST, ISO, and many more so that you can manage everything in one place, even if you are using multiple cloud platforms.

   This dashboard helps you **spot problems early, and stay ready for audits** without stress.

6. Now, if you scroll further down on the **`Regulatory Compliance screen in Microsoft Defender for Cloud`**, you will start seeing deeper insights into each standard like in this example, the **`AWS Foundational Security Best Practices`**. Refer to the following screenshot:

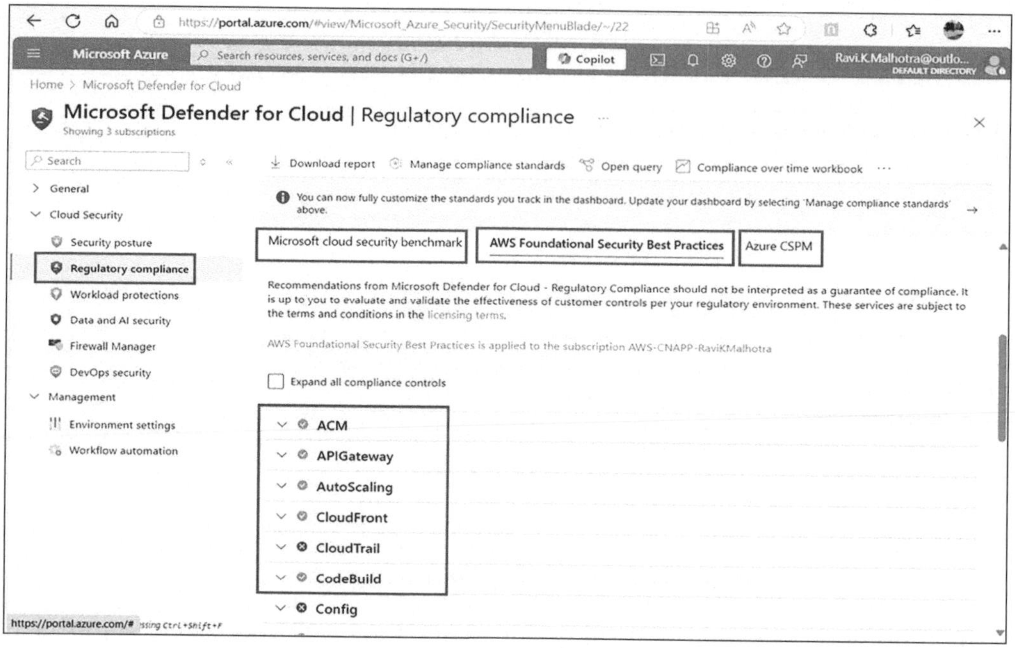

***Figure 10.2**: Regulatory Compliance Initial View - Part 2*

7. This section breaks down individual AWS services such as **ACM**, **APIGateway**, **CloudTrail**, and many more. Each one has a status indicator:

    - ☑ **Green check** means the control is fully passed.
    - ✗ **Red cross** highlights areas where action is needed.
    - ☐ **Empty rows** might mean no data is available or checks are pending.

    This view helps you quickly identify which parts of your cloud environment meet compliance, and where you need improvements. It is like having a checklist for each cloud service, all in one place.

    By expanding these sections, you can dive even deeper into specific controls and their recommendations, making it easier to fix issues, and stay audit-ready.

8. If you click on the "**Microsoft Cloud Security Benchmark**" tab–located next to the '**AWS Foundational Security Best Practices**'–**Defender for Cloud** will update the view to show compliance results, based on Microsoft's own recommended security controls for Azure environments.

    This benchmark is specifically designed for **Azure environments**, and covers a wide range of security areas such as **identity management**, **data protection**, **logging**, and **network security**.

    Just like the AWS standards view, **it breaks down each control into pass or**

fail status. You will also see a detailed list of Azure services, and whether they meet the required controls.

9. This helps you align your Azure resources with Microsoft's recommended security baseline, making it easier to stay compliant and secure.
10. This concludes the lab.

Lab # 2: Managing Compliance Standards: Enabling NIST SP 800-53 Standard

Every organization operates under different rules and regulations depending on its industry, location, and the type of cloud services it uses.

Microsoft Defender for Cloud makes it easier to handle these different needs by allowing you to enable and manage multiple compliance standards–tailored to your business.

By default, Defender for Cloud enables the **Microsoft Cloud Security Benchmark (MCSB)**. While MCSB provides excellent general coverage, many organizations–especially those in government or regulated industries–also need to follow **NIST SP 800-53 Rev. 5**, a widely recognized standard for securing federal systems and critical infrastructure.

In this lab, you will learn **how to enable NIST SP 800-53 as a compliance standard within Microsoft Defender for Cloud.** You will see how to:

- Access the compliance standards section.
- Add NIST SP 800-53 to your compliance view.
- Understand how this standard will impact your compliance dashboard.

By enabling this standard, you can align your cloud security posture with NIST's trusted guidelines, and track how your environment performs against its requirements. It is an essential step for organizations that need to meet government regulations or want a detailed, structured approach to cloud security.

By the end of this lab, your Defender for Cloud dashboard will begin showing insights, recommendations, and compliance scores aligned with **NIST SP 800-53**, helping your team stay on top of what truly matters in securing your workloads.

Let us dive in and configure it together, and follow these steps:

1. Log in to the Azure portal, using your administrative credentials.
2. Go to the search bar > type "`Microsoft Defender for Cloud`", and select the service to open the dashboard.

3. Once inside the dashboard, locate the "**Regulatory Compliance**" tab on the left-hand menu under '**Cloud Security**' section.
4. This is the initial view of the '**Regulatory Compliance**' dashboard as it appears in my instance of Microsoft Defender for Cloud environment. This screen is your starting point to see how well your cloud setup meets different security rules.
5. To begin, click on the '**Manage Compliance Standards**' button located at the top of the Regulatory Compliance screen.
6. This action will take you directly to the '**Environment Settings**' tab in Microsoft Defender for Cloud, where you can view all cloud accounts currently onboarded in your environment. The following screenshot shows the Environment Settings view from our instance of **Microsoft Defender for Cloud**.

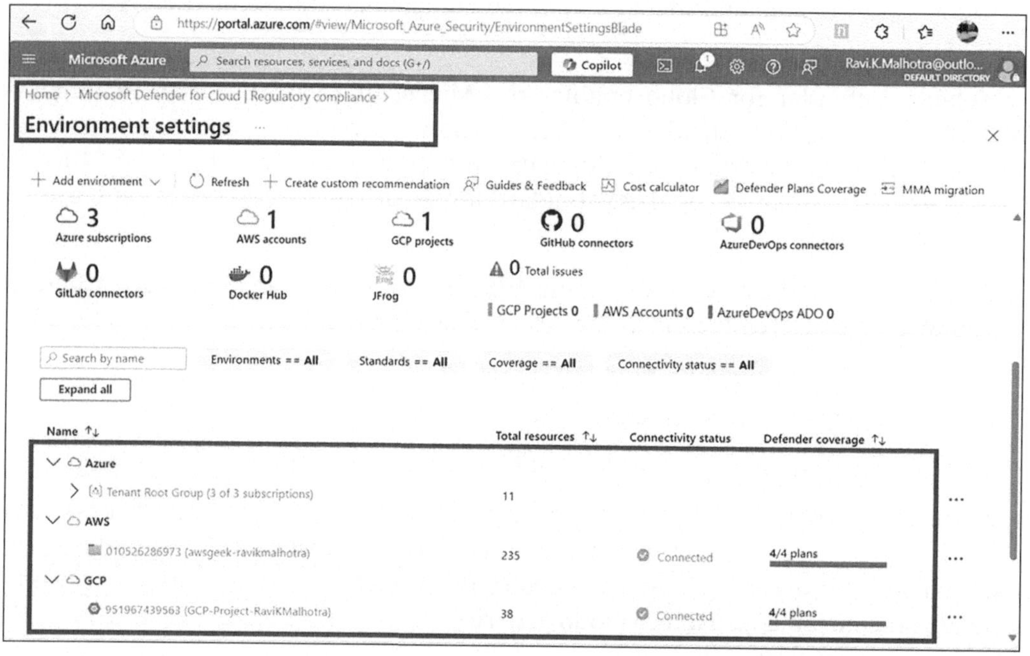

Figure 10.3: *Regulatory Compliance and Environment Settings Page*

7. Next, click on any subscription, you want to manage—here, we selected **one of our Azure subscriptions**.
8. This will open the '**Security Policies**' screen, where **Defender for Cloud** lists all the available compliance standards and recommendations.

   You will see which ones are already enabled, and which are available to add.

This screen also gives you the flexibility to create custom compliance standards tailored to your organization's specific regulatory needs. Refer to the following screenshot to see how this looks in our Defender for Cloud instance.

You will see two tabs near the top:

- **`Standards`:** Shows a list of **industry and cloud-specific compliance standards** (like Microsoft's benchmark, CIS, NIST, APRA, and so on).
- **`Recommendations`:** This tab provides **detailed security recommendations**, based on the selected standard(s).

In this view, the **`Standards`** tab is selected. Refer to the following screenshot:

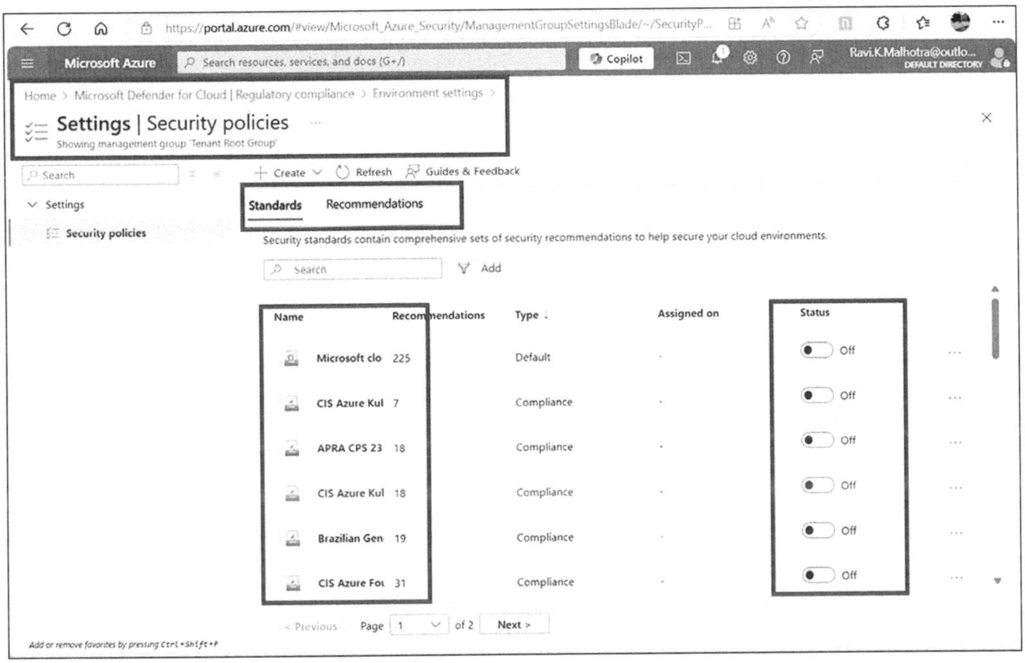

Figure 10.4: *Security Policy Screen for Enabling Standards*

0. In the search bar, **type 'NIST SP 800-53'** to quickly locate the standard within the list of available compliance frameworks. Once it appears, **toggle the Status,** and **switch to 'On'**. Defender for Cloud will begin assigning the standard to your selected environment. This may take a few moments. Once the process completes, you will receive a confirmation notification stating: "**`Assigned standard successfully.`**"

   Refer to the following screenshot:

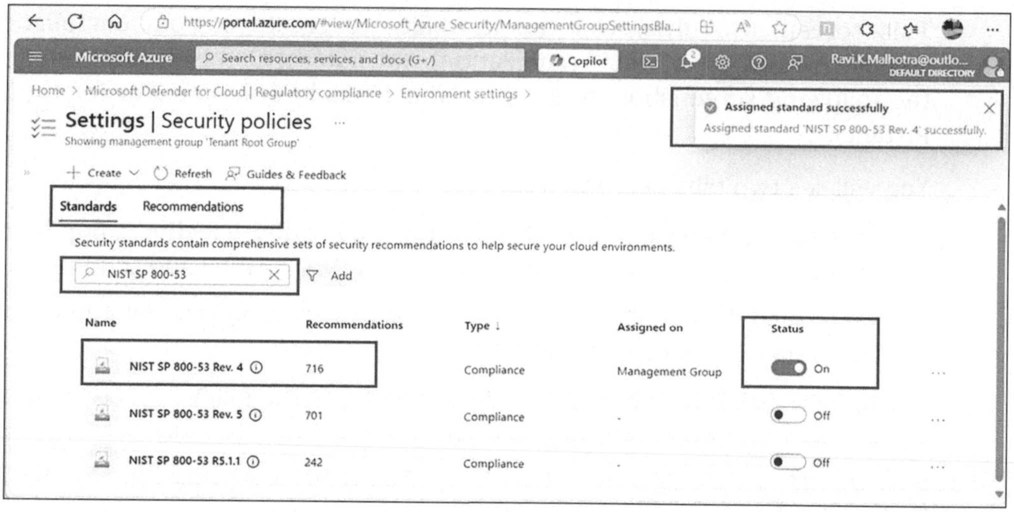

Figure 10.5: *Security Policy Screen - Enabling NIST SP 800-53 Standard*

10. Once the NIST SP 800-53 standard is enabled for your selected subscription, **`Microsoft Defender for Cloud` begins a thorough evaluation of your cloud resources** against the controls defined in the framework. This assessment process may take some time to complete, depending on the size and complexity of your environment.

    During this time, Defender for Cloud collects data, analyzes configurations, and **generates a compliance-based secure score specific to the NIST SP 800-53 standard**.

11. This concludes the lab.

    In the next lab, we will explore the secure score generated by Defender for Cloud, and dive into the detailed findings provided under the NIST SP 800-53 *compliance view.*

Lab # 3: Exploring Compliance Secure Score Generated by All Standards

After **enabling** compliance standards such as **NIST SP 800-53**, **Microsoft Cloud Security Benchmark**, and others in Defender for Cloud, it is crucial to understand how these standards influence your overall compliance posture.

`Microsoft Defender for Cloud` evaluates your cloud resources against each selected standard and calculates a compliance-specific secure score.

This lab walks you through **how to view, interpret, and utilize these secure scores**

to prioritize remediation, and improve your security alignment across different regulatory requirements.

By the end of this lab, you will gain a comprehensive view of how your environment measures up to multiple compliance frameworks, helping you drive more targeted security improvements.

Let us now dive in, and configure it together, as well as follow these steps:

1. Log into the **`Azure portal`**, using your administrative credentials.
2. Go to the search bar > type "**`Microsoft Defender for Cloud`**", and select the service to open the dashboard.
3. Once inside the dashboard, locate the "**`Regulatory Compliance`**" tab on the left-hand menu under '**`Cloud Security`**' section. This is the initial view of the '**`Regulatory Compliance`**' dashboard as it appears in my instance of **`Microsoft Defender for Cloud`** environment.

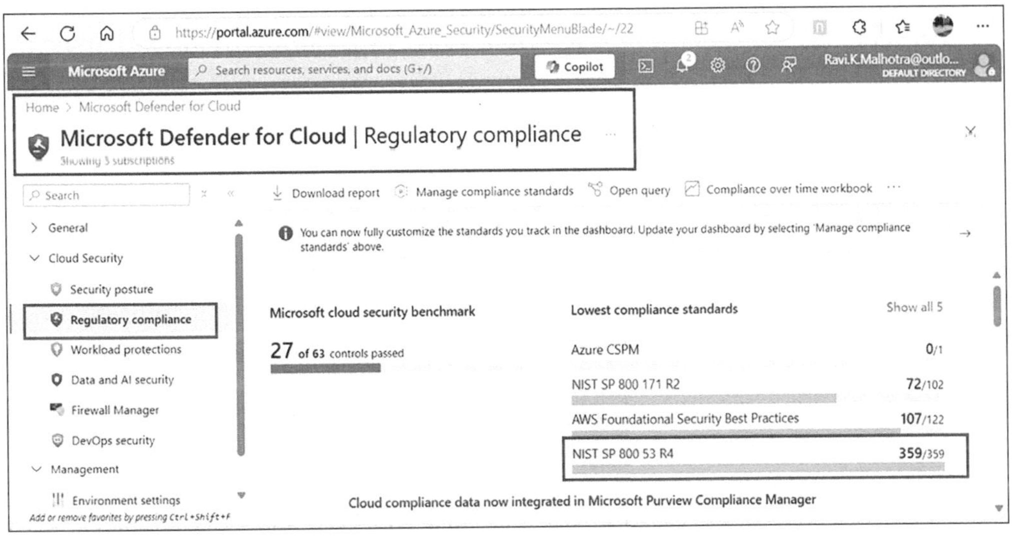

Figure 10.6: *Regulatory Compliance – NIST SP 800-53 Secure Score View*

4. The **`Regulatory Compliance`** option is selected under **`Cloud Security`** which brings up the compliance overview and details on the right pane.

   `Microsoft Cloud Security Benchmark`: Shows 27 out of 63 controls passed – this gives an idea of how well the environment adheres to this baseline benchmark.

   Under **`Lowest Compliance Standards`**, a list is shown with the least compliant frameworks at the top. In your case:

   - **NIST SP 800-53 R4** is listed with **359/359** – indicating **full compliance** with this standard across your evaluated resources.

- Other standards such as **NIST SP 800-171 R2** and **AWS Foundational Security Best Practices** are also shown with their respective control pass counts.

5. The bar next to **NIST SP 800-53 R4** is fully blue, representing **100% of controls are passed**, which is an excellent score.
6. This score reflects the evaluation of your cloud environment against all 359 controls defined under the NIST SP 800-53 Rev 4 framework.
7. This **dashboard is an essential feature for cloud compliance monitoring**. It helps security teams:
   - Quickly identify non-compliant areas.
   - Track progress across various regulatory standards.
   - Take action to improve secure posture, based on compliance scores.

   Your environment currently demonstrates a **strong alignment with NIST SP 800-53 R4** which is a major milestone in ensuring robust cybersecurity compliance in the cloud.
8. This concludes the lab.

Conclusion

Centralized compliance management is no longer a luxury—it is a necessity in today's complex, multi-cloud environments. As we have explored in this chapter, Microsoft Defender for Cloud offers a powerful way to manage, monitor, and enforce compliance standards such as NIST SP 800-53, CIS Benchmarks, and the Microsoft Cloud Security Benchmark—all from a single unified dashboard. Through hands-on labs, you have learned how to enable standards, monitor secure scores, and align your cloud workloads with regulatory requirements, without needing to jump across multiple tools or platforms. This not only improves security posture, but also builds trust with customers, auditors, and stakeholders. Defender for Cloud helps organizations stay proactive, not reactive, when it comes to compliance and risk reduction.

Now that you have mastered the fundamentals of managing compliance, it is time to zoom in on one of the most sensitive aspects of cloud security—**data**. In the next chapter, we will dive into **Data Security Posture Management (DSPM)**, a fast-growing area that focuses on discovering, classifying, and protecting sensitive data across cloud environments. You will also learn how to use Defender for Cloud and Microsoft Purview to uncover hidden data risks, ensure encryption is applied, and stay compliant with privacy-focused regulations like GDPR and HIPAA. Get ready to explore how visibility and control over data security can elevate your overall CNAPP strategy.

Points to Remember

Here are some **key points to remember** from this chapter on **Centralized Compliance Management Using CNAPP:**

- **Compliance is not Optional:** Every organization must meet certain regulatory standards, based on its industry, location, and cloud usage. Non-compliance can lead to fines, reputational damage, or even legal consequences.
- `Microsoft Defender for Cloud` **Supports Multiple Standards:** You can monitor against popular frameworks such as **Microsoft Cloud Security Benchmark, CIS, NIST SP 800-53, ISO 27001**, and cloud-specific benchmarks like **AWS Foundational Security** and **GCP CIS Benchmark**.
- **Centralized Dashboard for Compliance:** The **Regulatory Compliance blade in Defender for Cloud** offers a unified view to track how well your cloud resources meet the selected standards.
- **Secure Score by Standard:** Defender for Cloud generates a **separate secure score for each compliance standard you enable**, helping you to understand gaps, and track improvements over time.
- **Compliance is Dynamic, Not Static:** The secure score updates continuously as Defender for Cloud re-evaluates your cloud resources against compliance controls.
- **Customization is Easy:** You can **enable or disable** specific standards per subscription, and even **create custom compliance policies** to suit your organization's needs.
- **Compliance and Security Go hand-in-hand:** Compliance is not just about passing audits–it is about improving your actual security posture by aligning with the best practices.
- **Defender for Cloud Makes It Scalable:** Whether you manage one cloud account or hundreds, Defender for Cloud allows **scalable compliance management from a single console**.
- **Labs Help in Practical Understanding:** The labs in this chapter walk you through enabling standards, managing settings, and **viewing secure scores–real-world actions, you can apply in any organization.**
- **Next Step: Data Security Posture Management (DSPM):** After ensuring compliance at the infrastructure level, the next logical step is to **secure the sensitive data itself**. That is what the next chapter–DSPM–is all about.

Multiple-Choice Questions

1. What is the main purpose of the Regulatory Compliance section in Microsoft Defender for Cloud?
    a. To configure network security rules
    b. To store backup files
    c. To monitor compliance with security standards
    d. To manage user identities
2. Which compliance standard is enabled by default in Microsoft Defender for Cloud?
    a. ISO 27001
    b. NIST SP 800-53
    c. Microsoft Cloud Security Benchmark
    d. CIS AWS Foundations
3. What happens when you enable a new compliance standard like NIST SP 800-53 in Defender for Cloud?
    a. It deletes the existing standards.
    b. It immediately shows a secure score.
    c. It starts evaluating the cloud environment against the standard.
    d. It asks for a reboot.
4. Where do you go to enable or manage compliance standards in Defender for Cloud?
    a. Policy Alerts Tab
    b. Firewall Settings
    c. Environment Settings under Manage Compliance Standards
    d. Virtual Machine Overview
5. What does the secure score in Defender for Cloud indicate?
    a. How much storage is being used.
    b. Network speed performance.

c. Compliance level with security best practices.

d. Number of subscriptions.

Answers

1. c
2. c
3. c
4. c
5. c

Questions

1. What is the purpose of centralized compliance in Microsoft Defender for Cloud?
2. Which compliance standard is enabled by default in Defender for Cloud?
3. Where can you manage and add compliance standards in Defender for Cloud?
4. What does the secure score tell you in the compliance dashboard?
5. Can you enable multiple compliance standards at the same time in Defender for Cloud?
6. What is the benefit of customizing compliance standards per subscription?
7. Which tab shows the list of all enabled standards and their status?
8. What does the NIST SP 800-53 standard help organizations achieve?
9. How does Defender for Cloud display the compliance posture visually?
10. What type of benchmarks can be added for AWS and GCP in Defender for Cloud?

Key Terms

- **Centralized Compliance Management:** A unified way to monitor, manage, and track regulatory standards across multiple cloud environments.
- **Microsoft Defender for Cloud:** A security solution that provides visibility, hardening, threat protection, and compliance for cloud workloads.

- **Compliance Dashboard:** A visual area in Defender for Cloud that shows how well your cloud environment meets the selected standards.
- **Microsoft Cloud Security Benchmark (MCSB):** The default compliance framework in Defender for Cloud, based on Microsoft's own cloud security best practices.
- **NIST SP 800-53:** A widely adopted U.S. government security standard for protecting information systems and organizations.
- **Secure Score:** A numerical score that represents how well your cloud resources align with a chosen compliance standard.
- **Regulatory Compliance Blade:** A section in Defender for Cloud where users can explore active standards, and view their compliance status.
- **Environment Settings:** A configuration area in Defender for Cloud where users manage security policies for their cloud subscriptions.
- **Security Policies:** Rules and benchmarks (like NIST, CIS, and ISO) that help organizations ensure that their infrastructure follows the best practices.
- **Custom Compliance Standard:** A user-defined framework in Defender for Cloud tailored to specific business or regional needs.
- **Compliance Initiative:** A bundled group of policies tied to a specific regulatory or best practice framework.
- **Assessment:** An evaluation of cloud resources against compliance requirements, generating recommendations and scores.

Chapter 11
Understanding Data Security Posture Management (DSPM)

Introduction

Data is the heart of every modern business, and keeping it safe in the cloud is more important than ever.

Companies store vast amounts of sensitive data, customer records, financial details and intellectual property across multiple cloud platforms. Without the right security measures, this data can be exposed, misused, or even stolen.

This is where **Data Security Posture Management (DSPM)** comes in. DSPM helps organizations **discover, classify, and protect their data in the cloud**. It ensures that sensitive information is stored securely, access is properly controlled, and potential risks are identified before they become serious threats.

Microsoft Defender for Cloud, combined with **Microsoft Purview**, provides a powerful DSPM solution. It helps businesses **automate data discovery, monitor security risks, enforce compliance, and respond to threats**—all within a single platform. Whether your data is in **Azure, AWS, or Google Cloud**, Defender for Cloud gives you full visibility and control, reducing the chances of a costly data breach.

In this chapter, we will explore how DSPM works, why it is essential, and how **Microsoft Defender for Cloud** can help you build a **strong data security posture** in today's cloud-driven world.

To make this chapter more insightful, we have included **four (4) hands-on labs**, providing **live demonstrations**, using the **DSPM** module in **Microsoft Defender for Cloud.** These labs will help you gain **practical experience** in implementing **Data Security Posture Management (DSPM)**, and exploring its key capabilities. The following is the list of **all hands-on demonstrations covered in this chapter**:

- **Lab #1:** Enabling and Configuring DSPM in Microsoft Defender for Cloud for Azure, AWS, and GCP
- **Lab #2:** Understanding the Next Steps after Enabling DSPM
- **Lab #3:** Navigating Built-in Data Classification Rules
- **Lab #4:** Exploring and Configuring Data and AI Security in Microsoft Defender for Cloud

Structure

The following topics will be covered in this chapter:

- Introduction to DSPM
- Key Components of DSPM
- Why DSPM has become Essential in the Industry
- Microsoft Defender for Cloud as a DSPM Solution
- DSPM Labs

Introduction to DSPM

In today's digital age, Cloud Data i

s the most valuable asset for any organization, but in the cloud, it is also the most vulnerable.

Businesses store sensitive information across multiple cloud platforms, including **Azure, AWS, and Google Cloud.**

Without proper visibility and control, this data can become an easy target for cybercriminals, accidental exposure, or compliance violations.

Data Security Posture Management (DSPM) is the solution to this growing challenge. It helps businesses **discover, classify, and protect** the sensitive data, while ensuring it remains secure and compliant. Unlike traditional security tools that focus only on networks and applications, **DSPM is data-centric**—it looks deep into the cloud to find where the sensitive data is stored, who has access to it, and whether it is at risk.

With DSPM, companies can:

- **Automatically discover** all cloud-stored data, even in shadow IT.
- **Classify and label** the sensitive information such as financial records and personal data.
- **Detects risks** such as misconfigured storage, excessive permissions, and unencrypted data.

- **Ensure compliance** with security frameworks like **GDPR, HIPAA, and PCI-DSS.**
- **Respond quickly** to data breaches or unauthorized access attempts.

As cloud environments grow more complex, DSPM is no longer optional–it is essential.

Businesses need a security approach that adapts to modern challenges, providing real-time protection and deep visibility into their most critical data.

Key Components of DSPM

To build a strong cloud security posture, organizations need more than just firewalls and access controls–they need complete visibility and control over their data.

DSPM provides this by **combining intelligent data discovery, risk assessment, compliance enforcement, and real-time threat detection** into a single framework. Unlike traditional security tools that focus on securing networks and applications, **DSPM is designed to protect what matters most: The data itself.**

By continuously scanning cloud environments, DSPM helps organizations **identify the sensitive data, detect security gaps, monitor access permissions, and respond to threats, before they escalate**. It ensures that the **data is properly classified, securely stored, and only accessible to the right people**, significantly reducing the risk of breaches and compliance violations.

Let us explore the core components that make **DSPM a critical part of modern cloud security:**

Data Discovery and Classification

Before you can protect your data, you need to know where it is and what type of data it holds.

DSPM solutions scan cloud environments to locate and classify all the stored data, whether it is structured (databases) or unstructured (documents, logs).

Example: Microsoft Defender for Cloud, integrated with **Microsoft Purview**, can automatically scan **Azure, AWS, and Google Cloud** to identify **Personally Identifiable Information (PII), financial records, and confidential business data**.

Risk Assessment and Security Posture Management

Once the data is discovered, DSPM evaluates its security posture.

It **checks for misconfigurations, excessive access permissions, and compliance gaps** that could expose the sensitive data.

Example: If an **Azure Storage Account** contains unencrypted financial records, **DSPM will flag the risk**, and **provide remediation steps**.

Access Control and Permissions Monitoring

Not all users should have access to the sensitive data.

DSPM continuously monitors **who can access what,** and **detects overly permissive roles** that could lead to data leaks.

Example: If a database containing customer records is **accessible to all the employees**, DSPM will generate an alert, and **recommend** the **least privilege access controls**.

Compliance and Regulatory Monitoring

Many industries are required to follow strict data protection laws.

DSPM ensures that cloud environments meet **GDPR, HIPAA, PCI-DSS, and other regulatory requirements** by continuously checking for compliance violations.

Example: If an organization in the healthcare sector stores unencrypted **patient health records in a public cloud storage bucket**, **DSPM will detect and alert security teams to fix it**.

Threat Detection and Incident Response

Even with strong security measures, threats can still arise.

DSPM uses **AI-powered analytics** to detect **suspicious access patterns, data exfiltration attempts, and insider threats**. It can also **automate responses** to block threats in real time.

Example: If a user suddenly downloads large amounts of sensitive data outside normal work hours, DSPM can trigger an alert, enforce Multi-factor Authentication (MFA), or even block access, until verified.

DSPM is the future of cloud data security. By **combining data discovery, risk assessment, access control, compliance monitoring, and threat detection**, it provides a **complete shield for the sensitive data** across multi-cloud environments.

In the next section, we will dive deeper into how **Microsoft Defender for Cloud** integrates these capabilities to provide a **powerful DSPM solution for enterprises**.

Why DSPM Has Become Essential in the Industry

In today's **cloud-first world, data security is no longer just an IT concern–it is a business-critical priority**. Organizations store vast amounts of **sensitive data across multiple cloud environments**, making **traditional security measures insufficient** to prevent **unauthorized access, misconfigurations, and breaches**. This growing complexity has fueled the rise of **Data Security Posture Management (DSPM), a proactive approach that provides continuous visibility, risk assessment, and automated protection for cloud-stored data**. As **regulatory requirements tighten** and **cyber threats become more sophisticated**, DSPM is rapidly becoming **a necessity, not an option**.

As businesses migrate to the cloud, their **data footprint expands**, creating **new security challenges** beyond traditional network defenses. Unlike on-premises environments, cloud data is **highly dynamic**, moving across multiple locations, and accessed by various identities. This shift makes it **harder to track where the sensitive data resides, who can access it, and whether it is adequately protected. Traditional security tools focus on protecting the perimeter, but they do not provide deep visibility into cloud-stored data–leaving critical blind spots that attackers can exploit.**

This is where **Data Security Posture Management (DSPM) plays a crucial role**. By offering **real-time visibility, automated risk assessment, and proactive security controls**, DSPM **helps organizations identify sensitive data, detect risks, and enforce protection policies, before breaches occur**.

For instance, many companies unknowingly **store vast amounts of sensitive customer or business data in the cloud, without proper tracking or security controls**. This lack of awareness increases the risk of **data leaks, insider threats, and regulatory violations. DSPM solves these challenges by continuously monitoring, classifying, and securing cloud data–ensuring it remains protected, regardless of where it resides**.

In this section, we explore real world security incidents, industry adoption trends, leading solutions, and future challenges that highlight the critical role of DSPM in modern cloud security. Additionally, we examine major cloud security incidents where DSPM could have prevented or minimized the impact of data exposure.

Real-World Security Incidents That DSPM Could Have Prevented

In today's cloud landscape, data breaches and misconfigurations continue to expose the sensitive information, leading to financial losses, regulatory penalties, and reputational damage. Many of these incidents could have been **proactively identified and mitigated** with **Data Security Posture Management (DSPM)**. By providing **continuous monitoring, automated data discovery, and real-time risk assessment**, DSPM ensures that **misplaced, overexposed, or unprotected sensitive data** does not become a security liability.

In this section, we will explore **real-world security incidents that could have been avoided with a robust DSPM strategy**, highlighting how **Microsoft Defender for Cloud** helps organizations **stay ahead of threats in multi-cloud environments**.

Let us review some of the major incidents that disrupted the industry:

Marriott International Data Breach (2018–2022): 500M+ Records Exposed

- **What happened?** Hackers gained access to guest reservation databases containing passport numbers, credit card details, and personal information.
- How could DSPM have helped?
  - **Data discovery and classification**: Identifying and encrypting the sensitive data.
  - **Real-time monitoring:** Detecting unusual data access, and stopping exfiltration.

Tesla Insider Data Theft (2023): Employee Leaked 100GB Data

- **What happened?** A Tesla insider had stolen and leaked 100GB of customer and employee personal data, including salaries and social security numbers.
- How could DSPM have helped?
  - **Insider threat detection:** Monitoring anomalous employee access patterns.
  - **Data flow tracking:** Identifying unauthorized data movements.

Equifax Data Breach (2017) – 147M Records Exposed

- **What happened?** A vulnerability in Equifax's system allowed attackers to steal highly sensitive personal data, including social security numbers and financial records.
- How could DSPM have helped?
  - **Continuous risk assessment:** Identifying sensitive data at risk.
  - **Automated security policy enforcement:** Preventing unauthorized access.

Alibaba Cloud Database Leak (2019) – 1.1B Facial Recognition Records Exposed

- **What happened?** A publicly exposed Alibaba database leaked 1.1 billion facial recognition records used for surveillance.

- How could DSPM have helped?
    - **Data access controls:** Restricting public exposure of sensitive datasets.
    - **Misconfiguration detection:** Identifying databases with weak security.

Microsoft Defender for Cloud as a DSPM Solution

In today's cloud-driven world, organizations manage vast amounts of sensitive data across multiple cloud environments, including **Azure, AWS, and GCP**. While cloud providers offer robust security controls, **data security gaps still exist, making organizations vulnerable to misconfigurations, excessive permissions, and unauthorized access**.

Microsoft Defender for Cloud (MDC) serves as a **comprehensive Data Security Posture Management (DSPM) solution by providing:**

- **Automated Data Discovery:** Identifies the sensitive data across cloud storage services.
- **Real-Time Risk Assessment:** Continuously evaluates security posture and compliance.
- **Misconfiguration Detection:** Flags excessive permissions and insecure storage configurations.
- **Threat Protection:** Provides insights into the potential data breaches and policy violations.

Unlike traditional security solutions that **focus on infrastructure-level security**, **Defender for Cloud integrates DSPM capabilities to protect the data at its core**, ensuring visibility, governance, and compliance across hybrid and multi-cloud environments.

Key Components of DSPM

To effectively safeguard the sensitive data across **multi-cloud environments**, **Microsoft Defender for Cloud (MDC) employs a robust set of DSPM components** that work together to **identify, classify, monitor, and secure the data.** These components integrate seamlessly to provide **end-to-end visibility** into an organization's data security posture. Whether it is **detecting misconfigurations, enforcing compliance, or responding to threats**, each component plays a crucial role in **strengthening data protection across Azure, AWS, and GCP**.

The following sections outline these components, and their specific functions in MDC's DSPM framework.

- **Sensitive Data Discovery (Built into Defender CSPM and Defender for Storage)**
    - **Automatically detects and classifies the sensitive data** across storage accounts and databases.
    - **Supports multi-cloud environments** (Azure, AWS, GCP).
- **Microsoft Purview Integration** *(Data Classification and Governance Engine)*
    - Provides **deep content inspection** and **sensitivity labeling**.
    - Uses **predefined and custom data classification rules**.
    - Enables **data lifecycle management** (retention and encryption policies).
- **Defender CSPM (Cloud Security Posture Management)**
    - **Analyzes misconfigurations and security posture gaps** related to the sensitive data.
    - Maps security gaps to **compliance standards (GDPR, HIPAA, PCI-DSS).**
- **Defender for Storage** *(Storage-Level DSPM Component)*
    - Focuses on **data stored in Azure Blob Storage, AWS S3, and GCP Storage**.
    - **Monitors access patterns**, and **detects risky permissions and misconfigurations**.
- **Defender for SQL and Defender for Databases** *(Data-Level Protection)*
    - **Monitors database activities**, and detects **suspicious queries as well as anomalous access**.
    - Works across **Azure SQL, AWS RDS, and GCP Cloud SQL**.
- **Microsoft Sentinel (SIEM and SOAR for Data Threats)**
    - Collects **DSPM security alerts and events**.
    - Automates **incident response and threat hunting**.
- **Azure Policy and Compliance Controls** *(Security Hardening and Compliance Enforcement)*
    - Defines and enforces **sensitive data protection policies**.
    - Maps **data security controls** to **industry compliance frameworks**.
- **Microsoft Entra ID (Identity and Access Management for DSPM)**
    - Detects **excessive permissions** to the sensitive data.
    - Works with **Conditional Access and Privileged Identity Management (PIM)**.
- **Data Loss Prevention (DLP) Policies** *(Prevents Data Exfiltration and Leakage)*
    - Restricts **data sharing and unauthorized access**.

  - Enforces **encryption and access policies.**

Understanding Sensitive Data Discovery

In cloud environments, the sensitive data is often dispersed across multiple storage services, databases, and applications. Without proper visibility, **organizations risk data leaks, compliance violations, and unauthorized access. Sensitive Data Discovery** is a critical function of **Data Security Posture Management (DSPM)** in **Microsoft Defender for Cloud**, enabling organizations to **identify, classify, and protect the sensitive information** efficiently.

Key Capabilities of Sensitive Data Discovery:

- **Automated Scanning:** Continuously scans cloud storage, databases, and other repositories to detect the sensitive data.
- **Multi-Cloud Coverage:** Supports sensitive data discovery across **Azure, AWS, and GCP environments.**
- **Predefined Classification Rules: Uses Microsoft Purview's classification engine** to detect PII, financial data, healthcare records, and other regulated data types.
- **Customizable Sensitivity Labels:** Allows organizations to create and apply **custom classification rules** to align with the internal policies.
- **Risk-Based Insights:** Provides security teams with **visibility into data exposure**, access controls, and potential threats.

How Sensitive Data Discovery Works in Microsoft Defender for Cloud

- **Enables automatic discovery** of sensitive data stored across cloud platforms.
- **Identifies sensitive data types** (for example, credit card numbers, Social Security numbers, and API keys).
- **Maps discovered data** to compliance standards like **GDPR, HIPAA, and PCI-DSS.**
- **Generates security recommendations** to mitigate risks (for example, enabling encryption, and restricting access).
- **Integrates with Microsoft Purview** for advanced classification, governance, and policy enforcement.

Why Sensitive Data Discovery Matters:

- **Reduces Compliance Risks: Helps organizations meet regulatory requirements** through continuous monitoring.
- **Enhances Visibility:** Provides a **centralized view of the sensitive data** across cloud environments.

- **Improves Security Posture:** Identifies **misconfigurations, excessive permissions, and potential data leaks.**
- **Strengthens Data Protection: Enables proactive security measures** like encryption, access control, and threat detection.

By leveraging **Sensitive Data Discovery** in Microsoft Defender for Cloud, **organizations gain deep insights into their data security posture**, ensuring that sensitive information remains protected against unauthorized access, breaches, and compliance failures.

Data Security Posture Management in Defender CSPM

As cloud environments grow increasingly complex, securing sensitive data has become a top priority for organizations. **Microsoft Defender CSPM (Cloud Security Posture Management)** enhances data security by **offering continuous visibility, misconfiguration detection, and compliance monitoring** across multi-cloud environments. **Data Security Posture Management (DSPM) in Defender CSPM** builds on these capabilities by **adding automated data discovery, classification, and risk assessment** to ensure that sensitive information remains protected at all times.

How DSPM Works in Defender CSPM

When **Defender CSPM is enabled**, the **Sensitive Data Discovery feature is automatically activated**, allowing organizations to:

- **Discover and classify the sensitive data** across cloud resources such as databases, storage accounts, and Virtual Machines (VMs).
- **Monitor data access patterns** to detect anomalous behavior or potential insider threats.
- **Identify misconfigurations** that could expose the sensitive data such as overly permissive access controls or unencrypted storage.
- **Ensure compliance with industry standards like GDPR, HIPAA, and PCI-DSS** by continuously assessing security policies.

By integrating **DSPM into Defender CSPM**, organizations can **reduce data exposure risks, prevent unauthorized access, and improve their overall cloud security posture**.

Real World Use Case → Consider a **financial services company** operating in a **multi-cloud environment**. Without DSPM, sensitive customer financial data might be stored across different cloud platforms, without proper security controls. **Defender CSPM's DSPM capabilities** would allow the company to **discover, classify, and enforce**

protection policies on financial records, reducing the risk of breaches, and ensuring compliance with financial regulations.

Data Security Posture Management in Defender for Storage

Cloud storage services are one of the most **common targets for cyber threats** due to the large volume of sensitive data, they hold. **Microsoft Defender for Storage** extends **Data Security Posture Management (DSPM) capabilities** specifically to **cloud storage resources** such as **Azure Blob Storage, AWS S3, and Google Cloud Storage**.

How DSPM Works in Defender for Storage

When Defender CSPM is enabled: When **Defender for Storage** is enabled, it provides **intelligent threat detection and data security insights**, ensuring that the sensitive data remains secure. The **Sensitive Data Discovery** feature in **Defender for Storage offers:**

- **Automated scanning of cloud storage** to identify files, objects, and blobs containing sensitive information.
- **Real-time detection of suspicious activities** such as **unusual data access patterns** or **large-scale data exfiltration attempts**.
- **Data protection policy recommendations** to enforce **encryption, access controls, and retention policies** on sensitive files.
- **Integration with Microsoft Purview** for **advanced data classification and governance**, enabling organizations to define **data sensitivity labels and access controls**.

By **enabling DSPM in Defender for Storage**, organizations gain a **storage-level security layer** that works alongside **Defender CSPM** to **protect the data at rest, and prevent unauthorized access**.

Real World Use Case – Imagine a **healthcare organization** storing **patient medical records** in **Azure Blob Storage**. If an attacker gains access to an account with overly permissive storage permissions, sensitive data could be exposed. **With DSPM in Defender for Storage**, the **organization can identify misconfigured storage containers, classify medical records based on sensitivity, and apply automated protection policies–ensuring compliance with HIPAA and other healthcare regulations**.

Key Difference: Defender CSPM vs. Defender for Storage CSPM

While both **Defender CSPM** and **Defender for Storage** provide **Data Security Posture Management (DSPM) capabilities**, they focus on **different layers of cloud security:**

Feature	Defender CSPM	Defender for Storage
Scope	Covers cloud-wide data security posture	Focus specifically on storage security
Data Discovery	Detects sensitive data across VMs, databases, storage, and more	Scans cloud storage containers (blob, S3, buckets, etc.)
Threat Detection	Monitors **access risks, permissions and misconfigurations**	Detects anomalous file access, malware, and exfiltration attempts
Compliance Focus	Aligns with multi-cloud security standards	Ensures data protection and encryption compliance
Integration	Works with Microsoft Purview, Defender for Storage, and SIEM solutions	Directly integrates with Microsoft Purview for data classification

Table 11.1: *Comparison between Defender CSPM and Defender for Storage*

For **comprehensive DSPM coverage**, organizations should **enable both Defender CSPM and Defender for Storage**. While **Defender CSPM** ensures **organization-wide visibility and compliance**, **Defender for Storage** provides **in-depth protection for cloud-stored data**. Together, they create a **robust data security framework** that mitigates risks, detects threats, and ensures that the **sensitive data remains protected across cloud environments**.

DSPM Labs

To gain a practical understanding of **Data Security Posture Management (DSPM)** in **Microsoft Defender for Cloud**, hands-on experience is crucial.

These labs provide step-by-step guidance on how to enable, configure, and manage **DSPM capabilities** across **Azure, AWS, and GCP environments**. Each lab is designed to explore the key aspects such as **sensitive data discovery, classification rules, security recommendations, and compliance enforcement**.

By following these exercises, security professionals can effectively leverage **Defender for Cloud's DSPM features to enhance data security, minimize risks, and ensure regulatory compliance in multi-cloud environments.**

Lab # 1: Enabling and Configuring DSPM in Microsoft Defender for Cloud for Azure, AWS, and GCP

When you activate Defender CSPM or Defender for Storage, the **sensitive data discovery extension is automatically turned on.** However, if you prefer not to use **DSPM,** you have the option to disable this feature as well.

To **enable DSPM** across major cloud providers, including **Azure, AWS, and GCP,** follow these steps:

1. Log into the Azure portal, using your administrative credentials.
2. Go to the search bar > type "`Microsoft Defender for Cloud`", and select the service to open the dashboard.
3. Once inside the dashboard, locate the "`Environment Settings`" tab on the left-hand menu.
4. **Expand Azure**, then **expand** **`Tenant Root Group`**, which is a management group.
5. Here, you will see all your active subscriptions detected by **`Microsoft Defender for Cloud`**, along with the currently active plans.
6. Select the relevant **Azure subscription**.
7. **You will notice that Foundational CSPM is fully operational and enabled by default. This plan cannot be disabled.**
8. If Defender CSPM is not enabled, please enable it first. *Refer to Lab #1 – Enabling Foundational and Defender CSPM in Chapter #4 – Understanding* CSPM *for guidance.*
9. If **Defender CSPM** is already **toggled On**, select **`Settings`** in the **`Monitoring` coverage column** of the **Defender CSPM plan,** and ensure that the **Sensitive data discovery** component is set to **On**.
10. In our lab instance, **Defender CSPM is already enabled for the Azure subscription** "`Azure-Learn Train and Certs`". Refer to the following screenshot:

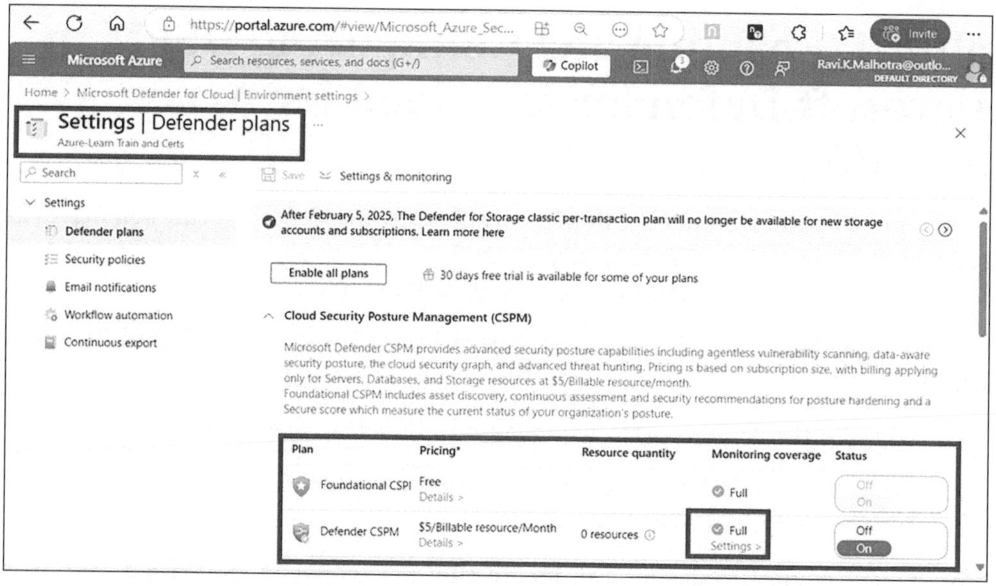

Figure 11.1: *Foundational and Defender CSPM Enablement Status*

11. In our instance, the **`Sensitive Data Discovery`** component is already set to **"On"** for the desired subscription.

12. To verify this, navigate to **`Settings`** in the **`Monitoring Coverage` column** of the **Defender CSPM plan**, and ensure that the **`Sensitive Data Discovery` component is enabled**. Refer to the following screenshot:

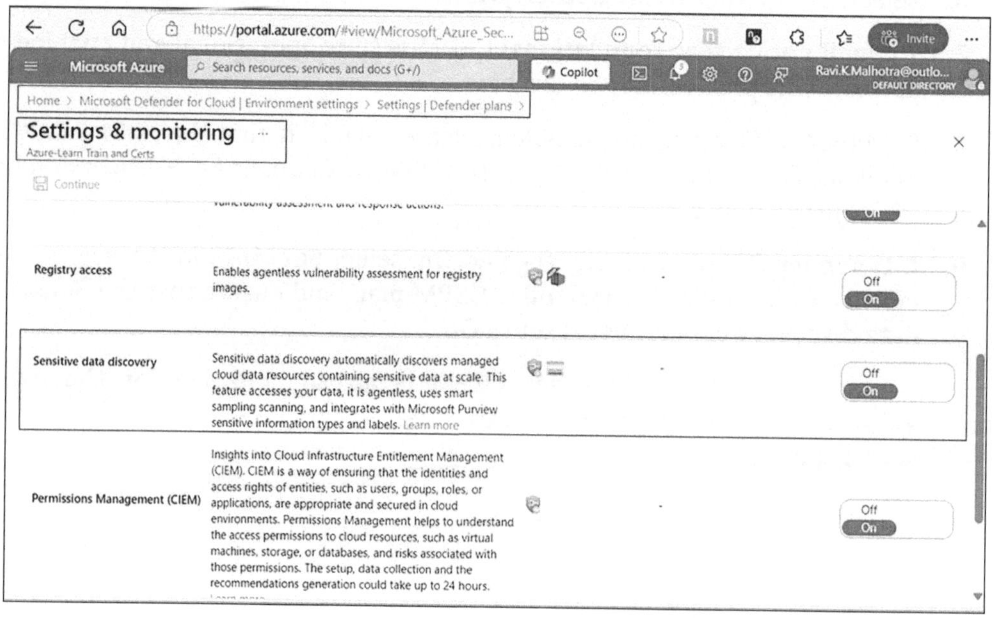

Figure 11.2: *Sensitive Data Discovery Status*

13. Once the **Sensitive Data Discovery feature is enabled** in **Defender CSPM**, it will automatically extend support to the additional resource types as Microsoft continues to expand the list of the supported resources.
14. Let us proceed to the next step.
15. Now, click on **Settings** in the **Monitoring Coverage column** for **Storage Defender**. Here, you will find the **Sensitive Data Discovery** feature. Toggle the switch to **On**, and then click the **Continue** button. Refer to the following screenshot:

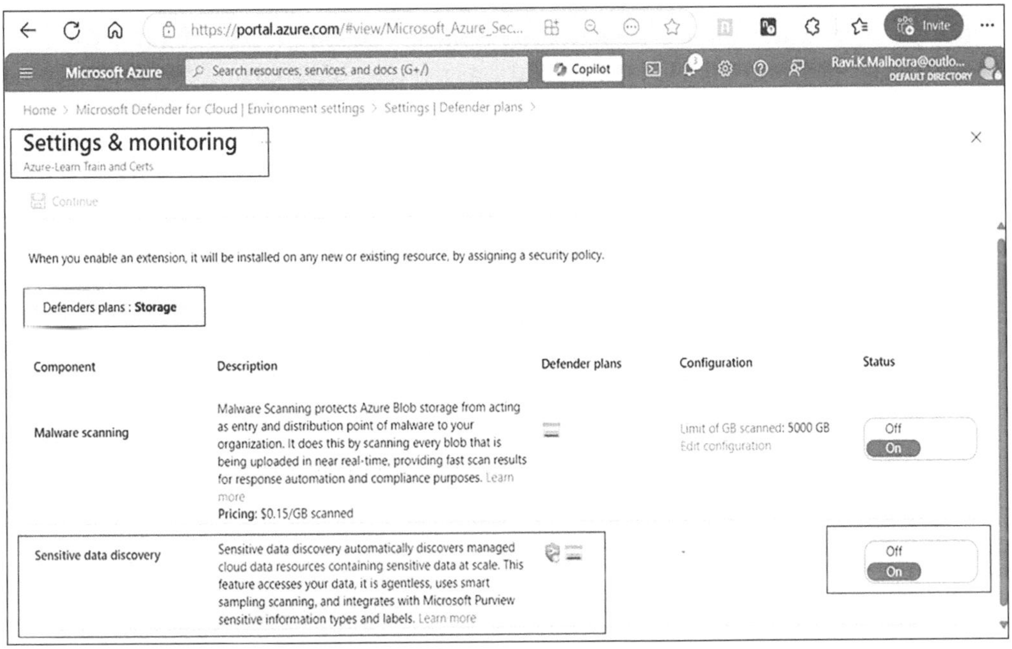

Figure 11.3: *Sensitive Data Discovery Feature in Storage Defender*

16. Now, we have successfully enabled the **Sensitive Data Discovery** feature in both **Defender CSPM** and **Storage Defender**.

    Enabling both ensures **comprehensive coverage**, allowing all the sensitive data across cloud resources to be **discovered, classified, and protected**. Additionally, keeping both features enabled helps to **address storage-level risks,** while also managing **broader cloud security threats**, ensuring a more robust data security posture.

17. This concludes the lab.

Lab # 2: Understanding the Next Steps after Enabling DSPM

Enabling Data Security Posture Management (DSPM) is just the first step toward securing sensitive data in the cloud.

To maximize its effectiveness, organizations must configure the key settings such as **data classification rules, scanning policies, and compliance insights**, to ensure that DSPM accurately identifies, categorizes, and protects critical information.

In this lab, we will explore what happens after enabling DSPM, how to define classification rules, and the vital configurations needed, before running data discovery scans.

By following these steps, you will **establish a strong foundation** for **proactive data security** across your cloud environments.

Steps to Follow after Enabling DSPM:

1. **Configuring Sensitive Data Classification Rules**
    - Importance of data classification before discovery.
    - Where and how to define **custom classification rules for different data types** (PII, financial, API keys, secrets, and so on.).
    - How **Microsoft Defender for Cloud leverages built-in classification.**
2. **Reviewing DSPM Dashboard and Insights**
    - Explore what happens right after enabling DSPM.
    - Where to find **initial insights in Microsoft Defender for Cloud (MDC).**
    - Understanding **active recommendations** and **security posture updates.**
3. **Understanding Automatic and Manual Scanning Options**
    - How DSPM starts identifying sensitive data across your cloud environment.
    - Differences between **automatic scanning vs. on-demand/manual scans.**
    - Supported cloud platforms (Azure, AWS, and GCP).
4. **Reviewing Compliance and Regulatory Insights**
    - How DSPM helps meet **GDPR, HIPAA, PCI-DSS**, and other compliance standards.
    - Where to check **compliance recommendations and security gaps.**
5. **Next Steps before Running Data Discovery Labs**
    - Ensuring that **correct classification rules** are in place.
    - Verifying **scan scope** for **different cloud resources.**

- Checking **Role-Based Access (RBAC) permissions** to allow DSPM full visibility.

By configuring **data classification rules, scanning policies, and compliance settings**, we ensure that **DSPM goes beyond just detection**—it actively helps classify, monitor, and protect the sensitive data across cloud environments. These **configurations lay the groundwork** for accurate data discovery and risk assessment, **enabling organizations to proactively manage** their data security posture. With these steps completed, we are now ready to move forward with **discovering and analyzing the sensitive data** across cloud resources in the next lab.

Lab # 3: Navigating Built-in Data Classification Rules

Data classification is the cornerstone of any **effective Data Security Posture Management (DSPM) strategy**. Before diving into custom rules, it is crucial to understand how **Microsoft Defender for Cloud** leverages **built-in classification rules to detect and categorize the sensitive data across Azure, AWS, and GCP**.

These predefined rules help organizations quickly identify **Personal Identifiable Information (PII), financial data, healthcare records, and other critical datasets**, without manual configuration. In this lab, we explore how to **navigate, review, and understand these built-in classification rules within MDC**.

Please follow these steps to:

1. Log into the Azure portal, using your administrative credentials.
2. Go to the search bar > type "`Microsoft Defender for Cloud`", and select the service to open the dashboard.
3. Once inside the `Microsoft Defender for Cloud` dashboard, navigate to the `Environment Settings` tab from the left-hand menu.
4. On the `Environment Settings` **page,** you will see a structured view displaying various configuration options. One of these key configuration items is `Data Sensitivity` which defines how the sensitive data is managed and classified within your cloud environment.
5. The `Data Sensitivity` **settings apply globally across all onboarded cloud accounts and subscriptions, regardless of whether they belong to Azure, AWS, or GCP**. This ensures consistent data security policies across your multi-cloud infrastructure.
6. Refer to the following screenshot to see the default view of the `Environment Settings` **page:**

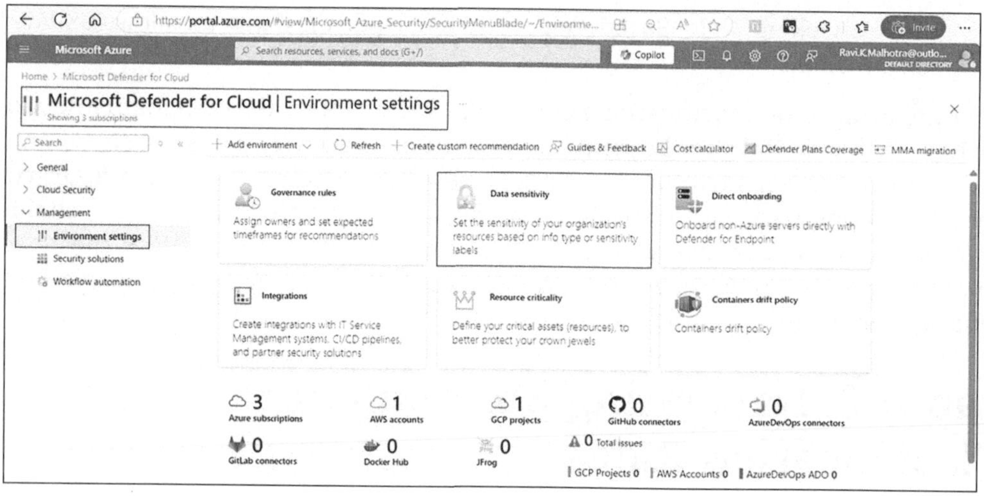

Figure 11.4: *Data Sensitivity Option in the Environment Settings*

7. Now, click on the `Data Sensitivity` tile. This will display the **default sensitivity labels** provided by the **DSPM module** in **`Microsoft Defender for Cloud`**. These built-in labels help to classify and protect the sensitive data across cloud environments.
8. If you need to create or customize additional sensitivity labels, you must manage them through **Microsoft Purview** which is beyond the scope of this chapter.
9. Refer to the following screenshot to view the **default built-in sensitivity labels.**

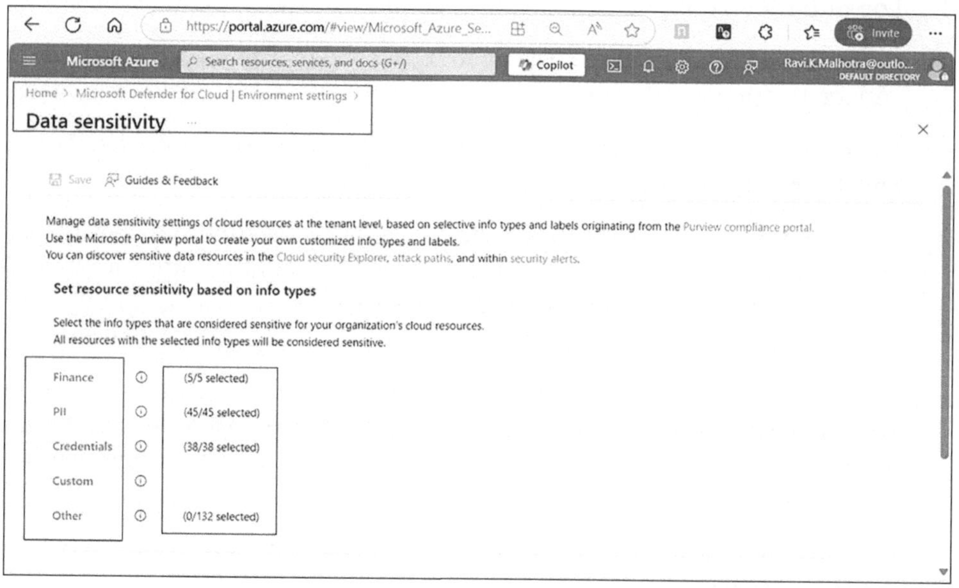

Figure 11.5: *Default List of Built-in Data Sensitivity Labels*

10. As you can see, the `Finance` label contains **five predefined sensitive information types (5/5), and all of them are selected**. You can click on the `Finance` label to view all the five information types. If needed, you can disable any of them, based on your organization's requirements.

11. In our instance, we have **unchecked two options: `EU debit card number`** and **`SWIFT code`**, and then applied the changes. Refer to the following screenshot to see the modified sensitivity settings:

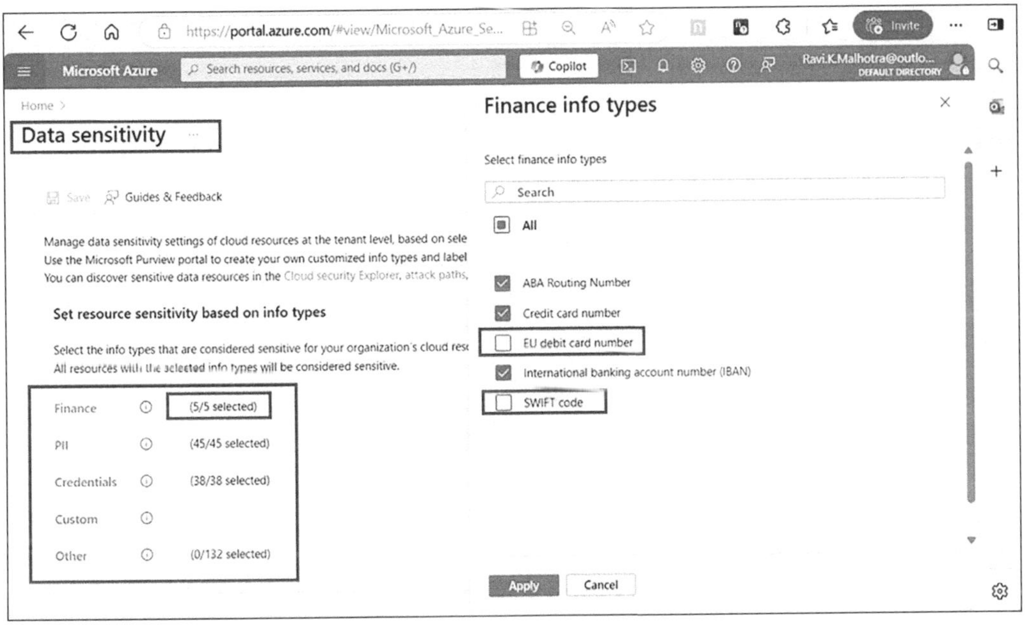

***Figure 11.6**: Modifying the Finance Info Type Sensitivity Labels*

12. Now, if you revisit the default view of the built-in sensitivity labels, you will notice that the `Finance` label reflects **`3/5 selected`, instead of 5/5**, indicating the changes made in the last step. Refer to the following screenshot for confirmation.

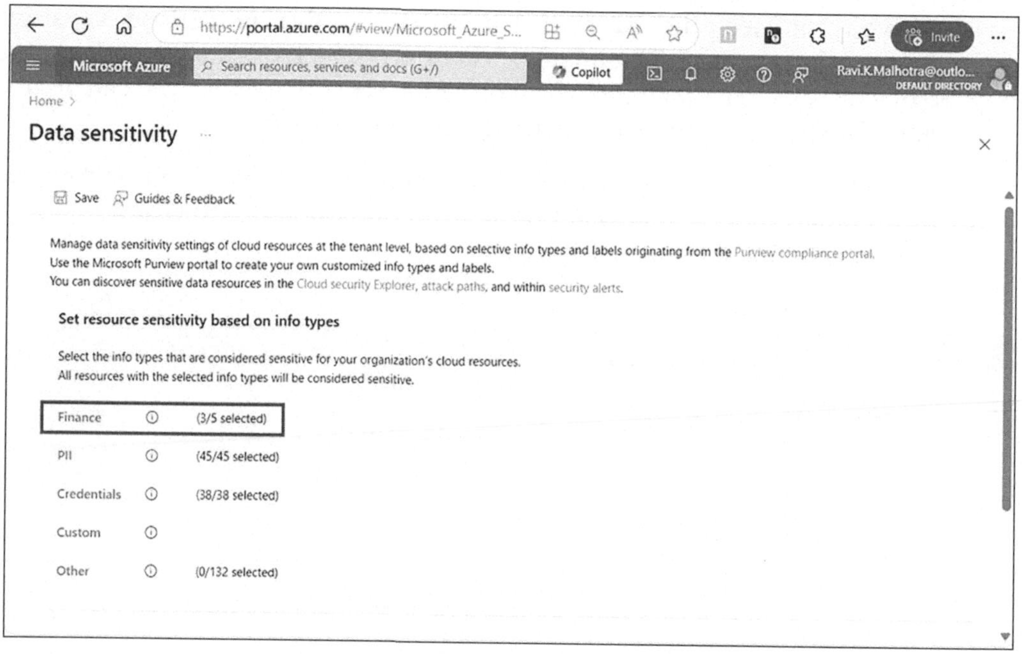

Figure 11.7: *Modified Finance Info Type*

13. This concludes the lab.

Lab # 4: Exploring and Configuring Data and AI Security in Microsoft Defender for Cloud

For any **CISO or Digital Leader**, one of the most **critical priorities** is detecting **publicly exposed sensitive and classified data** within their organization, and implementing **mitigation strategies** to prevent data breaches and compliance violations.

Traditional **Data Loss Prevention (DLP) solutions** have long served this purpose in **on-premises environments**. However, with the **rapid adoption of cloud computing**, **organizational data is now spread across multiple cloud platforms**, creating a **highly hybrid data** landscape. As a result, organizations **must rely on cloud-native security solutions** with **built-in capabilities** to automatically **discover, classify, and protect** the sensitive data across **Azure, AWS, and GCP**–ensuring proactive risk mitigation, and regulatory compliance.

Imagine that **your organization heavily relies on cloud storage for day-to-day operations**, storing vast amounts of **customer data** for seamless processing and business continuity. Suddenly, senior leadership mandates a **comprehensive compliance assessment** requiring you to address the following critical concerns:

1. **Inventory Assessment:** Identify and list all **storage accounts** across **Azure, AWS, and GCP**, ensuring complete visibility into your cloud assets.
2. **Security and Misconfiguration Analysis: Detect any misconfigurations** and **receive recommendations,** based on **cloud security best practices** to enhance the security posture of these storage accounts.
3. **Risk Prioritization:** Evaluate and prioritize risks associated with each **storage account**, **mapping them to widely adopted industry standards and compliance frameworks**.
4. **Database Visibility:** Identify and list all **managed and hosted databases** across your cloud platforms, **ensuring their security and compliance.**
5. **Internet-Exposed Sensitive Data:** Detect any **publicly exposed sensitive or classified data** such as **credit card numbers, U.S. Social Security Numbers (SSNs), and other PII**, that should not be accessible on public domains.

Meeting these compliance requirements manually would be complex and time-consuming. However, **Microsoft Defender for Cloud's Data and AI Security capabilities** provide a **centralized and automated approach** to efficiently address these challenges–offering deep insights, continuous monitoring, and proactive risk mitigation across your cloud infrastructure.

A **single, comprehensive solution** to address all the concerns raised by leadership is the **Data and AI Security module** in **Microsoft Defender for Cloud (MDC)**.

To help organizations **identify, monitor, and protect the sensitive data** used in **AI models and analytics pipelines**, Microsoft Defender for Cloud introduces the **Data and AI Security feature (currently in preview)**. This capability strengthens an organization's **security posture** by providing **deep visibility into data assets**, detecting **misconfigurations**, and ensuring **compliance across multi-cloud environments**.

The **Data and AI Security tab** in Microsoft Defender for Cloud serves as a **centralized hub for security insights** related to both **sensitive data and AI workloads**. It empowers **security teams** to **identify risks, monitor threats, and enforce security best practices** for **data assets and AI models** across **Azure, AWS, and GCP**. The following screenshot provides a real-time view of the **Data and AI Security dashboard** in our instance of **MDC**.

In this lab, we will **explore** the **Data and AI Security tab** in **Microsoft Defender for Cloud (MDC)**, and examine how it enhances the security of **AI-powered workloads**.

This module is structured into **four key sections:**

- **Data and AI Security Overview**
- **Top Issues**

- **Data Closer Look**
- **AI Closer Look**

We will dive into each of these sections to **understand its role, features, and impact on securing sensitive data and AI workloads.**

The **Data and AI Security Overview section** in Microsoft Defender for Cloud offers a high-level summary of the current security posture, highlighting identified risks, important recommendations, and a snapshot of your data and AI assets across cloud environments. In our instance, this dashboard has **detected three (3) `Storage assets`, one (1) `Managed databases`**, and **five (5) `AI services`**. Among these, **three sensitive data resources** have been discovered, with **two of them flagged as requiring immediate attention**. This quick-glance view helps security teams assess their overall data security status, and understand where to prioritize their actions. Refer to the following screenshot for a closer look at the findings in our environment.

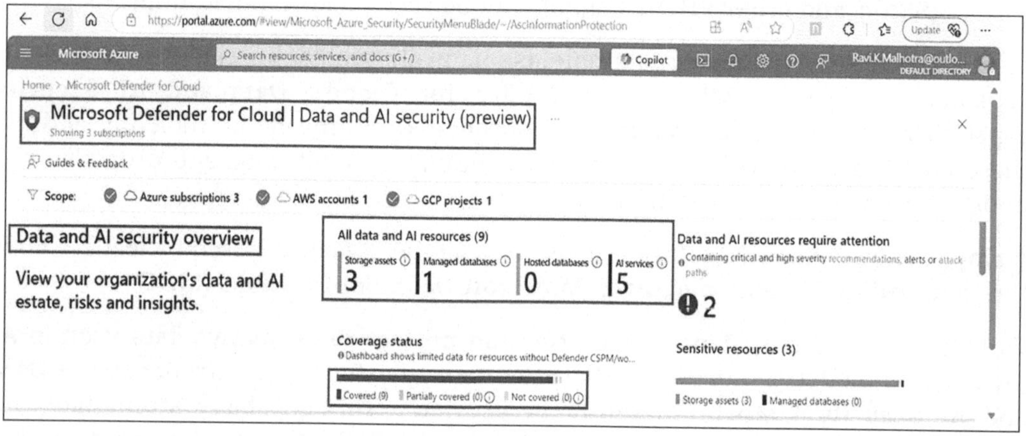

Figure 11.8: *Data and AI Security Overview Section*

Clicking on the **`Storage assets` count** under the **'All data and AI resources'** section navigates to the **`Inventory` page**, where you can view a detailed **list of storage object names, their respective cloud platforms (Azure, AWS, or GCP), and security recommendations** for each asset. This allows for a **comprehensive assessment** of storage security across multi-cloud environments. **Refer to the following screenshot from our instance of `Data and AI Security Overview in Microsoft Defender for Cloud`.**

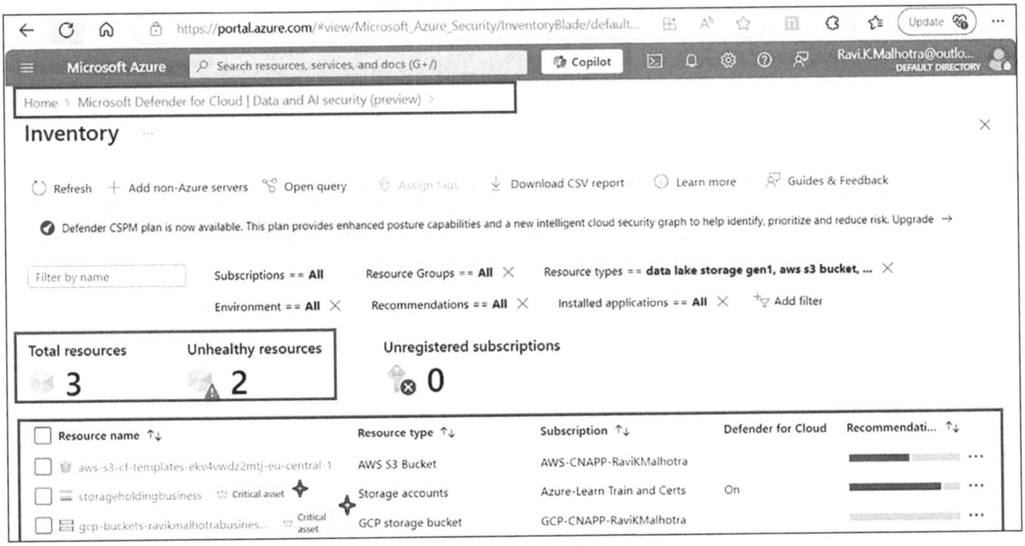

Figure 11.9: *Storage Assets Details with Resource Type and Recommendations*

However, clicking on the **`Storage assets count`** under **`'Data and AI resources require attention'`** redirects you to the **Cloud Security Explorer** page. Here, you will find a comprehensive list of all storage objects, along with a dedicated **`'Insights'`** column. This section provides **business-specific insights** such as **identified sensitive data types and the exact file names storing this data,** within the storage account.

In our instance of **`Microsoft Defender for Cloud`**, the system has detected **`US Social Security Numbers`** and **`Credit Card Numbers`**, along with their corresponding file names. Refer to the following screenshot for more details.

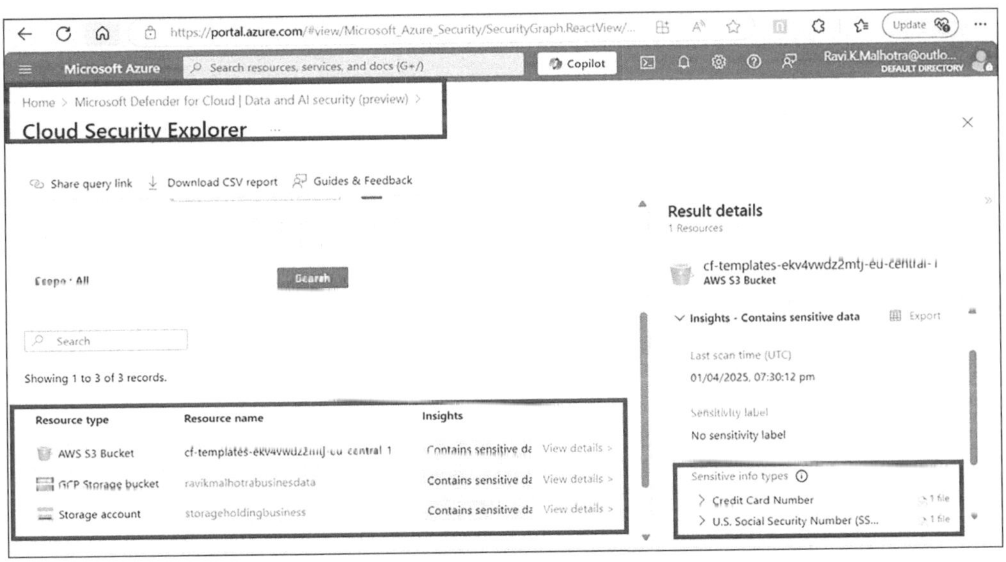

Figure 11.10: *Sensitive Data Insights inside Storage Objects*

Top Issues: Highlights the **most critical security concerns** related to data exposure, misconfigurations, and AI vulnerabilities. The **Top Issues panel** in Microsoft Defender for Cloud **offers a prioritized list** of the **most crucial security concerns** related to your data and AI assets.

It acts like a security radar–instantly drawing attention to high-risk areas that need urgent action. These issues are grouped by severity (High, Medium, Low), helping teams focus their efforts where they matter most.

In our **environment**, this panel provides a clear breakdown of **pressing concerns** such as **exposed sensitive data**, **misconfigured storage resources**, or **non-compliant AI workloads**. Each issue includes a short description, the impacted resource, and a direct link to the detailed recommendations and remediation steps. This makes it easier for security teams to take quick, informed actions, without needing to dig through scattered dashboards.

By addressing these top issues first, organizations can significantly improve their overall security posture, and reduce the risk of data exposure or compliance violations. Refer to the following screenshot from our lab environment to see how this looks in action.

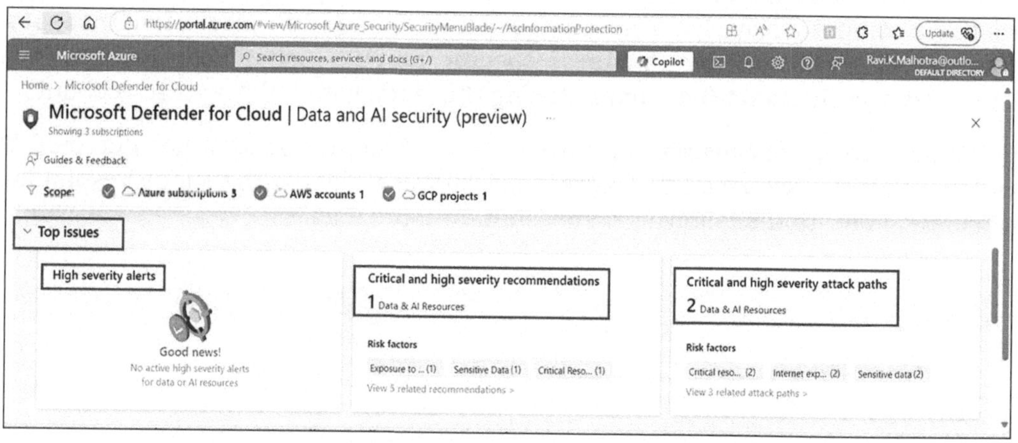

Figure 11.11: *Top Issues Panel in Data and AI Security Section*

Data Closer Look: Provides a **detailed breakdown** of security findings related to the **sensitive data**, including **classification and access insights**. The **Data Closer Look** section provides deep insights into the nature and exposure of the sensitive data across cloud environments.

In our instance of Microsoft Defender for Cloud, this view highlights **two vital and sensitive information** types–**`U.S. Social Security Numbers`** and **`Credit Card Numbers`**–each discovered in **three (3) different locations**. These sensitive data elements are detected across both Storage assets and Managed assets, reflecting MDC's ability to scan data repositories and managed databases services comprehensively.

Additionally, the **Data Threat Protection panel summarizes security alerts** by **severity** for both storage and managed databases. As shown in our environment, there are currently no active alerts, **indicating a clean posture** from a threat detection standpoint–though this can change dynamically, based on new findings.

The **Data Queries in Security Explorer** tile **flags one publicly available storage resource** that contains the sensitive data. This helps security teams quickly investigate and mitigate data exposure risks.

Lastly, the **Internet Exposed Data Resources** section **confirms** that **one storage asset is publicly accessible,** and **holds the sensitive data**, while no exposures are found across managed or hosted databases. **This visibility is necessary for organizations to take immediate corrective action to prevent data breaches or compliance violations.** Here is a Data Closer Look screenshot from our instance of **`Data and AI Security`** (**`Overview`**) tab:

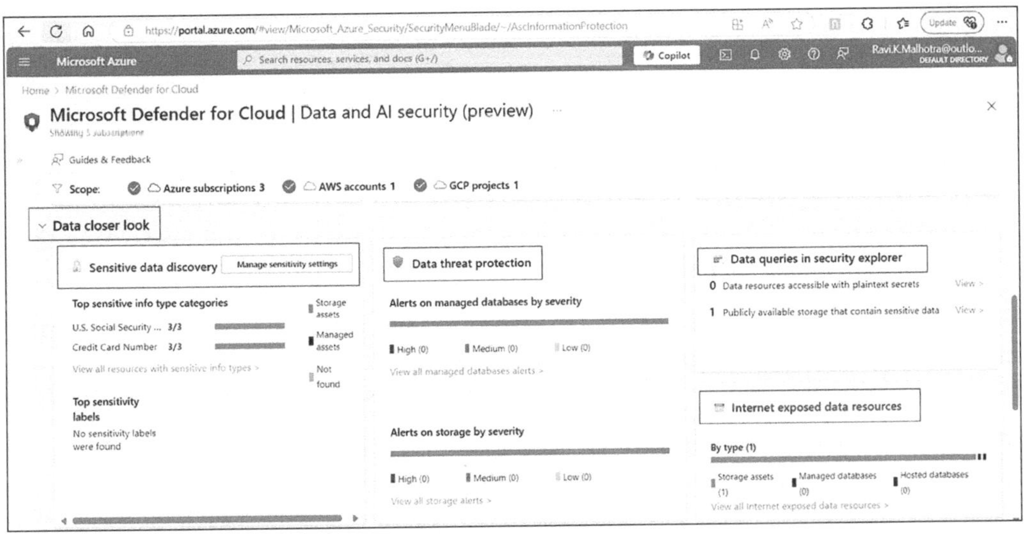

***Figure 11.12:** Data Closer Look Panel in Data and AI Security Section*

The **AI Closer Look section** in **Microsoft Defender for Cloud** offers **focused visibility into the security posture of AI workloads and services** across multi-cloud environments. It acts as a centralized dashboard where security and compliance teams can monitor AI services, detect risks like adversarial attacks, data poisoning, misconfigurations, and ensure alignment with compliance standards.

This section highlights each AI asset, along with important details such as the type of service, associated resource group, cloud platform, and recommended actions to improve security.

In our environment, **Defender identified five (5) AI services**, with **two (2) requiring immediate attention** due to critical issues. With these insights, **organizations can**

proactively secure their AI-driven workloads, **reduce risk exposure**, and follow the best practices for **data protection and compliance**.

Refer to the following screenshot for more details from our lab instance.

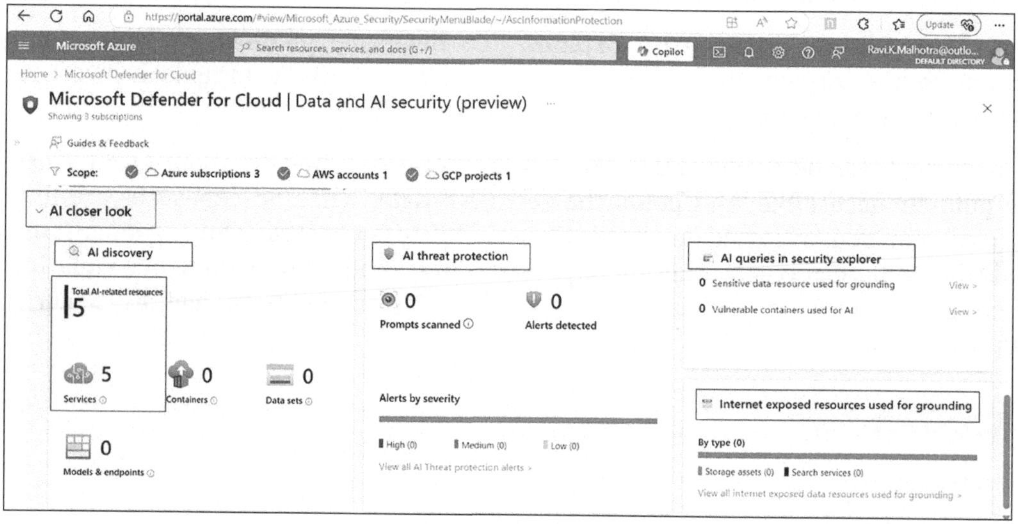

Figure 11.13: *AI Closer Look Panel in Data and AI Security Section*

Data and AI are at the heart of modern digital transformation, and **protecting them is no longer optional–it is essential.**

This lab demonstrated how **Microsoft Defender for Cloud's Data and AI Security module equips organizations** with the tools they need to gain deep visibility, prioritize risks, and strengthen the security posture of their sensitive data and AI workloads.

With **centralized dashboards like Data Closer Look**, **AI Closer Look**, and **Top Issues**, security teams can identify exposures, understand misconfigurations, and take immediate action across multi-cloud environments. Whether it is spotting an exposed database or detecting compliance risks in AI models, this module empowers organizations to stay ahead of threats, and ensure responsible, secure use of their most valuable digital assets.

Conclusion

As cloud adoption accelerates, **data security must be at the forefront of every cloud security strategy**. While traditional security models focus on **infrastructure hardening and network protection**, **modern threats demand a data-centric approach. Microsoft Defender for Cloud's DSPM solution** provides this critical layer of protection, ensuring that the **sensitive data is continuously discovered, classified, and secured across multi-cloud environments**.

By implementing DSPM, organizations gain **real-time visibility into data risks, enforce governance policies with Microsoft Purview, and leverage AI-driven threat detection** to proactively mitigate breaches. Whether it is **protecting Personally Identifiable Information (PII), financial records, or intellectual property**, **Defender for Cloud's automated risk assessments** and compliance mapping enable security teams to **stay ahead of evolving threats**.

This chapter marks the final piece in our **comprehensive journey through Cloud-Native Application Protection Platforms (CNAPP)**. From **CSPM to CIEM, KSPM, and now DSPM**, we have explored how each component plays a crucial role in **building a resilient cloud security posture**. By embracing these technologies, security professionals can **confidently safeguard their cloud environments, reduce risk exposure, and maintain compliance at scale**. As threats continue to evolve, so must our approach–and **DSPM is a critical step in that evolution**.

Points to Remember

Here are some **key points to remember** from this chapter on **DSPM in Microsoft Defender for Cloud:**

- **Data Security Posture Management (DSPM)** focuses on discovering, classifying, and protecting sensitive data across Azure, AWS, and GCP.
- **Unlike traditional security models**, DSPM is data-centric, ensuring protection at the data level, not just at the infrastructure level.
- **Automated discovery and classification** of the sensitive data reduces the risk of misconfigurations and unauthorized access.
- **Defender for Cloud integrates DSPM** to provide real-time monitoring, risk assessment, and security recommendations for the sensitive data.
- **Built-in integration with Microsoft Purview** enables advanced data classification and governance.
- **AI-powered threat detection** helps identify data exfiltration, insider threats, and ransomware activities.
- **Sensitive Data Discovery** automatically identifies and categorizes PII, financial, and healthcare data across storage services.
- **Misconfiguration Detection** flags excessive permissions, insecure storage, and unprotected sensitive data.
- **Access Control and Compliance Mapping** maps data security posture to GDPR, HIPAA, and PCI-DSS.
- **Real-Time Threat Protection** detects unauthorized data movement, abnormal access patterns, and exfiltration attempts.

Multiple-Choice Questions

1. What is the primary goal of Data Security Posture Management (DSPM)?
    a. Protecting cloud workloads from malware.
    b. Managing encryption keys for data protection.
    c. Identifying, classifying, and securing sensitive data across cloud environments.
    d. Monitoring network traffic for security threats.
2. Which component in Microsoft Defender for Cloud is responsible for deep data classification?
    a. Azure Policy
    b. Microsoft Purview
    c. Azure Sentinel
    d. Azure Key Vault
3. How does Defender for Cloud DSPM detect potential security risks?
    a. By analyzing cloud billing reports
    b. Through manual user input and static rules
    c. By continuously scanning for misconfigurations, excessive permissions, and access anomalies
    d. By blocking all external access to cloud storage
4. Which of the following is NOT a capability of DSPM in Microsoft Defender for Cloud?
    a. Automated discovery of the sensitive data.
    b. Continuous monitoring for data exposure risks.
    c. Automatic encryption of all data in cloud storage.
    d. Integration with compliance frameworks like GDPR and PCI-DSS.
5. What is the key advantage of DSPM over traditional security models?
    a. DSPM is entirely manual, reducing automation risks.
    b. DSPM focuses on data security, while traditional models focus on infrastructure security.

c. Traditional security models offer better compliance management than DSPM.

d. DSPM works only for Azure environments.

Answers

1. c
2. b
3. c
4. c
5. b

Questions

1. What is the primary function of DSPM in Microsoft Defender for Cloud?
2. Which cloud platforms are supported by Microsoft Defender for Cloud's DSPM module?
3. Which Microsoft service is used for deep data classification within DSPM?
4. Which feature in DSPM helps identify misconfigurations in cloud storage?
5. How does DSPM contribute to compliance management?
6. Which key security risk does DSPM help to detect in cloud storage environments?
7. What kind of data does Microsoft Purview help classify in DSPM?
8. How does Defender for Cloud detect excessive permissions in DSPM?
9. What makes DSPM different from traditional security models?
10. Which major compliance frameworks do DSPM in Defender for Cloud help organizations to align with?

Key Terms

- **Data Security Posture Management (DSPM):** A security approach that focuses on discovering, classifying, and protecting the sensitive data in cloud environments.
- **Microsoft Defender for Cloud (MDC):** A cloud-native security solution that integrates DSPM capabilities for multi-cloud protection.
- **Microsoft Purview:** A data governance and classification tool used for identifying and labeling the sensitive data.
- **Sensitive Data Discovery:** The process of scanning and identifying sensitive information across cloud storage and databases.
- **Security Posture Assessment:** Analyzing an organization's security configurations to identify vulnerabilities and risks.
- **Compliance Mapping:** Aligning security policies and configurations with industry frameworks such as GDPR, HIPAA, and PCI-DSS.
- **Data Sensitivity Labels:** Predefined or custom labels assigned to the data for classification and protection.
- **Excessive Permissions Detection:** Identifying over-privileged access to the sensitive data which may pose security risks.
- **Threat Protection:** Real-time monitoring and alerts for potential data breaches, unauthorized access, or insider threats.
- **Multi-Cloud Security:** The ability to secure the sensitive data across Azure, AWS, and GCP environments.

Index

A

C

D

T

V

W

Y

Z